THE TALE OF THE RING:

A KADDISH

Frank Stiffel

THE TALE OF THE RING:
A KADDISH

A personal memoir of
The Holocaust

BANTAM BOOKS
TORONTO · NEW YORK · LONDON · SYDNEY · AUCKLAND

WINNER OF THE SECOND ANNUAL EDITORS' BOOK AWARD

Sponsoring editors for the Editors' Book Award are Simon Michael Bessie, James Charlton, Peter Davison, Jonathan Galassi, David Godine, Daniel Halpern, James Laughlin, Seymour Lawrence, Starling Lawrence, Robie Maccauley, Joyce Carol Oates, Nan A. Talese, Faith Sale, Ted Solotaroff, Pat Strachan, Thomas Wallace.

Final illustration by Aurora Stiffel Berman

*This low-priced Bantam Book
has been printed from new plates.
It contains the complete text of the
original hard-cover edition.*
NOT ONE WORD HAS BEEN OMITTED

THE TALE OF THE RING: A KADDISH

*A Bantam Book / published by arrangement with
Pushcart Press*

PRINTING HISTORY
Pushcart Press edition published February 1984
Bantam edition / November 1985

Library of Congress Cataloging in Publication Data

Stiffel, Frank.
  The tale of the ring.

  1. Holocaust, Jewish (1939–1945)—Personal narratives.
2. Stiffel, Frank.   I. Title.
D810.J4S79   1985   940.53'15'03924   85-4044
ISBN 0-553-34214-2 (pbk.)

Published simultaneously in the United States and Canada

Bantam Books are published by Bantam Books, Inc. Its trademark, consisting of the words "Bantam Books" and the portrayal of a rooster, is Registered in U.S. Patent and Trademark Office and in other countries. Marca Registrada. Bantam Books, Inc., 666 Fifth Avenue, New York, New York 10103.

PRINTED IN THE UNITED STATES OF AMERICA
DH   0 9 8 7 6 5 4 3 2 1

DEDICATION

———

To my Father and my Mother,
murdered.

To Ione, my wife, with whom I was blessed
as a result of the murder.

To Aurora, my daughter, who in her own right, as a child
of a survivor, is the ultimate victim of
the murder.

ACKNOWLEDGMENTS

My sister-in-law, Mura Light-Stiffel, was the first person to read my manuscript. She encouraged me to look for a publisher.

My friends Naomi and Fred Weissenberg introduced me to Bob Hunter, without whose sensitivity, loyalty, and incredible editorial skill my manuscript would have never become a book.

A dozen large publishing houses rejected the manuscript on the grounds that you, the reader, were no longer interested in the Holocaust tales.

Then, Bill Henderson appeared on the horizon, the publisher of the Pushcart Press. His feelings did not coincide with those of the large publishers, and this is how the manuscript finally has become a book.

I thank my wife Ione, my daughter Aurora, my son-in-law and friend Steve Berman, my grand-daughter Nicole and some of my best friends, Edie Wyman, Phil Peagler, Ceil Shultz and Halina Greenwald, for their support and their faith in me.

And I thank you, the Reader, for investing your time and your money in this book, which is a living page of our history, where you yourself in one way or another have played an indelible part.

PUBLISHER'S NOTE

BANTAM BOOKS IS HONORED to present Frank Stiffel's memoir, THE TALE OF THE RING: A KADDISH, winner of the second annual Pushcart Press Editors' Book Award.

Frank Stiffel wrote his manuscript soon after he was released from Auschwitz. He prepared it from diaries that were written while he was in captivity. When on many occasions the authorities confiscated his diaries, he rewrote them again and again from memory.

For three decades, the manuscript lay unpublished in a desk drawer, until the author happened to mention its existence to Robert Hunter of Macmillan, who then nominated it for The Editors' Book Award. His nomination was co-sponsored by Robert Loomis of Random House and Terry Karten of Harper and Row.

This memoir of hope and horror reads like it happened yesterday—because at the time it was written it did happen yesterday.

Frank Stiffel now lives with his wife in Queens, New York City. He is the father of a daughter, Aurora, and he recently retired from The New York State Department of Labor.

CONTENTS

THE TALE OF THE RING:
A KADDISH

POLISH PATRIOT

My STORY BEGINS on September 1, 1939, a few hours after the first Nazi bombs had fallen on [1]Lvov, Poland and the first contingent of victims, who were wounded and killed on a trolley car going up Sloneczna Street, was delivered to the Jewish Hospital in Lvov, where I was finishing my summer medical training. With the smell of warm blood still in my nostrils and the picture of butchered bodies in my mind, I stood in the throng gathered around the statue of the 19th-century Polish poet and fighter for freedom, Adam Mickiewicz. We intoned the old, unofficial anthem: "We shall not surrender the land from which we stem: we shall not allow our tongue to be buried; we are the Polish nation, the Polish people, the descendants of the kingly tribe of the Piast; we shall march when the golden horn calls — so help us mighty God." As we reached the moment of the pledge, "so help us God," all the right hands went up in a solemn oath. Tears were stifling me as I kept thinking, "So this is it. So this is what the war looks like. So this is the fatherland, and I and the others, the Poles and Jews alike, are its children. We are all brothers. We have a common cause."

[1] At the time the town was Polish and called Lwów. Today it is in Russia and called Lvov. I will use current names of towns and cities throughout.

By now the throng had formed into a huge army of people who marched first to the French Consulate, then to the British one, calling on the consuls to urge their governments to declare war on Germany. While marching, the throng chanted, "Up with Hitler — up the light pole — let the miser lose his damned soul."

As I marched with the throng, I tried to figure out how I could help in this war, a war in which many heroes would be born and many heroes would die. In the society in which I had been brought up, the cult of the hero was tremendous. As a child I had had the urge to be a hero myself when I grew up. But now, most of this feeling was gone, washed away by the years of rejection by the Polish part of my society. There were thirty-one million people; the Jews were three and a half million. They told us day after day that we were cowards, that we were not Polish, that we should leave Poland and go to Palestine — and the result was that we had become the way they chose to see us.

The next morning, I got together with three of my friends, Adam, Salek, and Pentsak. Salek and Pentsak, like me, had studied abroad. I had studied medicine, first in Italy, then in Belgium and France. This was caused by a restriction on the number of Jewish students who were allowed in the medical schools in Poland. The same was true in the school of pharmacy and engineering, and this is why Salek and Pentsak had studied architecture abroad, first in Milan, and, after Mussolini's introduction of the Nüremberg laws in Italy, in Grénoble, France.

We were all twenty-three years old, and all coming from well-to-do Jewish business families. My father, an exporter of willowware furniture and baskets to America, and a part owner of the most modern movie theater in town, had tried hard four years earlier to have me accepted in a Polish medical school. He had even bribed an influential university professor to help me, but his effort had backfired the day Poland's first marshal Józef Pilsudski had died. It was in May, 1935; I was about to take my *matura* examination; and the professor who had taken the money, Pilsudski's man, had lost overnight all of his influence.

It didn't make much difference by now anyhow. Poland, although still governed by Pilsudski's political party, was in fact ruled by the fascist National-Democrats, the virulently anti-Semitic Endeks, who wanted to see the Jews dispossessed, expelled, or even destroyed.

Father, who had visited New York in the late spring, returned to liquidate his business in Lvov, and to transfer it to the U.S.A.

Meantime, he had sent my brother Max, a thirty-one year old lawyer, to New York, to mind the sales office father had opened during his visit to the World's Fair in the Flushing Meadow.

My other brother, Gustav, thirty-three, had been living in Palestine since 1933, where he had gone as an idealist, a pioneer, a *Halutz*, as it was known by its Hebrew name in the Zionist circles.

The oldest brother, Martin, thirty-seven years old, had been married for two years, and had an excellent position in Zloczow, a small town east of Lvov, where he was the director of the accounting office of the largest bacon factory in Poland. Martin's wife, Pola, the only acquired member of our family, came from a rich family of tea and coffee importers in Lvov, and she brought Martin as a part of the dowry, one half of a large apartment house. Pola's apartment house was the reason why Martin still was in Poland, instead of directing his boss' accounting office in New York, a job he had been offered and had rejected, because apartment houses could not be exported from Poland, and money obtained from selling one would have been frozen inside the country, due to terse government restrictions.

Mother, once upon a time a beautiful, matronly woman with blue eyes and very long blond hair, was now sixty-years old, and suffered from various post-menopausal complications, which made her feel physically not well, and unhappy and depressed.

Frankly, my family, I, and my friends had no business being in Poland at the time when a global upheaval was in the making. Some of the other Jewish students stayed in France or in Belgium, having decided that, should there be a war, they would join the Foreign Legion.

But the four of us were Polish patriots. We wanted to fight under the white and red flag of Poland.

We briefly analyzed the situation and made a quick decision. After all, heroes or no heroes, we had returned to Poland from abroad just for this one purpose: to join the army and fight Hitler.

We went downtown to the crowded recruitment post. We watched other young people arriving with mobilization cards in their hands, and we felt awkward. Then we saw a lieutenant. Adam looked and always acted very Polish. He stepped forward, stood at attention, and reported in a military fashion: "Sir, we respectfully ask to be drafted." The lieutenant asked why we hadn't received our mobilization cards, and Adam explained that we were university students and therefore not subjected to the regular draft. He added that the rest of us studied abroad.

"Then you are Jewish," said the lieutenant. He knew well what sector of the Polish population would send their children to foreign universities.

The lieutenant stood at the top of the stairs, Adam just one step below, and Salek, Pentsak, and I all the way down. The lieutenant seemed to us like a god on Mount Olympus, and we the mortals were humbly waiting for his decision. A captain joined the lieutenant. He asked what this was all about, and the lieutenant repeated, "Jews, Captain, sir. They want to join the army." Now there were two gods up on Olympus. The captain examined us carefully. Then, he made up his mind. He called a sergeant and ordered him to give us equipment. Each of us was given a military belt and a cap, and we were ordered to report as soon as possible to the army headquarters in Zloczow, some seventy kilometers east of Lvov. Happily we had been drafted.

My oldest brother, Martin, lived in Zloczow. His marriage had been a typical Jewish arrangement, through a matchmaker. I could never understand how my father, a so-called assimilated Jew who kept the major Jewish holy days strictly, but otherwise was quite more Polish than Jewish, could agree to a matchmaking for his oldest, his favorite son. It must have been because of my mother's strong wishes.

Mother had been visiting with Martin and Pola for some time now, so that when the war erupted, she was caught away from home. It proved to be a blessing. The night of September 3 my three friends, a few of Martin's friends, my father and I gathered in our house at nine in the evening, so that we all could start on our way to Zloczow.

Zloczow lay seventy kilometers east of Lvov, away from the approaching German army, and it was there that the Polish army headquarters had opened its temporary strategic office.

Old people wanted to go to Zloczow to avoid falling under the German occupation; young people went there in the hope of being drafted and sent to the front.

Father opened the heavy walnut cabinet where his prize wines and liquors were kept. He brought out a bottle of a seventy-year-old Armagnac that I had brought him as a gift from France, uncorked it, and served everybody. "We don't know what is going to happen," he said. "This might prove to be our last decent drink."

He called Marynia, our maid from time immemorial, and poured her a drink, saying, "Now, you will be the head of this house."

He looked around. It was a nice middle-class apartment: the parents' bedroom with beautiful, old lemon-wood furniture; the huge walnut dining room for special occasions, where we were now having our farewell drink; a studio which also served as my bedroom; a nice little dining room for everyday use; Marynia's little room; a huge kitchen; two bathrooms; a terrace in the front; a kitchen balcony with a separate exit at the back.

Marynia sobbed.

"No time for tears now," said Father, and he made a toast: "No war can be as terrible as the Great War. We have a solid government, and with the help of our good friends the French and the British, this war will be over by next spring. The German offensive will be stopped as soon as the autumn rains fall. They'll drown in the good old muddy roads of Poland. In the early spring we'll have a massive counteroffensive and a total victory."

We emptied our glasses solemnly. It was time to leave.

"We'll leave everything the way it is," said Father to Marynia. "We'll just take with us some silverware. It could be of help."

Since the trains were clogged with troops, all the horses had been commandeered, and the few automobiles were out of gas and abandoned along the highways, we had to go on foot.

In pitch darkness, we left the city through the Pohulanka Forest, and then we turned east, trying to get to the highway. It didn't take us long to realize that taking the silverware had been a capital error. We hung the heavy valise on a stick, and at first I carried it with Adam, then Salek with Pentsak, then I with Salek, then Pentsak with Adam, then I again with Adam. We hadn't even reached the highway yet.

I was fed up, and I said so to Father. I expected him to react. I almost wanted him to become violent, to start preaching about the sweat it took to earn the money that bought the silver. After all, I had not yet earned a penny in my life.

Father surprised me. "I should have thought of all that weight," he said. "It makes no sense. Drop it. Drop it right there. This is not the end of the world. When the war is over, I'll make money and buy new silverware."

I was confused. My three friends couldn't hide their joy. Our way had become much easier now, and we walked briskly for five hours.

At dawn, the German airplanes started raiding the road in two waves per hour. Each time the raiders appeared on the horizon, we ran into the potato fields or into the ditches, hid our heads in the Mother Earth, and covered them with our rolled jackets. The Germans made a game out of these raids. There wasn't anybody to shoot at them. The few soldiers on the road ran into the potato fields even faster than we did. The teams of Luftwaffe flew low, almost skirting the tree tops, and machine-gunned the road, the trees, and the fields. Occasionally, they threw a small bomb on an abandoned truck or horse-driven wagon.

Because of the slow pace caused by these raids, we didn't reach Zloczow until three in the afternoon. Martin's beautiful apartment had by now become a sort of way station where his friends and his friends' friends stopped overnight, before resuming their travels. Here, for the first time, I learned that many of these people were going toward the Rumanian border, hoping to sneak across the Dniestr River and forget all about the war, the fatherland, and the patriotic effort.

We did not find the army headquarters in Zloczow. If we wanted to catch up with the army, somebody suggested, we'd better continue eastward, the next largest town being Zborow.

My parents, Martin, and Pola tried to dissuade us from following the army. They wanted us to stay with them and wait for the events to happen. Yet, we still had that thing in us. We had come back to Poland from abroad to fight Hitler, and we were going to fight him. Adam, the only one who had not come from abroad, also wanted to fight for his fatherland. And so we said good-bye to the family, took small bundles of food and a change of shirts given us by Pola, and went to Zborow.

We left early in the morning and by nightfall had reached Zborow, where we found a synagogue, which was filled with refugees. Here we learned that the army headquarters weren't in Zborow any longer. Somebody said that it had moved farther to the east, toward the Russian border. Others thought that it was the army itself that had gone toward Russia, while the headquarters were already in Rumania. Whatever was said, it was just a rumor. Zborow was a poor town, and the head of the Jewish community didn't even have a radio. Now, we really didn't know what to do, so, as one of the refugees suggested, we decided to wait in Zborow and see.

We waited a day. And a second day.

On the morning of the third day, we stood in the town's marketplace, watching the Ukrainian peasants from the Zborow countryside come into town. They carried flails, scythes, sticks, and empty bags.

The reason for their gathering in the marketplace was not clear to us, so we just stood there and watched them. That morning, I had washed my shirt, and while it was drying, I was wearing a beautiful silken Russian rubashka that Pola had given me when we were leaving Zloczow.

An army ambulance arrived. Strangely, it came from the east, from the general direction of Russia, and was headed west, toward Lvov. It stopped in the marketplace, and two Polish officers came out to stretch their legs. I recognized one of them, an assistant at the Jewish Hospital in Lvov under whose supervision I had worked for a good part of the previous summer.

I ran toward him, my hand outstretched. "Dr. Rotter! What a pleasure to see you!" He shook my hand cordially and asked what I was doing in Zborow. I told him that my friends and I had been following the army, and that now we were waiting.

The other officer then joined the conversation. "So you are waiting!" he said. "And you are ready to give welcome," he added sarcastically, pointing toward my Russian rubashka.

Puzzled, I looked at Dr. Rotter, who said to the other officer, "Colleague, you're wrong to assume that. I know this young man very well." Then, turning to me, he asked, "Haven't you been listening to the radio?"

"There is no radio in Zborow. We haven't heard any news in four days. Since we left Zloczow."

"Then better brace yourself," said Rotter. "Today, the Russians have invaded Poland. I'm afraid that the war is over. It's all been a big, tragic joke. Our army has surrendered to the Russians. Soon, you will see the disarmed Polish soldiers going back home. I'm sorry, colleague." Rotter and the other officer returned to the ambulance and left.

The marketplace was now crowded with flail-wielding Ukrainian peasants. Some young Ukrainians installed a large machine gun on a promontory at the edge of the cemetery overlooking the town. It became finally clear what the reason was for the peasants' meeting in town. Although we were aware of the pogroms that had occurred at various times in Polish history, we were nice boys from good, middle-class Jewish families and simply couldn't believe that we were about to witness the mass murder of a whole town. The local Jews were less sophisticated. They had already heard some rumors about the Ukrainians who attacked a group of Polish cadets, closed them in a barn, and set fire to the building. And other rumors about peasants who cut off people's fingers to get a quick hold of their rings. In one respect the local Jews and the four of us were identical: we had no idea how to defend ourselves.

It was already afternoon, and it became obvious that the Ukrainians were waiting for the night to fall. Possibly, they needed the cover of darkness.

A short while later, a Russian tank arrived in town. It was huge, awkward-looking, and welcome. We ran to it. An officer was standing in its open tower. He spoke some Polish. We poured our fears out at him. We pointed to the machine gun up on the cemetery, and he promised to wait there, until the Russian Army would start flowing into town. It didn't take long for the Ukrainians to evaluate the new development. The machine gun soon disappeared, and the peasants dispersed slowly, almost unwillingly. They had missed their chance.

RUSSIAN OCCUPATION

LATE IN THE AFTERNOON, a group of Polish soldiers appeared on the road. They were unarmed and dirty from many days of retreat, but happy.

"Oh, what fine kids, the Russians," one of them answered when we asked about the first encounter with the invading Soviet Army. "They are not at all like we used to be told."

He didn't say more, but then it wasn't necessary to hear his story. The Russian Army started arriving in town. That evening, Russian tanks rolled through Zborow; on they came, day and night, day and night, for four nights and three days. Some of them stopped for an hour or so, enough time to spend their rubles in the stores reopened by the Jewish owners. They had a good supply of rubles, and they bought whatever there was for sale. All the goods were sold the very first day, and after that the owners kept the stores open only to give a warm smile to their liberators and to tell them that there was nothing more they could buy.

One day, a young artillery officer visited the local woman doctor complaining of an awful toothache. I had had some recent experience in dentistry, so I assisted the doctor in ridding the young man of his aching tooth. After having done this, I asked him some questions that had been bothering me for quite a few years. We didn't know anything about the Soviet Union, except some invectives uttered by the most patriotic of our gymnasium teachers, who had been members of Pilsudski's Polish Legion during World War I. I wanted to know about the freedom of expression, about the freedom of worship, about the Soviet class structure. To each of my questions, the young officer said only, "It's good in the Soviet Union. We have everything. And what we don't have, we will have." Obviously, I didn't learn much from him.

The next day, a *Politruk* (an officer in charge of political indoctrination) stopped for an hour in the marketplace to extoll the Soviet system. He lectured the people who gathered around him on every Soviet citizen's equal right to a decent life, to education, to work, and to a dwelling. I asked him about my own problem. How would the Russian authorities treat a medical student with a foreign university background?

He thought for a moment, and then said, "Show me your hands." He also asked an old peasant woman standing next to me to show him her hands. Then he stated solemnly, "Mother, yours are the hands of a working person. For you our Soviet fatherland will be a paradise. And you," he addressed me, "you have the soft hands of a bourgeois, and we'll make due accounts with you!"

On the very first evening of the Russian invasion — or rather liberation, as they called it — all the lights along the main road went on. This was a symbolic end of the war. My three friends and I reported to the town hall, where the Russians had established their temporary town command. We wanted to let the commandant know that we were there, four aspiring fighters, to help in fighting Hitler. It was our assumption that this was the purpose of the Russians' going westward with all their might.

Instead, we were told to surrender our military caps and belts, and the commandant also decided that my hunting knife was a weapon, and he confiscated it.

The huge Soviet Army was pouring in, without a pause. In rolled columns of tanks, cavalry, infantry, batteries of heavy guns, convoys of supply wagons, airplanes, and more tanks, and more guns. This gigantic army marched, and marched, and marched, and the very sight of its size would have made anybody think twice before offering it an armed resistance. Oh, I thought, this is the end of Hitler. Some of the soldiers with whom I had spoken assured me that this army would not stop before taking Berlin.

At noon of the fourth day, it was all over. The last wagons had disappeared down the road leading westward. Adam, Salek, Pentsak, and I still stood at the edge of the road, reminiscing on this show of might never seen by us before. At that moment, a strange figure appeared in the middle of the road, coming from the east. It was a lone Russian soldier, short and thin. The rifle he was carrying on his shoulder seemed so heavy that his legs literally bowed under its burden. He trudged past us, and then, as in an afterthought, stopped and turned back. He smiled shyly and asked something in Russian. Adam said we didn't understand him. He repeated his question, this time in Yiddish: "Is it safe to go west? Have they stopped shooting?" I felt this was indeed an anticlimax to the events of the last three weeks.

There was nothing for us to do in Zborow any longer. The mighty Polish army, the invincible infantry, the light artillery, and the swift, colorful Ulans, were no more. Some part of the army had crossed the border and fled to Rumania, emulating the example of the Polish government and the chiefs of staff who had escaped just before the arrival of the Soviet troops. If any war remained to be fought, it would have to be done by the Russians, but so far nothing pointed to a Russo-German war.

We returned to Zloczow. There, we found my parents, Martin, and Pola in good health but in miserable spirits. Martin had become afraid of his shadow. During the last few days, the bacon factory had been confiscated from its lawful owners, and a Soviet director had been assigned to run it. From the very first day, he had been stealing the goods, while making Martin personally responsible for the functioning of the business. Father was unhappy because, from listening to the radio, he had learned what we didn't know: the Russians had come here to stay and not to help Poland in her fight against Hitler.

And Father developed an instant dislike for the Russians. He considered them rude, mannerless peasants whose only interest was buying watches, boots, vodka, and women. In fact, he disliked them so much that he would rather have had the Germans, whom he remembered from World War I as cultured and courteous people.

Mother was unhappy because she didn't like to be away from home, and Pola was miserable because she could already forsee that the Russians would soon confiscate the apartment she and Martin lived in.

Some of these feelings proved to be correct; some others, all wrong. But in the meantime, my three friends and I decided to start on our way to Lvov, seeing no immediate need for Father and Mother to return.

It was a sad way back. People who had left Lvov two weeks ago, in good physical health and decently dressed, were trudging now along the road—dirty, ragged, barefoot, their limbs swollen and ulcerated. Some helped themselves with sticks made from broken tree branches. Some, like us, traveled on the grotesque peasant ladder wagons, makeshift carriages whose sides consisted of two ladders stood on edge. Passengers sat on the narrow floors of these wagons with their legs dangling through the bars of the ladder; they looked as haggard as their pedestrian comrades.

At one point, a wagon passed us on which we recognized two of our Polish classmates. Not so many years back, Adam and I had been their friends. Now they looked at us with hostility. The ambulance captain's words came back to my mind. They, too, thought that we were waiting for the Russians to come. Every Pole was now thinking that every Jew wanted Poland to cease to exist, to become Russian, to become conquered again, after only twenty short years of independence. I thought how wrong they were and how they still did not understand that a Polish Jew wanted to be a good Pole. Yes, this was all he wanted: to be a good Pole and to be given a chance to show it.

It took us over thirty hours to get back to Lvov. When we finally reached my home, Adam, Salek, and Pentsak thought they would stay overnight. When Marynia opened the door and saw us, she was jubilant. She kept saying, "Everything is bad, very bad."

We all sat down at the dining table, and Marynia told us how the janitor and his wife had come to the apartment and had told her that now they could take from us what they needed. They emptied our cupboards and the pantry. Marynia also told us that when the Russian Army was marching in the street, somebody had shot at them from the roof of the house opposite to ours. The Russians answered with grenades.

"There was a horse, and a wagon, and a peasant standing down there" — she pointed from the window to a heap of contorted steel and fragments of wood across the street. "Then there were just pieces of meat everywhere. People took away whatever was left from the horse. A piece of meat is still lying on our window sill." She pointed to a huge chunk of meat. "But I don't know whether it is the horse or the peasant."

The apartment looked ransacked, probably because of the many broken windows. It was cold, and there was no electricity. It really didn't feel like home. I felt helpless. Marynia thought that now that I was back, everything would return to order. But how? I didn't know how to fix things. Father had never let me take a hammer in my hand. I was destined to become a scholar or a doctor, nothing else. I hadn't even earned a penny in my life yet. Father had made it a point that I grow up despising money. My three brothers had a very well-inculcated notion of money and reality, while I, the youngest, was allowed to have dreams of perfection, to write poetry, and to live in a world of theory.

Marynia told us that if we wanted to buy bread, we'd have to be standing in line by four in the morning. The bread distribution started at eight, and there was never enough for everybody in the line. The house was cold and unfriendly, so we didn't even undress. We slept a couple of hours, then went to join the bakery line. Here, we were lucky. One of the salesgirls recognized me, and the four of us and Marynia got some bread. It amounted to one loaf and was black and wet, but it was bread, and, even more, it was my first personal achievement in the struggle for survival.

Some days later, Father and Mother returned, and together we set out to solve many urgent problems. There were windows to fix, but no glaziers around. We badly needed food supplies such as potatoes, cabbage, beets, flour, and lard. We could hardly get enough bread, let alone any other supplies. Mother was proud of her cooking. Now, she had to accept the idea that there would be none of it. Her pantry and the cabinets, not so long ago bursting with jars of preserves and cans of meat, now were empty. What's more, there were financial problems to contend with. Only two months before the war, Father had returned from a visit to the United States, where he opened an import agency in New York. Father had transferred a substantial amount of liquid assets to the new firm, and at the same time, he had invested in a couple of freight carloads of willowware. He had shipped the goods to the States just before the war, so that now we didn't have much ready cash. There was need for action.

Some of the problems were solved with relative ease. A neighbor of ours, a Mr. Schwartzbart, whom Mother used to ridicule because he was the only one who did the shopping for his family in a society where only the wives were the recognized shoppers, now proved the value of a man's direct involvement in the housewife's concerns. He knew where to find a handyman to fix things; he knew where to find replacement parts; he knew the prices of material and labor as they were yesterday, as they were today, and as they would be tomorrow. With Mr. Schwartzbart's help, our windows received brand new glass panels, and a peasant bartered two wagonloads of firewood for various pieces of Mother's clothing.

Then, the Pollaks arrived.

Adolph Pollak, a highly successful businessman, had been Father's good friend for as long as I could remember. Now, Adolph and Mitka Pollak were refugees from Warsaw. They arrived unexpectedly, but Mother immediately gave them our large dining room, which she converted into an additional bedroom. The Pollaks had with them their only son, Jasio, who was about twelve; Mitka Pollak's daughter from her first marriage, Marysia; and Marysia's husband, Nulek. We easily found a room for Marysia and Nulek, but then Adolph wanted us to find a room for their dearest friends, Dr. and Mrs. Szejnberg, and their son, Staszek, a medical student, who were about to arrive in Lvov.

The Pollaks had had one stroke of bad luck after another since a German bomb had fallen on their recently built movie theater in Warsaw on the very first day of the war. They had collected the most valuable things they had in the house and Mitka's innumerable fur coats and left Warsaw in two cars. As they stopped on the road to get some refreshments in an inn, a bomb fell on one of their cars, reducing it to dust. They continued eastward in one car and reached Pinsk at the time the Russians had occupied it. In the middle of the night, the Russians had confiscated their car and whatever valuables they found in it. Mitka put her sweater on, claiming that she felt cold. She was allowed to keep the sweater — and each button of this sweater was a huge, pure diamond! The biggest weighed fourteen karats. So the impoverished Pollaks still had enough capital to make plans for the future. And the future was now at hand.

Of course, money was still the first concern, but even people who had the money could buy hardly anything. The stores were empty, and there were no supplies coming in. Various large corporations, meanwhile, had been nationalized, and their employees had been given the right to organize their own food cooperatives. Pollak and Father contacted some of the cooperatives and started working for them as freelance buyers, which meant that the cooperatives made a truck and a driver available and gave Father a permit to travel in the countryside to purchase food, while Pollak and Father advanced the money necessary to buy the food. The supplies were resold to the cooperatives at the purchase price, and the freelance buyers could keep a part of the food as their wages. It was hard work, but it yielded the best food there was available. Again, Mother's pantry was filled with flour and fat, we had an ample supply of vegetables and meat, and there was even enough to resell, so that some money started coming in, instead of always flowing out. True, the janitor Wojciech had become a silent partner to everything, but it seemed worth it to keep him happy, because every janitor had by now become an official spy for the new regime.

So much for the simple everyday struggle for survival, which was just one of the most obvious symptoms. The real problem was much deeper.

As soon as the Russians had established themselves in the occupied territory, their political organization took over. Every inhabitant of Lvov had to register with the Russian militia in order to receive a passport. This was my first experience with a document called a passport that didn't have to do with going on a trip abroad; on the contrary, it was necessary if we were to stay where we were. Not everybody, it appeared, was entitled to a passport. Ex-owners of businesses, for example, were destined for deportation from Lvov, because they were members of the bourgeois class. Refugees, who by now numbered as many people as the usual population of Lvov, were also to be deported, because there might be German spies among them.

We were a part of the bourgeois class. However, I soon discovered that university students were entitled to a passport, their social origins notwithstanding, and their families also had the right to a passport. Quickly, I registered for French philology, passed the examination, and was accepted as a student. This resolved our passport problem.

Now, there was the question of protecting the Pollaks and their friend Dr. Szejnberg with his family. Father looked around and found contacts with the militia precinct. They were a Mr. Bergman and his common-law wife, Helena, from Warsaw who nevertheless had Soviet passports and friends in the militia who, for the right money, would procure passports for potential deportees. Through Mr. Bergman, Father arranged for passports for the Pollaks, the Szejnbergs, and quite a few other refugees whom the Pollaks recommended.

The Pollaks didn't stay with us for very long. They found two rooms in an apartment right under ours, on the second floor. It is true that they needed more room than they had with us, but it was even more true that they had a lot of secrets with the Szejnbergs, which they wanted to keep away from us.

By this time, Martin and Pola had also moved to Lvov and were staying with us. Martin found himself a minor bookkeeping job for one hundred and forty rubles a month.

During the winter, other worries arose. The Soviet political police, the NKVD, raided people's homes nightly. They checked papers, asked innumerable questions, then loaded people on horse-driven wagons and took them away. Soon, it became known that the abducted people were put on crowded and cold freight trains and that as soon as a train was ready, which sometimes meant up to three days wait, it left Lvov going eastwards. Soon, letters started coming from the deported people. They came from various locations, but from one territory: Kazakhstan. All we knew from the letters was: "We are living in labor camps; in order to warm up our huts, we must cut our own wood in the nearby forest; if we want to earn money to buy the black bread (and it is all we can purchase here), we must work as lumberjacks; the climate is terribly cold and the land is rugged; we all suffer vitamin deficiency, have ulcers, and are losing teeth." Everybody was sending to the deportees packages containing garlic and onion extract, salt pork, and canned meat. Most packages were received.

The majority of the deported people were refugees from German-occupied Poland, but there was always the fear that one night the NKVD might start taking away the local people. It became very important to have a job. Of course, there were not enough jobs in Lvov, but one could buy a certificate of employment, so that he would have at least something to show to the NKVD people when needed. Father and Pollak bought such certificates. Dr. Szejnberg didn't need one, because, as a physician, he had a legitimate job in a hospital.

The Russian liberators were not liked by the middle-class Jews of Lvov. They were called patronizingly "Fonky," which, I believe, came from the common peasant name Fonyia, and it was rarely that a God-fearing, middle-class Jew was found entertaining a Russian in his house, unless a part of the house had been confiscated by the Russian housing authority and allocated to a Russian. Such allocations were a daily routine, as the Russian housing law permitted four square meters of living space per person in a family, and if a family was composed of two people and had a four-room apartment, one or more tenants could be assigned to the surplus space. The Polish population hated the Russians on both a cultural and a historical basis, the Warsaw part of Poland having been occupied by Czarist Russia for a century and a half, until World War I.

The middle class of Lvov showed their dislike for the Russians in ways subtle enough to allow them to ridicule the occupiers without running into any danger. Peddlers would sell negligee fabric to Russian women, assuring them that it was the finest Western material for evening wear, and indeed, I did see Russian girls coming to a party dressed in nightgowns. Russian soldiers loved watches to such an extent that on many occasions I saw a soldier wearing a half dozen of them on both forearms. I remember once seeing a peddler shake a watch close to his victim's ear, and as the broken inside of the watch was rattling, he asked, "Can you hear this perfect tick-tock?"

The most popular part of the middle-class vendetta against the Russians was the derisive jokes. One was told of a Russian officer who had just taken possession of his newly allotted room and, after having spent some time in the bathroom, said to his host, "You have an interesting washing arrangement there. But it needs some improvements, because it's too low, the water runs too fast, and one has to pull the cord several times before the soap can be washed off the face."

During my student years in Belgium and France I came in contact with symbolist poetry. I translated poems of Baudelaire, Verlaine, and Verhaeren into Polish, and, influenced by them, I started writing my own poetry.

Now, in the university of Lvov, my skill as a poet had flourished. Yearning for a chance to express myself, I organized Polish, Ukrainian, Russian, and Yiddish poets into a literary club of the Russian university of Lvov. We had our monthly literary magazine, of which I had become the editor-in-chief; we had our debate evenings; and, well-aware of the gatherings of artists and literary men in the nineteenth-century salons, we created our own Thursday afternoon unofficial meetings, where poetry and chapters of prose were read, sandwiches of black bread with hard boiled eggs eaten, and soft Crimean wine drunk.

In order to be allowed public conferences and the magazine, we struck a deal with the Russian rector of the university, according to which half of our production could be as we wished it, provided that the other half would consist of praises of Soviet socialism.

Although our club had many Polish literary men, I was chosen to be the head of it. The Polish students feared exposure to the communist youth organization, the Komsomol, and chose secondary roles in the club.

At home, I had arguments with Father. He called the Russians "Fonky" and said that he would gladly exchange them for the Germans. Anytime. I argued, sometimes angrily, that the time might arrive when we would all be happy to kiss the ground where the Soviet boot had stepped. Father pointed to the deportations and to the news from Kazakhstan. I replied that surely Stalin knew what he was doing. And so on.

My life in the Soviet Lvov was a big surprise to me. Never before had I been so involved in what I was doing, and never before had I had the feeling of belonging that I had now. I could write, and I could listen to discussion regarding my work.

My position as an editor kept me always in public view and brought me, as one of the fringe benefits, a number of relationships with girl students.

One of them was Anka. I met her during the most important evening of my literary career. Our club had been getting ready for that evening for a long time. Three impressionistic announcements made by one of our members were posted, one in front of the university, and two in the lobby.

The night before the meeting, I had a strange dream. It consisted of two sentences said by a very sweet and very penetrating female voice: "Your posters have been taken down. Go immediately to the rector."

As I was approaching the university in the morning, I realized suddenly that something was not right. Then I remembered my dream, and I knew what was wrong: there was no poster in front of the university. Excitedly, I ran into the lobby. The posters weren't there. I proceeded to the rector. He said the posters were too impressionistic. The Komsomol had already intervened, and the matter was out of his hands. However, after I had reminded the rector of a number of prominent literary figures, including Professor Boy-Zelenski, who were invited for the evening, he took me to the Komsomol's office. He pleaded for me and promised in my name that our readings would be well-balanced, and that social realism would be well-represented.

The meeting took place. Every author read his poem or his piece of prose. I was scheduled to be the last one. This morning's argument, however, had cost me my voice, and when the time came for me to read, it was Fredek Szwarc who read my latest poem, "The Jews."

I remember it well in Polish. I wish I could translate it into English, but I'm afraid it wouldn't do. There was something to this poem — oh, it was crude, it could have used many more finishing touches — yet, there was something to it that not even I had recognized before this evening. As Fredek read in his beautiful basso, one could feel enormous tension in the air, and when the last words were spoken, "Forever they'll suffer and fear," something strange happened. There was total silence for a moment, and then everybody applauded and applauded. All those important faculty members patting me on the shoulder, and shaking my hand, and congratulating me. I felt like flying and yelling to the entire world, "A Poet was born this night, a Poet!"

I needed somebody to talk to about my wonderful experience, but there was nobody at home who might show an interest in my literary success. I never discussed with my family my extracurricular activities at the university. My parents didn't know that I was writing anything, let alone poetry. I would have been embarrassed to say to my father, "Here is your son the poet."

As I was leaving the university, Anka approached me and said, "Forever they'll suffer and fear." This was the beginning of our love story, which lasted, with interruptions, for some three months, then was renewed during the German invasion, only to end in the Nazi concentration camps.

A couple of days later, a daily newspaper described our event and mentioned me. Adolph Pollak was the first one to read it. He congratulated Father, and by the time I came home that evening, everybody knew. My parents sat at the table next to me.

"So, you are a poet," said Mother sadly.

"You never mentioned it," said Father.

"I was afraid you wouldn't understand me. You might have ridiculed me."

"We are proud of you," Father said.

And I felt so bad, so guilty, so unworthy. They were too old for me. The youngest of my older brothers was eight years my senior. All my life, I had felt an ugly, dark gap between me and the rest of the family. As a child, I wasn't allowed to talk in front of the elders. As a university student, in my first letter home from Italy, I had described the beauty of that country, and Father had answered in a stern typewritten letter, "You went to Italy to study, not to admire nature."

Since then, I had never tried again to cross the gap. And now, they had done it.

It was spring, 1940, and the legendary offensive by the Polish army against the Germans had failed to take place. People who had money decided to escape to Rumania.

One of them was Pollak, with his wife Mitka, and twelve-year-old son Jasio. They paid a guide; they were betrayed; they wound up in the jail of Kharkov; and Jasio, because of his tender age, was sent to the Pollaks' best friend, Dr. Szejnberg.

And when, finally, the Pollaks were let go, they discovered that Mitka's 14-karat diamond hidden in Jasio's heel, was missing.

An argument ensued, during which the Pollaks called the Szejnbergs to the rabbinical law suit, the Din Torah; the Szejnbergs refused to appear; and a long and precious friendship had badly ended.

Nobody knew it yet at that time, but the two families were destined to meet again in this world, for just one short afternoon, at the end of which they all would be executed, under the same wall, and by the same machine gun.

At that time, some people in Lvov started receiving mail from the United States. A letter came from Max, in which he described his arrival in New York and advised us that soon he would be sending a package. Mother was showing the letter proudly to all her acquaintances. She had a son in America — her favorite son — and now she would be receiving packages from him. But they never arrived. This was the only letter we received. Max never liked to write. Instead, he sent cables. They were coded, so that the Russian censor wouldn't know what they were all about. Father answered in similarly coded cables. Instead of using the word *dollars*, they used *baskets*. Most of the cables had to do with transfers of money from Lvov to New York. The cable business went on for some time. Father kept transferring small amounts of his money; Martin sold some of his valuables and had Father transfer his money; Pollak also had an amount transferred. And imagine, the Russian censor believed all the while that these people were all living out of baskets.

One day, we received mail from Berlin. It came from the Legation of Ecuador, and it was a notice that there were visas waiting for us there. All we had to do was to report to the German capital. Father inquired around, only to find out that we might as well forget those visas, as nobody, especially no Polish Jew, would be allowed to go to Berlin. Besides, to leave Russia, one had to get an exit visa from the NKVD. We assumed that the arrangements for the visas had been made by Max, and we were sure that he would try to help. Father sent a cable to Max. This time, the baskets probably meant visas.

It was in late spring 1940 that a thick letter arrived from Ecuador. We opened the manila envelope and found three passports bearing our names, our photographs, and the most exciting statement yet: we were citizens of the Republic of Ecuador! It all seemed perfectly clear: the Ecuadorian representative in Berlin, Señor Gomez, must have been made aware by Max that we couldn't possibly come to the German capital to pick up our visas and had advised his government accordingly. The good Ecuadorians had decided to help us in the simplest way possible: they accorded us their citizenship. Now all we had to do was to get an exit visa. Father knew at that time a family that had just received an exit permit, so it became apparent that a contact in the NKVD and a substantial bribe could get us the visas. Meanwhile, Martin and Pola had received their passports, and the rest of Pola's family had received theirs. Thus Father would make one combined effort for the entire group of some nineteen people.

I had been asking myself often whether I really wanted to leave the Soviet Lvov and go to an unknown Ecuador. I didn't have a clear-cut answer at that time. I finally had a place under the sun. I was an equal part of an equal society. I was productive.

On the other hand, my parents didn't belong there. They and Martin were unhappy and wanted to escape from a life they considered a nightmare.

Then there was the sense of adventure. The idea of crossing the entire Asian Russia, going to Japan, crossing the Pacific, and discovering the jungles of South America mesmerized me. As I was searching for the right answer to my dilemma, Father had quietly made his contacts, paid some advance bribes, and deposited our passports with the NKVD of Boryslaw, the town of my birth. The time was passing, I was becoming restless, Father was traveling back and forth to Boryslaw without knowing when he should start looking for somebody to buy our household furnishings, and Mother was all desperation about what to do with our miniature pinscher, Mousi. Months were passing, and strange rumors could be heard around the city. We all had radios, but all the foreign stations were jammed, so that we knew only what the Soviet government wanted us to know and what some unknown sources, seemingly with a free access to foreign transmission, spread around. At first, the rumors said that the Russian-German friendship signed in summer 1939 was not to be a long-lasting one. There was talk about the Germans being in need of the Ukrainian wheat and the Russians considering some sort of an arrangement. Then the rumor said that Russia had received an ultimatum from Hitler. We weren't told what the ultimatum was all about, but it was supposed to expire in two weeks.

In spring 1941 Father sent Martin to Boryslaw, to make sure that he would get our visas on the same day that they were ready. Then Martin called up. There was something wrong in the NKVD in Boryslaw. The contact Father had made had suddenly become inaccessible to Martin. Father was called to the NKVD in Lvov and interrogated regarding our passports. The ground on which we were walking seemed to burn our feet.

On June 19, 1941, Martin unexpectedly returned to Lvov. He was excited and pessimistic. He had our passports, but no exit visas. The NKVD man who was supposed to handle them told Martin that everything had gone wrong, and that we might even expect to be deported.

On June 20, I was seated with Adam, whom I had not seen in months, and two girls on the High Castle, an old park in Lvov, where the citizens had raised a tall mound of earth some three hundred years before to commemorate the Union between the King of Poland and the Principality of Lithuania. From our vantage point, we could see antiaircraft lights sweeping the starry sky. I said, "Today is the last day of the ultimatum." Adam dismissed this as an insignificant rumor. But by now, I hoped that it was not just a rumor but a fact. I feared that, given a couple of more days, the NKVD might pick us up.

When I returned home, I found a mobilization call for the next morning.

And at four in the morning, Lvov was bombed.

Father turned on the radio, and now, for the first time, we could hear, undisturbed, an impassioned speech by Goebbels. The Germans were coming. They were going to bring freedom to the nations oppressed by the barbaric Bolshevik hordes. They were carrying the sword and the cross.

CHAPTER

3

GERMAN INVASION

Eᴀʀʟʏ ɪɴ ᴛʜᴇ ᴍᴏʀɴɪɴɢ, I reported to the Russian Army recruiting office.

It was in an uproar. A disquieting air of uncertainty was hanging there, as people of all ages and in assorted physical conditions were reporting for medical examination. I ran across Adam, Salek, and Pentsak. I hadn't seen the last two since the time we had returned to Lvov over a year and a half before. We undressed and joined what was known in Lvov since the Austro-Hungarian times as a *schwanz-parade,* "the parade of tails."

We were taken into a large room where the Russian military medical commission was making its decisions. The potential recruit in front of me walked with the help of two crutches. The head doctor took a quick look at him, and said, "Eh, you're still good enough to drop a couple of bombs," and he dictated to the secretary, "Bomber!" The four of us were assigned to the infantry. We were given our classifications and told that we would be sent notices when and where to report.

I parted from my friends and went to the university. The classes were suspended. I learned that the secretary of the Komsomol had just been knifed to death in the men's bathroom. As I started on my way back home, shooting erupted all around me. I took refuge in the lobby of an apartment building. I was soon joined by other people. Everybody looked scared, but nobody knew any details about the shooting. We could see out in the street Russian tanks and armored cars rolling toward the eastern boundaries of the city. This was a retreat.

I felt a sharp pain in my chest. Then, it had all been a dream, this past year and a half. Then, it was good-bye to my Russian friends. The infantrymen ran along both sides of the street, close to the buildings, clutching their tommy guns and looking up. Snipers were shooting from the roofs. Now the soldiers were returning fire. A body fell in front of the door, making a juicy, smacking sound. A well-dressed, middle-aged man burst into the hall. "It's unbelievable!" he was saying excitedly. "They're shooting all over the city. It's the Ukrainian underground. The Russians are in full retreat. The Germans have already surrounded Lvov."

I looked at my wristwatch. It was one o'clock. I remembered Goebbels's speech. That was at four in the morning. My God, only nine hours, and everything's gone!

Early in the afternoon, the Russian exodus came to a standstill. Shortly after, the tanks, the armored trucks, the heavy guns and the infantry turned about-face and rolled westward, toward where the Germans supposedly were. The shooting lasted until four o'clock. Then everything subsided.

Now we were cut off from any news. The radio played patriotic Soviet music, while all the foreign stations were again silenced by the buzzing sound of the censor's electronic devices.

By evening, waves of German aircraft were bombing the city uninterruptedly. It was a repetition of the first days of September 1939, except that now some sort of resistance was offered by the Russians. A couple of times, we saw a Luftwaffe plane hit by the Soviet antiaircraft, and falling in a cloud of smoke. We also saw duels between two airplanes. It seemed to amuse Father. He stayed for hours on the terrace, watching the battle through binoculars. Mother didn't seem to be at all excited, but Martin was furiously pulling at a lock of his hair, which meant that he was nervous, and Pola was frankly defeated. She walked around the apartment mumbling in despair, "This is it. Now, we're all finished. Now, we're all dead." I wasn't nervous yet. I just wanted to have my chance for a couple of shots against the Nazis.

The bombings took on the aspect of a nightmare. Maybe I wasn't yet in the tragic shape of Pola, but I couldn't help thinking, "What for? Stop defending the city. Let them stop the bombing. Let them take over. This is no life, the way it is." I knew that one day I would regret having had such thoughts, but at the time I couldn't help myself.

On the third day, some of the people who had been inducted on the first two days returned. Two of them, dirty, in torn uniforms, stopped in our shelter to rest for a while. One of them was Jewish. He told us of the terrible butchery he had witnessed outside of Lvov. The newly mobilized soldiers were being sent without training to stop the German bullets with their bodies.

In the evening of that day, huge clouds of dark smoke came out of the chimneys of the large, modern NKVD building at the corner of Jablonowska Street. On the waves of the smoke flew burnt sheets of paper. The NKVD were burning their files.

Another day of bombing passed, and then, late in the afternoon, an unusual silence fell on the city. The streets were empty. No civilians and no army could be seen anywhere.

The night passed quietly. We were all in the cellar, fearing a sudden resumption of the bombings. In the morning, the rabble went around looting stores and businesses. Our janitor Wojciech and his family joined in, and a few hours later they returned, pushing a cart with some twenty NKVD typewriters on it.

The day was overcast with heavy clouds. A huge Russian tank rolled in from the northern corner of the street. It stopped in front of our house, and the three soldiers who were manning it got out and tried to fix the vehicle. After a while, they gave up and marched off eastward. A few minutes later, a German plane flew over the tank, and a moment later several artillery shells fell nearby.

"Did they have to leave it here?" Martin mumbled.

Two other Russian soldiers appeared in the middle of the street. They were marching together, their arms thrown over each other's shoulders, and, in drunken voices, were singing a military paean to Stalin.

Our street was built in a shallow canyon. In the low hills behind us, the armory of the light artillery was located, and the Citadel, a robust old fortress, was on the hill in front of us, where the Austrians, then the Poles, and now the Russians kept their ammunition.

Both the armory and the Citadel erupted suddenly in repeated explosions. It was like the New Year's Eve in Naples when I was a student, only now, instead of a fireworks show, it was the real thing. It lasted late into the night. Our street was drowning in fire and thunder from both sides. Chips of shrapnel were falling on the roofs and ricocheting from the walls of the houses. The entire population of our building spent this last night in the cellar.

Late at night, the explosions stopped, and a deep calm befell the city.

At five in the morning, a neighbor who stood guard at the gate yelled at us, "The Germans are here!"

We and the tenants of the adjacent buildings gathered in small groups, watching the first Germans arrive in the city. A soldier on a motorcycle stopped in front of the building across the street from us. He was neat and shiny, from the top of his helmet to the wheels of his cycle. Some women and older men standing in front of the building threw their arms around him. Someone in our group whispered, "He is not German! I know him! He's the son of the Ukrainian janitor of that building!" I risked going across the street, and from a closer distance I could see a minute Ukrainian flag painted on one side of the soldier's helmet.

Another soldier stopped his cycle in front of us and waved at our group. Father approached, and the solder asked in German, "Where is the Ford dealer's place?"

Mr. Altschuler, Father's friend, had had a Ford dealership before the war, but when Lvov was occupied by the Russians, Mr. Altschuler lost his business. Father explained the situation to the soldier, and he left on his bike, cursing. He might have had an old score to settle with Mr. Altschuler.

Later in the day, regular troops marched in. They were all neatly shaven, the sleeves of their military jackets rakishly rolled up. It seemed as if they had spent a day washing and shining their shoes before deciding that they were finally in a shape to stun the city. The first companies were Ukrainian. The Germans followed for the rest of the day.

We saw more and more Ukrainian inhabitants of Lvov coming out of the buildings and warmly greeting more and more young, uniformed Ukrainian invaders, and we felt desolate. I remembered that feeling from what seemed to be a long time ago, when *war* was still a word, and when Poland was still Poland: the old familiar feeling of not belonging.

On July 2 posters were affixed everywhere calling for everybody to report to his work site and threatening to take drastic measures against anybody disobeying the order.

Many people took the risk and stayed home. But just as many law-abiding citizens reported next day to work. A part of the surprise awaiting them was easy to foresee: there was no work. The other part couldn't have been foreseen. Small groups of armed Ukrainian militiamen burst into various shops and offices, looking for Jews and herding them all into the middle of the street. Some three thousand Jews were thus gathered, and now, to the accompaniment of insults, kicked and beaten, they were driven to the Brigitki Prison. There, a heap of bodies of recently shot prisoners covered the yard. The Ukrainians, controlled by a few German SS officers, ordered the Jews to start gathering the bodies, to clean them, and to prepare them for burial. While the Jews were doing as they were ordered, they were beaten savagely. The chief rabbi of the Lvov Temple, Dr. Levin, refused to clean the bodies, stating that religion forbade him to do so, and he was shot on the spot. Over a hundred and twenty other Jews were shot in Brigitki that day, while others were crowded into the Lenckiego Prison at nightfall.

Next day, the Ukrainians kept rounding up more Jews and throwing them into Lenckiego. From our terrace, I could see the open military trucks rolling through our street in the direction of "the Sands." The official name of that part of the city was *Piaskowa Gora* (the "Sandy Mountain"). Before the war, there had been a rustic restaurant there where Father used to take us for an occasional Sunday dinner in late spring or early fall. While the adults played Bocce before dinner, we the children played in the warm neat sand of the mountain. Today, shots could be heard from that direction all day long, and I could see live people lying face down on the floors of the trucks, some of them covered loosely with tarpaulin, being driven toward the Sands.

The pogrom lasted three days.

For three days, I watched live bodies being driven to the Sands, only to become a remembrance in the hearts of the people who were left alive, and who continued loving them, and hoping for their return.

For three days, I listened to the outbursts of machine guns, knowing that each bullet produced a short shriek, a gasp, and oblivion.

But, strangely, I felt no panic. I was pervaded instead by a bottomless sadness, and I felt like saying in my mind, "God! Do you see? And do you hear? And if you do, how can you permit this to happen?"

On the night preceding the German invasion of Lvov, I had had a dream. The by-now familiar, soft female voice was saying strange words to me, and as she was saying them, a picture developed in front of me to illustrate their meaning. The voice said, "The mourning mothers stand above their distressed sons, clad in grief, curved in anguish, their black arms stretched in mute despair, like wooden crosses in an old country graveyard. The wind howls in eternal dejection. The wanderer kneels down in front of the most pathetic, the most tragic of all the mothers and bends his head in an act of repentance." As I was seeing this terrifying scene, the voice finished by saying, "And you will live to tell."

After three days of pogroms, Father still remained stoical.

"It is true," he said, "that many people have been murdered."

He shook his head, musing. My cousin Lusia had been taken to Lenckiego Prison, never to be seen again.

"But the Germans didn't do it," he continued. "They have just given a couple of days of free rein to the Ukrainians. Now, it is over, and law and order will be back. This is not the end of the world."

The Germans had taken over. One decree after another appeared, mostly regarding the new status of the Jewish population of Lvov. Some decrees were signed by the Schupo — the *Schutzstaffel* (SS), or Police-in-Charge-of-Protection; some bore the name of the Military commander of Lvov; most were signed by the Gestapo — the *Totenkopfverein* ("Death's-head Organization") — whose black caps with a metal skull in the front could be seen more and more often. One of the first such decrees established a Judenrath, the Jewish Council that was to be responsible for putting into effect the rest of the Jewish laws. After that came the decree about the Jewish armband. During the Soviet time, we had already had a vague idea about what was going on in the German-occupied part of Poland, and of course, we knew that in some parts of the territory the Jews had to wear a yellow patch in the shape of a Star of David; in other parts, it was a white armband with a blue Star of David painted on it. But as long as it was happening there and not here, we didn't have to feel the full emotional burden of it. Now it was here.

One of the last sentences of the decree made us feel strangely excited. It said that the above laws did not apply to Jews of foreign citizenship. We had those passports sent to us from Ecuador. We actually were Ecuadorian citizens!

Father took a walk to the Schupo headquarters and soon returned with the good news. We were considered foreign Jews; we didn't have to wear the armbands; we didn't have to consider any future

Jewish laws as applying to us; in witness of which, Father triumphantly exhibited a paper bearing the rubber stamp of Schupo that made us practically invulnerable. Thus, when the day came for the Jews to put on the armband, I stood on the terrace, my heart beating anxiously, to see how the Jewish population was going to take it and how the non-Jews were going to react.

It was surprising to see the dignity with which the Jews wore the armband. From the very first moment, instead of being an object of ridicule, which I expected it to be, the armband took on the character of a symbol of honor. It was cut exactly to the measurements specified and neatly sewn to the left arm. The Jews wore it, seeming not to pay any attention to it; the non-Jews also seemed not to notice it.

A little later, everybody was ordered to surrender his radio or else face a death penalty. The radios had to be given up by Jews and non-Jews alike. The last link between us and the world had been broken.

Other Jewish laws followed: all Jews had to have working documents, or they would be deported to labor camps; no Jew was allowed to work in a profession; all Jews had to pay a contribution for the privilege of being left in their apartments.

These decrees were signed by various German authorities, but they were always countersigned by the head of the Judenrath, so as to make the Jewish Council responsible for what was happening to the Jews. At the beginning, it was Dr. Parnas, a Jewish lawyer, who signed the decrees. But when it came to signing for the contribution, it seems that Dr. Parnas refused to use his name, after which he disappeared, and somebody else became head of the council.

Now that we had no radios, the only news came from the official German bulletins. There were loudspeakers all over. Several times a day, the regular transmissions were interrupted, giving way to a special bulletin. An English boat was sunk, and the radio broke into a victorious tune.

But then, there were other sources of news. Many German officers lived in apartments belonging to Polish or Ukrainian families. There was always a radio in the officer's room. The only problem was to find a Pole who would have enough courage to listen to the radio when the German was out and who would be friendly enough to tell a Jew what he had heard. And in this way, a source of news was born, which came to be known as the JPP Agency. *JPP* were the initials for the Polish words *jedna pani powiedziala* ("a lady said"). The JPP news was our refuge from all the evils of the real world. While the German radio claimed incredible victories on all fronts, the JPP Agency assured us that after a two-hour-long heavy British bombing, the island of Crete had surrendered; that Mussolini had broken with Hitler; that the German offensive on the Eastern Front had first been stopped, then broken, and that the German army was now retreating in utter panic. In fact, going by the JPP Agency, things were so good that sometimes, as I was watching the German soldiers crowding the streets of Lvov, I had the urge to wink an eye at them and say, "Comrades, I know the truth. You are only masquerading as Germans, while in fact you are Russians."

By then, one German army could already see the roofs of Leningrad, the other was only a few short kilometers from Moscow, and the third was closing in on the Crimea.

Every Jew had to have a job and his Jewish identification card, on which his employer's address was shown. To make their jobs appear even more significant, many Jews also had separate employer's statements to that effect. The Jews who were employed by the armed forces were the luckiest: they were well protected and decently nourished. A few who were taken at the beginning to the Lenckiego Prison were even luckier: instead of being shot at the Sands, they were recruited as menial workers in the service of the Gestapo. Some were enrolled by the newly created Ukrainian Militia to do general household work in their armories and precincts. The majority worked for private industry, but here, too, there were various degrees of importance, as every industry was supposed to produce for the German war machine. Some were producing articles more important and others less important to the war effort, and the Jews working for such industries were, accordingly, either more or less protected by their employment.

Whatever the job might be, there was no salary or almost no salary, so that the jobs that offered food were the most coveted. We, not being considered local Jews, didn't have the need for either a job or an ID card. However, we needed money. Everything had to be bought on the black market, and everything cost a great deal. The "cafe society" of the early Soviet days had all but disappeared. There was no joking with this invader. The main job of the Ukrainian Militia was to make sure that every Jew knew his proper spot on this planet: they checked people's documents in the streets, raided apartments, and double-checked Jews at their work sites. At the slightest sign of doubt, a Jew would be sequestered and deported to a labor camp. In this, the Ukrainians were thoroughly helped by the Jewish Militia, some members of which did a good job as denouncers and enforcers. Very little was left of the Polish police, as the Germans did their best to impress on everybody that this was not Poland but the Ukrainian Territory. The Schupo and the Gestapo did very little actual street work at that time, except for an occasional little bout of fun, when a Gestapo man would catch a Jew and teach him how to behave in front of a German. On such occasions, one could see a couple of Gestapo men giving the orders and a scared Jew parading in front of them, back and forth, taking his hat off, putting it back on, greeting them in German, and, perhaps, directing at himself some newly discovered German invectives.

Our money was disappearing fast, and something had to be done besides the continuous selling of our valuables. I ran across an old classmate of mine, Wladek Pulawski, a Pole. In the old times, he had been an artist, a painter. Now, he was driving a Red Cross ambulance. He had the tool, and I had the imagination, and soon we started traveling out of Lvov whenever Wladek had a free day. We did approximately what Father and Pollak had done at the beginning of the Russian invasion: we bought bacon, meat, peas, and flour, reselling some in Lvov and keeping the rest for ourselves. It was the proudest moment of my life when Father said casually, "Franek, you are a big help."

One day, two men visited us. They were recommended by some friends of Pollak and introduced themselves as rich Polish merchants from Warsaw, Mr. Mikolajczyk and Mr. Nowak. They needed anti-typhus vaccines, which were produced only at the University of Lvov by Professor Weigel and which, appropriately, we now called *weiglowki*. Until then we hadn't known about the existence of weiglowki, let alone their commercial value. Also, we hadn't known that there was an epidemic of typhus in Warsaw. Mikolajczyk and Nowak explained that since the Warsaw Ghetto had come into being, the Jews had lived there in such crowded, filthy, and deprived conditions that their quarter was an incubator for typhus. The disease could not be cured. A sick person either died or survived. However, a weiglowka could protect one from contracting typhus; thus it had become fashionable for the rich Jews in the Ghetto as well as the rich Poles on the Aryan side to take a vaccine. Nowak and Mikolajczyk had all the money in the world. All they wanted us to do was to start buying all the weiglowki available and to keep buying them, in Lvov and out, while the supply lasted. They said that they would go back to Warsaw the same night, but that they would send to us their liaison, a certain Mr. Ostrowicz, who, from now on, would deliver the money and pick up the goods. We all went to work, Pollak, Father, and I. It didn't take long to discover that it would be hard work to buy the weiglowki. Working like detectives, we followed each shipment from the source to its destination. When we knew the whereabouts of a shipment, the next step was to find a contact, somebody who knew somebody. The last step was the price: the contact had to be paid; the vaccine had to be purchased; we had to make a profit; Ostrowicz had to make a profit.

We worked hard, and the business was developing. Ostrowicz visited us once a week, preceded by his usual telegram, "8:30 Lvov Wait Ostro." He was a neatly dressed, thin gentleman who, with his trim mustache, a pince-nez, and the general appearance of a bureaucrat, looked like Molotov. He never wasted any time talking. He just counted his weiglowki, waited till Father had counted our money, shook our hands, and left. Only on the fifth or sixth visit, when we tried to inquire about the situation in Warsaw, about the Ghetto, and about the difficulties connected with traveling, did Ostrowicz leave his usual demeanor for a moment, to tell us that should we ever decide to go to Warsaw, he would gladly accompany us.

At that time, I was seeing a couple of girls who lived a few buildings away from us. This was one of the few distractions I still had, since we were not allowed to listen to the radio or go to the movies. There were two sisters and a girlfriend of theirs, all crammed in a small apartment with the two sisters' parents. We used a small room with a large couch in it, where all four of us would lie down and engage in sexual foreplay, without ever going any further because of the crowded circumstances. It never occurred to me, and I don't think it occurred to the girls, that we were doing anything immoral. As I look at it today, from a perspective of over thirty-five years, I still am not sure whether what we were doing was wrong. We didn't know it at the time, but maybe our intuition was that the life spans of most of us were destined to be extremely short.

The special privileges of our family seemed so enticing that the ever-enterprising Adolph Pollak devised a plan that would give him, too, the status of a foreigner. He hired a professional counterfeiter and made him insert into the list of objects confiscated from him in the Kharkov prison three Ecuadorian passports. He even had the counterfeiter base the numbers of the passports on our serial numbers. Armed with the list, which also had the official NKVD stamp on it, Adolph presented himself in the Schupo headquarters and received his foreign certificate with even more ease than Father had. They considered him, an ex-prisoner of the NKVD, an avowed anticommunist, and perhaps even a martyr.

The decree about the ghetto was posted around the city. A day was specified, in mid-November, by when every Jew in Lvov had to move into the old Jewish quarter long known as the Behind-the-Theater Section, an agglomeration of many narrow streets bordered by rows of collapsing tenements a couple of hundred years old, where running water and flush toilets were often an unthinkable luxury. In the normal time, Behind-the-Theater was overpopulated. Now, the impossible was ordered and, what is even stranger, achieved. Jews emptied their apartments in the Aryan part of Lvov long before the deadline, hoping that whoever came first would be served best. It was not exactly so. Whoever had the money was served best. Everybody got what his pocket entitled him to. Most of the furniture was left behind in the former apartments, and there it immediately became the property of the innumerable new Polish and Ukrainian owners.

The city was strangely quiet. The Jews made believe they didn't see the Poles. The Poles turned their eyes in another direction, hopeful that the thing they didn't see did not exist. There was almost no show of deeper feelings. People had become robots, and they were doing what the masters ordered.

Of course we, the foreigners, didn't have to leave our apartments. However, there was something in the air that worried us. Also, we needed more money, as our purchases of the weiglowki had become more difficult every day. Through some acquaintances, Father found a Wehrmacht colonel who was interested in our collection of old Persian rugs that Father had been painstakingly purchasing all his life. The colonel, a handsome, distinguished-looking man in his early fifties, didn't beat around the bush. He offered for the entire lot an amount worth twenty American dollars, and when Father objected, he said, "I don't want to sound rude, but if you don't sell them to me, the fellows from the Gestapo will get it gratis." He probably didn't mean it to be a threat, but it certainly sounded like one. Father gave him all the rugs for twenty dollars, feeling that otherwise it might not even be the Gestapo who would get them some day, but possibly the janitor Wojciech.

After that, Father started looking for a decent Polish family who would take over our apartment with everything in it, on short notice, should the necessity arise. Again, he found a Polish engineer from Silesia, who loved our apartment and was anxious to get it one day but wouldn't pay a penny. He argued that either there was a need to vacate or there wasn't. If there was such a need, we would leave the apartment the way it was, no matter what; if there wasn't a need, we wouldn't relinquish the apartment to him. There was much wisdom in what he was saying. So Father made an agreement with him that should we be forced to vacate, the apartment with everything in it was to become his, in exchange for which he would take good care of Mother's miniature pinscher, Mousi. All this was like writing a last will and testament, but then we all felt as if we were living on the brink of doom.

Rumors were started that some of the Jewish population of the ghetto was to be deported. No one knew the real meaning of the word *deportation,* but it implied leaving the known for the unknown, which in itself was threatening. So we all hoped that these were only rumors. However, they persisted; then they became stronger; then a date was fixed: the first transports of Jews were taken away, and the first disquieting news started spreading about mass killings by electrocution. Of course, it was all nonsense, as everybody knew that, in the first place, it was impossible to mass-exterminate by electrocution, and second, the Germans wouldn't even try any mass extermination because of what the rest of the world would say.

When the deportation was in full swing, we were suddenly called to the Gestapo, all of us.

The entire Ecuadorian community of Lvov was there, some nineteen people, including the Pollaks. A bulldog-faced Gestapo officer faced us. He gave us a victorious smile and held an open sheet of paper, a letter as it soon appeared, in his left hand.

He cleared his throat and said to us, "Ladies and Gentlemen, brace yourselves! You'll need a lot of strength to withstand the news I'm going to give you now."

He read aloud. It was a letter from the Ecuadorian Legation in Berlin, signed by the same Señor Gomez who over a year before had advised us to come to Berlin to pick up our Ecuadorian visas. Now, Señor Gomez advised the Gestapo that there was a group of Jews in Lvov who had come into illegal possession of authentic Ecuadorian passports; that the police authorities in Quito were searching for the persons responsible for stealing such passports; that the pseudo-Ecuadorians of Lvov were to be considered Russian citizens of Jewish ancestry.

If thunder had struck us at this moment, we would have been less surprised than we were by the contents of this letter.

The bulldog-faced Gestapo officer requested that we immediately surrender all the papers issued to us by the German authorities, and everybody did so automatically. That is, everybody but me. Only a few days before, the Schupo had given us a renewal of our permit to live in the Aryan quarter. I had gone for the renewal, I had it in my pocket, and I decided to keep it.

After having collected all our documents, the bulldog-faced officer said almost cordially, "Now go home, all of you, and prepare yourselves nice armbands. As of this moment, you are considered simple local Jews, and the Law of Deportation will be applied to you accordingly."

CHAPTER

4

WARSAW

THE EVENTS OF THE NEXT twenty-four hours were a continuous flow of emotions, with surprise as their supreme ruler.

March 21, 1942, afternoon and evening: We are affixing our arm-bands and preparing one valise per each person to contain our best clothing and some valuables. Father fills a little cotton bag with Mother's diamond earrings, two diamond rings, his gold Schaff-hausen pocketwatch, and three hundred paper dollars. Mother fills a similar bag with two rings of rubies and diamonds, two diamond earrings, and two hundred paper dollars. Should one be lost, the other might remain.

March 22, 7 A.M.: They are knocking at our front door with their fists, their boots, and the butts of their rifles. We open. Six of them burst in, two of each: Schupo, Ukrainians, and Jewish Militia. They order deportation. Pola loses her head and walks around the room wringing her hands. Mother cries desperately, saying, "I will never see my Max again! And what's going to happen to Mousi!" Father embraces her and says, "It's going to be all right. This is not the end of the world."

I step forward, reach into my pocket, and hand over to the Schupo men the renewal slip signed by the Schupo headquarters just a few days ago. One of them reads it; they hold a short conference. One of them mumbles, "Must be a mistake." The other says, "We've got to verify it." The slip is returned to me. They are yelling at the Ukrainians and the Jews, "Raus! (Get out!) It's been a mistake!"

March 22, 7:30 A.M.: Father says, "It is a miracle!" Mother says, "I've been praying to God." Martin says, "What have you given them?"

I explain, and now we are holding a conference. It is clear that we have gained just a few hours. Deportation raids always end at three in the afternoon. If they leave us alone until then, they might come back tomorrow morning. I advance the idea of running to Warsaw.

But how?!

March 22, 3 P.M.: The raids for the day have finished.

March 22, 4:30 P.M.: Somebody rings the bell at our door. I open. It is Ostrowicz. Business? Extrasensory perception? Miracle?

March 22, 9 P.M.: We are at the railroad station, with our luggage and with Ostrowicz, who has bought the tickets for us.

March 22, 11 P.M.: We are seated in a compartment of the Lvov-Warsaw night express. The train is leaving Lvov.

It was a long ride. When it was dawn, the train stopped in a small town, and a girl entered. She was Jewish; the armband was clearly exhibited on her modest but clean overcoat. Her hair was neatly combed. A passenger barked, "What is this Jewess trying to do, traveling among people?!" I looked at him. There was a whole group of them, five, six, all men, sloppy, unshaven, disheveled. He repeated, "How does this Jewess dare to travel among people?!" And he stood up. The girl took a piece of paper out of her pocket: "This is my working paper. Every morning, I go to work in the next town. I have a travel permit from the Gestapo." The man stepped toward her. "You stink!" he yelled, holding his nose with two fingers. "Come, somebody, help me to put her in the right place!" he called to his comrades. I examined the group. They must have been black-marketeers returning from a shopping trip, as they had baskets loaded with food under their benches. One of them got up: "I'll help you." The two of them grabbed the struggling girl, opened the door to the bathroom, shoved her on the floor, and locked the door. "Such Jewish arrogance," another one in the group said. The car was crowded, but no one said anything. Other passengers made believe they hadn't seen a thing. Mother and Father were sitting on one bench; Martin, Pola, and Ostrowicz on another; and I on still another. I felt ashamed, so ashamed that I didn't dare to raise my eyes and look at them. No one said anything, and neither did I. "Oh sure, I know," I thought, "I cannot risk getting into an argument with the hoodlums who might discover that I, too, am Jewish." Yet, I was deeply ashamed.

The train arrived in Warsaw around eight in the morning. Ostrowicz took care of our luggage, then took us to the railroad cafeteria, and as we were having some coffee, he telephoned Mikolajczyk and Nowak, who asked him to take us to them.

We drove in two man-pedaled rikshas across Warsaw toward the suburb of Praga, where Mikolajczyk had a beautifully furnished apartment. Nowak was already there, too, and both of them gave us a very warm welcome. We had breakfast together, during which the new situation was discussed. Nowak offered to find us an apartment on the Polish side of Warsaw. This, he said, would involve getting false documents issued in Polish names and stating that the bearers were Roman Catholic. Father refused immediately. He didn't believe in changing his name and even less in conversion, even in the form of a phony statement on a piece of paper. It was surprising to see Father fighting so hard for his Jewishness — Father, whose only religious link with Judaism was the observance of the High Holy Days and Passover.

Then it was decided that Ostrowicz would lead us to the Warsaw Ghetto. This had to be done quickly, so we embraced Mikolajczyk and Nowak and left with them two valises with the fur coats belonging to Mother, Pola, Father, and Martin, and Mother's little bag of jewelry and money. We wanted to make sure not to put all our eggs in one basket. "If things get too hot there," said Father, "we'll have something of ours here with you two good people."

We went to the courthouse, which stood on the border of the Ghetto and the Polish side of Warsaw. It was easy to enter the building on the Polish side and to leave it on the Ghetto side.

Now we were in the Ghetto, with all its bustling traffic, noise, and commerce. The question was where to go now. The priceless Ostrowicz solved our problem: "I do know of two fine rooms, with two nice families, that you could take this very morning." This was just one more surprise: Ostrowicz was a Warsaw Jew, with a residence in the heart of the Ghetto.

The Warsaw Ghetto. I don't know how to begin describing this shameful monument to the depravity of Western culture. Had I been a tourist at that time, I might have compared it to the Hongkong, Singapore, or Macao I knew from the movies, with the natives hustling desperately to survive the day. But I was not a tourist. I was a Jew who had come to stay with other Jews, like myself, and who was to learn quickly that "they" and "I" were two different groups of people who could hardly hope to learn how to coexist.

It was a nice large room where Ostrowicz placed us, in a four-room apartment belonging to the Grinbergs, a middle-class Ghetto family. The mother was a housewife and the actual head of the family; the father made the family's livelihood by selling and buying anything, and by manufacturing — with the help of a small group of partners, each of whom had his own specialty — saccharine pills and American gold dollars. Their twenty-year-old daughter, Edzia, worked in a medical laboratory, and her younger brother, Moniek, worked for the smugglers.

As soon as we'd met, Edzia evaluated me as a person and as a Jew and said, "You will never be accepted by the real Ghetto people. You act differently, you think differently, you even speak differently." I didn't speak Yiddish, and this was to prove one of the most serious obstacles to my ever becoming a regular Ghettoan. To survive here, one had to become a hustler, and how do you hustle without a knowledge of the native idiom? It didn't take long for me to discover that for the locals, I was just another *Yecke*, which was their derogatory way of describing somebody the Germans had thrown on a heap of garbage, who was then discarded by the garbage collector as a piece of trash liable to damage his garbage bag. Events were moving fast in the Ghetto: people were telling each other recent news, underground resistance was being created — but I never had the slightest chance to become a part of any of it.

At that time, all roads led to the Ghetto. Within a couple of days, we had learned that the Szejnbergs were already there, and that he was working as a doctor, that the Pollaks had arrived a day before us, not wasting a minute after our dismissal by the Gestapo, but taking the train to Warsaw that same night; that even two of my friends, Adek and Witek, who had studied with me in the medical schools in Brussels and Nancy, were there.

The layout of the Warsaw Ghetto was as complicated as the life in it. Actually, there were two Ghettos — one called the Little Ghetto, the other the Large Ghetto — which were connected by a high, narrow wooden overpass above the wide Polish Avenue separating them. That overpass, the Bridge, looked like an umbilical cord running from the mother ghetto to the baby ghetto, where we lived. Under the Bridge, at both sides of the avenue, were two huge wooden gates closing off access to the Polish part. Polish traffic ran along the avenue, and standing up on the Bridge, a Jew could have a quick glance at freedom. Both Ghettos were surrounded by the Wall. The Wall was not necessarily a structure in masonry, as some parts of it were just wooden fences, while in many parts it was an eight-foot-tall barbed-wire separation. To gain legitimate access to the Ghetto, one had to cross either the main gate or one of the several secondary gates. All the gates were manned by the Jewish Order Service (comprised of Ghetto Jews), the Polish police (called the "Blues" because of their dark-blue uniforms), and the German Schupo, or SS. The portions of the Wall between the gates were guarded only by the Germans. Legitimate traffic between the Ghetto and the Polish part of Warsaw, called the "Other Side," was possible on the presentation of papers signed by the German authorities and stating that the bearer had an approved task to attend to.

The Ghetto was highly overpopulated. Nobody knew any real figures, because of the continuous influx of Jews deported from Germany and Czechoslovakia, as well as of refugees like ourselves from all over Poland. Some estimated the Ghetto population at a half million; some believed it was more like seven hundred thousand. Whatever it was, the Ghetto was crowded to such an extent that if one wanted to avoid physical contact with other people in the street, he had to walk sideways. And there was at least one significant reason to avoid such contacts: people were catching lice from other people; lice were carriers of typhus; and typhus was decimating the Ghetto.

The legitimate way to purchase food in the Ghetto was based on a system of coupons. Every inhabitant of the Ghetto who was registered with the Judenrath, the Jewish Council, received a book of coupons. There were specific coupons for all varieties of food and fuel: lard, eggs, flour, bread, coal, potatoes. However, all one could normally get was bread and molasses. For the rest, as somebody suggested, you could put your egg coupons on your lard coupons and fry them on your coal coupons.

When a Ghetto Jew died, his family was expected to advise the Judenrath accordingly and surrender the dead person's book of coupons. Thus a term was coined, *to surrender coupons*, meaning "to die." Needless to say, the very poor ones had a hard decision to make when they lost a member of the family, whether to keep his coupons or to surrender his coupons and acknowledge his death. When the former decision was made, a naked, nameless corpse was left out in the street, the genitals sometimes covered, for the sake of decency, with a page of an old newspaper and a stone to keep the paper from flying off. The official undertaker of the Ghetto, Mr.

Pinkert, had his hearses — wooden boxes on four wheels, painted black, and drawn by a horse or a couple of men — go around the city early in the morning and collect the dead bodies for a mass funeral later that day.

To stay alive in the Warsaw Ghetto meant doing what one was doing for a living, plus selling an occasional piece of jewelry or clothing. Thus Dr. Szejnberg worked as a physician but also had to keep selling his assets; Adek's mother worked as a dentist and sold an occasional brooch or earring. Members of the Jewish Order Service worked as policemen and had to receive an occasional bribe. This was the Ghetto's middle class.

The lower class consisted of the prostitutes and the beggars, the former being more important in the social stratification of the Ghetto than the latter, for the simple reason that they had something to sell. Prostitutes could be seen all over. On occasion, three generations of prostitutes — a grandmother, a mother, and a daughter — worked on the same corner, so that they might avoid the final slide down to the level of being beggars.

The beggars were an underclass, living beneath the social grid of the Ghetto structure. They were a group, and yet each of them was a clearly defined individual. They were known in the Ghetto under the name, *rachmunesim,* from the Yiddish word *rachmunes,* meaning "charity."

One was the little boy whom Adek and I called the Lark. We had a name for almost every rachmunes crossing our street in the Little Ghetto. The Lark, a tiny barefoot boy with terribly swollen feet, walked along our street every morning in his torn shorts, singing in a falsetto, "Szanowni Panstwo — Ja was bardzo prosze i blagam — Kawaleczek chleba — Pare groszy — Albo jedna lyzke zupy — Dajcie co kazdy tylko moze" ("Most gracious people — I do beg so much and implore you — A tiny crust of bread — a couple of pennies — Or just one spoonful of soup — Give what each of you can afford").

The Dancer of the Macabre pirouetted in from the Large Ghetto singing in a dismal voice the serenade of Mack the Knife. A female skeleton covered with dark, parchmentlike skin and a black sheet, she whirled away, letting the torn rags fly around her like terrifying bats, and leaving behind her the smell of death and the tomb.

The Silent Family also made their dignified, ghastly appearance. The barefoot man, his huge torso nude, pushed a baby carriage from which his wife, a little atrophied body with a big head, showed to the world around her an ever-smiling row of teeth. Their three naked little children walked silently behind. As they disappeared into the distance, they left behind them shudder and uneasiness.

The King of the Rachmunesim was a man who would not have dignified the Little Ghetto with his presence, a clown whose usual beat was in the neighborhood of the German guards or in the waiting room of the Judenrath, the craziest of the beggars, the one and only Rubinstein. When he spoke, he did so in verses or in songs, all of his own creation. Rubinstein was the poet of Ghettoan realism, the coiner of neologisms, the author of memorable maxims. His "Song of the Coupons" led the Ghetto hit parade.

The great Rubinstein said many significant things, but the most significant of all was his prophecy about the way the Ghetto was going to end: "The entire Ghetto will perish except for just three persons: the Judenrath president, Dr. Czerniakow, because he is a decent man; the undertaker, Mr. Pinkert, because he is needed to bury the Ghetto; and Rubinstein the Clown, because he's crazy."

How true his prophecy was remained to be seen.

In contrast to the rachmunesim, each of whom was a distinct individual, the members of the Jewish Order Service seemed to be all alike: their uniforms, their behavior, their way of thinking. They were the extension of the Gestapo's arm in the Ghetto. They abducted people in the streets so that the Gestapo could send them to labor camps; they whipped a child for smuggling a few potatoes into the Ghetto, unless the child had already been punished directly by a guard, usually by being shot; and they imposed on the Ghetto population the habit of paying them bribes just to be left alone. This was defined by Rubinstein as, "Datek na to i na owo i na Sluzbe Porzadkowa" ("Gift for one cause or another, and for Order Service, brother").

A separate group of the Ghetto population were its youngest poor, the street waifs. They lived by snatching packages from the people in the street and devouring them while running for their lives. Their philosophy was "What's in my stomach, is mine." Although they were usually able to abscond with a loaf of bread or a small bag of potatoes, I saw at least one waif trying to devour a package of starched collars.

The most select, the most important if judged by the effects of their activity, and the richest of all were the smugglers. When a Jew sold a piece of jewelry, the money was destined to go either to a functionary of the Jewish Order Service, as a bribe for not abducting the Jew for the labor camp, or to the smugglers' pool, for the purchase of meat or butter or just a loaf of bread. The smugglers' guild was responsible for feeding all the residents of the Ghetto, except for the poorest of the poor. Most if not all the members of the smuggler class originated at the very bottom of prewar Jewish society: pickpockets, burglars, murderers, counterfeiters, drug pushers, and crooks of all sorts — such was the basic texture of the Ghetto's smuggler class. They were adequately matched by the Polish smugglers' organization, because the goods had to be prepared and delivered to the Wall by the Poles at which point the Jews took over. When the bribing of the German, Polish, and Jewish police had been successfully arranged, late at night while the law-abiding citizens of the Ghetto slept peacefully, bags of flour and potatoes, halves of beef, and chickens, as well as high-class articles such as champagne and caviar flowed in profusion into the Jewish quarter, while refashioned furs and all sorts of industrial products went to the Other Side. Rubinstein called this operation *Szafa Gra* — "when the pianola is playing" — because he associated the sound of the pianola with the sound of silver coins flowing from the hands of the smugglers into the pockets of the Ghetto police authorities. Sometimes, an article served double duty, like the saccharine pills that our landlord, Mr. Grinberg, manufactured. These were packed into counterfeit government-monopoly boxes and exported to the Polish Warsaw, and they would return to the Ghetto as a genuine government article, to be sold at a premium to those who had enough money to aspire to the best.

During the periods of time when the smuggling traffic was especially successful, the Ghetto was rich in food, bread cost not more than twenty zloty (.70 U.S. cents) per loaf, and on Sunday, the large bar at the end of Sliska Street, near us, right under the Wall, was bursting with joyous ado: the Polish and the Jewish smugglers were getting together to cross-check their bookkeeping and make plans for the next week's activity over a bottle of vodka and with whores on their knees.

Sometimes a German guard took the bribe but didn't keep his part of the deal. Then shooting was heard at night, and a Jewish smuggler's dead body was found near the Wall early in the morning. On such a day, the carefree air of the Ghetto gave way to anxiety, and a loaf of bread went up to thirty zloty.

There were a few nightclubs in the Ghetto where *la dolce vita* went on all the time. The owners of such clubs catered to the most powerful of the smugglers, as well as to the German officers, who often brought here their tourist friends for a night of frenzy in this Jewish Harlem of the city. On occasion, the Ghetto nightclubs had German visitors during the day. These were groups of journalists who, accompanied by SS officers, would set some of the most miserable-looking rachmunesim under the nightclub's windows, which were bursting with the costliest foods from around the world, and take the incongruous photographs that were to appear in various German weeklies to illustrate the innumerable articles about Jewish perfidy.

That was the Warsaw Ghetto in the early spring of 1942, into which I and my family had been driven by the unexpected news that our Ecuadorian passports were just worthless pieces of paper.

From the very first day, it was obvious that an enormous amount of adjustment would be necessary if we were to survive both the physical and emotinal stresses of our new surroundings. Mother made her initial statement, which she was never to change: "This is my last stop. I'll never again see either Lvov or my son Max." Martin kept furiously twisting a lock over his forehead, Pola pulled her hair in silent acceptance of disaster; Father said, "It is not the end of the world"; and I felt like a tourist in a strange land whose language and habits I might attempt to learn, though without much hope of success.

At first, we had to sell some of the things we had brought with us in order to buy food and pay the rent. Soon the necessity of getting ID cards made itself felt, and bribe money was needed for the Order Service. This meant that some of the dollars we had in Father's little bag had to be sold for zlotys. Father quickly calculated that, at this pace, it would take less than a year to spend all we had. We could not legally register in the Judenrath for our books of coupons because we were afraid that the Gestapo of Lvov might be looking for us here, so that even a loaf of bread cost us a lot of money. It became clear that we had to start doing something to make a living. Thus, Martin found a job as an assembly worker in a German-owned calculating-machine factory, where for his work he received some staple food like bread or molasses; I found a job in the Stawki Hospital, helping in the pathology department, an extremely busy place because of all the people dying from typhus or hunger. My boss, Dr. Fenikstein, kept repeating all day long, like a sad litany, the cause of death: "Atrophy of liver; atrophy of heart."

Father was used to bigger operations. He got together with Pollak and a little man who had been in the dairy industry. They bribed the Judenrath into giving them a monopoly on a legitimate supply of cracked eggs and aged farmer's cheese, rented a large kitchen in the basement of a modern apartment building on Zelazna Street, along

one of the sections of the Wall, and started the
German beer cheese, calling their little factory, as we
itself, *Edelweiss*.

My free moments were spent mostly with my frie
sionally, we visited Witek, another friend, but he was
and therefore no longer qualified for our bachelor
these ran grossly along the same line as in Lvov, except that here we
had more of a social life. We had met quite a few local girls of our own
age or younger, with whom we had an occasional dance and sex party
in Adek's dental office, when his mother was out, or if it happened to
be a nice sunny day and we had time off, we visited one of the girls,
Lilka, and took a sunbath on the roof of her house, from where we
could see the Other Side and the Schupo man guarding the Wall.
Sometimes we saw the bad Schupo guard Frankenstein. Not even
today am I sure whether this was his real name, or whether he was
called Frankenstein because of the monstrosities for which he was
known. Frankenstein was the guard who would accept a bribe and,
instead of keeping his part of the deal, shoot down the smugglers. He
was the guard who specialized in catching the little street waifs who
tried to slip under the barbed wire with a few potatoes stolen from the
Other Side inside their shirts, and in shooting them dead in front of
the morning crowd. And finally, he was the guard who liked to hide
behind a chimney on the roof of the building across the Wall and
shoot at us while we were sunbathing. Thus he forced us back into
Adek's dental studio and the sex.

Sex had become a must for many nice girls who would never have
engaged in premarital activities of that kind before the war. There
was something in the air itself of the Ghetto which seemed to confirm
what Lilka once put into words: "I haven't lived yet, and it is the
end." Nobody liked to admit it seriously, but the atmosphere there
was one of anxious expectation of the ultimate fate, and sex seemed a
way to become immortal.

It was already late in May, and unpleasant rumors were heard from
time to time, about transports of Jews being taken out of the Lodz
Ghetto and exterminated by gas on the trains. Of course, we didn't
believe it: How can you take a couple of thousand people and gas
them on a train? Sheer nonsense. However, a rumor is a rumor, and it
makes you wonder and ponder and feel uneasy. These were not the
only rumors. Other news said that the Jews taken from the Warsaw
Ghetto to labor camps never reached any such camps but were killed
somewhere in the marshes. Of course, we didn't believe that either.
Why marshes? When they wanted to kill the Jews in Lvov, they killed

in Lvov. Nobody had to make believe that they were being taken away to any labor camps.

Then, instead of just rumors, there was some action. In fact, whenever the Germans raided a group of Jews to take them away, it was known officially as "action." For a few consecutive weeks, a Gestapo car raided the homes of prominent Jews. It always happened on a Friday, and always at about two in the morning. They took the Jew for a ride, then stopped the car and told the Jew that he was free to go. As he was going away, they shot him from behind. The next day, people in the Ghetto would tell each other that the victim had been a baker; that somebody had denounced him for financing the smuggling of flour into the Ghetto; that he had been tried and sentenced in absentia; and that what the raiders had done was just to enforce that court's decision. After a night of executions, the price of bread went up, and the prices stayed high. After the bakers came other prominent Jews, people mostly involved in the politics of the Ghetto then and before the war.

Then, a Gestapo ghost-car started into action. It would enter the Ghetto through the main gate and, while rolling in the general direction of the Pawiak Prison located in the heart of the Jewish city, its occupants, usually four Gestapo men, shot into the crowd, waving their revolvers in the air and laughing heartily. After the car had disappeared, Mr. Pinkert had his crew collect the bodies, and life in the Ghetto went on as usual. The Jews knew how to accept the inevitable, without lifting a hand in self-defense. They also had faith in the Warsaw Ghetto: How do you exterminate a city of seven hundred thousand Jews, especially as long as there are Germans willing to take bribes and there are Jews able to produce the money?

During the second half of June, the feeling of the inevitable permeated everybody. Bills were posted in the streets of the Ghetto calling for Jews with foreign citizenship to register at the Pawiak Prison, to be exchanged for German citizens living in various Allied countries. Within hours, many Jews emerged with all sorts of South American and Panamanian passports and went to Pawiak carrying their luggage joyously. One of them was Adolph Pollak, who had arranged for a phony foreign citizenship by using the services of a lieutenant of the Jewish Order Service, a certain Ehrlich. That man Ehrlich was known in the Ghetto as the most important contact between the Jews and the Gestapo. Whenever a really difficult transaction had to be made between a Jew and the Gestapo, Ehrlich was the man to see and he was the man to be paid. The fee, of course, was extremely high, for two main reasons: Ehrlich had to give most of the money to his German Sponsor, and a deal made with Ehrlich was foolproof. Pollak had such a deal with Ehrlich. It cost him a thousand dollars per person, and the three of them went: Adolph, Mitka, and the little Jasio. (Mitka's daughter Marysia had been uninterested in saving herself since she had learned of Nulek's death.) The Pollaks were overjoyed, and Adolph dismissed Father's warning that his name could be on the Gestapo's list because of our misadventure in Lvov. He had Ehrlich's personal backing. What could be better?

Next day, a rachmunes visited us. He had a message, and he wanted a tip. The message was from Pawiak Prison. It was a short sentence and our address scribbled on a piece of paper thrown from one of the prison's windows. The sentence was "Save us at the last moments of our lives. Adolph."

It was a shock to us. No matter how used we were to seeing death around us, until now it had been only a matter of statistics. Today, we were faced with a death threat to the Pollaks, to our life-long friends. Something had to be done immediately. Father took his little cotton bag and went to see Lieutenant Ehrlich. Within an hour, he was back. He was pale and distressed. He had found Ehrlich at a banquet, Father told us, and it had taken him half an hour to be received by the functionary. Ehrlich had listened to Father and had remembered the Pollaks. But he wouldn't do a thing to help. He also said something that Father did not quite understand, but that sounded threatening: "Go home, Jew," said Ehrlich, who was Jewish himself, "and enjoy the last moments of your life; the last moments of the life of the Ghetto."

The next day, young Szejnberg was picked up in the street, and his parents went to Pawiak, asking the Gestapo to take them with their son. In this way, the life-long friends whose closeness had been broken by the fourteen-karat-diamond affair were reunited again, to face together the last hours of their lives.

Toward the end of June 1942, the Stawki Hospital was ordered to evacuate. The site was going to become the *Umschlagplatz,* the center of transshipment. I still didn't understand the need for any such center. And what about the patients? Stawki was overcrowded with the sick, the disabled, and the dying. The evacuation order didn't make any plans for the patients. Their fate was now up to the hospital's administration and to the Judenrath.

I went to Father's factory. I wanted to share with him the outrage of this last order.

Father had his own problems by the time I reached his place. He and all the other occupants of the building were already out, with various pieces of their furniture scattered in the middle of the street. The Gestapo had evacuated the building, and its special unit, the *Sonderkommando,* was supposed to move in the next day.

A couple of hours later, bills signed by the Gestapo and the Judenrath were posted in the streets of the Ghetto. The signature of Mr. Czerniakow, the president of the Judenrath, was missing. During this time, there was a rumor that was then confirmed as fact: Mr. Czerniakow had been found slumped over his desk with a bullet in his head, an apparent suicide. The first of the three historic prophecies of the great Rubinstein had proved to be false.

The posters were official notice of the *Umsiedlung,* the mass deportation of the Warsaw Ghetto Jews to Smolensk, where they would be made to work at the military fortifications. There were priorities on the Umsiedlung schedule: the first to go would be the unemployed, the sick, and the antisocial elements. Every deportee was encouraged to bring twenty-five kilograms of personal effects, and any quantity of valuables and money. Bread and jam were to be distributed in a quantity sufficient for the duration of the journey. Volunteers for the Umsiedlung would be accepted, regardless of their status on the priority list.

All this seemed to point to two main developments: employed people would be left in peace, and the overcrowding of the Ghetto would be eased, thus making life there more comfortable.

Getting a job had become a pivotal problem for us. I had just lost my job in the hospital, and Father didn't have his business anymore. We approached some of the members of the Order Service who, in the past, had always been ready to exchange a courtesy for a bribe. We found that things had changed overnight. The proof of employment, issued by the Jewish Council's Division of Labor, had become insignificant, and most of the small shops working all over the Ghetto for private German firms had suddenly lost their privileged status, so that the Jews in their employ were not subject to the Umsiedlung. It had become imperative to find not only employment but employment in a firm defined as indispensable to the German war effort.

We were lucky: Astrawerke, the shop where Martin was employed, met the criterion of indispensability, although all that was assembled there were small manual adding machines. Having worked in this shop for a couple of months, Martin was on good terms with its German-Jewish foreman and with the German owner himself, and he was able to have us hired, Father and me, the same day. By the evening, we already had our very important work certificates, issued by our German employer and confirmed by the Gestapo. With these in our hands, we were ready to brave the new situation, and Pola and Mother, being covered as spouses of employed Jews, didn't have to worry.

Life in the Ghetto changed abruptly. The Wall was sealed hermetically at all its points. All smuggling stopped. Even the black market, the lifeblood of the Jewish city, came to an end.

On July 2, 1942, the Umsiedlung officially started. Seven hundred thousand people were talking. Seven hundred thousand people were discussing. Seven hundred thousand people were raising a deafening noise.

Suddenly the noise died out.

From the far end of the street leading to the Umschlagplatz, a column of people was slowly approaching. These were the inmates of the Ghetto jail run by the Jewish Order Service: petty thieves, minor smugglers, small businessmen who had run out of bribe money, individuals who were found in the street after the curfew hour.

These were followed by the sick, who, until yesterday, had been patients in the Stawki Hospital. They were dragging their feet wearily. Full acceptance was written in their extinguished eyes. Their bodies, swollen from hunger, seemed to be wishing to reach the railroad cars, to lie down, and to die undisturbed. And these were the healthiest patients. The bedridden were now being pulled by Mr. Pinkert's undertakers in their all-purpose carts.

The rachmunesim followed slowly. These beggars, dressed in rags or half-naked and barefoot, were now munching their own bread and jam. They seemed to be the only ones who could fully enjoy the new developments: finally, they, too, had something of their own; they were a part of the society.

As the first marchers were entering the gates of the Umschlagplatz, a new group appeared: children from Dr. Korczak's orphanage. They were walking in pairs, holding each other by the hand. All were dressed, girls and boys alike, in light gray, neat cotton smocks. Instead of shoes, they were wearing wooden sabots, which clattered sadly as they passed. The Ghetto seemed filled now with the same solemn sound that Polish children made with small wooden rattles on Good Friday, the day when church bells are tied in mute mourning of the Saviour's death. Dr. Korczak went with his children. And as the deaf clatter was being absorbed by the horrible fences of the Umsch-lagplatz, an uncontrolled weeping could be heard here and there in the watching crowd.

The Umsiedlung failed to follow the various points of the original posters. The posters had promised six pounds of bread and a pound of jam to every volunteer for deportation. The hunger in the Ghetto had become more severe than ever now that there was no smuggling, and many more Jews volunteered than the Germans had hoped for. So, according to the law of supply and demand, the provisions had been cut to three pounds of bread and a half pound of jam.

The poster mentioned the unemployed, the sick, and the antisocial elements, which meant the inmates of the jail and the rachmunesim. But now, SS units, helped by the newly imported Lithuanian and Latvian Militia, as well as the ever-obliging Jewish Order Service, were extending the "action" to practically anybody who didn't have a working paper confirmed by the Gestapo. It had become evident that the immediate purpose of the Umsiedlung was to empty the Small Ghetto and to reduce the size of the Jewish city to the Large Ghetto only.

Every day, early in the morning, we saw the police sealing our street block and raiding building after building. Now, all the Astra-werke employees living in the Small Ghetto formed a group that marched each morning, protected by two Order Service men, into the Large Ghetto, where the shop was. Along our route, we saw groups of people being dragged out of their homes, being beaten with the butts of rifles, and being shot for not responding promptly to orders that were thrown at them in the quick, hostile syllables of an unknown tongue. I watched all this with the cool eye of a bystander rather than with compassion, worrying about our safe passage to the work site, and about Mother and Pola, who remained at home alone.

And every day, as we were returning home after five in the afternoon, when the action was over for the day, we crossed streets littered with pieces of clothing and dead bodies. Obviously, Mr. Pinkert's undertakers were not very efficient anymore. I thought of the great Rubinstein. Were his prophecies completely wrong? I heard that he had already been deported. Was it now the turn of Mr. Pinkert?

At night, Warsaw was now constantly raided by the British, and a substantial number of bombs were falling on the Ghetto, where those various little German shops were producing articles that were seem-ingly necessary to the German war effort, such as the brooms and brushes, and our Astrawerke adding machines. We did not mind the raids. We loved them. We waited for them. They represented our way of hitting back. We wouldn't even have minded if a bomb had fallen on us, provided it killed a few of them at the same time. Father loved to go up on the roof during the night of an especially heavy air raid and to admire aloud the savage beauty of the bombings.

During the month of August, the German owner of Astrawerke succeeded in finding a building in the Large Ghetto where the entire work force of his shop could stay from then on. This was the last time I saw Lilka and Adek. She had decided to volunteer for the Umsiedlung. Adek, who had got a job at the airport, where he was working for the Luftwaffe, had just found out that his work did not protect his mother, as only the spouses of the workers were covered by the Gestapo certificates. So, in the wake of our moving to the new quarters, Adek had married his mother and had taken her to the airport, where the two of them would be living now as husband and wife.

The action was becoming more vicious every day. It was rumored that six thousand people were being deported each day, and it didn't take a mathematician to figure out that by now some two hundred fifty thousand Jews had gone to Smolensk. What sort of fortifications were these going to be? And what fortifications could old people, and sick people, and children be building? But the rumors didn't stop at the number of people deported. Now there was more disquieting news about a place near Bialystok where the transports were sorted, and from where the healthy specimens continued to Smolensk, while the sick and the weak were exterminated.

Meantime, a new Judenrath was formed, and one of its first acts was an announcement, countersigned by the Gestapo, that evil tongues were spreading false rumors about the plight of the deportees. It was forbidden, under threat of death, to propagate such rumors, and the inhabitants of the new Ghetto — as the Little Ghetto had already ceased to exist — were again reassured that all the roads led to Smolensk.

Then, one day, we learned that our own quarters had been raided and the women taken away. This was the first time in my life that I saw my father cry. He got up, weeping, and without talking to Martin or me, went toward the gate of the factory compound. We caught up with him, trying to force him to stay, but his mind was made up. "My poor wife," he sobbed, "my poor old sick woman. How is she going to help herself, all alone in the world?" He was going to go directly to the Umschlagplatz, to find Mother, and to join her in her voyage.

But then one of our Order Service men burst in, carrying the latest news: five women had hidden behind a double wall, and they remained in the house. Two of them were Mother and Pola.

That night we received permission from our German boss to sleep in the shop and to bring the five women in.

The next day, a young engineer from Warsaw, Mr. Zmigrod, came to the shop. He didn't know anybody there. He had just taken his young wife and entered the first open gate he saw. Nobody rejected them, just as nobody said anything when Witek and his wife came to stay with us, as well as a young dental student, Maria, whom I had once met through Witek. They had learned that I was there and thought that there might be a chance for them. So, during the day, they stayed with us in the shop, and at night they slept in a large wooden barrack in the yard behind the factory, hidden in the maze of luggage that we, the legitimate employees of Astrawerke, had piled up after having left our quarters to live in the factory.

The Umsiedlung, a German project which, at first, was marked by discipline and orderliness, has now become a savage hunt for Jewish game. It had become apparent that no certificates were being honored any longer, and that our remaining where we were was only a question of luck and of time. Each day that had passed meant to us six thousand more people deported, six thousand less people to be deported, six thousand people closer to our own safety. There was just one thing of which we were absolutely sure: the Umsiedlung would not go on forever, and once it stopped, we would not have any more problems until the end of the war.

In their wild hunt, groups of Lithuanians and Latvians, Jews and Germans, burst into our factory compound several times each day, verifying our status in the shop, breaking open the barn with our luggage in it, trampling over the soup our women were cooking on open fires in the yard of the compound, and scaring the souls out of Witek and his wife, who finally decided to volunteer for the Umsiedlung, their nerves not being able to take this nightmare any longer. Maria tried the short way out, and one morning I found her in the barn with a bellyful of sleeping pills. We had two Warsaw physicians working on the assembly line of the Astrawerke, and one of them pumped out Maria's stomach and saved her. Later that day, her eyes round with terror, Maria left the shop and roamed into the Ghetto like a sleepwalker, never to be seen by me again.

Thursday, September 3, 1942, 8 A.M.: The owner telephones to advise that he will not be coming in today because of a bad cold.

9 A.M.: A rumor starts spreading in the shop that Astrawerke has lost its status as being indispensable to the war effort.

9:30 A.M.: Martin asks the German-Jewish foreman about the rumor. The rumor is wrong. Adding machines are indispensable.

10 A.M.: The rumor persists. The German-Jewish foreman telephones the boss. He is reassured. The Wehrmacht needs the adding machines.

10:30 A.M.: Some of the workers say they've heard the same rumor from an officer of the Order Service. The foreman telephones the boss again. There might be something to the rumor. The boss has a lunch appointment with the Gestapo officer responsible for indispensability matters.

Noon: The foreman telephones the boss and cannot reach him.

2 P.M.: People here in the shop are becoming panicky. And yet, this is the first time in a couple of weeks that we haven't had any raid yet.

2:30 P.M.: The foreman telephones the boss. He is not available.

3 P.M.: The foreman telephones the boss. No answer.

3:30 P.M.: The foreman telephones the boss. No answer.

4:30 P.M.: The foreman telephones the boss. No answer.

4:55 P.M.: There has been no raid on us today. The day is as good as over. The action has probably already been finished for the day. The workers seem to be getting over their anxieties.

5:00 P.M.: The gates to the compound burst open. A substantial group of police of all designations invade the shop. A Gestapo officer steps briskly forward and yells, "Rrraus everybody!!! Everybody out! Schnell! Quick! Rrraus! Rrraus! Umsiedlung!!!"

5

TREBLINKA

BEFORE now, it had always been I who watched the others being dragged out of their homes and deported from the Ghetto. I had looked at them as though a member of the audience observing the actors in a play, seldom even trying to imagine what they could be feeling at such a moment.

But now, it was different. It was really happening to me. I looked around as we were driven by a horde of yelling Germans and Lithuanians, forced into a column, four abreast, and made to march to the sound of the whips and rifle butts falling upon us. A formation of Jewish workers passed by, marching smartly. They must have been going home from work, as we had, until yesterday. Some of them looked away from us. Some looked at us with curiosity, and I knew so well what they were feeling: "Another day has passed; another transport has left; maybe tomorrow, no more deportation." As for me, the whole thing was so far beyond my capacity to feel that I was unable to grasp its meaning. We marched crisply, I at the left flank, Father next to me, then Mother and Dr. Saks. Behind me, marched Martin with Pola, and the young engineer Zmigród with his pretty wife. I looked at Father and smiled. I knew that my smile in these circumstances must have seemed very stupid. He was serious. From time to time, he tried to take Mother under the arm, to help her in this excruciating march, but the German guard who walked near me yelled, "Was ist los?" ("What's the matter?") and waved his rifle threateningly.

It was not far to go. We were now approaching the Umschlagplatz. I was thinking how different the same place can be if it is seen on different occasions. It didn't even resemble the Stawki Hospital in which I had worked for three months and which I had known so well. Now it was a set of gloomy buildings surrounded by barbed wire and inhabited by a huge crowd of Jews who had been brought there before us. After our Astrawerke detachment of about one hundred and twenty people had been driven into this enclosure, feeling like cattle being readied for the butcher, we were left alone. Our little group, with the Zmigróds and Dr. Saks, entered the hospital building. People were everywhere: sitting people, standing people, lying people. The corridors, the wards, the stairways, all smelled of people and their excrements. People were sitting in their own feces, jealously clutching their bundles and their bread.

"How long have you been here?" I asked somebody.

He looked at me with distrust and didn't answer.

Someone else said, "Four days, five days — what's the difference?"

I wanted to know whether there were any transports leaving *now;* I felt nauseated; I wanted to leave this place.

There was a sudden uproar downstairs. Several men swiftly climbed the stairs past me. One whispered to the others, "Quick! Let's find a place to hide!"

The guards were chasing everybody out. A German in SS uniform stepped into human excrement, cursed, and didn't go any further in his search for Jews who might be hiding in some of those ill-smelling corners. I realized that the men who had gone upstairs would avoid this transport.

We were driven into a formation as before, four abreast, only this time it was all mixed. I could see in our immediate group maybe twenty or thirty people from the Astrawerke. An SS man with a huge belly and a leather whip in his hand gave the order. We were marched away, toward the railroad platforms. As we were passing by the big-bellied SS man, he noticed a blonde girl marching in my group. He stopped the group and motioned her out. They exchanged a few words, and she handed a document over to him. He glanced at it briefly, then motioned her back to the group. He might have taken her for an Aryan, I thought.

Now, we were led toward a long freight train. Our group was

stopped in front of one of the boxcars. On its side was still written the old military sign going back to World War I: "Eight Horses, or Forty Men." We were whipped into the car within minutes. I counted one hundred and twenty people. Just enough for most of us to have standing room, with only a few women, old or sick, able to sit. The door hinges jarred. The guards locked us in. The transport was ready for dispatch.

Mother sat on the floor, old and defeated. She wouldn't talk. Besides, what was there to talk about? When she had said, during our travel from Lvov, that she would never see Lvov again, that she would never see her son Max again, her words were prophetic. She had also said that she wouldn't leave the Ghetto alive. But was she now leaving the Ghetto, or simply traveling toward its annex?

Poor Mother. Tenderness for her flooded me. She and Father had always been so far away from me, so far in age, so far in understanding my hopes and my drives, that all my life I had been building a wall of silence between me and them, hurting them unwillingly by my aloofness. I would have liked now to pour this huge volume of tenderness, suddenly overflowing me, right into them, to soothe the aching effect of all the years that were gone without our having been able to express our emotions. All I could do was to caress her hair slightly with my fingers.

Father stood up against the back wall of the boxcar. His eyes were fixed on Mother. Never in my life had I heard him say to her, "I love you." Indeed never in my life had I heard them addressing each other by their first names. They had always called each other "Old Man" and "Old Lady," although they weren't old when I was a child. All these years, it had never occurred to me to ask myself this simple question, "Do they love each other?" As I remembered the scene in Astrawerke, when he wanted to join her for the Umsiedlung, I knew he loved her. And now, they traveled together.

Pola sat next to Mother. Unconsciously she kept pulling her hair, the personification of Tragedy, and I could hear her saying, "Now we are lost."

Martin stood against the locked gates of the boxcar, as if in a vain hope that it was all a mistake, that the car would open and a cheerful voice from the outside would call, "Come out, my good friends! You've just had a nightmare. Wake up to love, to life, and to laughter." He kept twisting a lock of his hair with a finger, his eyes fixed on the darkness of the car.

The car was hot, the air was foul. I could see a woman defecating directly under herself. A man urinated over another man, and an argument broke out between them. Mother said, "I'm thirsty," and I would have given my life for some water for her. But it had been an exceptionally beautiful September, and there was no rain in sight. Strange how much importance we had learned to give to rain in September. When the Germans had invaded Poland three years before, it was also in September, September 1. And everybody said, "Oh, just watch and see! Come the second week of September, the rains will fall, the roads will become muddy, and the German armor will drown — and that is when we'll hit them." The rains never fell, and we never hit them. And it was September again, and again there was no rain, and Mother needed water.

Suddenly there was lightning outside and thunder. "Must be from a clear sky," I thought. I didn't remember seeing the clouds. Rain fell on the train. I believed it was a miracle. I stuck an arm through the small rectangular airhole at the top of the boxcar wall. I squeezed my arm through the barbed wire that covered the outside of the slit and cupped my palm, trying to catch the heavy drops of rain. Not one drop fell into my hand. The eave of the car's roof was keeping the rain away. A heavy wind blew along the train, enveloping it in a nightmarish howling and giggling. I was not sure whether it was the wind that giggled, or the Lithuanian guards seated in the sentry booth behind the car. I prayed to God for a miracle.

"God," I said in my mind, "stop the train. Derailments, collisions, wreckages do occur. Let this train wreck. Let it collide. Let it jump off the rails."

But the train continued on its pitiless voyage forward.

The people in the boxcar had been affected by the heat, the lack of water, the imminence of danger, and the deep differences in their own individual backgrounds. Everybody hated everybody, and cursed everybody, and would have liked to survive at everybody else's expense. It wasn't a car full of Jews; it was Noah's ark all over again. Suddenly, these were not people but animals. Sick animals, dying animals, raging animals. The air of the slaughterhouse was all over us.

The train stopped in the middle of the night, the gate opened up, and two guards entered, a Lithuanian and a Latvian. They hit Martin, who was standing next to the gate, and asked him for his money. He handed over the little he had, and they proceeded to hit people, one by one, and to rob them. Father whispered, "What are we going to do?" I took his little cotton bag and hung it from the barbed wire that covered the airhole. The guards hit me for not having money for them and continued robbing other people. As they were getting ready to leave the car, I pulled Father's little bag in. A minute later, they searched the outside of the car, using strong flashlights. Probably my trick wasn't unknown to them.

As the train moved again, Father wanted me to keep his bag. "You saved it," he said. "We might still need it one day." I knew he was proud of me.

Dawn peered in through the air hole. The train came to a stop in the middle of the countryside. I could see, far away in front of me, the dark line of a thick forest. Closer, against the background of the forest, there was a peasant cottage, whitewashed, small, and simple. A peasant woman was bending over her plants, minding the garden. Outside, all was quiet, all was peace. I felt something like a spasm in my heart. I wanted to be a part of this universal peace that had always been denied me because I was a Jew. I was still allowed one last dream. I said to myself, "If I come out alive, I want to have such a cottage one day, with flowers in the front, and vegetables in the back, and peace in it and around it."

Two uniformed railroad workers were walking slowly along the train. They spoke Polish to each other. I recognized the Mazur accent. Then we weren't far from Warsaw, in spite of our long travel. Maybe it meant hope. Somebody yelled from one of the cars, "We are dying of thirst! Will you give us a drop of water?" The workers made believe they didn't hear him. Somebody else yelled a question, " How long are we going to stay here, before we move on?" The two workers stopped. One of them raised his blue Mazur eyes and said in his singsong accent: "People, poor people! If you only knew where you are going, you would like to stay here forever, and without water." The railroad workers wandered off, leaving the train in bewilderment.

It was already nine in the morning when the first twenty cars in the back were uncoupled from the rest of the train, and a locomotive pulled them away on a track parallel to ours. At nine-thirty, a second row of twenty cars was pulled away. As they were passing by, I recognized the Zmigróds in the vent of one of the boxcars. At ten o'clock, the irons jarred and jerked, and our portion of the train moved forward.

It didn't take long now. Within twenty minutes the locomotive moaned, and the train came to a full stop. Someone outside shoved the heavy doors of the box cars. From this point on, everything happened so suddenly, and so rapidly, and in such a shocking way, that even today, after over thirty-five years, I am still overcome by a mixture of emotions: blind anger and hatred, hope and misery, prayer and blasphemy were all drowning in a sea of hoarse commands, of whipping, hitting, kicking, and shooting.

It had taken on the shape of a square dance. I was again a student in Naples. Giacomino Biondi, a lieutenant of the Black Shirts, led the quadrille: gentlemen to the right — ladies to the left — vite! vite! vite! — Giacomino threw his orders energetically, and the row of ladies bowed graciously, and ran, and ran, and ran — vite! vite! — schnell! schnell! — run, you dog — you verfluchter hund — you sow.

All I could see was a moving body of martyred humanity. I didn't see Mother and Pola. When I finally started accepting the reality, the last women from the transport were disappearing into a long wooden barrack to the left of the square sandy yard where only the men were now kept in formation. Martin and Father stood next to me.

A man in front of me said in a colorless voice: "God! We are in Treblinka!"

I asked him, "What is Treblinka?"

He looked at me as if he had seen a tropical bird in the Arctic. "You don't know of Treblinka! It's even worse than Auschwitz!"

But then, I didn't know what Auschwitz was either.

We were standing along the barrack where the women had gone in. We must have been some six hundred men, all the men left from the last twenty boxcars of our train. It was already ten-thirty, and the September sun was burning unceasingly. A pile of loaves of bread was lying in front of us, some of the loaves bearing signs of having been bitten into. It must have been the bread belonging to the people on our train. I hadn't eaten anything in twenty-four hours, but I wasn't hungry. I asked Father whether he wanted some, but he wasn't hungry either. He said he would like a little water to drink.

There was a round wooden well, with a little decorative roof above it, in front of us and to the right, not far from the wide opening in the barbed-wire fence through which we had been chased into the yard upon our arrival. Two Ukrainian guards were standing at the well. I left the formation and approached it. A few others followed me. One of the guards twirled his rifle and hit one of the men with its butt. The other aimed his rifle, ready for firing. We all returned, running to our posts. I felt depressed. I wanted that water for Father. And I suddenly felt terribly thirsty myself. Father said, "Don't worry."

In the middle of the yard, fixed to two tall poles, was a huge placard, a welcome to Treblinka. It said in large, neat letters: "THIS

IS A LABOR CAMP. YOU ARE REQUESTED TO SURRENDER YOUR CIVILIAN CLOTHES AND DEPOSIT YOUR MONEY AND YOUR VALUABLES WITH THE CASHIER. YOU WILL TAKE SHOWERS IN GROUPS. AFTER THE SHOWER, WORKING CLOTHES WILL BE DISTRIBUTED AND ROOM IN THE BARRACKS ASSIGNED. FAMILIES OF THE WORKERS WILL BE EMPLOYED IN AGRICULTURAL JOBS."

And now, two Jews, obviously workers in this labor camp, walked slowly in front of us, calling in sad voices: "Surrender your diamonds. Surrender your valuables. Surrender your money. You won't need it here any longer. This is the end of the road. This is Treblinka."

They carried small wooden boxes in their hands, shaking them occasionally, encouraging us to throw our valuables in. Various people did.

Father whispered, "Oh, God! What are we going to do?"

I answered in a whisper, "Nothing. I'm going to keep your things."

The placard said one thing; the wretches asking us for our money were saying something else. And then, in front of us, in the hot white sand, I saw American dollars torn in half, and ripped Polish five-hundred-zloty banknotes, and pieces of jewelry, like orphans crying out for their departed owners.

A tall, blond, handsome German in an SS uniform, with a leather whip in his left hand, stopped in front of us, and his steel-blue eyes embraced the group in a swift glance. A little girl, a child of three or four, wandered in front of the group. She cried desperately, calling, "Mommy! Mommy!" With her long blond curls and her beautiful face shiny with tears, she looked like one of Titian's cherubs. The handsome SS man took the child in his arms, caressed her head, and gave her a candy he got out of his pocket.

He asked, "Do you see your mommy here? Look around. Do you see her?"

The child shook her head.

He put her down, turned to an elderly man in the first row, and said, "I make you personally responsible for this child. When you go to the bath, you'll take her with you. We'll find her mother later on."

A second SS man arrived, and they had a quick conference. Then the handsome one ordered, "Present yourselves to me, one by one, for work assignment!"

One by one, we stood in front of him at attention, each stating his age and occupation. In an elegant gesture, he motioned us to the left or to the right, one by one, one by one. Soon, there were two groups of us: a large group composed of people who looked old or tired or sick; and a small group of some two hundred younger men, or men who looked young. Father was in the former group; Martin, Zmigród, and I in the latter.

The command fell now: "Undress for the shower!" It was directed at Father's group.

I said, "I'd like to take a shower, too. I'm so hot."

A man next to me, who looked like a Ghetto smuggler, said, "Shut up, you shmok!"

The Ukrainians went into action. They yelled and used the rifle butts. The handsome SS man walked among the undressing men, letting his leather whip fall on them with an elegant motion. Father was not undressing quickly enough. I didn't want him to be whipped. I wished he could undress faster. By now, they had almost all disappeared into the barrack. Father was the last one to go. He walked slowly, naked but dignified, and they didn't hit him. I lifted a hand, and it clenched into a fist. Father waved to me. It was a good-bye. I felt an urge to ask him this last important question: "Father, is this the end of the world?" And, as if he had heard me, he shrugged his shoulders. And now I could almost hear him saying, "This is the end of my road. But it is not the end of the world."

Later that day, a feeling of guilt overcame me that I was to carry for many years thereafter. Long after that day, I told myself that had I known my Father was going to his death, I would have joined him. Today, I am no longer ashamed to admit the obvious truth: I knew where he was going. I must have known by intuition that we were drowning in a sea of death, and I wanted to steer away from it, toward some shore of salvation.

Our group was called to order by a big husky Jew with an armband saying, "Kapo," and with the raucous, gravelly voice of somebody suffering chronic laryngitis. He told us that we were lucky, that the Lagerkommandant needed two hundred able-bodied Jews to take the place of those workers whose productivity had fallen off, and that he had decided to give us a chance. Then he said that he needed immediately fifty unskilled laborers to take care of various odd jobs, and he asked for volunteers. Martin and I stepped out, followed by many others. Our intuition had become our guide. The ones who didn't volunteer, hoping for better work, were immediately rounded up, stood in front of a thicket of fir growth along one of the fences, and machine-gunned. We were led off to work.

Our assignment that first afternoon was in the *Lumpenkommando* — the "Rag Detail" — where we had to work at sorting clothing into uniform groups: dresses with dresses, jackets with jackets, shoes with shoes. Our group was divided into several teams of twenty people, each team having a Jewish foreman who, a stick in his hand, made sure that the work proceeded quickly and expertly.

Martin was marched away to another location, while I worked in a barrack positioned directly behind the barrack of doom, and parallel to it. The barrack was bursting with Jewish clothing.

While sorting, we were supposed to look for valuables and to report each find to the foreman. As we were working, the foreman kept yelling in both German and Yiddish, "Schneller! Schneller! Gicher! Gicher!" ("Faster! Faster! Quicker! Quicker!"), and whenever an SS man approached, the foreman ran into the barrack, hitting us with his stick. Sometimes, this was sufficient for the SS man, but sometimes, dissatisifed with our performance, he dropped in himself and hit us with his leather whip. All of this lasted until late in the afternoon, at which time all the teams were marched off into the camp, surrounded by the Ukrainian guards.

As we were marching, the chief guard ordered us to sing. It seemed unbelievable to me, but the old timers in the group — people who had already been there for two or three days — knew better, and they intoned a joyous song of the Ukrainian peasant festivals, "Szczoby nie Marusia." It was a dance tune, and it was incongruous with either a march or this sort of camp, but the guards laughed contentedly. It must have been just what they wanted.

It was still hot when the entire work force of Treblinka was gathered for the evening report. We were all waiting in formation along three sides of the yard, while the Ukrainian guards were getting together in the middle of it. I was dizzied by that awful thirst. I could hardly understand Martin when he whispered, looking directly in front of him, "Sonny, our folks are gone."

Martin always called me "Sonny," because he was fourteen years my elder. But I was now twenty-six. Going to be twenty-six in November. On November 23. If I lived that long. "Sonny, our folks are gone." I nodded my head, looking into the hot, white sand.

And there, watching me intensely, as if she were trying to call me back to my senses, was the Girl. I bent down and picked up a ring. It was a heavy piece of gold, set around a chunk of fluorescent tiger's eye stone with a soft cameo of a girl's face carved into it. Perhaps I had become an easy prey to superstition by now, but as I clutched the Ring, I had a vivid sensation of holding the Spirit of Life, and I could hear the voice I knew so well from my dreams: "This is me."

"Sonny, our folks are gone."

I clasped the Ring in my hot, sweating hand. And the Girl repeated, "It is really me."

The time had arrived for the evening report.

We were gathered in a U-shaped formation, four to a line, facing the center of the yard. My group was standing along the barrack where this morning's arrivals had been taken to death. Across the yard was another barrack, similar in shape and size, with a group of workers standing along it. Between these two groups, to my left, a third was standing, at the bottom of the U. Behind them was a long barbed-wire fence with a thicket of tall fir trees just behind it. This was the place where, earlier this afternoon, people who hadn't volunteered for unskilled labor had been shot.

While waiting for the report, I noticed a few details. The fir trees along the fence weren't alive. They were dead trees that had been cut away at the roots to become the woof for the warp of the barbed wire. The trees were just another fence with a make-believe life in it, holding forth a false promise in much the same way as the placard about the showers. Now I noticed another fence of fir trees, out at the other side of the entrance, across the railroad tracks. I could also see now, next to the entrance but in its own separate barbed-wire enclosure, a third, smaller barrack. In front of it, a small formation of perhaps fifty people was standing. They wore civilian clothing, like all of us, but on their pants, over the right knee, each of them had a large yellow triangular patch. I learned that they were the Jews who had helped to build Treblinka. They were all craftsmen, and all had been brought in from the little surrounding towns. Now they were considered permanent workers, had special privileges, like being able to move around unattended by the ubiquitous Ukrainians, and were known by the Jewish proletariat of the camp as the *Geyle Lattes* — the "Yellow Patches." Behind the barrack of the Yellow Patches, I saw a wooden sentry tower, from which two Ukrainians with a machine gun controlled this side of the camp. I noticed three more such towers in the remaining corners of the camp.

So, this was all? I knew better than this. This yard, with the three barracks and the four towers, was just a molecule. The real Treblinka must be lying behind the jealous fence of mummified firs. A continuous grinding sound was coming from there, something like a dentist's drill magnified to the millionth power. This sound was the real Treblinka. And the smell. The nauseating sweetish smell, similar to the one emitted by burning pork sausages. This smell, too, was the real Treblinka. And the shots. And the little explosions that sounded like grenades. They erupted sporadically there, at the other side of the firs. They, also, were the real Treblinka.

The administration of the camp was almost ready for the evening report. In the center of the yard, a group of Ukrainians stood in a single line. They wore SS uniforms, and each had a rifle. Next to them and to their right stood four strange figures. They wore impeccable white uniforms, but their husky bodies, huge hands, and oafish faces seemed awkward in all that unblemished white. Nobody knew who they were, but we were to see them, during the days to come, at each morning and evening report. Further away, stood the big Jew with the Kapo's armband and a dozen other Jewish foremen. The handsome, tall blond SS officer who had sorted us this morning was standing in front of the group. By now, I knew that he was known by the Treblinka Jews as the "Golem" and that his name inspired awe among the people here. But I did not know what a "Golem" actually was until it was later explained to me that a "Golem" was a figure from Jewish folklore, a mechanical being without a soul who if uncontrolled would easily fall into a murderous rage. The other SS officer who was helping the Golem this morning now counted us. He walked along my group, a leather whip in his left hand. As he was counting, "Ein-und-zwanzig, zwei-und-zwanzig," he punctuated his bookkeeping by slightly knocking the handle of the whip on the chests of the people in the first row.

Finally, the stage was set. An officer in a crisp white uniform, a slight figure with a pince-nez, marched in accompanied by two SS officers. The man who had counted us, and whom the Jews knew as "Franz," stepped forward, stopped at attention, saluted dutifully, and reported to the officer in white, "Eight-hundred men, Herr Kapitan! All present and accounted for."

We slept in the barrack through which the doomed ones had passed — this day and for many days and weeks before. The barrack was empty, except for us, lying on the earthen floor, body to body, exhausted yet unable to fall asleep, confusing our own sobbing with imagined sighs and whispers of the dead, having daydreams of bloody revenge, and nightmares of inevitability. There, at the narrow far end of the barrack was a locked door. This must be the exit from life, into a death without dignity.

There was a gas chamber beyond that door, people were saying. And there was another door, leading from the gas chamber into the ditches. But between the gas chamber and the ditches, there was a barber detail, where the hair was cut off of the bodies, to be shipped to Germany to stuff mattresses; and there was the dentist detail, where gold crowns were extracted; and there was even, they were saying, a chemical detail where it was attempted, on a laboratory scale, to salvage human fat to make soap out of it.

I couldn't sleep. My tongue was dry as parchment. It seemed to have reached the dimension of a calf's tongue. I had to get water.

There were some stray objects spread here and there in the barrack, among them an aluminum canteen. I took it and crawled out of the barrack. Out there, it was all darkness, except for a little field kitchen near the wooden well, where a small group of people were doing some work. On all fours, making sure that no guard could see me, I approached the group.

As they noticed me, one hissed, "Idiot! What are you doing here? They'll shoot you!" I could see the yellow triangle over his knee.

"Water!" I whispered back hoarsely.

A finger on his lips, he motioned me toward a pail filled with water. Still on all fours, I dipped my entire head into the pail, drinking the cool liquid like a horse. It had a strong smell of burnt skin, but so did all of Treblinka. I filled up the canteen.

A guard yelled out of the darkness, "Hey! What's going on there?"

A Yellow Patch yelled back, "Nothing! We are preparing the breakfast!"

"Then shut up!" screamed the voice.

By then, I was back in the barrack, giving Martin the water. As he drank avidly, he looked like a helpless baby, and I felt like calling him, "Sonny."

At four o'clock, we were up and ready for the morning report. The field kitchen was giving out something, and a number of people were waiting in line, some holding a plate, some holding a pot. We still weren't hungry. We still needed a lot of readjusting. What we did feel very strongly was a continuous, gnawing thirst. I drank again, and again filled up the canteen, which I then fastened to my belt.

After the report, my detail was marched back to the same barrack where we had sorted clothes the day before. Martin's group went to the adjacent barrack, also filled with clothes. Other, smaller groups went in various different directions. There was a group called the "Lime Detail" which went to work behind the firs mixing lime to be spread over the ditches of death. Another group was called the "Tower Detail," and I imagined that they must be employed in constructing additional sentry towers. There was also a "Ditch

Detail" and a "Garden Detail," and a few others, but obviously the largest group was the "Rag Detail," the Lumpenkommando in which Martin and I worked.

As I was going toward my work site, I could see several neat, colorful wooden cottages, in front of which young Jewish women were washing and hanging linens. Probably the SS lived in the cottages.

Later that morning, we were ordered to interrupt the sorting and were taken back to the yard, where one last group of a new transport was waiting in front of our barrack, and the yard was littered with clothing. We were whipped into quickly collecting the clothing and carrying it in large bundles to the sorting barracks. Each of us worked at a trot, to avoid a beating. I was told that any signs of beating on your face were a step closer to death. I ran across Martin. He had a huge bump on his forehead. I kept running in my direction, he in his. As I was trotting past two German SS men, one remarked, laughing, to the other, "Look at these Jews, how they work! They think they're going to stay alive!"

I now had a three-day-old beard. A thought occurred to me: Could I ask them to lend me their razor, so that I might die looking neat?

The group that waited in front of the barrack wasn't there any longer. We were led inside the barrack, to collect women's garments. Women didn't undress in the yard. Hidden under some clothes was a live infant. A Ukrainian caught him by the tiny arms and carried him out and beyond the firs. A worker was caught in the middle of the yard. It was a woman dressed like a man. A German SS man was whipping her while she was stripping naked as ordered. She cried that she could be as good a worker as a man, but she was soon whipped behind the fir fence. I thought about the little girl who had been looking for her mommy yesterday. When the Golem asked her whether she saw her mommy in the group of men, he had expected the child to betray her mother. Possibly other women before had tried to stay alive by passing for men.

Still later that day, an SS man led me to a huge hole in the middle of a forest within the camp. There a detail of Jews was making bricks. A guard indicated a wooden rack to me and ordered me to start carrying bricks to the opposite side of the camp, beyond the railroad platform.

I loaded the rack half full, and it still was very heavy. The day was hot, and I worked in my pants only, with naked torso and bare feet. I tried to trot in the hot sand, even with this heavy burden on my shoulders, so as not to be marked for death by the whip of a guard. I reached the platform onto which we had been discharged only yesterday. It seemed like a year ago.

I walked along a low concrete structure built on one of the sides of the platform. Some Jews were inside, working at sorting food. A foreman was yelling at them, "Schneller! Schneller! Gicher! Gicher!" marking his order rhythmically with a stick he held in his hand. Further down, a group of three foremen were having breakfast, helping themselves to some jars found in the bundles of deportees. I left the bricks at the spot indicated by a guard who was posted there and ran back for more bricks. As the time passed, the sun became hotter, and I dragged my feet at a slower pace in the burning sand of Treblinka. I felt dizzy from dehydration, and as I walked doggedly with my burden, both shoulders already two open wounds, I kept repeating automatically in my mind, *Avadim Hainu L'Paroh b'Mizraim* — "We were Pharoah's slaves in the Land of Egypt" — the sentence with which Father had started each Passover recounting of Jewish suffering and miraculous salvation three thousand years ago.

A Ukrainian guard stopped me. He was big and awkward and smelled of vodka. He told me in a kind voice that what I was doing was incorrect. That I was killing myself. He picked up some rags from the sand and slipped them under the arms of the rack, between the rack and my wounds. He said that this was the right way to carry bricks. Then he hit me with the butt of his rifle, right on the head. For a moment, I lost consciousness. When I came to, I heard the guard's voice: "Get up, you! Get up!" The words reached me as through a fog and through a distance, and I well remember my deep sense of regret that I was back there, to continue paying my dues.

That evening, we helped Mr. Zmigrod to die. Martin and I, and a couple more people from Astrawerke sat around him, while he swallowed a bottle of barbiturate pills, taking them, one by one, like a gourmet enjoying an hors d'oeuvre. He had decided today that he didn't want to live without his wife. Now, he was having his last cigarette. Later, he asked Martin to take it out of his mouth, as his hands were already asleep. And then he was lying in his last happy doze, which tomorrow no amount of kicking and hitting would be able to interrupt.

The next day was Sunday, and two transports of people had arrived, instead of the usual one. Twelve thousand people. As many as four entire little Polish towns put together. We worked that day with more intensity than ever, more carefully than ever trying to avoid being hit, more assiduously than ever looking down at the sand to avoid meeting the eyes of any of the SS guards. By intuition, we knew that looking them in the eyes could bring the thunder on our heads.

In the middle of the day, between the two transports, a group of workers, some thirty people, were driven into our barrack. Two Ukrainians calmly posted a machine gun on a tripod in front of the barrack, and one of them said to the protesting group, "Now, it's your choice. Either you go down there through the door, or you'll be shot here." I don't know which choice they made, because we were ordered back to work.

It took a very long time for the second transport to go through. We had already finished our work and had carried away the last group's clothing. Now, seated in the yard outside the second barrack, we waited for this group of naked men to go through our own barrack, so that we might finally go to sleep there.

One of them was arguing with the guards. He maintained that he was not Jewish. He argued that he had been caught in a raid while trying to buy some goods from the Jews.

The men were now driven into the barrack. The Pole climbed up the wall and proclaimed his innocence from the little air hole just below the roof.

"I am not a Jew!" he screamed. "Call somebody! Tell somebody about it!"

It was almost amusing to listen to him. He was innocent because he was not a Jew. Consequently, all the Jews were guilty of being alive, and therefore deserved to die.

Then the Pole stopped screaming. By now, they must all have passed into the gas chamber.

The night was quiet, with only the grinding sound of Treblinka in the background. A band started playing a tango by a popular composer of the times, Petersburski. This was the beginning of a new arrangement. That day, the Germans had picked a few musicians with their instruments and were making them play tangoes next to the gas chamber. And suddenly, through the stillness of the night, through the sound of Treblinka's bone grinding mill, through the sweet notes of the tango, a terrifying scream of several hundreds of dying people hit our eardrums and cut our souls like a sharp knife of guilt. I covered my ears with my hands and felt blood boiling in my brain: this was the way my parents had died only three days ago.

On Monday, I was ordered to carry some bundles further than I had ever been yet, all the way beyond the food warehouse, where the jewelry experts had their sorting stands. There all the Jewish valuables were carefully sorted, diamonds by the cut and the size, gold by the karat, money by the country of issuance. As pedantic as the administration intended to be with the valuables, there was always a lot of everything scattered about right in front of you, in the white sand.

As I was trudging away, I felt sick to my stomach, and I vomited. Immediately after, I had violent diarrhea. I did all where I stood, in the sand, but now I had to think of paper to clean myself. I looked around me, but there was no paper. Then I readjusted my thinking to the present situation, and I saw paper. A bunch of large, soft five-hundred-zloty bills, each of them worth some fifteen dollars, but in some other place in the world, not here. Here, this was what they really were: pieces of paper. I felt no hesitation as I cleaned myself with what would have paid a month's rent — in the outside world.

I picked up my bundle and trudged forward, toward the long row of dark fir trees. It ran all the way down, toward the main camp, and then made a sharp L-turn toward the place where I thought my barrack was. A moment later, I reached the end of the firs, and my heart stopped beating for an instant. There was a huge ditch. It was long, and wide, and filled with milky smoke, and with burning bodies. Groups of guards stood at its edge, here and there, some throwing in a grenade, some shooting from a tommy gun. And then I saw a scene. A scene of horror and pagan beauty.

Along the scarp, a nude girl was gently stepping down. Heavy black hair was falling down her neck. Around her, from the steaming Valhalla, half-burnt arms, hundreds of arms, thousands of arms, opened up in a hospitable gesture of welcome. Or were they raised to God, in a mute prayer for justice?

Among them, the fair girl was descending as the milky haze was lovingly creeping up her slim ankles, caressing her shapely calves, and lustfully clinging to her soft thighs.

She turned around and seemed to be softly swaying from the graceful lines of her hips. Her breast rose toward two guards up on the scarp, as if in a last protest. It seemed to be saying, "I have not known love. I have not lived yet. I am ripe with passion."

One of the guards slowly pointed his rifle at her.

And the fair girl dissolved in the light-blue oblivion of the milky haze.

The day after was Tuesday. Martin and I worked in different

details, but we always stayed together during the reports, and we slept next to each other. Our closeness was a new phenomenon. As long as I could remember, he had been so aloof, so distinguished-looking, and so much older than I, that as a child I wasn't even sure whether I should address him as "Martin" or as "Sir." During my growing years, he was already away from home, always in a good job, always consulting Father on various business matters, always nearly being "Sir" to me. It was only during the past few months that I had finally become convinced that he was just a brother. Yet even now, we were unable to communicate in words. For him, I was probably still the little baby brother; to me, he still must have been the fearsome oldest brother whose mere glance was sufficient to freeze me. So we didn't use many words now. But we learned to communicate just by being together. Just by being together, we felt the same guilt, the same shame, and the same helplessness, and we knew that soon we would be called on to share the same destiny.

Tuesday's evening report was different from the usual because of two things. First there was a short speech by the SS man called Franz. He addressed the entire work force directly, saying that we were all behind with our work, and that it was *Scheiss egal* to him whether it was us or another group, and that this was our last chance if we wanted to stay alive. The second new thing was the public punishment meted out to all the foremen by all the foremen. If we didn't meet the quota for our work, the foremen were responsible, and now they were all lined up, one behind the other in the middle of the yard, and were ordered to start punishing each other. A stick was handed to the second in line. The first in line bent down. The second hit him and counted aloud. As he reached the number ten, Franz stopped him, saying that he didn't hit the right way. He asked him to bend down, called a Ukrainian, and ordered a model beating. The guard took off his jacket, rolled up the sleeves of his shirt, spat into his hands, grabbed the stick, and applied fifteen hits to the shaking buttocks, while the beaten foreman counted his own punishment aloud. After this sample lesson, each foreman beat the next with all his heart. We enjoyed the scene. These foremen were the very same Jews who had whipped us all day long, yelling incessantly their "Schneller! Schneller! Gicher! Gicher!" and we just needed this little satisfaction, especially knowing well that tomorrow they would repay us with interest for their misadventure of today.

And so Wednesday, September 9 arrived.
We all looked sick and exhausted. All these days, we had drunk

enormous amounts of water but must have eaten only a few crumbs of bread. Some food could be found here and there, but we simply didn't care for any.

I had found a razor with some blades and a knife. I used the razor every night, so that I would be clean-shaven when I was killed. As for the knife, I didn't know why I had taken it. Maybe it symbolized a weapon, and maybe deep down I still hoped that I might be engaged one day in a direct, fair fight with an SS man.

The first train of the day arrived, and a group of the Jewish Order Service from Warsaw came on it. They left their car crisp and refreshed, as if they had traveled in a pullman. They stopped at attention, while their officer reported to the Golem. All this was done in such an efficient and professional way that I knew: this was our last day in Treblinka; these people will take over, and we will go.

In the afternoon, I was ordered to a new detail. A whole empty freight train was standing at the tracks, and everybody was carrying bundles to it. Now, the rags become clothes again were going to Germany as the loot of the victor. After I had carried a few bundles to the train, I noticed that there were two or three workers in each boxcar, taking the bundles from us and packing them nice and tight into the car. My plan of action was born and matured all in the same instant. I climbed into the closest boxcar, saying that the guard had ordered me to do so, and I started packing up the car. As I was doing so, I prepared a little hideaway for me and Martin. It was close to the opposite wall of the car, surrounded on all sides by a tall wall of bundles, and leaving a little square opening all the way up, under the roof. I had to make sure now that the other two workers wouldn't betray me. I asked them directly, whether they intended to escape. Both shook their heads. They were too old, they said, to start a new life. Their entire families had been destroyed. But they offered to finish packing, if I wanted to hide. I waited for Martin. There he was, coming with a big bundle of clothes, with that huge bump on his head, exhausted and miserable. I whispered to him to climb up, which he did, thinking that I wanted him to have a little rest. Within seconds, the two of us were crouching in my narrow pit, while the other two continued filling up the car. Martin was shaking. He didn't want to try to escape. He was nearly ready for death. He didn't have the strength to fight anymore. Then he quieted down. The work of filling up the train was finished. We heard people speaking in German, and then somebody was sticking a rifle with a bayonette in between the stacks of clothing. Somebody said, "In ordnung!" ("All in order!"). An order was given to seal the car. The hinges jarred. Somebody was shoving an iron bar across the outside of the sliding door. The Jewish foremen outside were yelling, "Schneller! Schneller! Gicher! Gicher!" The guards were hitting with the butts of their rifles. The Germans were whipping.

But for us, Treblinka was over.

CHAPTER

6

ESCAPE

T HE LONG WAIT had started. Martin, hidden among the bundles, his eyes closed, seemed to be asleep. I knew that he was trying to detach himself from the present circumstances — one way to avoid going insane. I felt absolutely cool. My existence under the German rule had brought out in me a precious component of my personality, which I never imagined I had: cold blood in emergency situations requiring an instant decision. Having started the escape, I thought now it was a pity I hadn't taken any of the riches with which Treblinka was littered: money, gold, diamonds. They could have been a big help out there where they still had value. Well, patience. I still had Father's little bag. It should see us through the initial period.

Silently, I squeezed through the bundles, so that I had now in front of me a narrow crevice between two boards in the car's wall. Through it I saw the far side of the railroad platform with its wall of firs. Nothing was happening here. The voices, the noise, the movement — all came from the other side, from the camp.

I hoped that the train would leave before the evening report. The SS man Franz always reported his "Eight hundred all present and accounted for." Could he possibly miss Martin and me during his evening count and order a search of the train? But then, I hardly believed that the eight hundred figure was a true one, with the constant killings and suicides. Could he possibly see the difference?

There was some activity outside, some voices were yelling, then there was a sudden jerk, and another jerk. The train was moving.

I kept my eyes glued to the wall of firs as the train rolled slowly along it. It was dark and soft. Now, we were passing a Ukrainian guard. He was so close that had I been able to stretch my arm through the crevice, I could have knocked away his rifle. The train proceeded along the open wing of a large gate. This, too, was interwoven with firs. I could now imagine the entire makeup of Treblinka: a labyrinth of barbed wire and mummified fir trees, a labyrinth leading inevitably to the great ditch of milky haze — except for the few chosen ones.

I looked at Martin. He was forcing his eyes to remain closed. The reality of the situation was too much for him.

The train continued rolling. I felt thirsty. My God, how unprepared was I for the escape. Not a drop of water in my canteen, no food, no money except what Father had left. Even our clothes — I still wore the same shirt in which they had deported me, a summer shirt made of cotton mesh. It was all threads and small holes, so that I couldn't even tell whether it was dirty. My pants were filthy, but there was a treasure in them: the little cotton bag, a razor, a knife, and the Ring. I caressed the Ring with my fingers and thought, "Some day, I'm going to have it engraved with 'Treblinka — September 4 through 9.' " And then there was my jacket. I kept it wrapped around my waist when I worked and put it on only for the reports and for the night, so that it was in slightly better condition than the rest. In the inside pocket, I had my old Polish passport. It had been three years now since the war started. Meanwhile, I had been a citizen of the Soviet Union, a citizen of Ecuador, a citizen of the Warsaw Ghetto — and I had had all the documents for such citizenships. Yet now, as I was leaving Treblinka, the only document I had was a Polish passport, with all its transit and student visas to prove that I had had a life once upon a time.

I shook Martin by the shoulder. He opened his eyes regretfully. How well I knew that feeling of resisting reality. We had to make plans.

"What now?" said Martin. He looked at me as if I had all the answers.

I shrugged.

"I've found a bottle of eau de cologne in one of the bundles," I said. "Maybe we can drink it?"

I tried some, but it tasted awful. I passed the bottle to Martin. He tried it and scolded me for making him thirstier than before. We traveled in silence.

We must have been traveling for not more than a half hour, when the train stopped. Dusk was falling as I peered through my crevice. I wanted to see whether we had stopped near the neat little peasant cottage I had seen six days ago. It was too dark to see any details. All I noticed was a little slope, some underbrush, and a forest further on.

The night fell. And in the midst of darkness, in our own boxcar, an argument exploded. It was conducted in a high-pitched hiss, in Yiddish, and it was coming from the other side of the car. There must have been three or four men who couldn't agree among themselves about what to do next. Their hissing had become a loud argument, and then I could see them, one by one, crawling up over the bundles. One of them yelled, "It's open!" Then I heard them jumping out of the train and running.

Martin shook with fear. He was sure that now we would be discovered. And he wasn't wrong. As I climbed to the top of our narrow hideout and lay under the roof, trying to figure out the best way to leave the car through the air hole, which was now facing me directly and which, miraculously, had no barbed wire over it, I heard voices outside. Two men were approaching, discussing in Polish which car the noise had come from. They stopped in front of our car.

One of them said, "This is it!"

The other asked, "Are you sure?"

One of them climbed up the wall of the car. It was too late for me to make a move. I remained lying on top of the clothes when a face appeared in the air hole, a flashlight swept the inside of the car, and an order was given in German, "Get out of there, you! I see you!"

By the accent, I knew that the man was Polish, a Mazur. I didn't budge. I felt that the light was weak enough to make him confuse me with the bundles of clothes.

The man yelled several times to get out, as otherwise he would shoot. Having satisfied his doubts, he jumped down and said to the other man, "But are you definitely sure?" The other one said, "Well, I thought . . . " His certainty was missing this time. Now this second man climbed up the side of the car and yelled into the air hole, in Polish. "Hey, don't be afraid, come out! We are Polish railroad workers. We want to help you!"

Silence was the answer, and the two left, still discussing the noise one of them thought he had heard.

It was time for us to go. I didn't know where we were, but there was little to speculate about. The train, as we had heard in Treblinka, was going to Germany, where the clothing would be given to the widows and mothers of fallen soldiers. We did not want to go to Germany, that much we were sure of.

Martin suddenly collapsed. He didn't want to go.

"Leave me here," he said to me. "Leave me alone. I want to die. Let me be. What do you want of me!"

I wasn't mature enough yet to understand that, given a choice between life and death, a person might prefer to die. I thought he was being unreasonable and started pulling him out of the niche. Finally, he gave in. Reluctantly and under protest, he reached the top of the load. He wanted me to leave the car first, but I didn't trust him. When I was out and down, would he decide to stay? I kept pushing him out. He slipped through the air hole, legs first, and now was hanging from the wall of the car, clinging to the lower edge of the vent and sobbing, "Let me alone. I don't want to go!"

I had no choice. I pounded my fist on Martin's fingers, and he let go. I slipped out after him. We were two lonely people in a hostile darkness. The riddle of life was hidden somewhere in that darkness, waiting for us to solve it.

"Juda, stoy!"

This was the first human voice we heard, as soon as we reached the underbrush.

Juda sounded German, and *stoy* was a Russian or a Ukrainian word. Together they meant, "Jew, halt!"

We ran, not knowing where to, but hearing several feet thumping behind us and somebody yelling, this time in Polish, in a pleasant Mazur singsong, "Good people, stop there! We want to help you!"

I decided to try. I didn't believe in any gratuitous help by now, but I wanted to see whether we would at least find out where we were. Martin stopped a little further off.

A group of six men surrounded us. Five of them were peasants in their late forties or fifties; one of them must have been not more than twenty. The oldest, evidently the leader, was the one who started the conversation.

"Where are you heading, poor people!" he commiserated with us. "This is the road to Malkinia. The town is full of Germans. You don't want to go there."

I said, "There is no place where there are no Germans."

"Oh, you're wrong! There are no Germans in Stoczek. There's still a ghetto there. Jews are still living in Stoczek."

It sounded like a story about a neverland.

"Where is Stoczek?" I asked.

"Ah," said the peasant, "this is the point. You are rich people. You just jumped off the train from Treblinka. You'll give us some money, and we'll lead you to Stoczek."

Calmly, I replied, "We're rich, all right. You'll take us to Stoczek, and then we'll pay you."

Another peasant interjected, "Enough of this idle talk! Let's take them to the police!"

"Oh, no, not till we get the money," the first peasant corrected him.

"And not the police," added a third peasant, "but directly to the Germans."

It was obvious that they were trying to scare us into giving them money. I thought, "If we give them some, they'll want more. There is no telling where they'll stop. We cannot give them anything."

Another peasant grabbed me by the arm, hissing, "Money! Money!"

I evaluated the situation: five older men and a youngster who hadn't said a word.

I said aloud, "I'll pay you your money."

I reached into the pocket of my pants where I had the razor and the knife. It was a short hunting knife, like those the boy scouts used. I took it out phlegmatically.

"Well then, good people, you know where we are coming from, and you know damn well that I'll kill the first one who touches either of us. All right?"

Maybe it was the tone of my voice, maybe it was the knife, maybe the combination of the two. The peasants sensed that I was not kidding, and they moved a couple of steps back.

I said, "And now, how do we get to Stoczek?"

They answered with silence. They hated us at this moment, because they felt defeated.

But then the young peasant said, "Oh, my God! This is a shame! Go, good people! Be on your way!" He pointed with a finger, "See this road? It leads to Stoczek. Some fifteen kilometers."

As we started on our way, the older peasants argued with the young man, and somebody yelled behind us, "Those lousy Jews! They're stingy even now!"

It was a quiet night. All we heard as we were quickly going on our road was the continuous grinding sound coming from Treblinka. The peasants in this neighborhood knew well what was going on. They had made an industry out of escaping Jews. I was sure that many other peasants were waiting around each train from Treblinka, to get what the Germans, the Ukrainians, the Latvians, the Lithuanians, and the Polish railroad workers might have overlooked. An old Yiddish saying came to my mind, *S'iz schwer zu sein a Yid* — "It's hard to be a Jew." It seemed so appropriate in our circumstances. It seemed strange to me that these peasants here knew the whole story, while people in Warsaw didn't know a thing. Or did they? Had Czerniakow, the president of the Judenrath, known what was going to happen and preferred taking his own life to . . . To what? To telling the truth to the people in the Ghetto, so that they might have the option to fight if they wanted to, rather than dying like rats? No, I just couldn't believe that he knew the entire ugly truth. Maybe an inkling? And how about the people on the Polish side of Warsaw? Did they know? Again, my guess was that they couldn't have known. Otherwise, they would have warned the Jews. After all, Polish anti-Semitism was far from being virulent enough to wish the extermination of all Jews. An occasional killing, yes. Plenty of beating, yes. But a total extermination? No, no, no! The Poles wanted the Jews to go to Palestine, after which they would do business together. Why, there was already the PKO in Tel-Aviv, the Polish National Savings Bank. Poles didn't want the Jews dead. In Warsaw, they didn't know of Treblinka.

From time to time, the road crossed a small village. All was asleep, only a few dogs barked at us, and then it was again the road, the night, and the far rumbling of Treblinka. It was clear to us that staying on the open road at night meant danger. A policeman, a German, anybody could make the arrest, and good-bye. But we had no choice. If we followed the road, and if we walked quickly, we might get to Stoczek before dawn. If we left the road, we might get lost altogether. So we stayed on the road, and when the dogs barked with more insistence, Martin whistled a tune, for courage.

It started raining. We must have looked pitiful — two quixotic figures, unshaven, lean, and in rags, defying the evil lurking in the darkness.

We were soaking wet when a little wooden country church appeared at the edge of a village. It looked peaceful and reassuring. I thought, "Is this Stoczek?" It was already morning. I didn't have a wristwatch anymore, and Father's pocketwatch was in the little bag, its spring broken. It indicated eleven o'clock, and I chose to believe that the watch had stopped at the very moment Father had stopped living. Now I didn't know the time, but it seemed like six in the morning. It was raining very hard.

"At what time are there services in church?" I asked Martin.

At his work, he knew many Poles and Ukrainians and was familiar with their religious practices. He didn't know, but he suggested that we try to talk to the priest. Maybe we could find out whether that was Stoczek and where the Jews lived. But it was too early to knock on the door of the parish, so we sat on a wooden bench right outside and waited. And it rained and rained.

It must have been an hour or more later when we took our first chance. Martin knocked on the door, and a middle-aged woman opened it. She was dressed. Obviously, the day started early for the priest. Martin explained that we had business to discuss with the father, and she said that the father was still asleep and that we would have to wait. We sat down on the drenched bench and kept soaking in the rain. At about eight, Martin knocked on the door again, and we were informed that the father was having his breakfast.

It must have been eight-thirty, when we were finally introduced into the nice, clean hall of the parish and asked to wait there. The priest came out. He took just one look at us, and he knew. The plump little man in sacerdotal attire closed his eyes and whispered a prayer, while Martin threw himself on his knees and sobbed, "Pardon us, Father, because we have sinned."

The priest drew a cross in the air over Martin's head and asked, "What can I do, my sons, to alleviate your condition?"

I let Martin do the talking. I was fascinated by his performance.

Still on his knees, Martin said, "Father, we are headed toward Stoczek, and we don't know how to get there. Will you tell us, please?"

The priest shook his head sadly. "You are the pilgrims," he said. "You are the wanderers, and the Lord in His wisdom will let you know which road to follow."

Again, he drew a cross over Martin's head. Martin stood up.

"Just a mere bit of information, Father," he said. "If you just told us whether we are going in the right direction."

"The law forbids me" the priest replied, "to give you any information. But just wait a moment."

He left us and returned within seconds, trying to squeeze into Martin's hand a five-zloty bill. Martin refused the money. We didn't need the five zloty. Besides, a loaf of bread cost over thirty zloty. We had to admit to ourselves that our Jean Valjean caper simply hadn't worked. We said good-day to the priest and left the parish. As we returned to the road, at least one miracle had happened. It had stopped raining.

We walked in the middle of the road, in the full light of the morning, not caring any more who might see us. We were simply too exhausted to worry. Curiously, there was not a policeman, not a soldier, not a uniformed creature in view.

A peasant wagon arrived from behind us. It was a typical Polish open wagon. One small, lean horse pulled it, and a peasant in his thirties and his wife were riding on it.

Martin said to them, "Praised be Jesus Christ." This was a greeting used by the peasants all over Poland.

"For centuries and centuries," said the peasant. This was the closing part of the greeting.

We were now walking along beside the wagon.

The peasant said, after a while, "Would you like a lift?" We accommodated ourselves on the narrow floor of the wagon, our legs hanging down through the bars of the step ladder side of the cart.

"Are you peddlers?" asked the peasant. There were quite a few black marketeers from Warsaw roaming the countryside in search of food products.

I evaluated the situation quickly and replied, "Yes, we are. This is how we've got into this jam. We were selling some food to the Jews in the Ghetto, and the SS caught us."

"Yes," added Martin. "They caught us as they were taking a transport of Jews. No arguments would help. We jumped off the train."

The peasant nodded knowingly. I wasn't sure whether he had bought our story, or whether our story was what he wanted to hear. It occurred to me suddenly that there were many Jewish converts in Poland and that, although Hitler requested for at least three generations of clearance before a person could claim that he wasn't Jewish, the Poles themselves, these very peasants, might recognize a convert as an honest-to-goodness Pole. Maybe this was why the priest had given Martin his blessings. Maybe this was why this peasant took our story so seriously.

After a short ride, the peasant told us that he was now going into the fields, for his day's work. We left the wagon, praising Christ once more. Shortly, there was another village. I consulted with Martin, and we decided to try to buy a little bread. We knocked at the door of the first cottage at the edge of the village. It was freshly whitewashed, had a large, neat courtyard and a fence in good condition, and seemed to be the home of a rich person. Nobody answered, except for a big mutt whose unfriendly barking scared us away. We tried the next cottage. It was a very small and a very poor little hut. A woman opened immediately and asked us in. We inquired about bread, and she invited us to sit at the heavy oak table. We rested on a long bench, while she served us a bucketful of milk and two huge slices of freshly baked black rye bread.

"We are just baking bread for the week," she explained, pointing to seven huge wheels of bread resting on the side of the oven. "My daughter and I," she nodded at a girl of eighteen, "are minding the hut, while my husband and son work in the field." She looked at us with compassion. "You look very tired. How far are you going?"

This was a friendly hut. We couldn't resist the temptation. Martin asked, "Would you let us rest until tomorrow morning? We are going to Warsaw, and it's far."

But she couldn't. This one room, with its baking oven and the heavy table, was all they had. Between the two women and the two men, it was crowded.

She mentioned the house next door: "That house is owned by a rich widow who lives there all alone. She has a lot of room and would find no difficulty in letting you stay."

That was the house where nobody had answered before. As we were giving some thought to our hostess's suggestion, a woman knocked on the window.

"Oh, this is the neighbor," said our hostess, as she opened the window.

The neighbor yelled angrily, "Send the Jews away! This very moment! If you don't, I'll call the Germans! The lousy Jews!" Our poor hostess stood motionless. We could tell that she suffered for us. We thanked her for her hospitality and wanted to pay. She didn't want any money.

"Guest in the house, God in the house," she said. This was a Slavic greeting that the first Polish kings had used a thousand years ago.

It must have been ten in the morning. The sun had forced its way through the clouds, and the air had become sultry. We were back on the road, avoiding passers-by whenever we were sure that we wouldn't lose the direction, and doing all we could to be inconspicuous.

At one point, two teenage girls joined us in our walk. They went barefoot, carrying their clean, shiny boots on their shoulders. We knew that they would put them on before entering a village. They praised Jesus, and we responded accordingly. We asked whether they were going to Stoczek. The girls whispered between them.

Then one, the more courageous, said, "No. We are returning home."

I asked whether they knew how far it was to Stoczek.

Again, they exchanged whispers between them and giggled, and the courageous one said, "We are going to be married."

We congratulated them and asked whether this was the right way to Stoczek.

The girl said, "We are preparing our dowry."

I assured her that we would contribute to the dowry, if she gave us the information.

She said, "Just come with us to our village. My mother will prepare you pierogi with cabbage for dinner, and father will take you to Stoczek," Martin asked where their village was, and the girl pointed away to the left. At that, we praised Jesus, got off the road, and went as quickly as we could to the right.

Behind us, we could hear both girls now yelling, "Come back, gentlemen! We'll take you to Stoczek!"

For more than an hour, we walked through the woods, suspicious of any human being. Later, we returned to the road. It was empty, and we regained our courage. After maybe a half hour, we reached a little town. At the entrance to it, to the right, there was an old wooden fence, and next to it, on the muddy sidewalk were standing two men with Jewish armbands.

"Are there still Jews in this town?" Martin asked. "Is this Stoczek?"

They gave us an inquisitive glance. One of them asked, "You from Treblinka?"

We nodded. Then, Martin asked, "Can we get a place to sleep? Some food to eat?"

"If you have the money," replied the man, "you can get anything here you wish."

We assured him that we had the money, and he led us through the breach in the fence into an abandoned garden, and then into a large, dilapidated cottage.

"This is the Stoczek ghetto," the man stated, showing us with a round movement of his arm a large room and a substantial group of men seated around a table. They all raised their heads and looked at us.

One of them said, "Treblinka?"

A slim little woman wearing a dirty black apron came from the kitchen to give us her official welcome: "Do you have money?" Again, we assured her that we did, and she continued: "You poor men, you look exhausted. Sit down, and I'll make you something to eat. My name is Freidka."

We were given chairs by the others. Somebody said, "You made it just on time. Tonight is Erev Rosh Hashanah."

Jewish New Year. An awful sadness came over me. On this day, the family had always stayed together. Mother put on her best dress, and our parents' bedroom was filled with the delicate fragrance of *crepe de chine*. Father, smoothly shaven, in a dark suit and a derby, held under his arm a little velvet bag with his prayer shawl and book. As he was ready, he called from the door, "Well then, old lady, shall we go to schul? It's getting late." At the same time, he reminded us, his four sons, that we too were expected to go. "Once a year, you might stand the sacrifice."

Ten days later, the Terrible Day of Atonement came. Before dusk, Mother lit up two candles. Then, swaying her hands around their flames and covering her face with her palms, she uttered the blessings and cried softly. I delicately kissed her face, all wet with tears, and felt humble and happy. And everybody wished everybody health and happiness. This would never happen again.

I glanced at our companions in distress. They must have been as lonely and unhappy as we were, but there was a definite lack of communion between us. I had the same feeling I had had when we first arrived in the Warsaw Ghetto: Martin and I were foreigners to them, a couple of *Yeckes*.

Freidka asked what we would like her to prepare for supper. This was the first time since the German invasion that somebody had asked me this question. She mentioned something about potato pancakes, and Martin and I jumped at the idea. Potato pancakes! We hadn't had them since Marynia left us, when Lvov was still under the Russians. It takes a lot of patience to grate raw potatoes, and none of us had had it. Now, Freidka was bringing us plate after plate loaded with pancakes. I don't know how many we ate, but that night awful cramps got me. My guts were twisting with pain, and there was no one that Martin could call to help me. We slept in a small empty shack that might have been used by Freidka as a stable for a goat, once upon a time. Lying on the floor, I bit the earth to forget my pain. Toward morning, it subsided, and a little later I felt well enough to do some laundry. Our shirts were in pitiful condition, and our suits didn't look much better. Freidka pressed the suits for us, and by the evening, we were again decent. Yet there was that smell of burning bodies in my nostrils, and I couldn't get rid of it. All the time, I had the impression that every pore of my body and every thread of my clothing were saturated with that nauseating smell. I asked myself a simple question: "How can we expect anybody to take us for Poles, if we reek of Treblinka?"

In Freidka's house, we finally had a chance to reevaluate our situation and do some planning. Nobody ever disturbed us here. There were no Germans in town, and only a lone Polish policeman visited the house once every evening, to get his bribe from Freidka.

On the third day of our stay, Freidka offered us a real bed. We should have stuck to our barn, but we didn't know it at the time and welcomed Freidka's generosity. After the very first use of the bed, we were filled with lice: head lice, and pubic lice, and, most terrible of all, cloth lice. My shirt, my summer shirt made of cotton net, had lice in each mesh, and washing at the well in the courtyard didn't remove them. We had to wait for an opportunity to get fresh clothes and a hot bath, and Stoczek wasn't a town where we could ever get either.

Freidka had a nucleus of guests who had escaped from Treblinka, had come to Stoczek, and had realized that there was no place for them to go. They cast their die on the future of Stoczek and expected to survive by staying here. The reason was that the Yellow Patches of Treblinka were fathers and sons of Stoczek families, and seemingly they had been promised by the SS that their families would never be touched. Freidka's other guests were the transients, the escapees who had a goal, or had money, or had both a goal and money. They came in during the day, ate and rested, and left early the next morning for their own secret destinations. Some of them carried luggage filled with money and jewels. They had plans for the future.

One of Freidka's favorite "steadies" was Goetz, a baker from western Poland, whose escape from Treblinka was quite unusual. Goetz had a good sense of humor, and he made me laugh through tears when he told me his short story. Well, he was in the gas chamber, together with a few hundred other men, but while the others died, Goetz remained alive. When the gassing was over and the naked corpses were being carried out by the crematory detail, a worker shuddered when Goetz winked an eye at him. Two Jews carried his "live" corpse to the far side of the ditch and covered him with other bodies. Later, the guards roamed over the ditch, looking for people who were not yet dead and shooting them. Goetz died a dozen deaths during that time. When the shooting was over and the guards were gone, Goetz waited for the night to fall, and then, in darkness, he crawled out of the ditch and under a barbed-wire fence and out into the fields and the forest. He wandered to a lone hut and knocked on the door. A young peasant opened the door, screamed with fear, "Jesus, Mary!" at the sight of a naked body in the middle of the night, and shut the door. Goetz sat sadly under a nearby bush, waiting for the Germans to pick him up. Meanwhile, the peasant, realizing that it was not a vision but a naked Jew, brought out a pair of pants and a piece of bread and cheese, and deposited it in front of his door. He also waved for Goetz where to go, and this was how he had come to Stoczek. Now his mind was made up: to stay here until the end.

From the transients, we learned something new: we could not go on the road and make believe that we were Poles, unless we had caps to cover our heads. It was a long time since we had stopped using head covers, in order to avoid taking them off in front of any German in the street, and it had never occurred to me before that the lack of a hat might be a clue for a policeman. We searched all Stoczek for two caps but couldn't find them. This became one more problem on the long list of our difficulties.

One day, a big peasant woman drove her wagon directly into Freidka's yard. She entered the house in a boisterous way, patting Freidka on the shoulder, saying hello to everybody in a husky voice, and attentively examining each of us with her shrewd eyes.

"New arrivals?" she said to Martin and me.

Freidka introduced us: "This is Mrs. Czylakowa. She's a good friend of the Jews. She likes to help." Then, knowing our intention to go to Warsaw, Freidka added, "Mrs. Czylakowa travels to Warsaw a lot," and, addressing the woman, she finished, "and these two men would like to go to Warsaw."

Mrs. Czylakowa embraced us cordially. Next to such a huge female, I felt secure.

I complained, "But we have no caps. How can we get to Warsaw without caps!"

This didn't seem to be a problem for Mrs. Czylakowa. She assured us that she would get us the needed caps and would pick us up from Freidka's in a day or two. She didn't mention any money.

"Well, it will cost you a little," Freidka explained later, "but really not much. She has helped before. It seems there is a Jewish woman living in her house, and everybody thinks she's Mrs. Czylakowa's cousin."

A few days passed, but there was no sign of Mrs. Czylakowa. The Atonement Day arrived and passed, and still no Mrs. Czylakowa. And then, one early afternoon, there she was, with her sturdy wagon, two caps for us, and with an offer that we couldn't refuse: "I'll take you to my house. You'll rest there for a few days. Then I'll take you with me to Warsaw. And in Warsaw, I'll introduce you to a Polish judge I know. He also helps the Jews."

It was a quick, hectic good-bye to everybody, and we left Stoczek under the full protection of our Mrs. Czylakowa.

As we traveled, she gave us a few tips. She had paying guests in her house who came from Warsaw for a little country vacation. As we would all have our supper at the same table, she would introduce us as two Polish railroad workers who were taken by mistake to Treblinka, and who had fortunately escaped. She would also pretend that she had known us for a number of years, which would eliminate any possible doubts. Armed with such pointers, we arrived at Mrs. Czylakowa's place late in the afternoon. We admired her property. The house was large, beautifully kept, built in bricks and stucco. The garden around the house and the fruit trees behind it made it look warm and inviting. We met Mrs. Czylakowa's guests soon, as supper was served very early. Of course, Martin and I immediately became the center of everybody's attention.

"Treblinka? You don't say! And is it true that they are making soap out of the Jews? And what good can such soap be, considering that the Jews are dirty. And are there separate camps for the Jews and the Poles? Because we've heard lately that some Poles are also being taken to Treblinka, but to the labor camp Treblinka."

Such questions and comments were directed at us throughout the supper, and hungry as I was, I couldn't swallow a bit of food. Mrs. Czylakowa saved us, saying that we were exhausted and needed rest. She took us to a large barn at the other side of the courtyard. It was filled almost to the roof with fragrant hay, and I don't believe it took us more than a minute to fall asleep.

It seemed as if I had been asleep not more than five minutes, when I was abruptly awakened. Somebody was shaking me violently. It was deep into the night. I must have been sleeping for hours. I recognized Mrs. Czylakowa.

"For God's sake," she hissed into my ear, "you've got to run into the fields and hide till I tell you. The Schupo are searching every house—somebody has shot a German policeman."

She told us that we would find a clump of trees far in the field, and that she would look for us there as soon as the danger was over. So we went into darkness, fearful of the invisible pursuer behind us and of utter loneliness in front of us.

We found the trees and lay under them as the night became dawn,

dawn turned into morning, and morning went on to become day. It was a gray, cold day with a penetrating little rain, something between a shower and a fog. It became late afternoon. We were hungry, and our teeth chattered from cold.

Finally, Mrs. Czylakowa arrived. She was accompanied by a young woman whom she introduced as her cousin. The woman brought us some food. Mrs. Czylakowa left us under the woman's care, promising to return soon. When Mrs. Czylakowa disappeared, the woman told us that she was Jewish, and that she was staying with Mrs. Czylakowa. We understood that she must be the person Freidka had described to us, and I asked for details. The woman shrugged.

"I've been staying with her for six months," she said, "and it cost me all the money I had. Now, not satisfied with this, she's sending me to Warsaw to do her black-marketing for her."

I asked about the Polish judge in Warsaw, and she said, "Oh, yes! Black marketeer, just like Czylakowa. Be careful with her. She's a witch!"

At this point, Mrs. Czylakowa returned to tell us that the Germans were still searching, and that we would have to wait until all was clear.

Mrs. Czylakowa picked us up late in the evening. She led us to the fence of her house and stopped us there. In a matter-of-fact voice, she told us that she would have to take us to Warsaw almost immediately, but that we couldn't go the way we were dressed. She wanted money so she could buy us new clothes and train tickets. I suggested that we enter the house, as I had a little bundle sewn into my pants and I would like to get it out and give her the necessary money.

She grabbed me by the pants and hissed, "You cannot come in. Show me where it is, and I'll get it out."

I didn't like the way the situation was developing. "I have in the bundle a diamond ring," I said, "not money."

And she, "I'll take the ring."

"At least, get a pair of scissors," I insisted. "You could rip the pants, otherwise."

She gave me a suspicious glance, but then decided that maybe I was right regarding the scissors.

"I'll be back immediately," she warned.

As soon as Mrs. Czylakowa entered the house, Martin and I ran until we lost ourselves far away in the fields. We didn't know what to do next. Martin suggested that Stoczek was our only hope, and we turned in the general direction of the town, walking all night through the fields, the woods, and the pastures. As we were approaching Stoczek, very early in the morning, shots could be heard from the direction of the town, sometimes singly, sometimes in salvos. They worried us, but we continued walking.

The shooting could be heard now not only from Stoczek but from all over. Still, we continued in the same direction. We were near the town. We could already see the little wooden bridge at the entrance to Stoczek. But now we could also see two military or police trucks and several uniformed men with automatic rifles posted on the bridge.

Martin and I communicated without words. We got off the road and into the courtyard of the first cottage we saw. We praised Jesus Christ and asked the peasant whether we could have a drink of water from his well. We swallowed the water while watching the bridge. The peasant gave us a curious look. We praised Christ again, thanked him for the water, and left the farm house, only this time in the opposite direction.

It didn't take much imagination to understand what was happening. Stoczek was being liquidated, and whoever wasn't shot there would go to Treblinka on the two trucks.

As we were walking along the edge of the road, a young peasant joined us. He was talkative, and we had a conversation. He told us that he was returning from Stoczek.

"Jesus!" he said, "What's happening there!" And he amply confirmed what we had already guessed.

He told us about people being chased out of their homes into the marketplace and being shot there in groups. He didn't understand why the Germans needed the two trucks. One was more than sufficient. We were just passing a little roadside chapel. Our companion took off his cap and crossed himself. We did the same.

He wanted to know about us, and we told him our story: we were merchants from Warsaw, who had come here to purchase some food for the black market, but when we saw what was happening in Stoczek, we decided not to do anything about business today.

"Can you hear the shots all around us?" I finished. "I believe that they are finishing them off everywhere."

The young peasant nodded. "That shooting comes from the direction of Wegrow," he said. Another blow. Wegrow was the town with a railroad station. We were heading there, to try for passage to Warsaw.

"We might not be able to get the train in Wegrow," I complained.

The peasant suggested, "Why go to Wegrow if you can get your train in Urle, which is much closer?" He pointed out the direction.

We passed by a few more little chapels or crosses, and each time all three of us took off our caps and crossed ourselves. Now we were entering a village.

"This is where I live," said the young peasant, as we parted.

We continued down the road, while our companion joined a group of older peasants and spoke with them. A second later, it was as if hell had broken over us. Peasants all over the village yelled, "Jews! Catch the Jews! Catch the Jews." and ran after us in hot pursuit. Our brisk march had changed into a sprint, and with the entire party of yelling villagers behind us, I had a definite feeling of empathy with a hunted hare. We, the Jews, had become fair game for anybody who cared to notice us. What still puzzled me was the incredible hypocrisy of the people. Why did they make believe that they took our story seriously if they recognized us so easily, and their intention was to hurt us? But if this was a game, like every game it must have its rules. Maybe one of the rules was "Make them feel that you believe so that their disappointment will be that much deeper and their pain that much sharper."

Still running, we reached the forest. "We've lost them," I thought. "We've lost them." And we had. Maybe they were afraid that these two ruthless Jews were waiting now behind the trees to shoot down the entire village. We slowed down. We both needed some rest.

We sat under a bush, and I thought that it would not be a bad idea to shave my face. I had my Treblinka razor with me, but there was no water. I shaved in short strokes, spitting into my hand after each stroke and wetting my beard with the spit. Martin thought it was not a bad idea, and after I finished, he shaved.

We walked again, but this time we followed a path in the forest instead of exposing ourselves to an open road. Suddenly a man on a bicycle appeared, coming from the opposite direction. He wore a dark gray civilian suit and dark glasses. He looked like a city man. He passed us on his bike without greeting us. As we made a few steps forward, we heard, "Hey, you! Stop!"

"German!" I said to myself. "He's not going to get us." With my hand, I felt the handle of the knife in my pocket. We turned around very slowly.

He was standing perhaps fifteen meters away, holding his bicycle with his two hands. I thought, "No weapon."

"Come here!" he beckoned.

Cautiously, we approached him.

The words were flowing from him. He wanted to give us a picture of what was happening, and he wanted to do it within a second.

"Poor people, where do you think you're going? Maybe some won't recognize you. I do. Don't even touch the main road! It's full of the SS. They murder and deport. They're everywhere!"

It was so very depressing; Martin sighed, "What are we going to do?"

"Wait until dark," said the man. "Sit still in the woods. When the raids are over for today, cross the main road, and go straight forward. The name of the village is Urle. And my name is Michalski. You'll find my house easily. You'll see the first large house in Urle. You can rest there, and tomorrow we'll discuss your next step."

Martin said, "We want to go to Warsaw."

"If this is your wish, I'll help you," said Mr. Michalski, as he was leaving on his bike.

He dipped into the woods. We crawled to the edge of the thicket, from where we could observe the main road. Mr. Michalski wasn't joking. SS trucks were roaring back and forth like furious bulls in a Spanish arena. And the sound of shooting was coming from all directions.

It was already long past five when the traffic slowed down and then subsided completely. Carefully we left our hideout. We quickly ran across the road and dipped into the forest at the other side. We found a path and followed it. Soon the forest ended, and we came to a pasture extending along a lively brook. As we sat, to decide about our next step, two little shepherd boys leading their cow back to the barn stopped near us and praised Jesus. We greeted them in the same Christian way.

One boy said, "Germans are killing the Jews."

I asked, "Do you know Mr. Michalski?"

"Mr. Michalski lives there," said the boy, pointing to a beautiful villa nearby.

The boys were puzzled because we knew Mr. Michalski. Maybe we weren't Jews, after all. They took their cow and left.

"Hey!" I called after them. "What's the name of the brook?"

One of the boys said, "Liwica."

"And where is the railroad station?"

"There! At the end of that road that goes into the woods. You've got to cross the brook to get to the road."

The boys were gone. The sun was almost completely down when we stopped in front of the tall, decorative, wrought-iron gate of Mr. Michalski's house. The villa was beautiful, drowning in flowers and in the golden bath of the setting sun. Most of all, there was an air of serenity all over it. We could see Mr. Michalski seated on a terrace and having a drink with another gentleman. I raised my hand to the bell, but then I hesitated. Martin and I looked at each other in a mute communication. Then, heads low, we went on our way.

For many years, I was sure that we chose not to go to Mr. Michalski feeling, "Who are we to intrude on a good person's peaceful existence." But now I am not so sure. Were we perhaps afraid that Mr. Michalski would betray us? I don't know the answer. But if you, Mr. Michalski from Urle, are still alive and if you happen to read these lines, for my sake and for yours tell me that you were our friend, that you wanted to help us, that you meant each word you told us; tell me that you were not just another dream.

The sun was setting fast behind the woods as we crossed the brook called Liwica and went on the road indicated to us by the shepherds. There were a few others going toward the station. We passed an old peasant woman and we praised Christ.

She returned our greeting, and said, "Jesus, Mary! What times! What people!"

Strands of gray hair hung from under a heavy woolen babushka covering her head and shoulders. The skin of her face was creased. She must have been very old.

"Germans are killing the Jews," she said, "and look at that peasant rabble: What are they doing? Jewish homes are still warm, and they are already looting!"

For a minute, we walked in silence. Then the old woman concluded: "Not even a featherbed or a pillow was left for me when I arrived!"

The old woman left the road and went home. We continued to the Urle station in what was now total darkness.

"We must assume Polish names," said Martin, "should anybody ask." True, it was very important to have such names. However, what good were the names, if there were no documents to back them up? I still had my Polish passport, and Martin his identification card issued by the Polish authorities. We could use our names and our papers for the time being. In Warsaw, many Poles had German names, and our last name sounded German. Besides, there was nothing we could do at the moment. We still had to overcome many immediate hurdles before we could get to Warsaw.

The first problem, assuming that we did reach Warsaw, would be to decide where to go once we got there. It would be past the curfew time, and we couldn't afford to be caught in the street.

We knew the Polish part of Warsaw from before the war. A thought occurred to me: "A hotel? On Chmielna Street?"

"One of those little hotels that rent by the hour?" Martin said. "That rent to the whores?" Yes, Martin thought that it was a good idea. In such hotels nobody ever asked for documents, and Chmielna Street was very near the Warsaw station. A short walk, and no problem with curfew.

The train ride to Warsaw was uneventful, and now here we were, free, anonymous, and vulnerable.

We went to Chmielna Street, as planned, and entered the first little hotel, at the corner of the street. The night clerk asked for documents. This was unexpected. Without losing my composure, I reached into my pocket and handed to him my passport. Martin waited until the clerk said, "All right." He produced his identity card. All was in order. The clerk didn't put our names in the register. He returned our documents, took our money, and ordered the bellboy to take us to our room. He did not seem to be interested in the fact that we had no luggage and that we looked like tramps.

We were hardly undressed when we heard a commotion outside. We went to the window. At the opposite corner of Chmielna Street two SS trucks were parked. Two German policemen drove a group of people out of a hotel, men and women, and lined them up in couples. An officer went from couple to couple, asking, *"Jude?"* — "Jew?" — and here and there a girl confirmed, *"Jude."*

They went from hotel to hotel, and soon the trucks were filled with betrayed Jewish clients. Martin was biting his lower lip, nervously curling the lock on his forehead. I felt like a piece of ice. There was nothing we could do to protect ourselves.

Ours was the last hotel on the list. When the policemen arrived, the clerk said, "I have no guests. Bad business!" and he showed them his empty register. They cursed, went back to their trucks, and left Chmielna Street. Martin fell on his bed, sobbing. I took his head in my hands. "It's all right," I said. "This is not the end of the world."

Suddenly, it was as if Father were with us. I touched the little cotton bag, and I felt my Ring. I took it out of my pocket and looked at it. The Girl on it — the soft, reassuring face with the compassionate eyes — she made me overflow with hope. Father was watching over us. And the Girl of the Ring was watching over me. I slipped the Ring on the fourth finger of my right hand. In a way, I felt engaged.

Next morning, seven o'clock: A busboy brings our breakfast, ersatz coffee and a slice of bread. He looks decent. I flash a twenty-zloty tip. He supplies shaving soap and the address of a second-hand clothing dealer.

8 A.M.: We take a riksha ride to the clothing dealer. Nice store, nice proprietor. We get completely dressed, except for the shirts. The owner gives us his home address. He'll have the shirts by the evening.

9 A.M.: Our riksha driver, who has been waiting for us all this while, refuses to take us. He says he's waiting for his fare. We explain that *we* are his fare. We look quite different, don't we? Martin again looks distinguished in his newly acquired navy blue overcoat and a soft Italian Borsallino. He tells me that I look like a Polish country squire, in my short leather jacket, riding pants, and high boots, a little hat with a feather, and my long, bushy Stalin mustache, into which my little French mustache has grown during the past month. Martin picks up a newspaper and reads the ads about rooms for rent. He finds something on Krucza Street. The riksha takes us there.

9:30 A.M.: I wait in the riksha downstairs, while Martin goes up to the eighth floor of the elegant old building to see the advertised room.

9:45 A.M.: Martin runs toward the riksha. He's excited. Is there a problem? Martin wants me to pay the riksha and go with him quickly.

9:50 A.M.: There is no elevator. We slowly go up the stairs.

"And who do you think opened the door," he asks, "but Linka Ber?"

I remembered Linka Ber. She came to Martin's wedding. She was the wife of one of Martin's best friends, who died a couple of years after Martin's wedding. Linka is Jewish.

"Linka Ber?" I ask.

"Here, she's Berska. She's a maid. It's a rooming house. We have a room."

Linka's boss, a middle-aged, smiling Polish lady, wanted to know just one thing: that her potential guests weren't Jewish. Any kind of documents would do. We didn't feel comfortable using our old papers. Martin assured the lady that we would present our documents in a couple of days, as we had just arrived from Lvov and had to undergo the complicated process of registration at the police precinct. This was all right with her.

Now we needed a source for counterfeit papers. Linka proved quite valuable in this. She told us about her brother Manek, who lived in the vicinity and who had all sorts of contacts. Manek, who loved both Linka and her six-year-old son, visited them every day, and she expected him any moment. Linka was petite, blond, pretty, and didn't look at all Jewish. Her son didn't look Jewish either. They didn't have to worry about being discovered ever, especially while living in this rooming house where every guest was either Polish or German. There was even a young German woman who was the secretary of a Gestapo officer.

I thought that Martin's finding Linka, just like that, through a rooming house ad, was significant. I felt that every little good thing that was happening to us was a miracle and was due to a special protection extended to us by the spirits of our murdered parents and the Girl in the Ring. If we wanted to survive, we had to believe in something special. However, while I was ready to plunge myself into mysticism with all of my considerable enthusiasm, Martin was a practical person who would bring me back to what he called reality each time I started dreaming.

Manek came that morning and we discussed with Manek our need for documents. He promised to have two sets ready in two days. These would cost us a hundred zloty each, because they were complete fakes. Better documents, original papers of a deceased Pole whose physical characteristics resembled one of us, would cost at least five hundred zloty, and it would take time to produce them. Manek spoke about hundreds of zloty as if they were peanuts. All we had at this time in liquid money was not much more than three thousand zloty. We had to find a way to earn an income.

When I mentioned this to Manek, he didn't seem to believe me. He said, "What do you mean that you have no money? You escaped from Treblinka, didn't you?"

They knew here in Warsaw, just as the Mazurs waiting at the Treblinka train had known. Manek really thought that we had a treasure but were too stingy to share it with him. He reached this conclusion that very first day and was never to change his mind about us.

At 8 P.M. on the same day, we went to the residence of the clothing dealer to pick up the shirts. I paid him whatever he asked, but then, in order to look independent, to look more Polish, I said to the man, "I hope you have not overcharged us."

And the man replied, smiling, "My dear sir, you can be sure that you have received everything at a bargain price."

There was something in the tone of his voice which told me that he knew about us.

The next day, I left the room only to buy some groceries downstairs. Until the day before, I would have entered any place, ready to show my own passport if requested. Today I was scared. Manek and Linka had told us stories about raids in the streets of Warsaw, where they had been catching the Poles to send them to Germany to work for German farmers, and how during such raids Jews who had been hiding on the Polish side were also being discovered.

Martin reacted even worse than I. He lay down on the bed and brooded, and I could find no way to distract him. Scared of his own shadow, he wouldn't even think of going out.

That same day, early in the afternoon, there was a knock on the door, and when I opened it, I saw a young woman, blue-eyed, with ash-blond hair, dressed in a satin, Chinese-style house robe. She said that she was our next-door neighbor and asked whether it was all right to come in. She walked with grace and self-assurance.

"I am Wanda Zakolska," she introduced herself, and took a seat. She had her own cigarettes and her own matches and now proceeded to light a cigarette. "I'm from Stanislawow," she said, "and you are from Lvov."

"How did you guess?" I tried to be funny. "Miss, or is it Mrs., Zakolska?"

Of course, my question didn't make any sense. The accent of an inhabitant of Lvov was so special that anybody would guess. I just needed a little time to set my thoughts straight and to avoid any errors in our conversation. But she didn't give me any time for this.

"I didn't have to guess," she said. "Oh, and it's Miss, and please call me Wanda."

"Wanda. What do you mean . . . ?"

"You haven't even introduced yourselves yet."

That was my present problem. I was not sure what name I was going to have. I told Manek that if the choice is ours, I would like to have the name Liwicki. Like the brook in Urle, where we had met Mr. Michalski, a decent human being. Martin wanted the name of Dobrzanski. One of our uncles had that name. He was a convert.

"Well," I started.

"You are Franek," she finished.

Now I was scared. Martin sat in his chair, rigid from tension.

Wanda smiled. She had a beautiful smile, but I couldn't enjoy it at that moment. She said, "I know you from Lvov. From the university. I listened to your poetry. I followed your literary journal. I was there, a student of Polish literature."

This was upsetting. If she wanted to, she could denounce us. Or, she could blackmail us. I had nothing to say, and I didn't say anything. Martin cleared his throat, as if he were getting ready to start a discussion, but then he must have changed his mind.

Wanda broke the tension with an easy "I, too, am Jewish. Just don't tell anybody in this house. They all think that I am a collaborator with the Germans. You see, a German officer dates me sometimes."

This was the beginning of our friendship, a friendship that started in a strange way and was to finish in an even stranger fashion.

Wanda had an answer for most of our problems. In need of money? Then we had to travel to Cracow and Lvov, to buy gold and jewelry there and to resell it in Warsaw. Yes, she did have contacts here. She might get some in Lvov. How to travel? No problem. She knew a clerk in the office of Orbis, the official Polish travel bureau. A twenty-zloty tip, and the tickets were ours. All we needed was enough money to purchase the goods and a set of documents.

We expected to receive the documents the next day. As for money, Martin and I thought that we would start modestly, investing two thousand zloty, and we'd see how it went. I couldn't help thinking of the several thousands of zloty that I had used in Treblinka to clean my behind. Once more, money was starting to have value.

However, Martin wouldn't travel. His nerves were a shambles, and he would be an obstacle rather than a help. Thus it was decided on that very day that I would be the traveler, and that we would leave, Wanda and I, the day after I received my papers. Wanda offered herself as my instructor for just this one trip, after which I should be able to continue on my own.

I appreciated Wanda's readiness to help, but I also didn't want to have to depend on her for too much. I started thinking of a way to develop my own business contacts. We had here in Warsaw Mikolajczyk and Nowak. They most certainly would buy the goods I might be bringing from Lvov. And if they could put me in touch with Ostrowicz, he could be of help in some way. But whom could I approach in Lvov? It had to be a Pole, and he would have to know the Jews in the ghetto who were still trading in gold and diamonds.

I don't know why the name of Tadek Opolski came to me. We had been classmates in gymnasium, and we didn't dislike each other, but that was about all. I knew his address because Tadek and his family lived next door to Adam. I wondered what had ever happened to Adam and his family.

Tadek. I really didn't know why it had to be him, but the same day I sent a telegram, "Planning to visit you on business. Answer if interested. Franek." And the very next day, a telegram came from Tadek, "Waiting anxiously." I had my Polish contact in Lvov.

It was not so simple with Mikolajczyk and Nowak. I telephoned, and Martin telephoned, and we left messages, but our friends didn't return the calls. Thus, when the evening of my first trip with Wanda arrived, I still didn't know whether we could count on these two gentlemen and left the matter with Martin, who would continue trying to contact them.

On the afternoon before the trip, I went with Wanda to the Orbis where, as Wanda had promised, a clerk sold us the tickets for a twenty-zloty tip. I prepared myself a small bundle with a change of laundry and a toothbrush, so that there wouldn't be any attention-attracting luggage with me. The train was scheduled to leave at ten in the evening. The curfew was at nine, so we left the house some twenty minutes before nine, and now we were in the waiting room of the Warsaw railroad station.

The illumination was just what I liked: semiobscurity. We bought a sandwich and a glass of tea and sat at a table in the buffet room. Two Polish policemen entered and started verifying everybody's documents. When they approached our table, Wanda opened her bag, took out her lipstick, and started putting it on. She gave the policemen an unfriendly look, bit her lower lip, and then her upper lip, and finally said, annoyed, "And what is it now? Are we supposed to be blackmarketeers? Or Jews?"

She reached into her bag for her papers and handed them over to them. I gave them my new identification card.

"Mr. Liwicki?" the policeman asked. I nodded. He saluted and returned the document. This was my baptism as a traveler.

Wanda looked at me, amused, and said, "Congratulations! You've been initiated."

It was already past ten when we were allowed to board the train. It was jammed with travelers, a feature which I appreciated. Wanda had other plans. She liked to travel in comfort. I followed her, as she pushed her way through the crammed cars, stepping on people's toes, kicking their shins, and ignoring their invectives.

Our journey ended in the dining car. At this hour, it was empty and dark, except for a dimly lighted little corner serving as the living quarters of the cook and the bartender. We headed directly to that corner.

"Good evening, Mr. Jan," said Wanda to the bartender. "I'm here again!" She shook his hand, introduced me, and ordered, "The usual."

We sat at a little table, and Jan brought us a bottle of Cukrowka, moonshine made out of sugar, along with some sausage and bread. As we were having a drink, Wanda explained that Jan would get a thirty-zloty tip from each of us, for letting us sleep here at the table. When I asked why everybody didn't do it, she winked at me: " 'Cause Jan doesn't like everybody."

We drank moonshine. It had an awful taste, but we had to drink it because, as Wanda pointed out, we wouldn't be honest-to-goodness Polish blackmarketeers otherwise. All Warsaw drank that stuff. It was also called *bimber*. I wondered why. The bimber started getting to me. I touched the tip of my nose. It felt like wood. The condition of the tip of my nose always told me whether I was sober or drunk. Now I was drunk. I knew I was going to act stupid.

Before I knew it, I was telling Wanda about the Ring and about the Girl and about my dreams, and their warnings and promises. Wanda listened to me attentively. I didn't know whether she, too, was drunk. She remained serious, while I expected her to ridicule me.

She said, "It's beautiful." After a while, she added, "I wouldn't be able to handle life in this way. Relations with people are usually tough and dirty. This is the only way I know how to survive."

We traveled all night long, and arrived in Cracow at seven in the morning. This was still the curfew time, and we had to spend one more hour at the station. Wanda knew how to avoid staying in the dangerous waiting room: "There is a beauty shop here and a barber shop. I'll go to one, you to the other. Whoever finishes first picks up the other."

It was a splendid idea. Lying under the barber's sheet, I was listening to the latest Cracow news.

"There's been shooting here in the ghetto," said the barber, while covering my face with foaming soap. "The SS trucks are working two shifts. The Jews are getting what's finally coming to them, hah? They are trying to hide in the Aryan zone, but no dice!" The barber's razor was shaving my throat. "Our police and the Germans have thrown a dragnet around the city."

The shaving was over, and I asked for a haircut. The barber

continued with the news: "The other day, that was a good one! A German *Feldfebel* ("corporal") got off the train. He had come for his furlough, from the Ukrainian front. And what do you know! One of our boys from the railroad militia recognized him. They had been together in grammar school in Cracow. The German Feldfebel was nothing but a Jew from here! Such a nerve! To serve in the German Army!"

The barber was giving me a shampoo. The aromatic soap was massaged into my scalp. The warm water was flowing down my cheeks and into the sink. For a moment, I felt safe. I fancied that all the evil recounted by the barber belonged to some dismal, remote past. The barber dried my hair with a warm towel. I opened my eyes. "What a satisfaction, huh? For a Polish boy to have a German soldier arrested!"

I was paying the barber when Wanda came in.

"Honeymooners?" asked the barber.

"How did you ever guess?" replied Wanda.

"If you need a room, you know," said the barber, "you cannot get one without a German permit. But I might be able to help you." He wrote an address on a piece of paper. "This is a nice lady. Her husband, an engineer, is in Auschwitz, so she rents the rooms. Of course, this is only between you and me. She has no license."

I looked at the name. "Mrs. Drescher? Sounds German."

"Oh, she's Polish, all right! Many Poles in Cracow have German names."

Since the train for Lvov did not leave until the evening, we needed a place to spend the day. There were many Polish families at that time in Cracow living off the money made by renting a couple of rooms in their apartments. Usually these were short-term rentals intended for business people. However, among the many travelers, there were quite a few categories of people, like Poles on the run from forced labor in Germany, or members of a resistance movement, or, last but not the least, Jews with false identity papers. Landladies didn't ask many questions. They wanted to know your name only so that they would know what to call you. For all the rest, they hoped that their guests would be smart enough not to get themselves and their landladies into a predicament. The service was good everywhere. The rooms were neat and nicely decorated, and if one wanted breakfast, he received it in bed.

Mrs. Drescher was no different. She asked us to sit down, told us about her husband, asked us not to reveal to anybody that she was renting rooms, advised us that we could even have three meals in her place, bade us good-day, and left us alone.

"Real honeymooners!" Wanda repeated the barber's comment, flinging herself into a comfortable armchair in the corner of the room.

Wanda was an unusual person. She was pleasant to be with, yet she was so outspoken that often I didn't know how to react. Of course, the situation was a bit awkward—from the standpoint of "normal times." Here we were, a young man and a young woman in a one-bed room, with many hours of free time before us. But the times weren't normal. Wanda seemed to be reading my thoughts.

"Don't worry," she said. "You'll get used to it. It may happen sometimes that we will have to spend the night together. All that counts is that we make an agreement and stick to it."

"Then let's make believe that you and I are sister and brother. I always wanted to have a sister."

Wanda laughed. She suggested that we go out for breakfast.

We went to a small dairy coffeehouse that Wanda knew, and we had a breakfast of bread and ersatz coffee. Afterwards, we went for a walk. I was against any pleasure walking, with all the shooting coming from the ghetto side and the barber's stories still fresh in my mind, but I would have felt uneasy about showing Wanda that I lacked courage.

Walking in silence, we finally reached the bank of the Vistula River. We leaned against a low stone wall protecting the banks of this largest of the Polish rivers and looked down. The gray water flowed slowly, carrying away the city's garbage. Wanda's eyes were now as gray as the water below.

She mumbled softly, "Filth." Then resolutely, almost cheerfully, she said, "I would like to tell you a story. You could turn it into a poem."

Wanda had lived with her parents in the city of Stanislawow. She had a Ukrainian friend who was an old schoolmate of hers. When the Long Night of Slaughter fell on the city, when the SS were murdering the Jews at the cemetary, this Ukrainian friend gave shelter to Wanda and her parents. When the immediate danger was over, he introduced Wanda to a Ukrainian policeman by the name of Sowa, who had contacts at the Gestapo, and who, for money, would arrange passports for the family and help them escape to Hungary.

That night, Wanda brought to Sowa the pictures needed for the passports, and the money. He let her in, locked the door, and started stripping off her clothes. She scratched him, and bit him, and escaped. Later that night, she and her parents fled to Tarnow. Before long, Sowa was there, too, with his Gestapo contacts and with his desire for Wanda. This was an ultimatum: either she yielded to him, or she and her parents would be deported. It was a basement room. A tin sink. A broken chair. An opulent bed. "Jewish," he said.

The next morning, Wanda's parents were taken away.

Wanda wept softly, and together we watched the gray waters of the Vistula carrying away the debris and filth of the city.

That evening, we left for Lvov. After a tiring nightlong trip in an overcrowded compartment—there was no dining car on this train— we arrived at eight in the morning. We left each other at the station, and Wanda was to pick me up at the Opolskis' before evening.

I felt like a tourist who comes on his first visit to an unknown city. It was not the same city that I had grown up in. It was not the city I loved, whose language I spoke, in whose character I delighted. I was now a stranger in a strange land, with just this one difference: I didn't have to ask anybody for directions.

Mrs. Opolski, Tadek's mother, hardly knew me, but she received me with warmth and hospitality. She made me take a hot bath and prepared a good breakfast. Tadek wasn't home. He was an engineer and worked in a factory located somewhere in the ghetto.

Mrs. Opoloski wanted to know about my family. She didn't know them, and suddenly I found myself at a loss about what to say. Here I was, a future businessman, a planner—and there, in my background, was a total loss. What was I to tell?

I said, "Everybody is perfectly all right. My parents are living on the Aryan side of Warsaw. They are well off. Still, I feel that our capital should be put to work, and this is why I'm here."

As I was saying all these lies, I was the victim of a variety of feelings and thoughts: Isn't it true that if you are in bad need of help, you will seldom find an outstretched hand? Isn't it true that those who need no help will be offered all of it? But it was also true that I was deceiving a kind human being who would have helped in any way she could.

In the evening, we made plans for the future. I was to advance the working capital with which Tadek would buy gold and jewelry while I was in Warsaw, so that he would have it ready for me each time I arrived in Lvov. Thus, in the future, I could come to Lvov in the morning and leave the same evening. At the present time, as I was already there, Tadek would try to buy whatever he could, for half of my capital, so I wouldn't go home empty-handed. The other half was to remain with him for the future purchases. Our profit was to be split in half. I stayed with the Opolskis for a couple of days while Tadek was looking for the goods.

All this time, Wanda was staying with somebody else in the city, visiting the Opolskis' only late in the afternoon. By the third evening, Tadek had already given me sufficient merchandise to make it worthwhile to return to Warsaw. Wanda was ready, and we left Lvov. The return trip had already become routine: a crammed overnight train from Lvov to Cracow; a day at Mrs. Drescher's; Jan's dining car from Cracow to Warsaw, with bimber and bread and sausage. It was all routine, except for the arrival itself.

It was seven in the morning when the train came to a full stop, perhaps a kilometer from the station. After a while, a humming of anger and indignation ran through the train. We went to the window and leaned out. We saw objects hanging from each of the tall lamp poles posted along the tracks. Reluctantly, we identified them as people.

"There must be at least thirty of them," said Wanda. I counted fifty.

Somebody said, "These are the Polish hostages!"

The train moved. Its windows were cluttered with people watching the improvised gallows. For a spell, it seemed as if the train was still at a full stop and a macabre procession of corpses were following their own funeral. There was a deep silence when the train stopped at the Warsaw station. Passengers left, one by one, scared to look above, unable to greet or to bid each other good-bye. Mass murder, until now reserved for the Jews only, had suddenly become public domain.

At home, I found a very upset Martin. I had been away for almost five days, and he thought me dead. And now, these hangings. He explained that posters with the names of the executed had been posted all over Warsaw. The hangings had been in revenge for a bomb that the Polish resistance had thrown on a group of German soldiers. Five Germans were dead. Ten Poles for each German. All professionals. I wondered whether this event might change something in Polish-Jewish relations. Martin didn't think so. He laughed bitterly when I mentioned a common cause.

"What cause?!" he said. "Do we have a cause? Does trying to slip unnoticed between the dawn and the dusk constitute a cause? While the Germans keep catching us like fish, one by one, the others hide and thank God that it wasn't them."

Wanda did not comment, but I couldn't help noticing an odd

expression in her eyes. The cold gray of steel shone through the familiar cornflower blue.

The same week, as I was crossing Wilcza Street, I ran across my old friend Adam. The meeting was so unexpected for both of us that we couldn't talk. We stood in the street, embracing and clapping each other on the shoulder. And only a few days ago, Mrs. Opolski had said that he had disappeared. Never underestimate Adam!

This called for a celebration. I invited him to our room, and he whispered his new name. It was still Adam, but the last name had become Arecki.

At home, I called Wanda to introduce Adam to her. My God! Adam is alive! She knew of him. I had told her about him when we left Lvov. I watched Adam as he was telling his misadventures. He had been a plump, pink-cheeked, handsome young man. Now in front of me sat a slender, mature man, with a gray complexion and a bushy mustache.

Adam had been thinking of leaving Lvov long before his family was deported. They were all dying of hunger and had no way to make a living. Adam had thought of joining the work brigade, as a Pole or a Ukrainian, and going to Germany. He registered, presented his false papers, and even passed the medical examination. All went well until he left the doctor's office and started dressing. A colleague of Adam's, a Ukrainian who had studied medicine with him, was there, too. While the Ukrainian was denouncing Adam to a guard, my friend left all he had and ran to Tarnow, and ran to Cracow, and ran to Warsaw, and still seemed to be running to who knows where.

Adam was hungry, but he did have a place to sleep. I gave him some money for food and brought him up to date regarding our situation. I figured that now we would have one more person to care for, and Adam could be of help. He didn't want to travel. He had had enough of that for the rest of his life. But he offered to cook for us. Poor Adam. Anyhow, he joined the group.

Martin had succeeded in getting in touch with Mikolajczyk. The gentleman said that yes, he had our parents' things, but that he was now terribly busy, and we would have to wait some time to call for them. He did us one favor, though: he put us in contact with Ostrowicz. Now we had a reliable broker for our goods, and in no time at all, Ostrowicz was able to sell everything, at a substantial profit. I was ready for my second trip.

I was supposed to go on my own, but Wanda had things to attend to in Lvov, so we traveled together once more.

While we were in Lvov, Tadek brought me some news from the

ghetto. Our neighbors the Gruners weren't to be found anywhere. Somebody mentioned that they might have escaped to Hungary. Most thought they were dead. A girl, though, had asked Tadek about me. A girl by the name of Anka. I became excited. Anka alive? I would have been excited about anybody I knew being alive. I was traveling and earning money — Father would have been proud of me. Now I felt that I would like to help people to leave the ghetto.

"What does she want?" I asked Tadek.

"She wants to get out of there."

Wanda had nothing against helping somebody. We decided that Tadek would put Anka on warning, so that she would be ready within minutes when we were prepared to get her out of Lvov. Tadek promised to bring her home from the ghetto when the moment arrived.

This time, we had to stay in Cracow for thirty-six hours, which meant sleeping in Mrs. Drescher's single bed. This made me sweat, even as we were arriving in Cracow. I liked Wanda too much to try anything with her. And now it was the evening. I watched Wanda carefully. She was seated in a chair, repairing a run in her silk stocking. Where in the world could she have gotten silk stockings during these times, I thought to myself. Possibly she received them from her German officer friend. Her ash-blond hair fell in a long wave on her delicate neck and partly covered her face. Then she smoked. She inhaled slowly, with dedication, then let the smoke out of her nostrils and carefully followed the smoke's course in the air. She was definitely pretty.

I said, "I'll sleep on the floor. Or in the armchair."

While I was bedding down for the night, she watched me, amused. "I suppose it must be quite difficult for a man, under the circumstances," she said.

Now, standing, Wanda leaned one leg against a chair and examined the other silk stocking. The skirt moved a little above her knee, showing a shapely, well-rounded calf.

"And what's the real truth about Anka?" she asked. She meant it as a rhetorical question, but I thought she deserved an answer nevertheless.

"Nothing at all. Once, a century ago, I thought I was in love with her. If I can help her, or anybody, to get out of hell, I'd like to do it."

"It's all right." She looked at me attentively. Then, becoming very serious, she said, "We can undress in the dark," and she turned off the light.

After that, I made several trips to Lvov on my own, as Wanda was involved in some mysterious dealings which sometimes made her disappear for many days. My trips brought in enough money to make a living, and I would have been satisfied to continue in this way until the end of the war.

Now the news from the Eastern Front was more reassuring, and the North African Front was doing very well. The war must finish one day, and there we'd be, safe and ready to tell the world what had happened to the Jews of Europe. There was a German saying, though, that categorized my hopes correctly: Das ist wie es sich der kleine Fritz forstellt — "This is the way little Fritz imagines it." In short, life is never this simple.

The problem was Martin. During my trips, he remained alone at night, and he became scared. He imagined hearing voices of people who were plotting against the Jews. And when sometimes it was the real voice of a real person, he still linked it to a plot. The last straw was a telephone call received by our neighbor, the Gestapo secretary, at midnight one night. As Martin listened to her, he could clearly hear "Jud! Jud! Jud!"

I returned from a trip the next morning, to find him highly upset, almost irrational. He wouldn't stay in the rooming house a day longer. The girl was a spy. She found out about hidden Jews and denounced them to the Gestapo. Last night's telephone call meant this to Martin: the voice on the other end of the line was reading names, and she was confirming the ones that represented Jews.

I reasoned with my brother. He spoke excellent German and knew that in some regions of Germany people pronounced the hard *G* as a soft *J*. Wasn't the girl simply saying "Gut" — "Good"? This suggestion was to no avail. He wanted to move out, because of the girl, because of the voices, and because of Linka's brother, Manek, whose appetite for what he considered our Treblinka money was becoming sharper each day.

Moving to Cracow for good meant many complications. In the first place, of course, there was the question of permanent living accomodations. I didn't know whether Mrs. Drescher would consider renting us a room permanently. And if she would, how were we to sleep in one small bed? We would have to take two rooms, especially as Martin now had his new documents, the real ones: a certificate of birth of a Pole who had perished during the war, but whose death was never registered. Martin's name was now Alfred Stelmachiewicz. He even had a real identity card issued by the Warsaw police on the basis of this birth certificate.

And my name was Liwicki. And Bronowski. And Matejski. And

Krupa. I had four sets of documents, all false, that I carried with me at all times. I thought that if I used a different name in each city, it would be harder for them to track me down, and I had to remember which name belonged to which pocket, so that I wouldn't make a mistake in identifying myself to the authorities. But I didn't have the name of Stelmachiewicz, which made it imperative for us to start introducing ourselves not as brothers but as business partners.

Another problem was that I still had to continue coming to Warsaw for business and would need a room. This meant more expenses.

We solved the problem of moving Martin to Cracow by establishing what, in a way, amounted to a regular business organization. Adam, who wouldn't leave Warsaw, would be from now on in charge of sales. I would continue to be a traveling buyer, with Tadek remaining a local buyer in Lvov, and Ostrowicz was to be the runner, the man who would transport our goods from Cracow to Warsaw and our money from Warsaw to Cracow. Thus my traveling would be limited to the Cracow-Lvov-Cracow route. On the basis of this plan, we moved to Cracow.

This time, Mrs. Drescher didn't have even our usual room free, but she gave me another address: the Gunther family. It was a large, old apartment on Zyblikiewicza Street. The address itself made us feel immediately at home, as in Lvov we had also lived on a Zyblikiewicza Street.

The Gunthers were a beautiful Polish family. Mr. Gunther was an ex-district attorney. The daughter was a painter. And Mrs. Gunther was the sweetest lady I'd known, except, maybe, for Mrs. Opolski. The Gunthers rented almost all of their rooms to permanent guests, who even had their meals there. Luckily for us, two small rooms had lately become vacant, and we moved in the same day as two business partners in need of a basic convenience: a private room for each.

Wanda and I left on what was to be our last trip to Lvov. Things were becoming bad. Each day it was increasingly difficult to travel, with all the raids on the trains, with all the Poles without working papers being caught and deported to forced labor in Germany.

When our business in Lvov was finished, Tadek asked, "And how about your friend Anka?"

This was her last chance. Wanda didn't object to Anka's traveling with us. It was decided that Tadek would bring her with him today, ready to go.

Anka hadn't changed much. Her slim face was still framed with a smooth, long wave of shiny black hair; the cool green eyes and the thin lips gave her an appearance of aloofness and independence. She wore a smart green tweed coat and a green felt hat with a little feather.

She hardly smiled when we shook hands.

"I knew that something had to happen," she stated. "It simply couldn't continue this way any longer."

The way she put it, I suddenly felt like God's special messenger who was dispatched to Lvov for one purpose only: to save Anka.

We didn't have the time now to discuss any details. We just had to go and hope for the best. Anka didn't even have any documents. But what she did have was her luggage: two huge valises of personal effects. Wanda and I exchanged a glance of disbelief, and I had the feeling that I was getting into very serious trouble with my "save Anka" program.

Our first difficulty arose as we were waiting at the railroad platform for the train to arrive. Wanda went to the restaurant to get some cigarettes. I was standing with Anka, her luggage separating us. A man in a porter's uniform addressd me: "May I see you for a moment, sir?"

"What about?"

"I think it would be best to discuss it privately."

I glanced at Anka. She looked terrified.

I said to her, "Will you excuse me for a moment? I'll be back soon."

I followed the man to the stairway leading to the railroad offices. We stopped there.

"We'll have to arrest you," said the porter in a courteous voice. Three men in civilian clothes joined us. One of them identified himself. They were the police. I had become very cool, and my mind started working with speed and precision. Here was a challenge, and I would overcome it.

"What do you want of me?" I asked indifferently.

"We charge you with smuggling Jews out of Lvov."

"How's that?"

"We've been watching you for some time. You and that blond lady. And surely today we've caught you red-handed."

A companion of his interrupted: "Enough talk! Let's go down to the precinct."

"And I thought you were businessmen," I said. "You must have some solution in mind."

The spokesman for the group called the other two men away,

leaving me with only the porter. They had a quick conference. Then a uniformed policeman with a rifle joined them. Their discussion had become lengthy.

Meanwhile Wanda came back with her cigarettes. She had a good nose for trouble and knew immediately that something had gone wrong. She stepped to me, gave an unfriendly look to the porter, and asked in the sharp, matter-of-fact voice she liked to use in rough situations, "What's going on? What does this one want?"

At this moment, the plainclothes man returned and whispered into my ear, "You can board the train. We'll talk to you later."

The train was just entering the station. There was a general commotion as all the passengers got ready to be the first ones to board it and get a seat, and there was certainly no time for explanations. I took Wanda by the hand and led her to Anka. The three of us, holding the two huge valises, made a frontal attack on the narrow door of the car, sealing it for an instant to other competitors. Thus we found seats in a dark compartment. But there was still no time for explanations, as the compartment filled up with other passengers.

The car was now filled to capacity; even the corridor was crowded with standing people. The situation would have been perfect for travel, except for that one little problem of mine. I was curious: How would they find me in all this whispering crowd — people always whispered in dark trains — and all this darkness? The train moved. Anka looked at me. It was an important moment for her. She seemed less tense. Suddenly, I realized: she didn't know the first thing about what was happening!

For an instant, I myself felt like the beneficiary of a little miracle: so far they had let us alone.

And then the door of the compartment opened. I looked at the dark rectangle as if I were hypnotized. Then, an arm entered the compartment. It stretched, slowly and inexorably. A hand shot out of it. A finger out of the hand. And it pointed at me. I got up and followed my destiny.

The policemen were waiting at the far end of the corridor, near the toilet. The one with the rifle took a strategic position, closing that part of the corridor to the traffic. The others surrounded me. The spokesman said, "Fifteen thousand zloty."

I laughed heartily. I had on me ten thousand zloty in one bundle of five-hundred-zloty bills. I certainly did not have any intention of parting with this money.

"You must be kidding! Fifteen thousand! And for what? For helping a Jewish girl out of her misery?!"

"So she paid you for it, didn't she?"

"She didn't pay me anything! I'm doing it from the goodness of my heart. I am a businessman, but Jews are not my merchandise."

"Look," said the spokesman, "we still can put you under arrest!"

"So you can. And then what? The girl will be kaput! My fiancée and I will be in trouble. And you will have no money."

"Ten thousand," said the man.

"I can give you a thousand zloty."

"Are you crazy or what! We're not working for a thousand."

"Three thousand is all the money I have on me. I don't like to part with all of it, but to conclude this unpleasant affair, I'll give it to you."

The policemen had a whispering conference. The decision was made: "Three thousand and your wristwatch."

I liked this settlement. I told them that I would leave the money and the watch in the toilet, so nobody would notice that they were accepting a bribe. I needed to be alone, to get the three thousand out of the bundle of ten thousand.

When I left the toilet, one of them entered, while the others watched me. He came out and nodded. They all shook hands with me and asked that I keep them in mind whenever I could use their services.

That night, I couldn't put my mind to rest. I had paid them off, but how was I to be sure that they had really let us off the hook? How could I be sure that another raiding party wouldn't be waiting for us in Cracow? Meanwhile, the two girls traveled peacefully, and I didn't have a chance to share my problem with them. With them? I couldn't share any problem with Anka without making her frantic. I would have liked to tell Wanda, but I couldn't with all the people around.

But nothing more happened. We arrived undisturbed and attempted to make ourselves comfortable at home. My difficulties started immediately. I wanted to ask Mrs. Gunther whether she could recommend Anka to somebody who had a room for rent. Anka refused to live by herself. She was insecure, she was scared. The only thing she could envisage was staying with me, as my wife, and she introduced herself to Mrs. Gunther as such. Martin had a different opinion about this whole business. He took me aside, and said that I must make a choice: Anka or him.

"Maybe she has class and all," he said, "but she looks so Jewish that you wouldn't be able to cross a street with her. If she stays, I return to Warsaw."

Wanda didn't like her either. She plunged in the soft featherbed after we had unpacked, her face drowning in the foam of her ash-blond hair, and she said mockingly to Anka, "How about exchanging your bed for mine?"

This was the crux of it. The bed. The only bed. I had never had any sex with Anka. This meant that from now on I would have to sleep in an armchair, while the two girls would use my bed. The situation was too complicated to try to solve immediately. I proposed that we consider it transitional and promised to try to find a solution that would suit everybody.

The time had finally arrived for me to tell them about my adventure with the police in Lvov. When I finished telling the details, Anka said, "Then I owe you three thousand zloty and a wristwatch." She took out a notebook from her bag and made the entry. It seemed unbelievable. "I'll write down every penny you spend on me, and when the war is over, I'll repay you." She was serious about it.

I asked about her parents.

"Father is working in the Janowska camp. He's in the garbage detail. Mother's gone. When they took us to Janowska, we were separated from the men, and I was sitting with Mother under the barbed wire when Rokita, the Kommandant of the camp, came by. He walked around picking a woman here and there to work in Schultz's army uniform shop. He took me by the hand and led me away. I walked as if I were in a dream. I don't think I even said good-bye to Mother. But she found a way to squeeze a couple of pieces of jewelry into my pocket. Her diamond ring." Anka's voice sounded wet with tears, but her tears were dry. "I miss Mother."

"When did this happen?"

"More than a month ago. After that, I worked at Schultz's. The last two weeks, I worked the night shift, and the boss was making passes at me. Two nights ago, he really meant business, and he stopped only because a Gestapo inspector arrived. It's strange. I wasn't scared at all. When he was almost at the point of taking me, all I could think of was whether he was destined to be my first man."

The next day I took Anka to dinner in a small restaurant I knew. We sat in a corner, a record player was playing "Lilli Marlene," the atmosphere was pleasant, and Anka seemed completely relaxed, so much so that she even started humming the tune. I felt it was a good start and hoped that after a week she might not look so terribly Jewish to Martin. The question was how to make her lose her fear.

Across the room from us, a couple were sitting at a little table. She was a cheaply dressed, good-looking blonde, a better sort of a Cracow whore. He, in spite of his civilian clothes, looked unmistakably

German. I tried to avoid looking in their direction, remembering the old wisdom of Treblinka: your eye will attract his eye. It didn't help. With the corner of my eyes I could see the German glancing at us. I was cool. Anka, oblivious, was humming her tune.

The blonde whispered something in the man's ear. He nodded and turned his cold eyes on Anka. I felt the danger in the air. I knew that the only way to fight danger was to face it. I looked straight into the man's eyes. He started rising. It must have been a question of seconds, but to me it was an eternity. I saw him rising and rising, and I felt my hair becoming gray by the split second. "It takes him years to get up," I thought. "I'll be an old man by the time he takes us in."

The man was leaning against the pink marble of the table top.

Anka said, "I almost feel like dancing." Her entire world seemed to be wrapped up in the tune of "Lili Marlene."

Anka continued, "It's like being a movie actress. Hidden danger around me. And I feel happy."

She had mentioned many times before, during the Russian occupation, that she wanted to be a movie actress.

The German stretched his big body.

Anka raised her glass.

The blonde burst into laughter. The spell was broken.

The German shrugged and sat down.

I said casually to Anka, "Shall we go?"

I told her everything at home. This was it. She refused to leave the room. This meant many things. It meant that I had to do all the shopping. It meant I had to buy dinner in a small dairy restaurant nearby and bring it home for Anka to eat. It meant I had to watch her making her petty entries in that little black booklet of debits and credits. It meant I had to stop traveling because she was afraid to stay alone. It meant I had to sleep with her, on the condition that I wouldn't touch her. It meant I had to listen to her praises of her huge diamond, which was worth so much, but which would never be sold because of its sentimental value.

One afternoon, as I was waiting in the dairy restaurant for my containers of soup and potato pancakes, my eye caught two familiar faces from Lvov: Rebecca and Piotr. They were about to leave. They, too, saw me, but none of us knew how to act. As they were passing by, Piotr said something to Rebecca. He said it aloud, for everyone to hear. He spoke Ukrainian.

I left a few minutes later and caught up with them in the Planty Park. Rebecca was delighted to see me. Piotr continued to talk in

Ukrainian. I understood Ukrainian, as did everyone from Lvov, but I didn't speak it. His insistence on speaking Ukrainian seemed ridiculous to me. Rebecca asked whether they could visit us. However, Piotr said he didn't want to be seen entering an apartment building with me. Our meeting was short and furtive. They wanted to get my address and leave all explanations for later.

That evening, they visited us at the Gunthers. Piotr explained that he was being adopted by a Ukrainian lawyer, a friend of his father's; that they already had the original papers, and considered themselves Ukrainian; and that of course we shouldn't acknowledge each other if we should happen to meet in the street, but that sometimes they might pay us a visit.

Anka's continued confinement at home bored her. To combat the boredom, she had an occasional idea about adding Aryan touches to our Jewish personalities. This was how she came up with "Project blond hair" for me. She told me which chemicals to buy. Then studied the instructions and went to work. The result was disastrous: my hair, my modest light brown hair, became a vivid green. Now, whenever I went out, I had to keep my head covered, to avoid attracting attention.

The Gunther's apartment, perhaps unknowingly to the owners, was a shelter for Jews as well as for members of the Polish underground. In one of the rooms lived a black-haired, black-eyed Jewish girl from Lvov, whom Anka recognized as Zula Ginczanka, a poetess whose lyrical creations had appeared in the Zionist daily *Chwila*. Her husband, a handsome young man with a mustache, was staying in a separate room, and the Gunthers knew him as Zula's friend.

Zula's daily visitor, known to the Gunther's as her fiancé, was one of the heads of the Polish underground. And Mrs. Gunther's daughter, the painter, courted Zula's husband fervently. Of course, Zula had very special documents: she was Armenian. This was convenient because of her strongly Oriental face. When Zula realized that she had been recognized by Anka, she had her husband pay us a short visit to ask us to forget Zula. On this occasion, I learned what the Gunthers thought about my new hair: "They refer to you as 'that green parrot,' " Zula's husband said. I started thinking of shaving my hair completely, but who would have dared to go to a barber in this condition?

Toward the end of November, Anka prepared what she thought was an unusual birthday gift for me. She asked me to buy a bottle of wine, and we had a birthday party, together with Martin and Mrs. Helena Bergman. We had not seen Helena since the days of Russian occupation in Lvov, when she and her common-law husband had provided Father with contacts in the Russian militia so that we could obtain passports to protect some of our friends from deportation. She had just arrived from Warsaw to try and get her son out of Auschwitz, where he was serving time as a Polish political prisoner. Anka fixed some canapes, which we had with the wine, and after Martin and Helena had left, we had another bottle of wine.

Then, Anka said to me, "Your birthday present!" and she got fully undressed.

"Your birthday present," she repeated.

I finally understood, but it was too late. I had had too much wine and simply fell asleep.

Quite a few things happened during the end of November 1942. Ostrowicz arrived from Warsaw. With his mouth expressing continuous disgust, and with his pince-nez, he still looked like Molotov but had become much slimmer. His wife and daughter had been taken away, and he had lost all interest in life. However, he would continue working with us, to fill up the gap between life and death. We gave him our goods and asked him to pick up our things from Mikolajczyk and Nowak. Ostrowicz, always a precise businessman, didn't want a written list of the effects. He learned by heart what the two gentlemen had in safekeeping for us and left. It was our understanding that he would be back in three days.

Next evening, Rebecca arrived. We hadn't seen her for some time. As Mrs. Gunther ushered her in, she was all joy and smiles. But as soon as the door closed behind our landlady, Rebecca broke out in a desperate sobbing, and kept repeating, "Piotr is gone! Piotr is gone!" It took me a little time and some bimber to make her tell the story. She and Piotr wanted to pay a visit to his mother in Lvov and took the Carpathian local train. At one of the small stations where the train stopped for a short while, the Gestapo and the Ukrainian police suddenly raided the train, chased all the passengers into the waiting room at the station, and proceeded checking documents. They were looking for Jews. There was nothing wrong with Rebecca's documents, and they let her go. Piotr's documents were just as good, but the policeman noticed something sewn into Piotr's collar. He asked Piotr, to take off the jacket, and ripped the seam. At this point, Rebecca hid in the toilet. She knew what was in the collar: a Mezuza, the diminutive parchment scroll with Hebrew blessings. The police began looking for Rebecca, who kept switching from toilet to toilet. In the evening, when the raid was over, Rebecca escaped from the station and continued her journey by walking along the highway, hiding in the ditches whenever she saw traffic. All that night and all the next day she walked through field after field. She had finally arrived in Cracow an hour ago, exhausted and miserable. I offered her a corner in our room. But she wasn't through with her story. The next day she told us the rest: she was pregnant.

Martin who was usually scared of his own shadow, proved to be of tremendous help to Rebecca. He suddenly remembered that he saw a doctor's name in the local newspaper. A name familiar to him. With all the courage he could muster, Martin went to visit the doctor. Within an hour he was back with good news. The doctor was a friend of his, a Jew working in a private hospital in Cracow whom everybody believed to be a Pole from Lvov. Martin took Rebecca to the hospital the same day, the abortion was performed the next day, and Rebecca was out five days later. All without charge.

Wanda then arrived in Cracow. We hadn't seen her for some time. I often wondered about the dealings in which she was involved and about the secrecy that surrounded them. I still remembered the day when we had met. Wanda had mentioned that she was having visitors who were Gestapo officers. I didn't believe that Wanda was some sort of a collaborator, yet, those Gestapo officers . . .

Wanda liked to stay with us for a few hours when she didn't have anything special to do. Now she was seated in an armchair, knitting a woolen scarf. She was the personification of peace and happiness, so pretty, so blonde, so satisfied with her work.

Mrs. Gunther knocked on the door. There was a telegram for us. I thought it must be from Ostrowicz, who was already a few days late. I opened it. It was from Adam. It was short and cryptic: "Don't give money to Wanda." I read it a couple of times before giving it to Martin.

Finally, Martin read it aloud, and I asked Wanda: "What does it mean?" There was no money that we were supposed to give to Wanda. Yet Adam wanted to say something of importance. Was it a code? Money. What did money represent?

Wanda remained cool. She didn't understand the telegram. She didn't know about any money.

Now, I wondered, what does giving money to somebody mean? Trusting somebody! Suddenly, I was afraid of Wanda. Who was she? What was her business? I was thinking feverishly, but I didn't dare to say aloud what I thought. I hoped I was mistaken. But Adam meant to warn us. That evening Wanda left Cracow.

And the next morning Ostrowicz arrived. He was even slimmer and paler than the last time we had seen him. He took off his coat, sat down, and cleared his throat. All this was usual for Ostrowicz. What he had to tell us was not.

"It's a miracle I'm here," he said, "because of your two friends. I went to Mikolajczyk and gave him your message. He was very nice to me. He promised that he would have not only his valise ready that evening but also the one that was at Nowak's place. He asked me to return at six o'clock sharp. I did. Polish police were waiting for me in the hall of his building. I tried to bribe them, but to no avail. They said I was denounced, and the record was in the precinct. But they did me one favor: they returned me to the Ghetto instead of delivering me to the Germans. That is why I'm still alive. I worked on the debris detail for several days, and finally, yesterday, found a way to escape."

He cleared his throat again, reached into his inside pocket, and handed me a bundle. "This is the money for your goods. Twenty thousand zloty." Even when faced with death, Ostrowicz remained a man of precision and honesty.

"Mr. Ostrowicz, are you going back to Warsaw?" Martin asked.

"Yes. Tonight."

"I'll join you."

This was unexpected. I understood Martin. He was afraid of Wanda. He didn't want to be near Anka. Maybe he didn't want to be near me. Martin asked me to settle accounts with him. We split the money in half. I kept Father's gold watch, and Martin took Mother's jewels. My Ring, of course, remained with me. It had relatively little value as a jewel, but to me it was all-important.

Martin promised to keep in touch. When he left, I didn't know that it would be a very, very long time before we would run across each other again.

Christmas was approaching, and Anka and I thought it necessary to find a place to spend the holiday season. Otherwise we were afraid that Mrs. Gunther might wonder what kind of Poles we were, without family to stay with at Christmas.

I found an ad in the *Kurier*. It was for a little villa in the mountains. Just perfect for us.

Helena Bergman was still in Cracow, and she came with me to meet the owner, Mr. Nowaczynski. He was a nice man. He told us that his maid was staying in the villa, and that some other guests were already there. He didn't know them, but he would take me up to the mountains so that I could see the villa and so that he could meet his other guests. Of course, he mentioned that one could not be too careful, with Jews impersonating Poles, and I reached for my papers. Mr. Nowaczynski stopped me midway, saying, "This is not necessary. We Aryans can smell each other at a mile's distance."

The next day, I went to the villa with Mr. Nowaczynski. It was a couple of hours' ride to the village, called Rickiciny Malopolskie, and from there a long and steep walk up the mountain to the villa.

Frankly, it was not a villa but a large cottage. The room we were to have was extremely small, but it was all right for our purpose. Miss Wladzia, the maid, seemed a very independent, but not very friendly, woman of forty. As for the other guests, after only a short glance at them, I disliked them. They were two men and a woman, and all three seemed to be uncouth low-class Warsaw peddlers. Mr. Nowaczynski took me for a walk and asked what I thought. I said I liked the place, but he wanted to know what I thought about the other guests. I didn't want to share my impressions with him and said, "They're all right."

At the end of the week, Anka and I were getting ready to leave Cracow. I advised Mrs. Gunther and asked Helena Bergman to let Martin have my address, as she was leaving for Warsaw.

Mrs. Gunther was very sweet. She came to the room, and said, "Please don't go! It is so dangerous nowadays to travel on the train. We'll prepare a nice holiday, and you'll stay with us. The other guests are staying." But my mind was made up: we were going to "spend the holidays with the family," and so it had to be.

That day, Wanda arrived in Cracow. She asked me to take a walk with her. We went to the Planty Park. The trees were stripped of leaves and the benches were abandoned on that cold December afternoon. We sat on a bench. A squirrel watched us for a moment with expectation. Then, as we didn't make a move to feed it, it swiftly disappeared into the hole of a tree.

"Christmas is coming in a week," said Wanda absent-mindedly.

"Wanda," I asked, "who are you?"

At first, she seemed startled. Then, she gave me a sad look: "One day soon, you might find out."

"Wanda, are you working for the Gestapo?"

She gave me no answer. She took my hand and kept it in hers for a while.

Then she said, "I just came to tell you that this might be the last time we see each other. I want you to know that I care." She pressed my hand. "And keep believing in your Ring."

I saw her eyes fill with tears. Her small lips were trembling with emotion. She bent toward me and gave me a kiss. Then she rose and left quickly. Musing, I followed her with my eyes. Her graceful silhouette was soon absorbed by the dusk. I shivered in my light coat and rose reluctantly. I had to go home, to take care of Anka.

The evening before our departure for the mountains, "Cyganerja," an elegant nightclub, now used by the Germans, was bombed, and some five or six officers were killed. At first, it was thought to be a bravura act committed by the Polish underground.

Soon, it became known that the bombing was done by an organized Jewish group, and people were talking about a girl — an ash-blonde who didn't look at all Jewish—who had befriended a Gestapo officer, with whom she had gone to the nightclub. She had carried the bomb with her.

Now, she was dead, and the Gestapo were pulling their dragnet around this hitherto-unknown Jewish organization.

That evening I roamed in the heavy fog that was enveloping the empty Planty Park. I sat on the humid bench where Wanda had said good-bye. I fancied seeing close to me the ash-blond head, the cornflower-blue eyes, and the small lips that would never smile at me again. I mourned for Wanda, and at the same time, I wanted the dead girl to be Wanda. But I will never know for sure. This was the end of the phenomenon that I had known as Wanda.

Rokiciny Malopolskie is a secluded little village at the foot of the Tatra mountains. Anka and I dragged our heavy luggage up a snow-covered hill, on top of which, in splendid isolation, stood Mr. Nowaczynski's wooden cottage. In a panoramic view from up there, the eye could embrace the rolling fields and pastures, now disappearing under a fluffy featherbed of snow, and the surrounding high mountains decorated with a growth of old, dark green firs. The village itself remained hidden down in the valley, where the Tatra train made its short stop.

The maid Wladzia introduced us to the other guests. There was Szczepan, a tall, clean-shaven man in his early thirties, with scarce light-brown hair, cool green eyes, and a gold tooth in the front of his mouth, which gave an air of perpetual sarcasm to his smile. His wife, Anna, a short, dark woman in her late twenties, had one feature strikingly similar to her husband: a gold tooth in the front of her mouth. And there was their best friend, Marian, a husky character in his mid-twenties who, with the rolled-up sleeves of his flannel shirt and a hatchet for splitting firewood in his hand, was a picture of the Polish peasant, except for his accent, which betrayed his origin in the Warsaw streets.

Szczepan caught up with me an hour later, as soon as I left our room after having unpacked some of my things. He told me that the three of them were planning to celebrate their Christmas holiday with Wladzia, and they were also planning to invite the mayor of the village and his wife to the Christmas Eve vigil. He wanted to know whether we would like to join them. He was wearing gray flannel trousers and a black quilted Russian jacket, which maybe because of its round stand-up collar, gave him the air of a clergyman. I quickly accepted the offer and wanted to give him our share of the expenses, but he raised his hand, as if he wanted to stop me from running in the wrong direction, and said, "No hurry. First of all, we've got to buy all that's necessary, and I'm counting on your advice."

This was a problem I had hoped to avoid. What kind of advice could I give to this Pole? We had never had any Christmas party at home. However, I had to say yes. I asked where we would do the shopping, and Szczepan laughed.

"This is a wild country! Once a week, we go down to the village to buy bread for the week. We carry it back home on our shoulders, up the hill. Then we visit the nearby peasants and barter pieces of clothing, bedsheets, and tablecloths for their eggs, butter, flour, and, occasionally, a chicken. This is how we do our shopping."

I remained perplexed. "Why clothing?"

"Because the peasants don't believe in money these days." said Szczepan.

This presented an immediate difficulty. Mr. Nowaczynski hadn't warned me. How were we to purchase even the staple foods? I shared my worries with Szczepan, and he was willing to help.

"We'll figure out the price of each article, and you'll pay us for whatever you'll want to buy." He told me that they had brought with them a couple of trunkfuls of clothing, just for the purpose of bartering.

I tried to evaluate the trio. Szczepan gave me the impression of being a cool, shrewd con man, calculating and ruthless. His wife, Anna, was so terribly gray and drab, that the only impression she made was one of a gold tooth shining in the dark. Marian was a primitive, both in his ways and in his language, and my best guess was that these three Poles were Warsaw upstarts who had become rich on the Ghetto smuggling. I even suspected that the goods they had brought here for bartering must have been Jewish clothes.

We sat down at the kitchen table, all of us, with Wladzia presiding, to discuss the meals for the party. We would have, said Wladzia, several kinds of noodles: with white cheese, and with poppy seeds and honey, and with buckwheat and fried onion. And boiled dumplings of grated raw potatoes. And fried dumplings of grated boiled potatoes. And for desert, *kutia,* which is boiled wheat with poppy seeds and honey. We couldn't get fish in Rokiciny, and meat, of course, was not permitted on Christmas Eve. The menu sounded like an awful lot of potatoes and cereals, and Szczepan, being a shrewd public relations man, asked whether Wladzia could invite some more peasants for the Christmas Eve meal. That, she was afraid, would not be possible, as it was really a family holiday. But she suggested that if we wanted to arrange a *Gwiazdka* — a "Little Star", as Christmas gift-giving was called in Poland — she could invite a few peasant families for a drink at six in the evening. Szczepan was willing to part with a few articles from his two enormous wooden chests, just for the sake of good neighborly relations, and a Gwiazdka was approved.

The next morning, Szczepan, Marian and I went down to the village to get fresh bread and flour. The bread was baked by the village miller, so we waited for our turn in the small mill. When it came to paying, the miller advised us that this was the last time that he could sell either the flour or the bread.

"From now on," he said, "I will have no wheat or rye. If you want bread, you will have to bring your own grain, and I'll keep a part of it as payment for grinding and baking."

This made our situation really bleak, and it made me brood as we climbed the steep hill, snow up to our hips, and bags of huge bread loaves and flour on our shoulders. I had no particular plan as to how long we would stay in Rokiciny, but now that we were here, I wished we could stay for the rest of the war. The village was small, hardly populated. And our nearest neighbors were a Polish lady and her twenty-year-old son, who lived in a villa about a kilometer from us. This was the place to be when the Germans were raiding and deporting people from the cities.

My problem was that not only did we not have any goods to barter, but even assuming that Szczepan would sell us a part of the food they acquired, how long would our money last if I couldn't make it work?

Meanwhile, the three women were busy decorating a *choinka,* the Christmas tree Marian had chopped down in the nearby woods.

There was no brooding here. Anka seemed finally to be in the surroundings of her choice. She confided in me one day that, some time before, unknown to her parents, she had taken lessons in catechism from a Polish priest in Lvov, as she had intended to convert. This news would come in handy at this time, when some basic knowledge of Catholic religious rituals and folk customs seemed indispensable.

At six in the evening, we gathered around the Christmas tree, where four stuffy peasants, one of them the mayor of Rikiciny, received their "Little Stars" from Szczepan and had a couple of glasses of vodka with us. After that, they left to join their own parties, and Wladzia announced that the Christmas Eve dinner was ready.

We sat around the kitchen table, covered for the occasion with a white table cloth and set with the various dairy dishes. I sat at one end of the table and Szczepan at the opposite end. The Christmas tree was right behind Szczepan, and with such a background, and still wearing his black Russian jacket, he definitely looked like a clergyman. Everybody at the table was very solemn and ate very slowly. I thought of the books I had read describing the life of Polish peasants, and I found that the almost aritificial solemnity of our group and the unhurried way of eating had been faithfully described in the Polish literature. What I could not understand was that these people around the table were not peasants, and still they acted as such for the occasion. Even Anka did. Probably, even I.

The dinner was coming to an end, and I felt uneasy thinking of the next step: singing the Christmas carols. This was the Polish way: you ate your Christmas Eve meal, and then you sat under the tree and sang the carols. I knew a few popular ones from grammar school, but they weren't sufficient. I knew that the celebration was supposed to last until midnight. I was angry with myself for not having invented a sore throat, so that I wouldn't have to face this disaster. I hoped that Anka would be of help.

The dreaded moment had arrived. Wladzia intoned the first, the most popular, the only carol I knew in its entirety, *Wsrod nocnej ciszy* — "Amidst night's silence". It wasn't fair! *I* should have started that song! We all joined Wladzia in splendid harmony.

Anka started a second carol. I also knew a few verses of this one.

The third was started by Marian, and from this point on, I could only hum. We went this way for some time, but then everybody seemed to have run out of carols. There was a short moment of silence, and suddenly Szczepan reached into his pocket, pulled out something that looked like a little black prayer book, opened it, and began a new carol. He read the words, unable to decode the tune, and while doing so, he started chanting softly.

An incredible thought crossed my mind: "He looks like a cantor!"

At midnight, Wladzia wished us a merry Christmas and went to bed. The rest of the company remained at the table cautiously scrutinizing each other.

Then I risked, looking at Szczepan, "Sholom Aleichem?"

The faces at the table, the room, and even the Christmas tree brightened up.

And Szczepan answered, "Aleichem Sholom."

Our life in Rokiciny revolved around searching for raw foodstuffs and trying to convert them into edibles. We couldn't count on Szczepan's selling us food, because once he had learned that we were Jewish, his generous intentions toward us had given way to indifference — maybe even to annoyance. He could have used Polish neighbors as added security. Other Jews in the house could only mean trouble.

Thus, while the peasants, lured by Szczepan's bartering power, brought him big chunks of fresh butter, beef, pork and chickens, we combed the mountains to find a person who would be willing to sell us bread, potatoes, and eggs. Our diet had become not only scarce but almost strictly vegetarian. We borrowed a cookbook from Wladzia and tried to create meals, but whether because of a lack of some of the recommended ingredients or because of our inexperience, the most frustrating things were happening to us daily.

The book said that as soon as dumplings hit the surface of boiling water, they were ready. We plunged the promising balls of raw dough into boiling water, and two minutes later they hit the surface. Have you ever eaten hot, raw dough? So much for the dumplings.

Once I made what the book called potato pudding. It was supposed to come out as a cake. I mashed boiled potatoes, added sugar and eggs, poured the mixture into a baking mold, and kept it in the oven until a crust formed. I followed the book precisely: baking time, cooling time, everything. Then I brought it to the table and solemnly turned the mold upside down to slip my cake onto the platter. It was a tempting heap of mashed potatoes, but we wondered why I'd had to put all those eggs and that sugar into it.

In our search for food, we found a local family by the name of Kun. There was the father, who was ailing; the mother who suffered hyperthyroidism; and their seven-year-old son, Jozek, who badly needed a tutor to help him learn the three R's. I had become Jozek's teacher and the Kuns' frequent visitor. To show their gratitude, they had become our brokers in the matter of a food supply. From that point on, we didn't lack the staples.

It was much more difficult for us to get meat, but for a different reason. Once the Kuns got a rooster for us. He was beautiful, with his variegated elegant tail and his proud posture. He and I became friends at first sight. I sat in a chair, and Caesar (I immediately gave him a name) came to me, picked my knee with his mighty beak, and accepted bread crumbs from my hand. When I brought him home that day, he fought a bloody fight with Wladzia's rooster, won, and became the pasha of a twelve-chicken harem. I couldn't possibly eat Caesar!

Another time it was a baby piglet. There was a law that each newly born piglet had to be registered with the Germans, as the peasants had to surrender most of their pigs when they reached the age of slaughter. This was why a peasant would occasionally consider selling a suckling pig, to avoid raising it and then giving it away for nothing. When I brought Gudzio (this was a purely onomatopoeic name) home, he immediately became everybody's darling. Wladzia gave him a bath of soap and water twice a day, Anka tied a colorful ribbon around his neck, and Gudzio, like a little dog, trotted around the house all day long. At night, he slept with Wladzia. We couldn't possibly eat Gudzio, either.

Through all this, our relationship with Szczepan, Anna, and Marian was cordially aloof: we didn't ask for anything; they didn't give us anything. I often tried to analyze their interrelationship. What was Marian to Szczepan? What was Anna to Marian? My best guess was that Szczepan and Marian were fifty-fifty business partners, with Szczepan being the brain and Marian the muscle of the business. I never learned from Szczepan about himself, but from Marian's incomplete allusions I put together at least a part of the story.

Szczepan had been a lieutenant in the Jewish Order Service, and in that capacity he had been able to accumulate a little treasure. When the moment arrived when even the Order Service lieutenants were imperiled, Szczepan had made a painful decision: he himself put his parents and his only child on the train to Treblinka, thus making it possible for himself and Anna to escape alive. Whether he was able to salvage any of his treasures, I didn't yet know at that time.

Who was I to pass judgement on Szczepan? I only could hope that, had it been me, I would have gone with my wife, my child, and my parents to death. Or, maybe in a moment of miraculous revelation, I would have found a way to save everybody. But I wasn't Szczepan and there wasn't enough in common between us to understand his motives.

Anna was Szczepan's faithful shadow, and as I noticed with envy, she was also a good cook.

Marian had been a truck driver in the Polish Army. Caught by the invading Russians in 1939, he had been thrown in jail, where he had spent over a year and a half, and from where he had been freed by — the most incredible of all choices — the SS. They thought him a Pole, and he maintained this identity thereafter. Obviously he had known Szczepan from the smuggling era of the Ghetto.

Our intellectual life in such chance company was nil. Or was it? Because Anka had suddenly discovered a wonderful new world: the world of freely expressed, freely spoken about, and never glorified sex. Now, she talked about it, and she delighted in it. Szczepan had two gods: Mammon and Phallus. He lived by a rule once quoted by him:

> "There's no doubt at all, I gather,"
> Said Grandma, while gently rocking,
> "Fuck, my child, without love, rather
> Than you should love without fucking."

Anka, an exquisite representative of the upper middle class of Jewish society in Lvov, a girl, who in normal times might have lived a whole lifetime without ever hearing a four-letter word, was now indulging in the juiciest slang of the Warsaw streets, sometimes just to make me feel embarrassed. In front of Szczepan, she discussed the techniques of lovemaking that she had been using with me. She told everybody of the times when, frustrated by our wretched life, I would suddenly become impotent, leaving her for a night with unfulfilled desire. I felt that, had it not been for Szczepan's wife, Anka would not have hesitated to sleep in his bed.

During this time, I prepared my first notebook of wartime recollections in which Treblinka, of course, played a preponderant role. I set down names and dates, as well as I could remember them. However, I had enough common sense never to mention Martin. I finished my notes in the middle of January 1943 and hid the booklet behind one of the beams in the roof. It was also there that I deposited my Polish passport and three sets of false documents, leaving on me only the set issued in the name of Liwicki.

According to a local custom, the curate visited houses for Epiphany and blessed them. Wladzia set the table, and Szczepan provided mountain moonshine and home-made cookies. The priest, accompanied by a choir boy, arrived late in the afternoon, and we did everything Wladzia did: we kissed the curate's hand; we kissed the crucifix; we paid a contribution. And then Szczepan took over and invited the priest for a drink. We talked a little, and the father told us that he was a refugee from western Poland. Then he inquired about us. Our conversation was quite friendly, and when the priest was leaving, he said, "Well, I hope that everything is going to work out fine."

Jews, the people of the Talmund, are addicted to a strict analysis of the words people utter on important occasions. We analyzed the father's parting remarks, and we all agreed: we didn't like it at all.

At mid-January, Mrs. Kun came to see me. She was terribly excited, but I was sure it was only her thyroid. She wanted me to listen to the dream she had had the night before. In that dream, she had seen a group of men in uniforms. Black uniforms. The men were rough with us. Then they took us away. Mrs. Kun's eyes were popping out of her head as she was telling me her dream.

"You must leave here immediately!" the good woman cried. "Tonight!"

She clasped my hands and begged me again to leave everything and escape. And how was I to tell her that there really wasn't any place for us to run to?

Or was there?

Only a week before, a letter had arrived from Martin. He had written that Mr. Bergman had found him a nice, quiet job in a German bookkeeping firm. And that Mr. Bergman could help me, too, if I wanted to come to Warsaw — provided that I came without Anka. I hadn't even answered the letter.

My relationship with Anka had evolved into almost a purely business arrangement. I spent so and so much for food, she put her share in the book and would repay me after the war. Even our love life was a mixture of distilled love and grossly mishandled sex. Among all the lice that had infested me in Stoczek, one part still remained with me, the tiny body lice that enter under the skin and that tortured me from the inside. My whole skin ached, and sex had no attraction for me under the circumstances. Anka complained about it daily to Szczepan and Marian, but frankly, I was not sure whether she had a good cause for complaint: she was basically frigid. Nevertheless, nobody could tell me to leave her in the mountains and come to Warsaw for the good life. After all, I belonged to a generation that still admired such chivalric heroes as Don Quixote and Cyrano de Bergerac.

Moments after Mrs. Kun had left, Marian burst in from the porch. His eyes were huge with terror, and he screamed, "The Germans are coming!"

Chapter

7

RECAPTURE

Szczepan was perfectly cool. He was used to handling emergency situations. He asked that I hide with Anka in the attic, while he tried to discuss the matter with the police. The three of them, it seems had excellent sets of documents, and there might be a chance — who knew, a slight chance.

There was a little corner in the attic where a small wooden wall had been nailed to the beams, creating a little hidden space, similar to a tent. This was where Anka and I slipped, hoping for the best.

Soon voices were heard downstairs, and a minute later the head of a German shepherd poked into our hideout. A voice behind the dog said in German, "Get out of there!" The dog kept looking at me in such a funny way that I almost could hear him say "Jew! You're under arrest!"

We got out with our hands up. Standing there were a Schupo with an automatic rifle and a local policeman with a huge revolver.

Downstairs there was another Schupo and the rest of our group. We were searched, but not very carefully. When they looked into my right pocket, I kept my little bag in my left fist. As they went into the left pocket, I slipped the bag into the right pocket. They searched the pants, and then the boots. I suppose they were looking for arms. They confiscated our documents and asked the basic information:

name, religion, our reason for being in Rokiciny. For a moment, I thought that they might simply be looking for Poles hiding from being deported to German labor camps. In a way, such a development would be a salvation for us, as we didn't have much money. Of course Szczepan didn't see it with my eyes. He said to the Schupo who seemed to be responsible for the raiding party, "Could we, please, discuss it in private?"

The Schupo looked at him curiously. Then he ordered us and the other two out of the room. His conference with Szczepan mustn't have been successful, because they came out after less than five minutes. Szczepan was pale and somber; the Schupo was smiling maliciously.

It was twelve noon when we were put into two sleighs and driven to the Schupo precinct in Rabka, a nearby town. I looked sadly back. The chimney of Mr. Nowaczynski's cottage was smoking. My beautiful rooster Caesar, at the head of his harem, was looking at me from the middle of the snow-covered courtyard. The local policeman traveling in our sleigh said, in answer to a question by Anka, "The schoolmistress denounced you. But if you are Polish, you will join a group that is leaving tomorrow to work in Germany."

Now we were lined up in the Schupo precinct, facing a funny-looking, very short lieutenant. He stood astride, his hands on his hips, his chin up. He wanted to look us in the eyes, but each of us was taller than he, and he had to bend his body slightly backward. The first in line was Szczepan, a very tall man. The officer, swaying backward in front of him, yelled, "Jew?" and after Szczepan had given a negative answer, he slapped him in the face. In order to slap him, the officer had to stand on the tips of his toes. The scene was ludicrous.

He now stopped in front of each of us, slapping us for not being willing to admit that we were Jewish. I felt sorry for Wladzia. The poor soul was being slapped for no reason at all. She was crying bitterly and twisting her hands in desperation. She didn't know what had befallen her, especially as she still didn't think that any of us was a Jew. The officer slapped me, and I looked at him with pity. Although I am less than five feet seven inches tall, he still had to stretch on his toes.

When this part of the ritual was over, we were searched again. During the search, I slipped my little treasure bag into the leg of one boot, and they missed it. However, they did notice my Ring, which I had been wearing on my finger since my escape from Treblinka. They ordered me to take it off, and they confiscated it. I felt a pain in my heart. It was like being separated from somebody very close. They also took away our documents, which were being studied by two Ukrainian policemen. It puzzled me. There were never any Ukrainians in the Schupo station in Lvov. One of the Ukrainians called me to the desk, took my fingerprints, and compared them with the ones on my identity card.

"Can you see the difference?" he pointed out some lines to his colleague. "The two prints came from two different hands!"

I felt like laughing. I myself had put my imprints on this piece of cardboard, for which I had paid Manek one hundred zloty.

We were lined up once more, and the officer asked me why I was hiding in the attic if I was not Jewish.

"Because I don't want to go to any forced labor camp," I answered, hoping that I might provoke him into performing a small miracle and send us all on the first available train to Germany. Instead he jumped up to my face and slapped me again.

Then, seemingly satisifed, he said, "Now you'll go to the Gestapo Academy, and if they give you a clean bill of health, tomorrow you go to Germany!"

A local peasant dressed in the traditional garb of a Tatra mountaineer then took over. He must have been a plainclothes man, but he looked like a costumed ballet performer. He received some papers from the Schupo officer and ordered us to follow him, while two armed Schupo men marched behind our group. We approached a large, modern building, which had been a resort hotel before the war, and was now the famous Rabka Gestapo Academy, called "the School" by its students. The faculty of the School was composed of many German Gestapo officers and enlisted men. The student body was made up only of Ukrainians, from both the Polish and the Russian part of the Ukraine. The cleaning of the School was done by the local Jews, who were concentrated in a small labor camp attached to the School. There were about one hundred Jews in the camp, the rest of the Jewish population of Rabka and the surrounding region having been shot on the spot during the deportation action. The chief administrator of the School and the camp was a Gestapo officer by the name of Rosenberg, who could be seen taking his walk in the camp, a huge revolver in his hand and a police dog at his side. Herr Rosenberg, the story went, had personally executed a whole Jewish family in Rabka because of their sin of having the name of Rosenberg too. The School was known for one more thing: nobody had ever yet come out alive from its little basement jail, located directly under a long, low brick building: the pigsty, where the prize hogs of the Gestapo Academy were bred.

It is difficult to explain why the Rabka Academy was so little known to the general population of the region, while the Zakopane Gestapo Headquarters had the renown of being a death trap. Both were equally terrible and equally dangerous. It is my feeling that Rabka didn't have as notorious a reputation because its executions concerned the Jews only, while Zakopane specialized mostly in the peasants who failed to register a hog or sold foodstuffs on the black market.

As we entered the School, two students took over and ordered us to line up in the warm, spacious, and clean center hall. At first, we lined up along one wall. This was found to be unsatisfactory, and with kicks and blows, each of us was ordered to face his own little portion of the wall, away from the others so that communication among us would be impossible.

A student was crossing the hall, and I turned my head toward him. His hair was flaming red. He gave me a nasty look. He didn't like my green hair. With one hand he grabbed me by the hair and hit my head twice against the wall. I felt blood running down my nose.

"Did you want to ask me something?" he taunted me.

I thought I might as well.

"Are we going to be sent to Zakopane?" I asked.

"We have our own *zakopane* right here," he replied with sarcasm, and he pointed down. *Zakopane* in Polish means "buried."

Now I knew what to expect.

From a radio behind one of the closed doors came the tune of "Ritorna a Sorrento," sung by an Italian tenor.

We waited and waited. Each student that passed by thought it was his duty to kick me, or to hit me, or at least to curse me.

At last, one of the many doors around the hall opened, a student came to me, kicked me on the shin, and led me inside a room.

It looked like a doctor's office. It was neat, and it had shiny white walls, a little white table, a white chair, and a white cabinet. A German officer was leaning against the table.

"Your face toward the wall, and hands up," ordered the student.

"Are you a Jew?" asked the German.

"I'm a Pole."

Another student entered the room.

"Refresh his memory," said the German.

The two students stripped me naked. I noticed the leather whip in the German's hand. It whistled through the air, and I felt a burning sensation in my face. The German hit me again, and blood dripped down my cheeks. The students hurled me on the chair, face down, and tied me to it with a rope. They pushed a rag into my mouth, and the flogging started. The students were hitting with sticks, the officer with a whip. The first strokes were the most painful. Each stroke cut into my muscles, chopped them in half, and again in half, and soon I thought of my body as a heap of chopped meat, a juicy Tartar steak. The rest of the blows acted as anesthetics. They rendered my nervous system insensible, they paralyzed me. But even as they were tearing off pieces of flesh, something much more sensitive, much more important to my survival was being laid bare. This was the very moment when I realized that if I wanted to be able to take this degree of punishment, I had to detach myself from my body. I felt now like an indifferent observer, a bystander watching an execution. That heap of bloody flesh under the white wall was not me. The blows falling on that human body were not touching me.

Four sticks were broken, and the whip was torn. The students unfastened me from the chair, and I fell to the floor. Somebody pulled the rag out of my mouth.

The officer asked, "Are you a Jew?"

I said, "I'm Polish."

A student's heel smashed my nose. Through a red fog I saw the white room splashed with my blood, and my torturers above me. I could hardly weep or breathe. I moaned softly.

"Get him ready for the doctor," ordered the officer.

A student brought in a pail of water and poured it over me. The fog disappeared.

"Stand up!" ordered the German.

It took me an enormous effort to stand up and lean toward the wall. A student let in a civilian man, a Polish doctor.

"Examine this man!" ordered the German.

The doctor examined my penis.

"Well?" asked the German. "Is he or isn't he Jewish?"

"Not necessarily," replied the doctor. "As far as I'm concerned, he might very well be Polish." He wanted to help.

The officer wasn't satisfied. He sent the doctor away and sent one of the students to fetch another expert.

Now a skinny, poorly dressed creature was led in. He was the Kapo of the little Jewish camp in Rabka.

"You swine Jew!" the German addressed him. "See whether this here is a Jew!"

The creature bent over me, his eyes almost touching my penis. Then he stood at attention and reported, "This is a Jew, Herr Sturmfuhrer!"

The German sent him away. Now, looking at me mockingly, he asked, "Do you still think you are a Pole?"

I watched him silently. The students led in the rest of our group. They were lined up so that they faced me. The officer said to them, "This is what you will look like, if you don't tell the truth."

"I am a Jew," said Szczepan quickly.

"Me, too!" said Anna in a rush.

The students seemed disappointed. One of them said to Szczepan, "You and this whore are shrewd Jews. Saved yourselves a lot of beating."

"And you!" the German addressed Anka and Marian.

Both said they were Polish.

Now, Szczepan, Anna, and I were led out to the hall, while Anka and Marian stayed in the room. I noticed that Wladzia was missing. Szczepan told me that a Gestapo officer had taken her away in a car. She would have had no difficulty proving that she was Polish.

We waited a long time. Finally, the door opened. Marian came out almost crawling. His face was one open wound. The skin was torn off his feet. Anka's face was in a bath of blood.

The students took us out. It was already night when we crossed the yard, going toward a low, long brick structure. One of the students put a key into the lock and opened the door. Bad air blew at us.

"In!" yelled another student, leveling his rifle at us.

I was the first in the group to look into the dark doorway. A narrow, steep stairway led down to something that looked like a cellar.

I thought, "This is it. They'll shoot us now, one by one."

I closed my eyes and felt a blow over my head. I rolled down the stairs. The rest were thrust in after me. The door slammed. We were left alone in complete darkness.

"They haven't shot us," commented Szczepan.

While I was lying on the floor, unable to move, Marian was murmuring next to me, "The sons of a bitch. They're gonna blast us." The others groped their way around, trying to visualize the appearance of our new living quarters.

"It's like a small room," said Szczepan. "I can feel something in the middle. Something like a wooden structure."

"It's a death cell," said a woman's voice.

"Who's that?" Szczepan inquired.

"I'm a Jewish girl," the voice answered. "I'm lying on the bunk. Just wait a while, and you'll be able to see in the darkness."

Indeed, after a couple of minutes it became possible to discern the shape of a large wooden structure that occupied about two thirds of the small cell. This was the bunk the girl had referred to. We all lay on its hard boards. My body was aching everywhere, and I wanted to be left alone, on one spot, without having to move again. Szczepan, who remained intact, was most inquisitive. Now he could see the strange girl's shape huddled in a corner of the bunk. Szczepan asked her about the place we were in.

"They'll shoot us tomorrow," she said. "When I was brought in, they had a whole group ready for execution. They took them out, and I saw them being shot, one by one. I saw them from that little air hole, up there." She pointed to a tiny window with heavy iron bars on the wall opposite the bunk, immediately under the ceiling.

"So why do you think they'll take us tomorrow?" Szczepan wanted to know.

"Because they put a group together, and then they shoot them." She reflected for an instant. "No, maybe not tomorrow! Because you can tell when there's going to be an execution. They empty the cell, and a couple of Jewish women from the camp come down and wash it. Then they let everybody in and order them to undress. And then they take them out and shoot them. This was the way they did it when I arrived. It was all done before dawn."

"And when was that?"

"Three days ago."

"And you could see them?"

"Yes, I could see. When it's light out, you can see. The Jews from the camp dug the ditch. I saw them working. When the people were going toward the ditch, the Ukrainians kicked them and hit them. Then they made them kneel down, one by one, and a Ukrainian shot each person, with one revolver shot in the back of the head. I saw them falling into the ditch." Her voice was indifferent.

"How old are you?"

"Eighteen."

"The sonsofabitch!" moaned Marian. "They're gonna blast us, for sure!"

"I'm scared!" exclaimed Anna.

"Shut up!" Szczepan quieted her.

"I'm scared," said Anka.

"They hit you," I remarked. "Did you say you were Jewish?"

"No. I don't even know why. It will make no difference."

"But you do have guts."

"No. I'm just scared. What should we do now? Pray?"

I sat, with difficulty. The idea itself made me frantic. "Pray? For what? To whom? Do you really want me to pray? Then I'll pray to you!"

Engulfed by the ultimate fear, she yielded to the old superstitions. Closing my mouth with her hand, terrified, she exclaimed, "You are blaspheming!"

The door upstairs jarred open, and many heavy steps were heard on the stairway. The door to the cell opened, and a German officer entered, accompanied by three students.

"Whose is this Ring?" he asked. As he raised the Ring in his fingers, the students illuminated his hands with torchlight.

Anka recognized it. "It's his," she said, pointing to me.

The Gestapo man handed the Ring over to me.

After the party had left, an almost religious silence fell on the cell. By now, Szczepan, Anna, and Marian also knew the history of the Ring.

Anka whispered, "Maybe there is a chance?"

And I felt a soothing wave of hope wash my aching wounds.

It was almost morning, when the short Schupo lieutenant paid us a visit, accompanied by a party of six students. We were lined up at the foot of our bunk, and the lieutenant jumped from one to another, slapping generously and repeating a strange question, "Where is the sixth one?"

"What do you mean?" I asked, after he slapped me.

"You swine Jew!" he yelled angrily. "You made me almost believe that you were a Pole, and now you continue lying! A comrade of yours murdered the policeman we left to guard your cottage! Who is he? Where is he?" and he slapped me again.

It was amazing how I had got used to being slapped. Once upon a time, a year and a half before, a slap had been an insult. I would have become bloodthirsty at a slap. Now, it didn't matter. If it had mattered, there would be no way to remain alive.

"I don't know any sixth comrade," I said calmly.

"The Gestapo will take care of you tomorrow!" foamed the little man, as his party was leaving the cell.

It was an unusual complication. We all agreed that something like this could keep us alive for a little longer.

I felt very thirsty. It was Treblinka all over again.

"Nobody will give you any water here," said the strange girl. "No water and no food."

Szczepan grabbed the iron bar at the air hole, lifted himself to it, and collected some dirty snow from outside. I held the snow against my lips, treasuring it there to prolong the enjoyment.

It was early morning now. Szczepan, hanging at the air hole, was giving us up-to-the-minute news.

"A group of Jews are passing, with shovels," he informed us.

"Hey!" he yelled at them. "Are you going to dig a ditch for us?"

They didn't answer, but passed by as if they didn't know that we were in the cell.

A little later in the morning, they took Marian, Anka, and me upstairs to the interrogation room. The Gestapo pressed us for an admission that we were Jews, and for information regarding the mysterious sixth person. The case seemed even more complicated than we had thought. The local policeman guarding the cottage had been murdered all right, but nothing was missing from the cottage. The Gestapo insisted that what the sixth person was after must have been some documents linking us to the underground. This theory cost us further beating, whipping, punching, and kicking. This time they carried Marian downstairs because he couldn't walk any longer.

In this way they continued for two more days, taking us upstairs again, day and night, and day. There was not a drop of water for anybody, and not a crumb of bread. It really didn't matter anymore whether we lived or died, but I still didn't feel like giving in. I had been born a mystic, and now the return of my Ring made me cling to a straw of hope.

On the fourth day, they devised a new tool of torture for me. There were two pulleys fastened to the ceiling that I hadn't noticed before. The students twisted Marian's arms and mine and handcuffed us in the back. They tied ropes around our wrists, threw them over the pulleys, and pulled on them. Marian and I were hanging, our arms twisted back and up and to the sides. It was difficult to breathe. The Germans asked us the same question for the hundredth time, and again we stated that we were Polish. The students flogged our bare feet with sticks. At each blow, I felt that I was becoming shorter.

I thought a ridiculous thought: "They'll make me so short that they won't be able to find me anymore."

I heard the annoying question, "Where is the sixth one," and I felt like answering, "Between the fifth one and the seventh one." These were only thoughts that were never shaped into words. I made myself separate from me and again became a curious observer. There I was, with my arms up, my slim, massacred body stretched painfully, aching and bleeding. I looked like Christ. This idea made me feel better. It made me feel superior to them.

I looked up, to my right hand. The Girl on the Ring smiled softly at me. I didn't mind their beating me. Not any more.

The flogging finished, the ropes were lowered, and the handcuffs were taken off. The German sat me at the little table, gave me a piece of paper and a pencil, and ordered me to write what he dictated to me. He started the dictation: "I am an idiot Jew who wouldn't admit the obvious." He stopped the dictation, took the piece of paper, reached into the drawer in the table, and brought out my notes about Treblinka. He had known all along that I was Jewish and had played with me as a cat plays with a mouse.

That evening, we were all taken upstairs, but to a different room this time. There was our Gestapo prosecutor, the short Schupo lieutenant, another Gestapo man, and some four or five students. The prosecutor had our confessions ready and ordered us to sign them. Everybody signed, but when it was Marian's turn, he refused to sign. One of the students raised his fist, ready to make it fall on Marian's head. I stopped him.

"Marian, dumb Marian," I said to him. "Don't you see it's a game? Sign the paper. Save yourself further bruises."

Reluctantly, he did. But afterwards, he remained angry with me forever, insisting that if it hadn't been for me, he wouldn't have admitted anything and would have been let go, as a Pole.

The prosecutor stood up. He cleared his throat and read a lengthy paragraph about our guilt and our sentence. Now it had become official: we were to die at dawn.

We were spending our last night in our little dark cell.

Marian never stopped moaning, "The sonsofabitch, they got us now, and they're gonna blast us for good!"

The strange young girl was lying in her corner, indifferent to everything, unaware of the borderline between life and death.

Szczepan was fucking Anna who kept asking, "Is it all right to do it, before facing God?" to which he finally answered once and for all, "As long as I fuck, I live."

Anka was silently praying.

Coldly, I was chewing my entire life's bitterness.

The dawn found us still waiting for the supreme moment. A small detachment of Jews marched by the air hole, and Szczepan called at them, "Hey, are you here to dig our grave?" They carried shovels and spades on their shoulders. None of them looked toward the cell.

"If they're gonna blast us, let them do it fast," moaned Marian, "I can't stand the suspense."

"They won't do it today anymore," said the strange girl. She got off the bunk and urinated in the barrel standing in a corner of the cell. "They do it at dawn early. And a couple of hours before, they take away your things and clean the cell."

She was right. The morning came, and the day, and nothing happened.

Then the evening arrived, and there we were, still waiting.

Then, late at night, we heard many feet stomping on the stairway. I thought, "This is it," as Anka grasped my hand and squeezed it nervously. The door was unlocked, and five students entered the cell. One of them, holding a torch, lighted the cell. Two others carried a large metal container of hot soup. The fourth carried metal bowls, and a fifth a few slices of bread. I thought of the last supper. Marian moaned, "Now?" The students laughed heartily. No, not yet. They just wanted us to have a bite to eat. Only the Germans shouldn't learn about it. As we were eating, they watched us closely. I had on my head a fur cap belonging to Anka. One of the students said to me, "You look like a Cossack. You and that one," pointing at Marian, "are made of tough stuff. What a pity that you are Jews!" This must have been intended as the highest compliment he was able to bestow on anybody.

"Are you scared of dying?" another student asked.

I shrugged. "We all die, sooner or later. The date makes no difference to me."

"And you won't be scared when you see me shooting your comrade? And when I tell you to kneel down and to bend over the ditch, and you see your friend still kicking at the bottom of the grave, and you know that in another second it's going to be you — will you still not be scared?"

"It might just offend my sense of aesthetics," I replied. "It's an ugly scene that you've depicted."

"Like a real Cossack!" the student sighed with admiration.

"Will you let me go with him to my grave?" Anna begged.

He laughed aloud. "Are you kidding? You aren't going to a ball. There is nothing sentimental about dying. We're just making room for the better people. You'll die when your turn comes."

"She's looking for dignity in death," I explained. "But dignity cannot come from you. Each of us has to display his own dignity. You can kick me to death, but if I have dignity, my death will be dignified."

In the morning, a worker from the Jewish detachment stopped in front of the airhole. He gave a piece of bread to Szczepan who by now had taken up residence at the little window, the only link between us and the world. The worker whispered hurriedly, "The Ukrainians love you! Keep up the good work."

Half an hour later, the cell was unlocked, and the students asked everybody to leave. We were lined up against the wall of the pigsty, and an armed student was left to guard us. Another student ordered Anka, Anna, and the strange girl to get some pails of water and rags and to wash the cell. This time, it looked exactly the way the strange girl had described it, except that it was already morning, and we had not been ordered to undress.

While the women were cleaning the cell, our guard whispered to us, "I listened to the radio. Our troops are advancing to Smolensk."

"Who, the Germans?" I asked with indifference.

"No, the Russians," he replied. "They might be here in six months."

It sounded unbelievable. He, a student in the Gestapo Academy, referring to the Russians as "our troops!"

The girls finished washing the cell, and we were led back downstairs. It was now quite different from what the strange girl had told us at the beginning. She tried to modify her predictions. "Maybe they'll shoot us in the evening," she theorized.

But then, late in the afternoon, something new happened. A few Jews from the camp came running to our air hole. They were smiling and congratulating us.

"Great news!" one of them exclaimed. "A telegram from Berlin! They've commuted your death sentence to concentration camps!"

"Impossible!" cried Szczepan.

"I saw it with my own eyes!" said the Jew excitedly. "I clean the office, and I was there when the telegram arrived."

"And the Ukrainians," said another Jew, "the Ukrainians have already asked the commandant to let you stay in our camp. They love you!"

Less than an hour later, five students visited us. One of them, the bloodthirsty type, yelled joyously, "Hey, you sonsofabitch. So you'll stay alive! And I was getting ready to have the last waltz with you!"

It was obvious that he liked the idea of our staying alive. Another student added that it was true that the bloodthirsty fellow was to have been our executioner. He also told us that they would try to convince the commandant to keep us in Rabka.

In the evening, a few Jews returned to the air hole, bringing a bottle of milk and slices of bread. They said this would be the first time in the history of the Gestapo Academy in Rabka that anybody had come out alive from the pigsty cell.

The Ukrainians returned the next morning to bid us goodbye. The commandant, Herr Rosenberg, couldn't keep us in Rabka because we were political prisoners and belonged to the Gestapo headquarters in Zakopane. One of the students said that he would be our sentry on the truck.

"And it's good for you," he added, "because some of us are sonsofbitches and would have you travel in handcuffs and on your knees."

Home is where you hope and you suffer. We had got used to Rabka and felt sorry to leave the School.

The entire student body came to bid us farewell when we climbed on the truck that was going to take us to Zakopane. They wished us luck. They had really come to like us, or had got used to us the way we had got used to the School. It was with a sense of sadness that I watched the walls of the School disappear behind us. Once more, we were traveling toward the unknown, and the unknown was exactly what we were afraid of.

I knew Zakopane from before the war. It had been a beautiful summer and winter resort village, high in the Tatras, where Father had taken me for winter vacation.

The Gestapo Headquarters were located in one of the most luxurious hotels in Zakopane, and it was a pity that we had heard so many ugly things about this place. Now that we had come out alive from Rabka, I couldn't help thinking that a bad surprise might be awaiting us in Zakopane.

We were marched into a plush hall and then, one by one, registered by a Ukrainian. I wondered whether he, too, was a student, but I decided against it. This place was run by professionals. The Ukrainian noticed the Ring immediately and confiscated it. I did not suffer this time, feeling that the Ring had already played its crucial role in my life.

After the registration, we were led down to the basement. A tall, rawboned German turnkey stopped us in front of a small door.

"The men step in here," he ordered in a heavy, phlegmatic voice.

I sent a good-bye smile to Anka and entered a small concrete room filled with an intricate system of metal pipes.

"I'm afraid it's a gas chamber," observed Szczepan.

"I told you so." Marian moaned again. "I always said that they would blast us eventually." One of his eyes was black and blue, and he looked like a sad fox terrier. In spite of our problems, I felt like laughing at him.

As it turned out, it was not a gas chamber but an honest-to-goodness bathroom, where showers were showers, and where the turnkey soon fetched a Polish prisoner who acted as the prison barber, cut our hair short, and gave us a shave. He also told us that this was a transit prison, where the Jews had one cell and the Poles another, but where the Jewish and Polish women stayed together. He told us that there were very few Jews in this prison. He confirmed what we already knew, that now and then a prisoner was shot in Zakopane, especially political prisoners, but that by and large, the prisoners were shipped from here, once a month, to other prisons or concentration camps.

After the shower, naked and dripping wet, we were led into the Jewish cell. Our clothes had been taken away for delousing, and now, in my hand, I was squeezing the little bag with my treasure: still a couple of thousand zloty, Mother's ring, and Father's gold pocketwatch. I didn't know whether Anka still had the large diamond ring her mother had left her, and that she didn't want to sell because of its special sentimental value. The cell was nothing but a corner of the basement corridor, where two walls of steel bars had been installed, thus creating a small, windowless, and now completely dark room. Somebody in the cell invited us to sit on the floor. Somebody else noticed that we were naked and cold and gave us a rag to cover ourselves. After a while, I started discerning human shapes. I inquired how many they were and was told there were three men. One was Reichert, the other Krug, and the third one who spoke like neither a Jew nor a Pole, but in a local dialect, was introduced to us as Janosik.

Reichert was the most talkative. He told us that there were no bunks in the cell, but that we could sleep on the floor almost as much as we wanted to. The light would go on, he said, four times a day: twice when they brought the soup, and twice when they led the prisoners to the toilet. Reichert was satisfied. If they let him stay here until the end of the war, he would have no objections. The only problem in this cell, he said, was Janosik, with his white woolen Tatra suit and his continuous crying for his lost freedom and his beloved mountains. He was so decidedly a local native that Reichert still didn't know how the Germans ever did understand that he was Jewish.

"Other peasants sold us out!" cried out Janosik. "Me and my mother. They were envious because we had a cow, and a good small farm, and an inn."

"Can you hear his speech?" said Reichert. "All the time, he cries for his mountains and says that he'll die from nostalgia."

"Where did you come from?" asked Krug.

"From Rabka," replied Szczepan.

"Nobody has ever come alive from Rabka," said Janosik. "This sounds like a miracle!" There was a minute of silence, then Janosik added, "I have dreams, strange dreams. Airplanes and old shoes. It all means going in transport. They'll take us someplace one of these days."

"They sure will," said Reichert. "They always do."

Janosik couldn't be dismissed so easily. "But it could be a bad transport. My dreams are telling me it's going to be a good transport. I also dream of black bread."

Dreams, symbols, superstitions. Man will use any means he can create to make his survival more probable.

The turnkey arrived with soup. Dazzling light flooded the cell. We quickly examined each other. Janosik looked like a legendary Tatra robber. Reichert was very short and husky and had a pair of light blue, smiling eyes. Krug was the most Jewish of the three, in his black suit, with the curved shoulders of a Talmudic student and with a serious, pale face.

The soup was soon eaten, the bowls taken away, and the lights turned off. I wondered about the women. Reichert assured me that they were all right.

"Janosik's mother is there," he said. "She also looks like a local peasant. They are treated well. The turnkey is a nice person. The girls call him Grandpa. He never hits or curses, and when he's drunk, he sings Lili Marlene."

The cell was silent. Only Janosik sobbed about his mountains.

"What do we do now?" asked Szczepan.

"You sleep," answered Reichert.

"Is it already night?"

"I don't know. But does it make any difference?"

I don't know how many hours or minutes had passed. The light flooded our cell again, and Grandpa threw in our deloused clothes.

Then it was dark again. I had the uneasy feeling of a pig being kept for fattening up before the slaughter. For two days it had been soup, and sleep, and toilet, and sleep, and soup, and sleep, and toilet, and sleep. For amusement, we told each other our recent histories. Until now, I had thought that I was the only one who had something to tell, but I had discovered that every Jew alive could write a book of adventures.

Reichert had come originally from a little town near Posen, in the part of Poland that currently belonged to the Third Reich. The few Jews who lived around Posen before the war had been deported to various Polish ghettos some time ago, but Reichert had preferred to remain the master of his own destiny. He had left his little store, where he sold kerosene and herrings, and had escaped with his family to the Tatra mountains. Here, however, the Germans caught up with them. Reichert lost his family, but he, with several other men, among them Krug, had been able to escape into the woods. It had been tough at the beginning. They had slept on the trees or in the bushes and had eaten raw potatoes stolen from the fields. Slowly, they had started organizing themselves. With tools stolen from the peasants, they had built a large underground room, which they furnished with bunks, chairs, and a table taken from empty Jewish homes. They had easily obtained the bedding, the pots and pans, and the silverware they needed by robbing the peasants who had robbed the Jews. The day they brought an iron stove into their room, the room became an apartment. They cooked their meals at night, so that the smoke coming out of the underground chimney wouldn't betray them.

Later they made a deal with a peasant, who every few weeks sold them potatoes, flour, and lard. The agreement was that they would leave him the money in a prearranged place in the bushes, and he would leave the food at the same location. In this way, the peasant didn't know where they lived and couldn't betray them, whether willingly or by coercion. For a while, they had had the feeling of total security. All they had to do was to sit still and wait for the war to finish.

But their food supplier told them one day that other peasants in the village had learned about them and had denounced them to the Gestapo. The peasant offered them shelter in his own hut. They accepted his offer, and that same night, the Gestapo came to pick them up. While their companions fought back Reichert and Krug tried to escape, but they were caught by the local police and thrown into a local jail. Here Reichert hanged himself, but Krug, an orthodox Jew who didn't approve of suicide, cut his rope. The Gestapo had taken over from there. Now Reichert and Krug had become some sort of celebrities. German journalists and Gestapo officers had taken them several times to their underground home, taking pictures and asking them a thousand questions, fascinated by the Jewish Robinson Crusoe story.

After having told us all this, Reichert added, as an afterthought, "And the peasant who denounced us is in the other cell, for stealing our belongings."

On the third day, Grandpa started taking us, the people from Rabka, one by one, to interrogation upstairs. First, went Szczepan. They didn't bring him back to the cell before they took Marian, as they wouldn't allow us to communicate during the interrogation. I was the last to go.

Grandpa brought me into a warm, small office where a pretty German girl sat at the typewriter, and a middle-aged, politely smiling Gestapo officer paced the room.

The officer stopped in front of me, and said, "And now, we'll be asked a few questions, and we'll answer them in the most truthful way we know."

He spoke in a soft voice, and his speech was delivered in a patient, slightly mocking fashion, as if he addressed a child.

Suddenly I felt inside me a wave of warmth. This man didn't want to continue destroying me.

And the officer concluded, "And should we try to hide the truth, then there is a Wonder Stick in our closet, whose magic touch will make us tell the truth."

I assured him that there was nothing more to hide, and that I had already been touched by a Wonder Stick. At this, he threatened me jokingly with a finger and said, "Careful now! We shouldn't talk like this, should we?"

The questioning started. I repeated my Treblinka adventure and the odyssey that followed. To account for the time between my escape from Treblinka and my arrival in Rokiciny, I told him that I had been practically living on the Warsaw-Cracow train, using it as my hotel, my restaurant, and my business office. The officer wanted to know my real name, but this was about as far as my truth telling would go. He asked about my family, and I assured him that no one was left alive. I told him that the other prisoners from Rabka were just chance acquaintances, including Anka. This was the agreement we had made, before leaving Rabka.

As I was telling my story, the pretty typist was efficiently putting everything down. The questioning shifted now to the personal belongings of the group, and to my amazement, I learned that the Gestapo had found buried in the garden of Mr. Nowaczynski's cottage a chest filled with jewels, gold coins, and foreign money. The officer asked whether it was mine. I said I wished it were, and I thought that Szczepan had been more than ready to face adversity. I didn't believe that all this wealth could have belonged to Mr. Nowaczynski. The officer proceeded to enumerate my own belongings, saying that I could claim them when the war was over. And at this point, he took the Ring into his hand. It lay in his palm, still mysterious and fascinating. The sweet face of the Girl was turned toward me. Her eyes were soothing me.

"Whose is this Ring?" asked the officer.

Automatically I extended my hand, and he put it in my palm. The Ring was once more with me.

My personal characteristics followed.

"Five foot seven, one hundred ten pounds, slim," dictated the officer. "Big ears."

The girl corrected him, "Medium ears."

"Green eyes."

"Blue eyes," corrected the girl again.

"What is the matter with all these Jews," the officer feigned desperation, "that each of them has to have blue eyes? Don't they realize that it messes up the entire Aryan theory?" He looked at me carefully, and said to the girl, "Do you really think that his eyes are blue?"

"Yes," she said, "blue."

I intervened: "My mother used to call them sea blue."

He looked with pity at my beaten-up face and said, "And that blue under your eyes? Would you call it *gendarmerie* blue?"

With self-assurance, I answered, "Gestapo blue, sir, Gestapo blue."

This was the only police interrogation of my life that left me with a feeling of warmth and friendliness. I didn't know the officer's rank or his name, and I regret it. But I did know that, although a Gestapo man, he was a humane person. Even my cell, after this interrogation, suddenly seemed bright and joyous.

The days were passing, and we, undisturbed, could feel our wounds healing in the cozy darkness of our cell. My smashed nose was still painful, and my broken ribs bothered me when I was breathing. All this damage had been done during the very first questioning in Rabka. The soles of Marian's feet were still terribly ulcerated, making it extremely difficult for him to walk. He worried about the transport. Nobody knew much, but one thing was sure: sooner or later we would go on a transport.

We discussed the transport and tried to imagine where people like us could be sent. Polish prisoners had it better: they would be shipped to Germany, where they would work for a farmer until the war was over. Could we hope that, by force of gravity, we would be shipped with them? We hoped — a little — even against hope. To work for a farmer would probably mean to have enough food. Food was all that counted at that moment. Our bodies would heal much better if we had more food. It was the first time in months that I had felt really hungry.

But maybe the Poles would go not to Germany but to a concentration camp. Then, by the same force of the same gravity, we would go there, too. I daydreamed (if it can be called so, in that pitch-dark cell of ours) about going back to a concentration camp. The only one I knew was Treblinka. All right, we were being reshipped to Treblinka. I had a plan ready. I knew how to escape, so I would escape from there. But this time, I would carry with me a lot of money and diamonds. I'd come out rich and would have no difficulty surviving in Warsaw.

But what if the Poles went to a concentration camp and the Jews were shot in Zakopane? After all, my Gestapo officer could be as nice as they came, but he did not make his own decisions. After having passed through all this, we still might be blasted, as Marian liked to say.

And so, between speculations, daydreams, and dream interpretations, another week passed. Or was it more than a week? Or maybe less. I didn't know. In the darkness, time lost its validity. There was no today, no yesterday, no tomorrow. There was only the here and now, and the transport.

One morning arrived that was different from all the rest of the mornings. Grandpa turned on the lights, opened our cell, and told us to take with us everything we had. To me it meant my little treasure bag into which, this time, I had slipped the Ring. I had hidden the bag in my left boot. In the corridor, the other prisoners were already waiting, the Poles separately, and the women separately. Janosik recognized his mother and broke out sobbing. I waved a quick hello to Anka, and she smiled back at me. The girls were kidding Grandpa, and he was trying to give them courage. Nobody knew yet where we were going, but we were about to start on a transport. Soon we were put into formation, by twos, and were handcuffed to each other. I was paired with Reichert, Janosik with Krug, and Marian with Szczepan. We were marched outside, where we were embraced by the crisp, cold, dazzling whiteness of the snow, and the purest blue of the sky of Zakopane in mid-February. We climbed into a couple of trucks and were driven to the railroad station. Here we were led into a separate car — not a freight car this time, but a regular third-class passenger car — where we were kept isolated from the civilians. This was how the normal, not-imprisoned population was to be known to us from this point on: the civilians.

And the train departed.

It was beautiful to watch the mountains and the forests and all that snow along the train's route. We were moving slowly, almost reluctantly, as if the train itself had not yet made its decision as to our final destination.

We knew that we were traveling along the very foot of the mountains, but we didn't know whether we were going westward or eastward. Going to the west would mean Germany, would mean a farm, would mean plenty of food. Going to the east might mean working at Smolensk, digging ditches, suffering cold and hunger. This was how we, the prisoners, commented on the train's movement. The train stopped in Nowy Sacz, the capital city of the Principality of Podhale, and another group of handcuffed prisoners joined us. They had no idea either where we were going. The only ones who knew were the Ukrainian guards, but they wouldn't tell us. And so, between hope and desperation, between the dream of a farm and the nightmare of Smolensk, it was already late in the evening when the train stopped, and we were told that this was where we would be getting off. I looked outside. It was impossible! But this was it. We were in Cracow.

As we were crossing the empty streets of Cracow, which were covered with dirty snow, I was trying to recapture my past in this city, so recent and yet so far away. We crossed the Planty Park, and I imagined seeing Wanda. Down there, in the maze of the streets, other friends might still exist, maybe free, maybe bearing new names and identities. And sweet, old Mrs. Gunther, and her daughter who called me the green parrot. Now my hair was all gone, and when it became long again, there would be no trace of green in it. It would be all gone and forgotten, just like my own past.

I remembered returning to Lvov. I had found it hostile. Not so Cracow. I thought that I would still like living here, if, through a miracle, my handcuffs were to disappear at this very moment. But handcuffs don't disappear, unless you're a magician. How I would have liked to be a magician! How I would have liked to have the power to make things happen, and then unhappen!

Our column marched wearily until we'd reached a complex of concrete buildings surrounded by a tall, massive wall. The windows were almost entirely covered by something that looked like flat steel armor, fastened to the wall, and running up at a seventy-five degree angle, so as to leave an opening at the upper part of the window for the light to penetrate into the rooms. Or rather, the cells. Because this was the notorious Gestapo prison of Cracow, the ancient, the dreadful Montelupich.

The heavy steel gate in the wall opened to swallow us, and to spit us out into a grim corridor, where the Ukrainians, in pitch-black uniforms, searched us thoroughly, then ordered us to wait, faces toward the wall, for the warden to receive us. Again, I was lucky. My little treasure was still with me.

The time was passing slowly, and nothing was happening.

Then the women were marched away. And again, we waited.

It was already two in the morning when the warden saw us in his office. He wore his Gestapo uniform, but because of the late hour, he remained half-dressed only. His jacket was wide open, he wore no tie, and his big belly was overflowing his tight riding trousers. And he looked Jewish, by God, did he look Jewish! He had a fat, huge nose in the middle of a three-chinned face, and his thick lips with a cigar in between and the heavy lenses of his eyeglasses made him look exactly like a caricature of a Jew in the *Sturmer,* the official Nazi newspaper. He held his hands in the pockets of his trousers as he questioned Szczepan: "What's your name?"

"Cohn." That was the first time I had heard Szczepan's real name. But I wasn't sure at all whether it was real. Szczepan must have had too many sins on his soul to be willing to disclose his real identity to the warden of a Gestapo prison.

The warden was in a joking mood, in spite of the late hour.

"Do you know the story of the little Cohn?" he asked Szczepan.

There were so many cute anti-Semitic stories about the little Cohn that the answer chosen by Szczepan was the most sensible one: "No, sir, I don't know."

The warden didn't tell him the story. He asked instead, "Do you know why you're here?"

"For impersonating a Pole."

The warden laughed with joy. Szczepan's answer brought to his mind another cute anti-Semitic story. He said, in German, "Itzik, Itzik, sei nicht witzig. Was ist rund kann nicht sein spitzig", which means, "Isaac, Isaac, don't be smart. What is round can't be a dart."

Good-humoredly, he threatened Szczepan with a finger and proceeded asking us the routine questions. When this was over, a Ukrainian came with a basketful of sliced bread and gave each of us a slice. Then the Poles were separated from the Jews and led away. We waited a bit longer, but it was our turn now, and we were all taken to the same cell.

I am still not sure, even today, whether that large basement room — at night covered with straw bags for sleeping, and during the day filled with seventy-nine standing prisoners — should be called a cell. However, this is what it was called then: the Jewish cell of Montelupich. It had two long, barred windows, covered from the outside by the slanted steel aprons. In the left corner of the cell, opposite the entrance door, stood three large garbage cans that served as a toilet. Once a day, the prisoners were led to the real toilet, outside the cell, and this was when they also emptied the three cans. There were no bunks here; as I have just mentioned, the prisoners slept on straw bags laid neatly one next to the other, wall-to-wall, so that they covered the entire floor of the cell. Two prisoners slept on each bag, and the sleeping room was so skimpy that when one man wanted to turn over, his entire row had to turn with him. In the morning, the prisoners piled the bags neatly in one corner of the room and swept the floor mirror-clean, so that during his daily inspection of the cell, the German guard wouldn't pretend to have tripped over a forgotten strand of straw and dispense bodily punishment to a selected representative of the cell for an attempt on his life.

The addition of our group signified that there would now be some ninety prisoners in the cell, and even less breathing room than before. Our group had been swelled substantially by the addition of one man from Zakopane who — God only knows why — had stayed there in the Polish cell, and the group of several men who had joined us in Nowy Sacz. At this late hour, we didn't expect anybody to make room for us, so we just lay down under the toilet cans, trying to get some sleep before morning.

Early the next morning, one of the old prisoners called the reveille. Everybody got up. The straw bags were collected and neatly piled, one on top of the other, in the far corner of the cell. Two dilapidated brooms were then produced, and two men swept the cell. We didn't know anything about this prison's routine, and we expected that somebody would give us some pointers.

A pale, gaunt young man with an old woolen stocking on his head asked me, "Where do you come from?"

"Zakopane."

He yelled, "Zakopane" and other prisoners surrounded us.

Most of the prisoners around us were pale, like the young man with the stocking decorating his head. Most of them were emaciated and had festering wounds on their faces, heads, and bodies, and some could hardly stand on their feet. Many were dressed in torn rags, like the Warsaw Ghetto rachmunesim. One prisoner struck me as being completely different from the others, inasmuch as he was obviously strong and healthy, but even his garb was quite unusual: he wore the uniform of a German soldier. The idea struck me like lightning. I remembered my first trip to Cracow with Wanda, and the news given me by the barber.

I asked the man, "Weren't you a soldier in the German Army?"

He answered heatedly, "Not a soldier. A noncom! That sonofabitch of a schoolmate of mine sold me out!"

"Son of a gun! But why did you decide to come home for your furlough?"

"How did you know?"

"The barber told me."

"Who?"

"Never mind."

I had to stop the conversation, as an unusual commotion could be felt in the cell.

One of the prisoners, perhaps the head of the cell, said to us, "There is going to be an inspection. Stand in the back row, and do whatever we do. When we say our morning prayer, move your lips, as if you were praying, too, so they won't punish you."

We fell into five rows.

The key jarred in the lock, and the door opened. We straightened to attention. Two Ukrainians in black uniforms entered, along with a German. As they were coming in, the German noticed a piece of straw on the floor, made believe that he had stumbled over it, and yelled, "You Jewish swine! Again you have made an attempt on my life! You do it every day! I'll teach you how to clean your cell! I'll teach you how to sweep the floor! Rrraus! Rrraus! Out! Out!"

As we trotted out into the corridor, he whipped us over the shoulders, and it became a question of honor for me to run under his nose swiftly enough so that his whip wouldn't touch me.

In the corridor, we were ordered to jump, froglike, its full length,

Frank Stiffel's mother and father

Truskawiec, Poland, 1925.

Pola and Martin Stiffel, after their marriage

Lvov, Poland, July, 1939.

"Mourning Mothers"

Illustration by the author's daughter, Aurora Stiffel Berman

"The Mussulman—Liberation of Auschwitz"
Illustration by the author's daughter, Aurora Stiffel Berman

Frank Stiffel (fourth from the right, second row)
and some of his group of Jewish survivors

Rumania, 1945.

Ione Sani

Rome, 1946.

Ione Sani and Frank Stiffel at their marriage ceremony

Rome, 1946.

Ione, Frank, daughter Aurora, and dog Kira

Rome, 1948.

Frank Stiffel and his family today

Photo by Steve Berman

maybe some thirty meters, and as soon as we reached the end, we turned around and jumped toward the opposite end. As we jumped close to the German or to the Ukrainians, they hit us as an incentive for greater speed. The exercise lasted perhaps a half-hour, and then we returned to the cell.

We fell into five rows, as at the beginning.

The German, standing in front of us, yelled now, "You filthy sinners! You have taken your morning exercise without first saying your prayer! I'll forgive you this time, but in the future, God will not forgive you! You'll pay dearly."

He waited awhile for his rage to simmer down. Then he ordered shortly, "Morning prayer!"

The cell intoned in unison:

> *Wir Juden sind schuld an allen,*
> *Am Krieg und Unglueck,*
> *Wodurch das Deutche kostbare Blut*
> *Vergossen werden musste.*
> *Fluch ueber uns Juden!*

> We the Jews are guilty of all,
> Of war and distress
> Through which the costly German blood
> Had to be spilled.
> Curse on us, the Jews!

I was moving my lips, as if I were reciting the prayer along with the rest of them. It was unbelievable that here I was, here we all were, catering to the sick whim of a madman. I was drowning in shame.

They left us alone after the prayer. The time had come for us to start meeting our other comrades in distress. I looked around me. The closest to me was a distinguished-looking, bald-headed, slim fellow, probably twenty years my senior, wearing riding trousers and boots, like myself. He was the one who had stayed in the Polish cell at Zakopane. I introduced myself. He shook my hand.

"My name is Stefan Blankenheim. Where are you from?"

"From Lvov."

"So am I! So am I!" He seemed to be truly happy to have found a landsman. He reflected a little and added, "And that young girl in Zakopane, Anka, was she with you?"

"Yes. But how do you know about Anka?"

"My wife was in the cell with her. And I had a system through which my wife and I communicated. She told me there was a girl from Lvov."

We definitely had various points in common. Besides, he was warm and friendly, and we made an instant friendship.

"How come you were in the Polish cell?"

"A complicated story. I'll try to tell you. As you well understand, we could not continue staying in Lvov after the Umsiedlung had begun. So we got ourselves very good Polish papers, and I applied for a job in Zakopane. I'm an electrical engineer, and as it happened, they could use me. I worked for a German company. They had respect for me, and it looked like an arrangement that was going to last forever. And a few weeks ago, a crash! My wife was recognized by a former student of hers — she's a teacher — a Ukrainian fellow from Lvov who came looking for a job in Zakopane. They took me in, but with all the respect and everything — I don't know, maybe they themselves couldn't believe I was Jewish — anyhow, they kept me in the Polish cell."

Somehow there was a strange kind of strength in this physically delicate man, a strength that was contagious. When he spoke, there never was any stress on doom and death; the only inevitability that Stefan had accepted was the inevitability of survival. It is difficult for me to tell whether my philosophy of life was similar to Stefan's before we met, and that was the reason for our friendship; or whether I contracted it from him, like a benign disease, and our friendship was just its unavoidable result. All I know is that from that time on, I knew I would survive, no matter how hard my trials might still be.

Meanwhile, Reichert was giving juicy explanations about Janosik, who had attracted even more attention than the German noncom, and Marian and Szczepan told our story of Rabka and mine of Treblinka. Suddenly, the seventy-nine prisoners lined up around the cell and did something I would have never expected. One by one, each of them stepped up to me and touched my arm, or my shoulder, or a piece of my clothing. In their plight, they had become superstitious, and now it seemed to them that their luck might change because I, a survivor of Treblinka, maybe a messenger of God, had come to this cell.

While this was going on, the man who seemed to be the leader, gave us some quick information about what to expect next. The coffee would shortly be distributed. A guard would give each of us a bowl of the hot liquid out of a barrel, and it had to be drunk by the time the prisoner again got to the head of the line. Any unfinished liquid would be poured over the culprit's head by a second guard watching the line.

When the coffee was served, everything went according to our guide's description. Obviously the routine of everyday life was unshakable. Two Polish prisoners brought a large metal barrel of boiling-hot coffee. They put it at the door to the cell, and while one Pole handed to each prisoner a metal bowl (many a bowl actually being a chamber pot), the guards ladled out the hot liquid, which the prisoner, walking fast along the line of other prisoners, tried to drink quickly. He joined the line again, at the end, and kept drinking, while the line moved all the while toward the coffee barrel. As soon as the first prisoner had reached the barrel again, he had to surrender the bowl, and whoever had not finished his "breakfast" by the time he reached the barrel again had the remaining part of it poured on his head. If, by ill chance, some of it dirtied the floor, the prisoner washed it up and, when the distribution was over, received ten strokes of the stick on his behind. These prisoners were always hungry, and yet they hated the food distribution; if given a choice, perhaps they would have chosen hunger over these meals.

After breakfast, the door was locked again, and I hoped that this was the end of our difficulties for the day. But the old timers informed me that this was only the beginning. In fact, some twenty minutes later, the German who had previously stumbled on a straw ordered us out for our daily gymnastics. We fell into two rows and were led into the prison's courtyard, which was covered with snow and mud. Here, we fell into a single line and were ordered to do the frog jump, just as we had done earlier in the corridor, except that had been for punishment, and this for health. We squatted and jumped and squatted and jumped, one behind the other, around the prison yard, in slow, rhythmic movements that became spasmodic each time any of us had to jump in front of the whip-yielding German. After a half-hour, we were ordered to stand up. In mud up to our knees, we stretched, thankful for the intermission.

A new order was yelled out: "Air drill. Flier!"

We fell in the mud, face and all, while the German circulated among us, whipping to the right and to the left and yelling, "Head down! Cover your head!" forcing us to immerse our heads and eyes in the cold mud. My nostrils were filled with the slimy dirt when he called off the "alarm." Now he wanted us to run, and as we were running, he would call, "Flier!" and down we would go, and "Alarm off!" and up we would get to run again.

When this was over, the German said that he had promised the cell new games. So now, the games. We formed two lines. At his signal, the last prisoner in each line quickly crawled between the legs of the men lined up in front of him and, having reached the beginning of the line, stood up with his legs astride, while the last man began his crawling. When the race was over, the German chose the winner and gave him a cigarette as a prize.

Now, at a trot, up the stairway and down the stairway, and along the corridor, we returned to the cell, out of breath and soaked to the bone.

Once in the cell, Stefan Blankenheim fell to the floor, pale and in a cold sweat. I took his pulse. It was very quick and uneven. He was in a bad state. As he lay on the floor, his teeth chattered. He had a heart condition, but he had decided not to give in. I gave him a massage and made him feel relaxed.

Somebody asked, "What are you, a doctor? A medic?"

I said that I had a pretty good idea of how to take care of some diseases, and a man let down his pants and showed me his buttocks. One half was just one enormous festering wound.

Somebody commented, "Many of us have been fixed this way. It's from the beatings." I shrugged. What could I, or anybody, do? There wasn't even a piece of gauze. A short, plump man in his early forties, dressed neatly and with care, said that he might be able to get some dressing and a disinfectant. He didn't look like one who has just come back from an hour of gymnastics.

Another prisoner explained, "Mr. Bielinski is not like the rest of us. He's an old convert, a Catholic. He has privileges."

And Mr. Bielinski kept saying that he might try to convince a guard to get us a few things, but that money was needed for a bribe. Or some jewelry.

I hid behind a toilet can and got out some money. I didn't want anybody to see my little bag. I gave a bill to Bielinski, and he promised to talk to a guard at lunchtime.

At noon the lunch was served. Actually this was the dinner, because at six in the evening we would receive only another bowl of coffee. Again, as in the morning, two Polish prisoners brought a barrel of potato soup, which was boiling hot and which, like the coffee in the morning, had to be consumed while the line of prisoners was moving forward. Lack of spoons and the thickness of the soup made it very difficult to eat fast. Holding my chamber pot by the handle, I tried to pour the boiling mass into my mouth, with the least burning possible. This whole business of eating at a trot, and eating from a chamber pot, to boot, was humiliating. But that was exactly the point. They wanted us to feel humiliated. I thought of the first day of the Jewish armband in Lvov, and the dignity that the people wearing it displayed. I applied their example to the chamber pot. And it wasn't a chamber pot any longer. It was a mug.

Stefan was a warm person, and he liked people. The first benefit of my friendship with him was the new ease with which I learned to approach people, following his example. The next few days were spent in talking to our cellmates and learning more about them.

The skinny young man with a stocking on his head was one of a group of forty who had been associated with the nightclub bombing. None of them knew any details of the affair, or if they knew, they wouldn't tell. Their leader was kept in a separate cell, incommunicado. They had occasional news about him from the Poles who brought the coffee, and it seemed that he was getting the most sophisticated set of tortures available to the Gestapo, and that he still had not talked. I wondered what there was to talk about, if the bomb had already been exploded, forty youngsters had been caught, and the leader was in prison, too.

I thought of my own experiences in Rabka and the unknown sixth person, and I knew that as senseless as it was, the Gestapo wouldn't accept anybody's word without submitting him to these trials.

All the youngsters were extremely proud of the fact that they had been involved in something that had kept the Gestapo on their toes. When I asked the skinny youngster whether they belonged to an organization or were backed by anybody, he swelled his emaciated chest proudly, swept his arm around as if he wished to embrace the entire group of forty, and said, "We are Zionists."

When he said this, an odd feeling seized me, as of a remembrance of a very old and very dear emotion: "I am Israel, your people, oh God, Amchu." Your people were not dead yet.

All signs seemed to predict that our stay in Montelupich would be a lengthy one. Here nobody had dreams about old shoes and airplanes, and even Janosik had to admit that it might be a long time before he would see his beloved Tatras again. This spurred Stefan and me into arranging some sort of cell activities that might help us a little to avoid complete stultification. We felt that even a slight intellectual interest could at least partially obliterate the destructive effect of the physical damage that was being inflicted on us daily. When we advanced the idea to the cell, we were surprised by the response. The Zionist group was all for it, as one man, but even the others, the unorganized individuals, seemed to acquire a new will to live at the mere suggestion that we might do something for our brains.

The question remained: What was it to be, and in what way was it to be conducted? We took a poll: they wanted to learn about electricity from Stefan, and about anatomy and the French language from me.

In order to conduct regular classes, we needed paper and pencils, and here Bielinski proved to be of great help. This little plump man took himself very seriously. He had converted to Catholicism some twenty-five years before, and the guards considered him a natural liaison between them and the Jewish cell. When he discussed a bribe with a guard, it was not a bribe, but a little souvenir for the guard's fiancée, and he always stressed in a very serious way the importance of his request for gauze and peroxide, or for pencil and paper, by saying: "Kost was kost!" — "The price is no barrier!" — knowing darn well that we could command very little money.

Thus, the day came when we had medical supplies to treat the festering wounds and school supplies to begin the classes. When I think of it today, it seems unbelievable that people under these most trying circumstances, uncertain of what the next hour would bring them, sick, hungry, and scared, found within themselves enough fortitude to be interested in learning.

During our stay in Montelupich, there was an occasional new arrival of two or three people caught with false papers. Each kept swearing to God that he was not a Jew, each kept clinging to the last straw of hope, against all the odds. Occasionally, they had news from outside. The ghetto in Cracow had been liquidated, and the few remaining Jews were concentrated in a labor camp nearby. New arrivals from Cracow told us about a Jewish collaborator, a certain Spiro, who was the head of whatever remained of the Jewish comunity. Some had news from the Warsaw Ghetto: it had shrunk to a mere nothing. Nobody knew of Lvov. The disaster was general. A universal cataclysm. And in the midst of it, these new arrivals still tried to survive by assuring us, the Jews, that they weren't Jewish, as if Bielinski might tell the guards, "Look here! That one there is an honest-to-goodness Pole! Let him go! Kost was kost!"

Occasionally, a Polish prisoner would slip in a note from Stefan's wife, and we learned that the women's cell had a Zionist group, too. Once a note came for me from Anka. She was now enthusiastic about Zionism. A glorious idea could survive in a rotten cell of Montelupich. But we, the people, would we survive to carry it out, to offer it

to the world at large, to say, "Anachnu po!" — "We are here!" —
We are here to stay, and you cannot deny us our existence.

There was no talk about a transport, but one day our Zakopane
group was taken to the showers. This was something new and
unusual: nobody in the Jewish cell was ever allowed to take a shower.
While we were in the bathrooms, we heard female voices at the other
side of the wall, and soon we established contact. They were the
women from Zakopane. I even exchanged a hello with Anka, and she
assured me through the wall that she was now an ardent Zionist.
After the shower, we were taken back to the Jewish cell, but not for
long. Late in the morning, our names were called again, and we were
told to take with us all our possessions. When we left the cell, we
didn't know where we were going, and the other prisoners didn't
know either. But they were superstitious. They knew that the man
from Treblinka could have only good luck, and that those who went
with him would have good luck, too. But those who remained behind
would have bad luck. Clustered in the middle of the cell, our fellow
prisoners wished us a mute, sad farewell.

We were taken into a small cell with one bunk in it, on which was
seated a Polish prisoner, a husky man of twenty-five. He greeted us
with a smile, and said, "So, we're going to Auschwitz."

I felt a cold shiver running down my back. Auschwitz. The man at
Treblinka had said, "This is Treblinka. It's even worse than Auschwitz." Then, I hadn't known the first thing about either camp. Now
I knew of Treblinka from first-hand experience and of Auschwitz
from what other people had said. I knew that Auschwitz was mainly a
Polish camp, and that Poles suffered there a lot. I didn't even realize
that Jews might go to Auschwitz, too.

Now this Pole, Tomasz, told us that we were going to Auschwitz,
and he knew what he was saying. This cell was the Auschwitz cell.
From here, one could only go to Auschwitz. He showed us all the
signatures on the wall of those who had passed through this cell on
their way to Auschwitz. He himself had already been there, and now
he was going back. The SS had brought him to Cracow to be a witness
at another Pole's political trial. He had done his witnessing, and now
he was "going home." He referred to Auschwitz as home.

Szczepan asked him about the Jews, and Tomasz said that there
were many Jews there.

"Once you survive," he said, "you have it made." And he clarified
this statement. Not all Jews were given a chance to survive. Most

were led directly to the gas chambers. But Tomasz was optimistic about us.

"The Jews from large Jewish transports go to the gas, but this is a very small transport, and it is a mixed one." He meant Poles and Jews. "I don't think they will gas you. You are probably political prisoners."

Tomasz's reasoning seemed sound and lucid. We probably got out of Rabka alive because they thought we were involved in politics. We decided that we might be allowed to live in Auschwitz, and we put our signatures on a wall. This time, I wrote my real name.

Early in the afternoon, we were led out to the yard, where a tarpaulin-covered SS truck waited for us. The women were brought from their cell, and we waved hello. Two German SS men searched us, and my little treasure still remained with me. One by one, we climbed on the truck and sat on the two benches running along its two sides. Two German SS men took seats at the ends of the benches and laid their automatic rifles on their knees. The back of the truck was closed, and we left Montelupich.

What does one think about, while traveling on an SS truck from Montelupich to Auschwitz? We were forbidden to talk. We were even forbidden to look at each other.

I could feel Anka's presence somewhere on the bench where I was sitting. "What have I done to you, Anka," I thought, "taking you out of the ghetto in Lvov to put you through all the torture of Rabka and the indignities of Montelupich, only to see you transported to Auschwitz, to something which might be only a hair less bad than Treblinka?" I felt guilty about having wanted to help her. I felt guilty because I hadn't joined Father when he was going to his death. I acted the coward, and all I had attained was a short delay, seven months' delay, and now I was going to die anyway. At least I could have died with him, with honor, and wouldn't have to feel guilty now.

And I was thinking of the kids in Montelupich. What guts. What beautiful guts! They struck back. Why didn't I ever strike back? God, how I hated myself! I was helpless. We were all helpless. We were so helpless, because we were thinking all the time. This Pole here, this Tomasz, he was not helpless. He was rough, and strong, and happy with his life in Auschwitz. He did not waste his time thinking.

The truck came to a stop, the back of it was opened from the outside, and our two SS men jumped down. There was an exchange of words, and some documents changed hands.

We were ordered out. Quickly we jumped down and lined up. The women were assembled in a separate group and were led away. Anka and I had just enough time to smile at each other.

We were standing outside of the main camp of Auschwitz, also known as Auschwitz One, or the Mother Camp. There was a long wooden barrack to our left, where the administration made its daily accounting, and a large, wide iron gate in front of us with an arch above it, on which was written in neat Gothic characters, *Arbeit Macht Frei* — "Work makes you free."

A new chapter of my life was about to begin.

CHAPTER
8

AUSCHWITZ

IF THERE WERE STILL ANY DOUBTS in my mind regarding my position in this world as a Jew, Auschwitz was the place to dispel them. Here I was an animal, and a thing, and a fuckin' this, and a fuckin' that. And here these lessons did not come directly from the masters. They were given to us twenty-four hours a day by a well-trained staff of other prisoners, who had climbed to their triumph in camp society over the bodies of thousands of the poorest of the poor, the proletariat of Auschwitz.

Perhaps I can give a better idea of Auschwitz by comparing it to a city, or a country, or the whole world. Auschwitz One was the capital city of a complex of camps known as Auschwitz. It commanded a whole province of minor camps, such as Buna, Janina, and Kobier.

Birkenau was the ugly twin of Auschwitz One. Birkenau was where the gas chambers and ovens were; Birkenau was where the regular Jewish transports were taken, their occupants to be gassed immediately or to wait their turn in primitive ugly wooden barracks. The bunks of these barracks resembled huge baker's racks and, because of the overpopulation of the place, held five people per bunk.

The society of Auschwitz was a prime lesson in social stratification. The German word for prisoners is *Haftlinge*. The Haftlinge of

Auschwitz One were like city dwellers, whereas the Haftlinge of the smaller camps were similar to either provincials or peasants. In the *Lager* ("camp") itself, the population was divided into those who worked in the Lager and those who were marched off in the morning to various work details outside the Lager. The former, the insiders, were considered better off than the latter.

Within the inside population, there were many, many layers. The highest-ranking functionary among the Haftlinge was the *Lagerkapo*. These functionaries were usually chosen by the German authorities from among the German Haftlinge, or from Poles who claimed German blood. There was one Lagerkapo per camp, and he was responsible to the SS *Lagerkommandant* for the internal order of the Lager. He ruled the Lager through a battery of *Blockaltesters* ("barrack elders"), each of whom was responsible for the affairs of one block, or barrack.

Every Blockaltester had a *Schreiber* ("secretary"), who was actually his alternate and his liaison with the population of the block. Such secretaries weren't officially recognized, as this was a purely nepotistic appointment, often assigned by a homosexual Blockaltester to his lover.

Each block had several rooms, or wards, each housing one hundred or more Haftlinge, and each room had a supreme ruler, called the *Stubendienst*. *Stubendienst* translated into English simply means "room servant," the implication being that a Stubendienst was responsible for cleaning his room. Well, this he was, but he didn't do it with his own hands; he used two, three, or four helpers, according to the size of the room, who were responsible to him for the cleanliness of the *Stube*. These helpers, like the secretaries of the Blockaltesters, might be the Stubendienst's lovers or might serve him personally in various other ways, like doing his private laundry, cooking his meals, cleaning his shoes, and making his bed. Occasionally a helper massaged his boss, read his palm, or told him jokes. Such helpers' main duty was to make sure that each Haftling in the Stube kept his own bunk in perfect order. They did, however, sweep and wash the floors, unless a less well-to-do Haftling wanted to do it for them in exchange for a bowl of soup.

All the rest of the inside population were just simple workers. However, they were much better off than their brothers who worked outside the Lager. Haftlinge who worked outside could be easily recognized because their uniforms and shoes were the worst in the Lager; and their bodies, especially their heads, were full of festering wounds inflicted on them by their foremen and their work-detail

Kapos. Such Haftlinge, after the evening report, usually went to the ambulatory clinic to have their wounds dressed and would leave the clinic with a white paper bandage around their heads, which, in combination with their skinny bodies and starved faces, gave them the appearance of desert nomads. This probably accounted for the name by which this ultimate proletariat of Auschwitz came to be known: *Mussulmen,* or Muslims.

The outside society of Auschwitz had its own functionaries, Kapos who left the Lager in the morning — at the head of their work details and tramping to the rhythm of a joyful march played by a Haftlinge orchestra at the main gate — for a day of hard work and terror, and reported at the gate in the evening that so and so many of their Mussulmen were being brought back on stretchers, dead from heart attacks.

These Kapos, like the Blockaltesters, had their assistants, usually boys in their teens, whom they called *Pipels* (pronounced Peepels), and who served the Kapos' personal needs, often including the sexual ones. The work of the Mussulmen was controlled by the foremen, who were responsible to the Kapo, and who, to avoid problems of their own, wielded wooden clubs with unheard-of generosity. However, the gods of an outside *Kommando* ("work detail"), the real masters of life and death over the Mussulman population were the SS *Posten* ("guards"), who decided who would be killed that given day and in what way. The killing could be done either by a Posten, in which case it was usually "Haftling shot during an attempt to escape," or by the Kapo at a Posten's recommendation, in which case it would be a killing by beating, which was known officially as a "heart attack."

As in the regular society we all know, in Auschwitz "The squire could be recognized by his boots," as an old Polish proverb pictures-quely suggests. The Haftlinge were dressed according to their means, with the Mussulmen wearing the worst rejects of the Lager's gray-blue striped unforms; its most dangerous, oversized shoes, which were made out of hard, thin leather and heavy wooden soles, and which were inevitably missing the shoestrings; and the much-too-large, torn, striped caps, the so-called *Mutzen.* The functionaries dressed according to the degree of their importance, the most impor-tant ones having their clothing custom-made by one of the better Haftlinge tailors, and the least important ones having, at least, custom-made Mutzen. In fact, it was usually by the Mutze and the shoes that one could tell a functionary.

Besides the main Auschwitz society, there was a separate society, all of its own. That was the *Krankenbau* ("hospital complex"). The hospital was composed of four blocks.

Block 28 consisted of admissions and infirmary; x-ray; the laboratory; oto-rhino-laryngology; dentist; optician; pharmacy; dietary kitchen; two small patients' wards; a ward upstairs where the *Krankenpflegers* ("medics") — or, for short, *Pflegers* — lived; and the morgue in the basement, where the bodies collected from all over the Lager were deposited during the day, to be loaded on a crematory truck each evening.

Block 19 held patients suffering from contagious diarrhea, an endemic disease of which most Mussulmen would die.

Block 20 hosted psychotics and gave shelter to sick Haftlinge with important contacts in the Lager, who were assigned to this Block for a prolonged period of recovery.

Block 21 specialized in surgery. Occasionally, a patient with diarrhea might be referred to the surgery block, or vice versa, depending on whether he had a contact that could help him in one block better than in the other.

In addition, there was Block 10, a mystery block inhabited by women only,where, the rumor went, all sorts of gynecological researches were being conducted by German doctors, who were liberally helped by some of the Polish and Jewish Haftlinge doctors.

The Krankenbau had its own hierarchy of functionaries with official titles like KB Kapo (Krankenbau Kapo), who was the chief doctor (Haftling doctor, that is), and the KB Blockaltesters, Stubendienste, etc. But for all practical purposes, almost anybody working in the Krankenbau was a functionary. Even the lowly Pflegers working in the morgue were considered functionaries. Each and every Krankenpfleger was well-off enough to have a pair of good shoes, a well-fitted uniform, and a smart Mutze. And these three possessions definitely put them in Auschwitz One's class of functionaries.

Even before entering the Lager, as we were standing in front of the gate, I could tell that if there was a similarity between Auschwitz and Treblinka it must be one of philosophy rather than structure. While Treblinka presented to the inexperienced eye a picture of utter chaos, Auschwitz struck me as a place where rigorous discipline was the overlord. Through the gate, I could see the main street of the Lager, a wide, straight avenue, bordered at both sides by a row of neat, two-story brick buildings, the blocks, and I could guess that there were other such buildings behind these, farther to the right and farther to the left. It was still early enough, and the bulk of the Haftlinge population was still at their outer Kommandos, so that the Lager appeared almost empty and sleepy.

As we were led in, a dwarf wearing a Lager functionary's uniform ran out of the sentry's booth and cursed us in excellent German. I didn't know what his function was, but in his ugliness, both physical and verbal, he appeared to me like Cerberus, the uncomely guardian of Hades.

Once we were inside, our SS guide handed our papers to a tall, handsome Haftling, and from that point on we were in the hands of our equals. The man led us into a wooden barrack standing parallel to the portion of the barbed wire beginning at the gate. This was the barbershop and the bath. The functionary who led us in now ordered us to undress and to surrender everything we had. To stress his order, he dispensed a powerful slap to Marian. We all undressed as quickly as we could, as there was little doubt that the man meant business. Stefan kept his belt in his hand. It cost him a blow on the head, and the man seemed curious to know whether Stefan had difficulty understanding German.

Then the chief barber, a tall, slim man in a white cotton suit, came over and asked each of us to open his mouth. Thinking at first that he was a doctor, I said, "Aaah!" but he just called me a fuckin' Jew and asked whether I was hiding any jewels in my mouth. I wasn't.

We remained completely naked, and there was nothing more I could do to protect either my treasure or the Ring. I left my little bag in my left boot and mentally said good-bye to Mother's ring and Father's gold pocketwatch, as this was the last part of them to leave me — and I also said, "We'll meet again," to the Girl of the Ring, as I was about to start the independent life of a Haftling, where I would have to count on my own power of cunning rather than on the purely metaphysical help of my friendly spirit.

After the chief barber's private inspection was over, we were ordered into an adjacent room, where several Haftlinge barbers were impatiently waiting for us. One of them grabbed me by the arm and pulled me to his bench. He had bright red, very short hair, and his face was covered with freckles; I disliked him as soon as I set eyes on him. As he was clipping my hair, he asked pertinent questions. Where was I from? And how come they had brought me here from Lvov? And when he heard I had been brought from Rabka, he wanted to know what I had been doing in Rabka. While he was shaving my armpits, he wanted to know what it was like to live on the outside now. And when he finally reached my groin, he realized that I was Jewish. He drove the blade of his razor into my pubic skin, yelling, "You're a sonofabitch of a Jew!"

I said I had thought that here, in a concentration camp, all prisoners were equal, and he laughed, "All, except you fuckin' Jews! You'll get here what you deserve!"

When the tonsorial operation was over, we went to the shower room. I had no confidence in the German concentration camp showers, and now that the redheaded Haftling had said that we would get what we deserved, I looked with suspicion at the shower heads, expecting them to start emitting gas at any moment. But it was a legitimate bathroom. All the shower heads, some twenty of them, were operated at the same time by one Haftling. We all stood under the shower, and the Haftling turned the water on. It was ice cold, and it made us hiss. He obliged and turned on terribly hot, almost boiling water. He seemed to be having great fun with us. Another Haftling came in carrying a gray paste in a pail. He packed some of it into my hand and said, "Soap!"

Our showering was over, and we were chased out of the barrack. Naked, barefoot, and wet, we were assembled in formation in a side street, between two brick barracks. Stefan was philosophical about it.

"We'll catch pneumonia," he said, "and this is obviously what they want us to do."

Some time later, another Haftling came out of one of the brick barracks and yelled to somebody we couldn't see, "Hey, Hans! Bring out the shoes!"

A fat, toothless creature came out carrying a bunch of shoes. They were made of hard, stiff sheepskin, and had heavy wooden soles. They had no shoestrings and were much too large, even for a man Szczepan's size. Hans sympathized with us. He said that the shoes would move as we walked, and that our feet would get ulcers unless we "organized" shoestrings. Organizing things, organizing food, organizing one's life — *organizing* was probably the most important word in the Lager's vocabulary. I would soon learn that organizing meant getting; and doing; and making somebody else do; but most of all, it meant stealing without being caught. Because if you were caught stealing, then you were a thief, and as a thief you would be severely punished. As an organizer you were respected.

I put on my shoes and had to admit that Hans was right on all counts. They were awfully large, and as I walked, their vamps cut into my ankles like two razor blades.

Another Haftling took over and ordered us into still another barrack. We lined up in the corridor, and two Haftlinge gave us our Lager clothes: torn drawers and shirts, socks in pieces, and the striped uniforms, composed of pants, jackets, and caps, which were either much too big or much too small. We looked like a bunch of circus clowns. We tried to exchange the ill-fitting pieces of clothing among ourselves but it didn't help. The lack of shoestrings and belts was one of the most depressing factors in our new situation. I suppose that it was carefully planned this way, so that our descent on the humiliation scale, started with the soup served in the chamber pots at Montelupich, would smoothly continue at Auschwitz.

We were kept in the corridor for over an hour, while a continuous heavy traffic of Haftlinge went by us. Some of them were dressed better than others; some had uniforms made of a heavy material that looked like wool, while ours were of thin cotton, with rips and patches all over them. Each Haftling had a little colored triangle on his left chest and on the right leg of his trousers, and a number printed under the triangles. Most of the triangles were red, but some were black, and a couple of times I saw a green triangle and a purple one. A man passed by who had a yellow triangle inverted on top of a red one, together forming the Star of David. This was the first Jewish Haftling we had seen in Auschwitz.

Tomasz, the Pole who had come with us from Montelupich, was well known in this barrack. Everybody greeted him, everybody slapped him on the shoulder, everybody was nice to him. He was at home. Szczepan asked him to tell us about Auschwitz, and Tomasz, evidently in a good mood, gave us a lecture.

"The most important thing in Auschwitz," he said, "is to have a function. Become a barber, a Kapo, a Schreiber, a Stubendienst, or a butcher — it makes no difference. As long as you have a function, you'll organize, and you'll be well off. Otherwise you'll become a Mussulman and go with the smoke."

He also told us that each color of the triangles had a meaning. For example, a red triangle denoted a political Haftling; a black one an *Aso,* or *Asozialer Element* ("antisocial element"), a term that could be applied to many kinds of people: saboteurs, homosexuals, prisoners of war; a green triangle meant a convicted criminal; and an inverted yellow over red, a Jew.

A tall, well-fed and well-dressed Haftling, definitely a functionary, ordered us to follow him. Tomasz explained that this was the Schreiber, and that we were now going to the *Schreibstube* ("administrative office") where our documents would be prepared. The office was a large room with several desks and a large legend in German on one of the walls: "Jeder Mensch hat seinen . . ." next to some paintings of birds. Stefan guessed that it must mean that every man had his bird, his cuckoo: that every man was crazy. We were called to various desks and were asked to repeat our personal characteristics once more, while the secretaries wrote them down, crosschecking them with the information we had previously given in Zakopane and in Cracow. Finally, a short, plump Jewish Haftling took over, and pricking my left forearm with a little tool resembling a fountain pen, he tatooed my new lease on life, the number that from this point on would be me officially, instead of my last name. He stamped on me in his neat, legible handwriting: 107455. I call this number my new lease on life because it was an indication that I would be kept alive for the time being — I had become a Haftling.

We were ordered to fall in, and a big, fat Polish Haftling took us to the very first two-story brick block of the Lager. This was the *Quarantane*.

A description of the physical qualities of the Quarantane is simple: it was a two-story barrack with quite a few rooms filled with rows of three-tiered wooden bunks, each of which was equipped with a skimpy pallet and a torn cotton blanket. Each bunk was intended to sleep two Haftlinge. Off the corridor there was a large bathroom with a concrete washing trough running the entire length of its wall. The block had its Blockaltester, a five-foot-tall yelling and jumping German with the green triangle of a criminal; its Polish Schreiber, who was a homosexual, and whose Pipel, a young German Gypsy, served as both his alternate and his lover; and a full staff of Stubendienste and their various helpers.

A description of the Quarantane as an institution of indoctrination is much more complicated. Its general goal was, of course, to brainwash us so completely that we would forget that we had ever been human. But let us not forget that whenever two human wills clash and one is made to submit to obedience by the other, it still remains unclear whether apparent yielding really means yielding. The Germans had a plan, according to which we, the Jews, were to be reduced to the level of heartless, brainless, and soulless robots, and they proceeded to work on us to this end. But had they taken into consideration the possibility that we, the Jews, also might have a plan, and that our plan might have been to cheat the Germans into believing that we were becoming just what they wanted us to become, while remaining intact within ourselves? Therefore the Quarantane was a game of poker, where they played the card and we played the bluff.

Our fat new leader took us to his Stube and ordered each of us to pick a companion and a bunk, and to wait near the bunk till he gave us further information. I took a bunk with Stefan, and we waited for further instructions. Finally the Fat One came back and told us that he was the Stubendienst, and that we were to maintain our bunks in perfect order, with the pallet neatly squared and the blanket beautifully flat over it. Everybody sweated hard, trying to satisfy the Stubendienst, but there was not enough straw in the pallets to make them square, and the thin, torn blanket just didn't want to cover the shame of the mattress. The Stubendienst walked from one bunk to the other, giving us pointers and hitting us over the neck.

This went on till midnight. Then the Fat One got disgusted with our lack of progress and ordered us to undress, as our new clothes were being taken to be deloused. Our protests didn't help, and soon the entire population of the Stube was naked and shivering. It was cold, and we were hungry and tired. Some of us sat on our bunks. The Fat One slapped those who were seated and ordered all of us to stand in the narrow passage between the two rows of bunks, each pair next to their bunk. Some hours passed by. An old man from Czechoslovakia fainted. The Studendienst and his helpers took him out to the corridor and laid him down on the concrete floor. The man regained consciousness and began moaning. The Stubendienst yelled, "Shut up, you fuckin' bum!" The man moaned until dawn. By then, our clothes had returned from delousing, and the Czech was dead. His body was left in the corridor. *"Leichenkommando* will pick him up later in the morning," said the Stubendienst. *Leichenkommando* was the morgue detail.

We had hardly had time to lie down when the reveille came. While the Stubendienst still slept in his bunk, his helpers went around the Stube, pushing us out of our bunks and chasing us out to the bathroom to wash up in the trough. We washed up rubbing our torsos with ice-cold water; then we put on our uniforms and went back to yesterday's lesson: making a perfect bunk.

At seven in the morning, the Stubendienst picked two of the new arrivals and sent them with a helper of his to the Lager kitchen, from which they brought a barrel of hot water with a few herbs in it. Breakfast was ready, and we lined up for it. The tea was served in soup bowls, one bowl for two Haftlinge. The procedure was similar to that in Montelupich: with our bowl of tea in hand, Stefan and I joined the end of the line, trying to share and to finish the liquid before we reached the beginning of the line, where we had to surrender the empty bowl.

After breakfast, the two Haftlinge who had brought the barrel from the kitchen washed it in the trough and carried it back to the kitchen. The rest of us were ordered to remain in the yard, because we were forbidden to go inside the block during the day. We were supposed to learn the Lager routine, and the lessons were to be given to us in the yard.

Our Stubendienst was our instructor.

"First," he informed us in his phlegmatic voice, "you sonofabitch civilians will learn how to salute your superiors."

We fell into formation, and the Fat One yelled: "Mutzen aaauf!"

This meant that we were to put our caps on our heads, and that this operation was to be performed in one harmonious movement. The next command was, of course, to take our caps off in a similar motion.

"Mutzen aaab!" yelled the Fat One, and our right hands brought the caps down to the seam of the right leg of our trousers. The operation itself was not difficult. But because of the linguistic and cultural variety of our group, harmony of movement proved difficult to attain. As one grabbed his cap, someone else already had his down to his leg, and a third trainee had lost his head covering in midair. The Fat One was radiant. With his roaring but mocking voice, he referred to us as the sonofabitch fuckin' intelligentsia and the whorish professionals, and he kept schooling us in the *"Mutzen auf!" "Mutzen ab!"* movement for over an hour. After that, promising an early return to the salute exercise, he switched to regulation marching. This, in itself an apparently simple activity, also proved to be a complicated chore because, not having belts or any other support for our pants, we kept losing them during our march, which brought derision on the culprits as well as blows over the shoulders. After a good hour of that, we were dismissed for the time being.

Finally, we had time to rest. At least this was what we thought. We were not allowed to enter the block. It was very cold, and as one long wall of our block was drowning in late winter sunshine, it was logical for us to gather under that wall in groups of three and four, trying to lend some of our body warmth to our fellows. As we were thus enjoying the moment, a window opened on the second floor, and the Blockaltester, the funny-looking short German with the green triangle of a convicted criminal on his chest, yelled, "Disperse, you sons of a whore!" This we did, only to gravitate back to the cozy wall after a couple of minutes. This time, a window on the first floor opened, and the Blockaltester beat us from there with a stick. He dispersed some of the people for a moment, but most of the crowd remained, preferring the risk of a stick to the certainty of freezing. After a couple of minutes, we were again all gathered under the wall. The Blockaltester, meantime, had devised a completely new and shockingly refreshing system. He had opened several windows on the second floor and with the help of his Schreiber and the Pipels, he poured pails of ice-cold water over our heads. He achieved what he wanted: we gathered in the middle of the yard, where his antics, we hoped, couldn't reach us. At first, small groups of three or four were formed, standing close to each other back to back, and sharing their natural body warmth. Soon the groups clustered together, and a huge human oven had been formed. Back to back, belly to belly, we were warming up ourselves and our neighbors.

But the Blockaltester and his helpers didn't give in so easily. They were now around us, all over us, with their sticks, beating the group indiscriminately as they shrieked at us that this sticking together was definitely unhealthy for us fuckin' bums.

As soon as we had dispersed, our Stubendienst, the Fat One, took over. He made us fall into formation, and he delivered a short speech. We were about to perform our first Auschwitz work assignment. The yard was covered with little pebbles — he called them "dirt" — and he ordered us to clean the yard by picking up these pebbles, one by one, with our hands, and piling them up in one corner of the yard. It had to be done quickly and competently, because Herr Blockaltester wanted his yard nice and clean.

This was a monotonous job of bending and picking, and picking and bending, and piling, and piling, and piling. When the yard was about clean, the Fat One emerged from the block, looked around, and yelled, disgusted, "You sonofabitch fuckin' intelligentsia! What do you think you are doing?" Somebody explained that we were doing what he had ordered us to do a couple of hours before. He gave the man who had answered a sonorous slap on the face and patiently explained that we, the fuckin' new arrivals, hadn't understood a word of what he had said, that his order had been to pile the pebbles in the opposite corner of the yard. So we transferred our pebbles, one by one, to the corner he indicated.

At noon, the Stubendienst and the Schreiber took four Haftlinge and went with them to the Lager kitchen to fetch dinner.

They returned with two wooden barrels of turnip soup. The soup was mostly hot water, with a piece of turnip here and there, often rotten, of the giant kind the Polish peasants fed to the pigs. The Haftlinge formed a double line, and each pair of men received one bowl, into which the Schreiber poured half a ladle of soup, smacking his lips, and calling it wiener schnitzel. No spoons were given, and we were faced with a vital problem: no one wanted his companion to have a spoonful of soup more than he got. I had Stefan Blankenheim for a partner, and we didn't have this problem: he wanted me to have more because I was younger and needed the food because I was still growing; I wanted him to have more because he was older and weaker. But most of the people counted the gulps their partners swallowed; with the width of their thumbs, they measured the diminishing level of the liquid; and in many instances, the partners resorted to jumping at each other's throats.

When the distribution was finished, a little soup was still left at the bottoms of the barrels. When the Schreiber called us to form for seconds, Stefan and I didn't even try, seeing that there might have been soup enough for five people, whereas the line must have included twenty times this many.

The men in the line had become rough by now. They were pushing each other, so that the strongest occupied the most advantageous places. The Schreiber enjoyed the moment. Like an Angel of Justice, he moved along the front of the line, here and there hitting a shaven head with his long ladle, now and then kicking a shin that got in his way. Finally, he decided that these men didn't deserve any seconds because they had been so greedy. He looked around and his eye fell on a tall, terribly skinny Jewish Haftling.

He beckoned to him and said, "You are a nice sonofabitch. Come! The soup is all yours!"

The man didn't know what had hit him. Beaming with joy, he ran to the barrel, stuck his bowl and his head into it, and tried to collect the most nourishing part of the soup, which was always at the bottom of the barrel. Standing so, with his torso in the barrel and his behind at its edge, he was too much of a temptation for the Schreiber. There was a swift pull at his legs, and the lucky creature landed in the barrel, his head in the soup, his legs up in the air. As a reward for this moment of distraction, the Schreiber allowed him to carry the barrel to the trough and clean it there, before taking it back to the kitchen.

After dinner, the Stubendienst let us into the block to wash the bowls and to use the bathroom. After that, we were again back in the yard to study our Lager routine and to spread the pebbles all over the yard again, to make it once more thoroughly dirty.

We then fell into formation, four abreast, and were introduced to another daily activity of the Lager: the *Lausekontrolle* ("louse control"). Every Haftling took off his jacket and shirt, pulled down his trousers, and approached the Schreiber, whose helpers proceeded to examine the seams in the clothing and our groins.

It was almost five when this was finished. By that time, work details of regular Haftlinge were returning to the camp from their day's work. Our Stubendienst ordered us to fall into formation and explained what was going on in the Lager.

"This is going to be the evening report," he said. "Nobody is going to bother with you here, in the Quarantane, but you must do everything the regular Haftlinge are doing, so that once you leave the Quarantane, you'll be well prepared for Lager life. At this time, all the Haftlinge stand in formation in front of their blocks. They are counted by their Blockaltesters, who then report the number to the SS *Scharfuhrer* ("sergeant") responsible for the block. All the Scharfuhrers then report to the Lagerkommandant, the SS head of Auschwitz. This is done at the plaza near the main gate. If the account is correct, the report is over soon, and the Haftlinge are allowed in their barracks. But if something goes wrong, you'll be kept outside at attention, even if it should take a whole night—and believe me, that has happened many times!"

Our first Auschwitz evening report happened to be a short one. And we were the happiest group of people alive when we were finally allowed to enter the block, wash in the cold water, and rest in pairs on our hard and narrow bunks.

In a way, however, our nights resembled our days. In the Quarantane, the lights were never turned off for the night, and at some time during the night, a foot inspection was conducted by the short Blockaltester and his Schreiber. They went from bunk to bunk examining our feet for cleanliness and for socks. It was cold, and many a Haftling thought it a good idea to sleep with his socks on. This proved not to be such a good idea after all. Anyone who was caught was dragged out of his bunk, made to undress completely, and ordered to take a full bath in the trough, which was filled with ice-cold water. While he was taking a bath, another culprit who was waiting his turn scrubbed him with a hard rice brush.

Finally, at one in the morning, we were left alone by the official Lager authorities. Still, it was difficult to sleep because of the unofficial rulers of Auschwitz: lice by the thousands; fleas by the millions; contagious diarrhea, which made people run to the bathroom almost incessantly; and the king of them all, the ever-present companion of all big wars, His Majesty the Typhus. I wouldn't know what to answer today should anyone ask me which was the most terrible. They were all terrible, all very intimate, and all very constant. You slipped your hand into your sock and brought out a fistful of fleas. You scratched your shirt and found lice under all your fingernails. You felt a pain in your belly, and a minute later your pants were full of a foul, semi-liquid, bad-smelling mass. You got a fever, and you knew it was probably typhus. And the most important, most vital decision you often had to make was this: How do I prefer to die? By beating, by shooting, by gassing, or by God-sent natural blessings such as diarrhea or typhus.

Learning the Lager routine and gathering the pebbles were just a minor sort of nuisance. Our real problem was the hours of idleness, when our thoughts, left free to meander in the labyrinth of our remote civilian past, dipped into memories of the foods we had once delighted in. As our diet consisted of the morning tea and the noon turnip soup, bread being reserved for full-fledged productive Haftlinge, thoughts of an unfinished portion of goulash when I was a little boy, or of a rejected slice of bread and butter offered by Mother at four in the afternoon, made me feel like a criminal who, having committed an unforgivable sin, was now condemned to pay for each and every malfeasance with denial of the basic necessities.

We all talked of food, we dreamed of food, we fantasized food, we shaped our life around images of food. Some could not exist on imagination alone and went into action. These men wouldn't stop at anything where food was involved. A stronger Haftling forced his weaker partner to yield him a couple of spoonfuls of his soup. An enterprising man looked to the outside for his additional supply of belly fillers. Most of the inhabitants of the Quarantane were Poles, and they often had friends in the Lager who would help them out with a piece of bread or with such luxury items as shoestrings, belts, or spoons, which they sometimes exchanged with other Quarantane dwellers for their soup, knowing that, anyway, the shoestrings, the belts, and the spoons would eventually be confiscated by the Blockaltester and his Schreiber. All of these were definitely *Verboten* ("prohibited") in the Quarantane.

But many, possibly most, of these Haftlings didn't have anybody to help them, and driven by nightmares of hunger, they would steal a rotten turnip from a truckload being unloaded in the vicinity of our block. Honesty — full and uncorrupted honesty — was, we were told, the number one ingredient of survival in Auschwitz. Such people, in their momentary weakness, violated the rule of honesty, running the risk of untold punishment. Once a Russian Haftling, a Tatar, was caught stealing a turnip, for which he was beaten to death by the short Blockaltester and the Schreiber. It was a lesson to us. We knew from this time on that we could not afford to steal. What we had to do, instead, was learn how to organize, that is, to steal without being caught. The Lagerkommandant himself confirmed the importance of organizing: once, in a speech directed at the Haftlinge population of Auschwitz, he said, "The diet in this Lager has been calculated scientifically so that its consumer should stay alive not less and not more than three months. Therefore whoever has been here longer than that and is still alive and functioning is, by definition, a thief." Yet, not having caught such culprits redhanded, he could not mete out to them the punishment called for by his insulted calculations.

As time passed and the end of the Quarantane approached (the prescribed time being four weeks), the Haftlinge started discussing their future plight in the Lager. Most Poles didn't consider this a problem. Some of them knew Kapos or foremen who would claim them the day the Quarantane had run its full time. Others counted on the ones who knew somebody. Still others had an occupation that counted high on the Lager's occupational ladder. They were butchers, or carpenters, or locksmiths — or they said they were, following the instructions of their friends.

For Jews, the story was substantially different. They didn't have a living soul to help them with advice or a slice of bread, and few of them had any knowledge of a craft. Most Jews declared themselves to be tailors, feeling that handling a needle was the simplest occupation to learn, especially as the few real tailors in the Lager happened to be Jewish. But how many tailors did the Germans need in one Lager? Many of the Jews were professional men. Even in the professions, there were degrees of importance. We figured that Stefan Blankenheim should have no problem because as an electrical engineer, he could always be used as an electrician's helper. But what about people who in civilian life had been lawyers, teachers, or physicians? We had a few medical doctors, and the highest they ever got in the Quarantane was to become Lausekontrolle experts, because the Blockaltester decided that, as doctors, they knew about lice and typhus, and as Jews, they were even more intimate with lice and knew where to look for them. By this time, we knew about the existence of the Krankenbau, but we could hardly believe that the Polish administration of the Lager would accord to the Jews the privilege of dispensing their medical knowledge in the Auschwitz hospital. This was the first time in my life when I felt that my Father had made a terrible mistake in choosing medical studies for me instead of a good, sound practical skill. But I couldn't have known, and he couldn't have known.

The day finally arrived when we fell into our last Quarantane formation, and the Blockaltester announced, "Today is the end of your bumming it up. Various Kapos have paid us a visit to pick up the cream of the crop. The lucky ones will immediately follow them. The rest of you sonsofabitch will get what you deserve. If you're lucky, you'll become unskilled laborers in some decent sort of Kommando. If you're not so lucky, then God help you, you sons of a whore!"

The Kapos were there and waiting for the end of the report. Most of them already knew whom they wanted and for what. They called out, "Electricians! Mechanics! Carpenters! Masons!" and as prearranged, their men stepped out and joined those who had called them.

When the occupation of tailors was called out, a number of Jews stepped forward. They were all thoroughly questioned, and most of them were sent back. Stefan Blankenheim stepped to the electrical Kapo and told him about his qualifications. The Kapo asked Stefan to design some electrical circuits on the spot, gave him an oral examination, thought for some time very seriously, and finally decided to give him a chance, threatening to send him back to the Quarantane should his qualifications prove inadequate.

This was a minor miracle. I congratulated Stefan and embraced him, hoping that this was a good sign for me, too. Marian was accepted as an automechanic, and on his recommendation, Szczepan was allowed to join him. Janosik, Reichert, Krug, and I were all that was left of the Zakopane people, and we were now just part of a large group of human leftovers who were to become either the lucky or the unlucky unskilled Auschwitz labor. Nobody cared for the "fuckin' intelligentsia."

A handsome-looking German Kapo wearing a green triangle stopped in front of the group. With his finger, he picked forty of us and ordered us to fall into formation. He evaluated us with a strange smile, somehow belied by his cool green eyes, and said, "I'm Kapo Rudi. Your new Kapo. I'll take you with me to Kobier."

How can one possibly render the essence of what the Quarantane really was? And yet, to describe one day in the Quarantane is to describe the entire four weeks there, because each day was like every other day, each night like every other night. It all consisted of the "*Mutzen auf*!" and "*Mutzen ab*!" training; of marching, and stopping, and "Right face!" and "Left face!" and "About face"; of sticking someone's head into a barrel of soup and hitting hungry people with a yard-long ladle; of keeping us in the cold and pouring cold water over us. It consisted of continuously calling the educated Haftlinge, "fuckin' intelligentsia" and putting them under the control of persons who in civilian life made their living by hustling, by stealing, by mugging, and by murdering.

The functionaries' techniques had a purpose, and they often brought a quick return. Each person has a certain "the worst" within. Some professionals and intellectuals gave in and found themselves poaching for raw potato peels, forgetful of the long years of training which were supposed to have made better people out of them. In a climate where all that counted for most people was to find a way to survive physically, the luxuries of spiritual or intellectual sophistication and social etiquette had to be put aside. And in this way, between the continuous hunger, the name-calling, the physical and emotional disciplining, and the constant threat of death, the four-week Quarantane was extended to Eternity, and unless a person had either unusual strength of character or a substantial quantity of enthusiasm, by the time the four weeks were over the person was not a person anymore; and from a civilian larva, through a Quarantane pupa, an ugly Auschwitz moth was born, ready to do what was ordered and to die an infamous death.

I was lucky: I had an ocean of enthusiasm in me, and I had Stefan Blankenheim for a mentor. While the others were fighting for an additional bowl of soup, which they really seldom succeeded in getting anyhow, Stefan and I liked to make believe that we were the audience in this strange theater of oddities. We observed, and we discussed what we saw, and suddenly we had an interest in life, and the hunger and the other primitive or refined tools of brainwashing stopped affecting us. I must add that Stefan made it even more possible for me to become immune to the contagion of the Quarantane by often making believe that he had diarrhea or a stomach ache, so that he had a logical explanation of why I should finish his part of the soup.

Stefan was very close to his wife. They had been married for over twenty years and had no children, which made them indispensable to each other. When they were in Zakopane, they had found a way to communicate daily. In Montelupich, where any communication was almost impossible, Stefan and his wife still were able to find a way to send an occasional note to each other. Here, everything stopped, and it was evident that Stefan didn't really care about staying alive. Yet he didn't want to give in either, and having found in me trainable material, he dedicated his Quarantane existence to helping me face the worst he could think of: intellectual death. To achieve this, everything and anything proved of value. When we were collecting our daily pebbles, he discussed with me their origins, their components, and the reason for the shape of these pebbles; when the short Blockaltester announced during an evening report that the entire population of the Quarantane had committed *"Ein Sabotage"* by hiding one spoon under somebody's straw pallet, Stefan dismissed the possibility that each of us might be beaten within the next few minutes and instead discussed with me the point that *Sabotage* is of the feminine gender, and that our German functionary should have said, *"Eine Sabotage."* By sticking to our own habits, painfully acquired through family life and years of schooling, we had found our own way to fight the danger of succumbing to the brutal routine of Auschwitz.

CHAPTER

9

KOBIER

SOME FIFTY KILOMETERS southwest of Auschwitz lies an obscure little village by the name of Kobier. Because this entire territory was covered with a heavy, centuries-old forest of oak and needle trees, the Polish name of the region was Puszcza Pszczynska, which to an untrained ear sounds like a lot of hissing, but which in fact means the "Thick Forest of the Town of Pszczyna," and to my ear sounded like a million oak leaves humming in the fresh breeze. Before World War II, this territory had belonged to Poland, and at that time the name of the village was Kobierz, implying that the locality as well as its population was Polish. In real life, the situation was not this simple — the same being true for every locality close to the Polish border, whether it was west, bordering Germany, or east facing the Soviet Union. The population of such localities, in order to avoid thorough confusion, adopted both Polish and the language of the bordering country and, according to who was the ruler at a given moment, proclaimed itself Polish or otherwise. At this time, during the early spring of 1943, the population of Kobier was German.

The SS administration had built near Kobier, in the middle of the woods, a minuscule labor camp, in which one hundred and twenty Jewish Haftlinge, led by three German Kapos, one Czech cook, two Polish horse-team drivers, and an SS Lagerkommandant — an *Un-*

terscharfuhrer ("corporal") — toiled as lumberjacks, draining-system installers, and agricultural workers. Our two SS trucks, loaded with forty Jews of many national origins, many languages, and many cultural backgrounds, were now rolling toward the camp of Kobier, and as we were crossing small picturesque villages, whose orderliness and neatness suggested a German rather than a Polish population, each of us was trying to guess his immediate future. What would Kapo Rudi be like? What role would the two armed SS guards be playing in our everyday life? How exacting would our work be? And, last but not least, was the three-month survival rule also valid there, in that small, God-forsaken labor camp, or was it intended only for the Mother Camp Auschwitz?

It was the second half of April. The old linden trees edging the road were covered with their first buds, and the pastures and fields were green. Maybe Kobier meant just agricultural work. To work on a farm! Heavy work? So what! A farm meant plenty of fresh air and sun, and the smell of freedom, and food! Lots of food! Milk! And fresh bread! Just imagine: the air, and the sun, and the food.

Reichert pulled me by the sleeve. "It seems that Kobier is a mill," he said. A mill. How splendid! A huge old water wheel. Or a windmill! Don Quixote, Spain, romance! It was so good to dream while the trucks were smoothly rolling across the beautiful agricultural country. I hoped this journey would have no end.

A Haftling seated near me smiled at me. He had a big round face and wore thick eyeglasses. He said in German, "My name is Richard. I've spent ten years in prison for being a communist. It makes me so happy to see this beautiful nature around me. I haven't seen a blade of grass in ten years!"

Richard was a German Jew and was now thirty years old. Once upon a time, he had wanted to be a teacher of literature. French literature. He spoke fairly good French, and we engaged in a conversation. He recited a poem by Verlaine, and I answered with Baudelaire. We were friends in no time. We even expressed hope that maybe now we would stop being called the "fuckin' intelligentsia." Another passenger cut in. He was a book publisher from Cracow. Goldberg. His twin brother was traveling on the second truck. Goldberg, too, was full of hope.

"Mill, farm — what's the difference?" he said. "As long as they make us work productively, and let us alone."

Another young man, short and skinny, wearing a piece of string around his left ear to substitute for a broken arm of his eyeglasses, said that he was a French Jew, but that he had been arrested for being a member of the French underground. He had already passed through a number of prisons and now just loved all this air, and the fields, and the woods — at this moment the trucks entered a road edged at both sides by heavy forest.

Soon we turned into an unpaved country road, and a few minutes later a small camp surrounded by barbed wire and guarded by four watch towers appeared in the middle of an empty field. The trucks slowly crossed a short wooden overpass bridging the ditch between the road and the camp, and we stopped in the middle of a rather small yard bordered by three low wooden barracks and boasting a water pump close to the righthand barrack. The whole thing slightly resembled Treblinka, but there was no bad smell and no grinding noise in the background.

The involuntary shiver I had felt on arrival disappeared. As we were ordered down from the trucks and fell into formation, I noted some more details of this little Lager. To the left of the yard, where the trucks had stopped, was the Krankenbau, which was just a small wing of the barrack occupied by the three Kapos, the foremen, and the other functionaries. The barrack to the right contained the kitchen and a ward where one group of the Haftlinge lived. The barrack at the far end contained only Haftlinge quarters. All this was within the barbed-wire enclosure. Beyond the fence, to the left, were the barracks in which the forty or so SS guards lived, and at the opposite side, beyond the right fence, stood the cottage of the Lagerkommandant.

Kapo Rudi entered the Krankenbau, carrying with him our documents, and I understood that the Schreibstube must be located within the Krankenbau. We waited in front of the barrack for a half-hour, after which the doctor came out to see us. He was wearing a Haftling uniform, just like ours, only nicely fitting and made of better material. Also, his cap was set at a smart slant. Yes, he was a functionary in spite of the Star of David on his chest.

In a rude, slightly bored voice, the doctor ordered us to take off our shirts and pull down our pants. He checked us for lice, and I must admit, he did it himself. When this ritual was over, the Schreiber ordered us, one at a time, into the Krankenbau, to verify our papers. This was a lengthy procedure, and meanwhile I could see the drivers of our two trucks getting their receipts for the delivered merchandise — ourselves — and leaving the Lager.

Finally, I was called into the Krankenbau. I faced a small group of Jewish Haftlinge — exactly three of them: the Schreiber, a German

Jew who also doubled as a tailor, fixing the SS uniforms of the Postens and fitting the Lager uniforms of the functionaries; the cobbler, a French Jew of Polish origin, a very short and very husky creature with the huge nose of a Polish peasant and a rudeness never yet seen by me in a Jew; and the doctor, a Czech Jew, whose unpleasant face and cold eyes didn't make me feel at home.

The Schreiber glanced at my papers and exclaimed, amused, "Hey, Doc! You've got competition!"

The doctor took my papers, studied them for a while, returned them to the Schreiber, and said, "We've got all the help we need. Assign him to Rudi's Kommando."

The Schreiber wrote my assignment, smiling and mumbling, "No favors for a colleague, eh?"

And the cobbler, lifting his potato nose from the little bench on which he was repairing an SS boot, examined me with his protruding eyes and smirked, "Another *farhurte doktor?*"

This was the epithet he reserved for me for the rest of my stay in Kobier. From now on, instead of being just a generic member of the fuckin' intelligentsia, I had advanced to the level of a *farhurte doktor,* a "whorish doctor," and had been assigned to Kapo Rudi's *Waldkommando* (forest detail) as a lumberjack.

Most of the one hundred and twenty Jewish Haftlinge of Kobier were divided into three large work details; the *Waldkommando,* whose members worked under the leadership of Kapo Rudi, and all of whom lived in the barrack at the far side of the Lager; the *Feldkommando* (the agricultural workers), under Kapo Alfred, a broad-shouldered man with a red face and a big nose, who, standing in the front of his Jews, booted legs astride, hands on his hips, and a black Mutze on his head, had the appearance of a movie pirate; and the *Abflussgrabenkommando* (the drainage workers), also belonging to Kapo Alfred. The members of the last two work details lived mostly in the barrack to the right of the Lager, near the kitchen.

Besides these three large work details, there was a small detail composed of ten French Jews, all of them very tall and strong, called *Entwurzelnkommando* (the uprooting workers), whose task was to uproot large, damaged trees with the aid of dynamite. This detail was headed directly by an SS corporal. Then there was a minuscule work detail called the *Kutcherkommando* (the horsecart workers), which consisted of two horse-driven peasant carts handled by two young Polish Haftlinge, one by Zbyszek, the other by Zdziszek, who were the drivers and were responsible for the horses. Each cart was manned by two Jews, whose duty was to load the carts with the timber logs prepared by the lumberjacks at the edge of one of the forest paths and to carry them to the edge of the highway, where the logs were neatly built into one-cubic-meter heaps. These, in turn, were carried away on SS trucks one evening a week. Both Kutcherkommandos also had the task of picking up the soup from the Lager and delivering it to the work sites of the other work groups. All these were the out-of-camp work details. In the Lager, of course, there were always some three or four Haftlinge helping the Czech cook Rudolf with such basic kitchen chores as potato peeling, carrying barrels of water, and doing the general cleaning of pots, barrels, and the kitchen premises, all of which had to be sparkling clean, as Rudolf, besides the basic soup of stone-hard old corn which he prepared daily for the Jewish Haftlinge, was also fully responsible for the SS mess.

Of course, I wanted to know whether having been assigned to the Waldkommando meant something good for me, or something bad, or nothing at all. There must have been an answer to my worries, but nobody could give it to me. The Haftlinge whom we had found in Kobier, the old timers, either wouldn't commit themselves to any prognosis or told outright lies. To our cumulative question, "What is life in Kobier like?" there was a standard answer: "Wait, and you'll see." When we wondered what had happened to the forty Haftlinge whom we were obviously replacing, there was a shrug of the shoulders. And to my specific question, "How is it under Kapo Rudi?" the answer was "Under Kapo Alfred would be much worse." Thus all I knew for sure was that only by obtaining a function right now, inside the Lager, could I hope to have a slightly easier existence, and this hope, for as long as the local doctor considered me his potential competitor, had to be relegated to things impossible. Thus, with my heart heavy with worry, but with a seed of hope left somewhere in its corner, I reported to Kapo Rudi for further orders.

My new life started at four-thirty the next morning. Dressed in my pants only, I washed vigorously under a stream of cold water from the water pump in the middle of the yard in the icy air of the Polish April. By doing so, I made myself conspicuous, as most of the other Haftlinge left their barracks fully dressed, and their washing was something of a symbolic ritual consisting of touching the cold water with the tips of their fingers and rubbing their sleepy eyes with this scant quantity. The only ones who washed the way I did were the French "uprooters" and a few quite healthy-looking specimens, who, as I was to learn shortly, were the foremen in the three main Kommandos. One of those individuals came near me, looked me over carefully, and asked, "To what Kommando have you been assigned?" When I informed him that it was the Waldkommando, he nodded pensively, evaluated me with his cool eyes, said, "Then I'll see you later," and entered the barrack next to the kitchen. I asked a tall, skinny Haftling with a face all black and blue, who the man was, and he replied, "Erich, Kapo Rudi's foreman." Having thus informed me, the Skinny One shambled away. Most of the Kobier Mussulmen had that clumsy, shambling walk.

At five-thirty, the Haftlinge gathered in small groups on the *Raportplatz* — this was the official name of the Kobier Lager's yard. Each Haftling had under his arm a red enameled bowl and, in the highest buttonhole of the jacket, a spoon. This made us feel essentially different from the subhumans we had been in the Quarantane. Now we were workers, an official part of the concentration camp's labor class, and as such, we were entitled to our food rations and to the tools from which and with which humans in the Western world consume their food. However, a look around me did little to keep alive my illusions about this laboring class. The old timers looked like walking skeletons and were covered with bruises.

Reichert came to me to say hello. He was older than I, and probably wiser, having had all that experience in his underground forest residence. I asked whether he had an opinion on our new surroundings.

He sighed, "Well, each of the workers has his own bunk, his own bowl, his own spoon, and even his own drinking cup!"

I looked around again. True, they carried red enameled drinking cups attached to their belts, and I had no drinking cup, no belt, and no shoestrings. How come?

Reichert, as if he were reading my mind, continued, "It will take us a few days to organize ourselves and get the rest of the basics. Still, what I don't like is that all those Mussulmen are so taciturn. Whomever I've asked about his Kommando has told me to wait and see."

There was not much longer to wait. Shortly, we'd see.

"What's your Kommando?" I asked Reichert.

"Field."

It was a pity. It would have been nicer to stay together, the few of us from Zakopane. Reichert and Krug had been assigned to Kapo Alfred, along with Janosik, and I was the only one from the group to work under Kapo Rudi. All I could do was wish good luck to Reichert and to myself.

Two Haftlinge brought a barrel of hot greenish liquid and placed it in front of our barrack. There was now a barrel in front of each barrack.

"Come on and get your tea!" one of them yelled.

There was no rush, no competition. I got my portion of the liquid, tasted it, and spat it out. It was nauseating and bitter.

An old timer said to me, "Don't be particular. Learn to drink it. This is one of our medications against *Durchfall*." *Durchfall* was the contagious diarrhea.

"I already had it in the Quarantane," I said defensively.

"Never mind the Quarantane," he replied. "You'll get it again. Everybody has it here. People shit until they die."

As soon as he said this, he left me in a rush, to join a long line of Haftlinge in front of the latrine placed in the far corner of the Lager, next to my barrack, right along the barbed wire. I shrugged and turned away to watch the other activities in the Lager. The Haftlinge were mostly finished with their breakfast and were gathering into larger groups, apparently by their work details. I didn't know which group to join. I didn't know my future co-workers yet.

Now, a short Haftling with gaily smiling light blue eyes came out of the Kapos' quarters and walked crisply toward the middle of the Raportplatz. He looked energetically around the Lager, put a big whistle to his lips, and blew into it. It was like a miracle. Within seconds, all the Haftlinge fell into formation and were ready for the morning report. I watched for Kapo Rudi and quicky joined the group of people in front of him.

The Lagerkommandant came out of his cottage outside the barbed wire and entered the Lager through the main gate. He was fully dressed in his SS uniform, but his eyes seemed still half asleep. A company of SS Postens gathered meantime in front of the gate. They were all armed with automatic rifles. There must have been four dozen of them.

Kapo Rudi counted his group quickly and reported the number to the short man who had whistled before. Kapo Alfred counted his two groups and also reported to the short man. The short Haftling, as I learned later, was the Lagerkapo Theo, the most important Haftling in Kobier. Theo now counted the rest of the Haftlinge: the cook Rudolf and his few helpers, the two Polish horsecart drivers and their four helpers, the doctor, the Schreiber, and the cobbler. The count was finished.

Kapo Theo sprang to attention in front of the Lagerkommandant and yelled: "One hundred and twenty Haftlinge, all present and accounted for."

The Lagerkommandant waved his hand with indifference. The morning report was over. We were about to embark on our first day's adventures.

Kapo Alfred roared, "Feldkommando!" and immediately afterward, "Abflussgräbenkommando!" and something like sixty Haftlinge formed quickly into two separate groups.

Kapo Rudi yelled, "Waldkommando!" and about forty of us fell into formation in front of him. The ten giant French Haftlinge fell into their own small formation, without anybody's telling them to; the drivers went phlegmatically to their horse teams, followed by their Jewish helpers; and the remaining men went back to their respective work sites. They were to stay in the Lager, and there seemed to be no rush regarding their activities.

Rudi called a few men. They stepped out of our group and joined the Kapo. These were his foremen and his Pipels. They all knew their routine. They went to a small shack behind the Krankenbau and brought forward a heap of hatchets, saws, and barking adzes, all the tools used by the lumberjacks. Each of us was ordered to grab a tool, and a moment later, we were leaving the Lager, the tools on our shoulders, and crossing the small wooden bridge between the main gate and the country road to start a ten-kilometer march into the heart of the ancient Pszczyna forest.

We marched five abreast, with our foremen and the Pipels in the first two rows. They were not carrying any tools and were all decently dressed and apparently well fed. There was a climate of intimacy between them and Kapo Rudi, as well as between them, Rudi, and the dozen SS Postens walking in front, behind, and at both sides of us. They exchanged the latest news, told each other jokes, and only occasionally paid any attention to us, the common folk.

After a couple of kilometers of leisurely marching, Kapo Rudi, after having held a serious conference with his functionaries and the *Postenkommandant* ("chief of the guards"), decided that we would sing a few German marching songs. They had even decided which songs were to be sung: "In Hamburg da bin ich gewesen," which was a sentimental song of a girl who had left her ever waiting mother to go to Hamburg, where she had become a whore, and was now ashamed to return home in spite of her brother's encouraging letters; "In dem Feld es bluhmt ein kleines Magdelein, und ihr name ist Eeerika," which was the story of a sweet, innocent German maiden; and "Es war ein Madel von kaum achtzehn Jahren, sie kannt kein Kummer, sie kannte keinen Schmerz," which was the story of an eighteen-year-old girl who suddenly learned that her beloved had been ruthlessly shot on Russia's green steppes.

I didn't know any of these. Some of the old timers knew a few words; but the Kapo and the Pipels knew all of them, and now, following Rudi's healthy tenor, they intoned the tearful words of the songs, while we the workers mumbled something that was supposed to sound like German words and the unfamiliar tunes. However, I was quick to notice that not all the foremen were really aware of what they were singing. There was one who looked like an Arab from Morocco, short, black-eyed, and with an olive complexion, who was singing words that were definitely not German, and I was not sure whether they belonged to any of this world's languages.

In fact, after a while Kapo Rudi ordered him to shut up. "You, Marcel," he said, "might be a good boxer in Algiers, or wherever you come from, but you are a lousy singer. You are spoiling the harmony."

I soon found out that Marcel had been brought to Auschwitz from North Africa. An Arab Jew. Then there was another foreman, called Dutchman, as he had been brought in from Holland. At home, he too had been a boxer, and now his specialty was singing a South African Boer marching song, of which we quickly caught two words, "In Transvaal" and "Imperiaria," and each time he finished his Dutch crooning, we all picked up and sang with him: "Imperiaria, Imperiaria, Imperiaria, Imperiaria, poom poom poom poom poom in Transvaal poom poom poom sharee poom" — the whole thing sounded to us just like this.

Erich was the foreman who had spoken to me in the morning. He, of course, was a German Jew and knew his portion of the patriotic marches.

The Pipels, who weren't German, knew what was good for them, and they had learned all the songs by rote. There were three of them to service Kapo Rudi: Max, a fourteen-year-old Dutch Jew, little and plump, with eyeglasses over his tiny nose and an air of terrible importance about him; Adolph, also a Dutch Jew, who much later confided in me that he was twenty, but, owing to his lack of a beard, had been able to convince Rudi that he was not a day older than fifteen and was rewarded with the function of a Pipel; and Raoul, a sixteen-year-old Frenchman with a pair of doelike eyes and plump, inviting lips. The three Pipels and three foremen were not enough to fill the first two rows of the marching column, and Rudi was always on the lookout for four more potential march singers, whom he usually picked at random from the rest of the group.

Now, his eyes fell on me. He asked, "Hey you there! Do you like to sing?"

During the last couple of years I had had enough experience to know that you never say no to a Kapo.

"Yes, Herr Kapo!" I announced in the most confident way I could.

He made me switch places with another Haftling, and now I was able to express my joy at being in Kobier by singing some more sonorous murmurandos.

Our column was marching on a wide country path in the middle of a beautiful forest. Here and there lingering patches of snow still could be seen, but entire families of tiny field flowers were announcing the coming of the spring. From the somber thicket of the wood came the smell of fresh mushrooms. Some twenty meters in front of us, a band of deer crossed our path. I would have loved this morning march, if not for the fact that my stringless shoes were hurting my feet at each step, and my beltless pants were continuously slipping down toward my knees. The shoes, though, were the real problem. I couldn't help noticing that Rudi, his foremen, and the Pipels wore decent civilian shoes, while the rest of the group had those damned large things with sharp lambskin vamps, which were cutting into our feet below the ankles at the slightest movement. Most of the group had shoestrings, and that helped. I had none. I was sure that the clumsy, heavy way of walking of most Haftlinge in Kobier must have been caused by their shoes.

Our Kommando had reached a large clearing in the forest, and we were ordered to stand still. The Postenkommandant yelled an order, and our SS escorts spread around the clearing, forming what they called a *Postenkette* ("chain of guards"). Rudi quickly informed us that it was prohibited to cross the *Kette,* and that anybody attempting to do so would be shot without warning, as this would be considered an attempt to escape. I thought it was nice of Rudi to tell us all this, although I couldn't imagine who in the world might try to escape into this junglelike forest, not to mention the fact that it was hardly possible to slip out unnoticed between two guards posted fifty steps from each other. While the guards were taking their positions in the Postenkette, most of the Haftlinge threw their tools on a heap in the middle of the clearing and rushed into the bordering bushes, dropping their pants while running. I remembered the old timer's warning: Durchfall.

Rudi interrupted them, by calling in a civil way, "Meine Herren! Start Working!"

Most of them already knew their assignment for the day. In foursomes, they had the task of sawing down certain marked trees, debranching and barking them, and, at the end of the work day, carrying them to the edge of a path in the middle of the forest, where sometime tomorrow the two drivers and their helpers would load the lumber on their carts and carry it to the highway for further transportation in the once-a-week SS truck. The few of us who had arrived yesterday were told by the foreman Erich how to recognize the trees marked for cutting: they must have had their peaks broken by the wind. He also informed us that it was *Verboten* even to touch the healthy trees, and that the culprits ran the risk of being shot. And finally, he advised us that the fresh lumber should never be mixed with the dry lumber, as the stacks of the former were destined for paper mills, while the latter was just fuel. I had now become part of a foursome, and while my partner and I were sawing a tree, the other two men clung to the trunk with their bodies, making believe that they were pushing it powerfully to help us in felling the tree. This was a necessary expedient, because a Haftling should never be seen not performing some sort of work. Idleness, whether voluntary or due to the circumstances, was a crime punishable by at least fifteen strokes of a stick on your behind, and this everybody wanted to avoid. Yet it was not sufficient either to be good or to make believe that you were good. The Algerian foreman, Marcel, stopped for a moment near my team, yelled something in what he thought was German, hit each of us on the head with his sturdy stick, and walked over to the next team.

And so, while we were sawing, cutting, barking, and being beaten by a foreman or a Pipel, the morning passed like a dream, and the driver Zbyszek arrived with his horse, and his two Jewish helpers, and a Posten to guard them, and two tin barrels of soup. My first Kobier dinner was about to be dispensed. Everybody received his bowlful of soup, sat down in a small group or alone, and ate quietly, while Rudi and his cohorts lay down to sleep and the Postens stood their guard.

The soup was different from the soup in the Quarantane. It had substance. It was filled with stone-hard kernels of old corn, which had to be swallowed without chewing. I didn't mind: corn is corn, and what is good for fattening the hogs would be sufficient to give us Haftlinge the necessary load of protein and starch. After having finished my soup, I still had plenty of time to lie down on the humid grass and take a rest. The earth smelled good, and I wished I could return here one day, after the war, for a picnic. I closed my eyes and probably fell asleep immediately. Rudi's whistle woke me up.

The afternoon work seemed much harder than in the morning. My arms were tired, the palms of my hands were afire, my back was aching, and my feet hurt always more and more. Also the tempo of the work seemed to have become quicker. The foreman and the Pipels rushed from team to team, yelling and hitting. Then, seemingly, our day's work of cutting and barking was over, and Rudi ordered us to place the tools in a heap. When this was done, he looked at his large wristwatch and said, "We have exactly one hour to carry the logs to the road. Start going!"

The old timers knew Rudi's ways. Each grabbed a log — possibly a light one — threw it on his shoulders, and trotted along the dark path in the woods. The Postens, Rudi, the foremen, and the Pipels stood along the path, flogging the workers.

I wasn't used to this new activity yet. I grabbed a log that proved much too heavy and, without the bark, much too slippery to be easily lifted onto my shoulder. I sweated, trying to find a way to manage the unwieldy timber, and as I was exerting myself, the foreman Erich approached with a menacing look in his cold eyes, and the only button holding my pants gave out. A disaster was on hand, when a miracle happened. My arms had suddenly learned the trick of an instant pull and thrust, and the log was comfortably resting on my shoulder. Erich glanced at my pants, mumbled, "We'll have to organize you a rope for them," and left me alone.

The hour that followed was a long hour of lifting, running, stack building, and again running and lifting. My shoulders were sore and my feet swollen. And my belly started bothering me. I felt an unpleasant pricking and would have liked to follow the example of some other Haftlinge who had already squatted under the bushes many times to relieve themselves. But they had done it before, during the regular working hours. Now everybody was running, and I couldn't afford the risk. Finally, the carrying came to an end, each of us picked up his tool, and we fell into formation and started on our way back.

It was a slow and lazy march back. The Haftlinge were tired, the Postens bored. Kapo Rudi looked several times at his large wristwatch. Finally, he said to the Postenkommandant that it was too early to return to the Lager. They must have had some sort of a timetable that they were supposed to follow, because the head Posten compared time with Rudi and nodded. Rudi ordered us to stop. We fell out of formation, and everybody was allowed to sit on the grassy scarp over a drainage ditch running along the road. For a while, they left us alone, and it was a pleasant moment — maybe even more pleasant than when we had first entered to the woods early in the morning. Richard, the communist German Jew whom I had met yesterday on the truck, sat near me. His round face was all joy.

"I don't care," he said, "about the work, the beating, the insecurity. For ten long years I've been dreaming about a time like this. The fields, the trees, the grass. And the smell of this humid good earth. Even if they kill me, it will be a different kind of death than in the courtyard of a prison."

I felt very much the same way. But I also had reason — valid or invalid — to know that they would not kill me. "They'll never kill me," I said aloud.

Richard looked at me in a way that seemed a mixture of pity, tenderness, and regret. Maybe he would have liked to help me understand my situation and to accept the inevitability of death, but he didn't feel entitled to dispel my illusions. I could read all this in his face.

I said to him, "I escaped from Treblinka."

But Richard had never heard of Treblinka, and so my strongest trump proved ineffective. I wanted to tell him about Rabka, and Montelupich, and most of all about the Ring. I could tell that Richard was a sensitive person. I looked around me and decided that, in fact, he was the only sensitive person in this group of hostile, ugly strangers. My belly pricked me again. Now Richard was trying to find a logical reason for me to have said that I would survive.

"We'll be getting enough food here," he said. "I've already inquired. A bowlful of soup at noon. Three quarters of a pound of bread in the evening, with either margarine or a tiny slice of sausage. This is because we are considered a heavy work detail. The whole Lager of Kobier is considered so. You work here six days a week, full time, from six in the morning till six in the evening, and the seventh day, on Sunday, from six till two in the afternoon only. That is heavy."

Yes. I thought it was heavy. Especially now that my feet were one big open sore, and my hands were covered with big, burning blisters.

Kapo Rudi interrupted my flow of thoughts. He exclaimed to the Postenkommandant, who was smoking a cigarette at the edge of the road, at the other side of the ditch, "How about having some entertainment?"

And, as the Kommandant nodded slowly, Rudi yelled, "Itzik! Come on! Give us a performance! Quickly, Itzik!"

A five-foot tall, unnaturally skinny (even for the Lager), bowlegged, freckled, fiery-headed creature jumped out of a group of Haftlinge, marched to the middle of the road, took his Mutze off, made a deep obsequious bow intended for Rudi and the Postens, and intoned a song. I don't remember the words, but it was all about his mother being fucked by a Cossack and asking him for more and more. The Postens and functionaries must have heard this song who knows how many times before, as some of them helped him with the words, and all seemed to enjoy Itzik's performance tremendously. When the song was finished, the Postenkommandant asked Itzik for the Jew story. They understood each other well, as Itzik chanted sadly in response, "Oy, me motherfuckin' sonofabitchofajewbastard drop dead melousy jew!" He said all of the obscenities that an angry man usually yells at his adversary, and he, Itzik, said them to himself — that was the Jew story the Postenkommandant and Itzik must have agreed upon. The Kommandant loved it, and Itzik had figured out that it might be a ticket to life. A Haftling sitting near me on the scarp, which had now taken on all the appearances of the family circle in a legitimate civilian theater, whispered, "Itzik is a moron. He doesn't know what he's doing."

I thought of the Great Rubinstein in the Warsaw Ghetto. How much do these morons really understand, and how much do they want us to believe they do? And I thought of the legend and the paintings on the wall of the Schreibstube in Auschwitz: "Every man has his birdie." Did this mean that each of us knows what is the best way for him to survive? I, too, had developed some sort of survival procedure. I knew from Treblinka that I shouldn't look into my persecutor's eyes; I knew from the first days of the German occupation of Lvov that I should never ask the question "Why?" No, that I had known long before the Germans had come to Lvov. I had learned it from my Polish co-citizens: a Jew should never ask why, because each *why* would cost him a slap, physical or moral. From Stefan, I had learned to create for myself a make-believe world, so that the boredom of continuous violence wouldn't succeed in brainwashing me. I realized that this was exactly what Rubinstein had been doing in the Ghetto and what Itzik was now doing here.

Meanwhile, the performer turned three quick somersaults and jumped back into the crowd of onlookers.

Rudi summoned other performers. Out came an odd couple: Jankel and Ayzik. Jankel was round all over. He had a short, bulbous body, a basketball face, and a potatolike nose, and his eyes stuck out of his head like two golf balls. Ayzik was a tiny bit taller than Jankel; he had the skinny, curved shoulders and the big, sad eyes of a Talmudic scholar, and his face was pale and serious and was decorated with the thin, slightly curved nose of a bird. The two men composed their lips in a thoroughly artificial smile, bowed as deeply as Itzik before them, faced each other, and put a right arm under his partner's right arm. They started their dance. Each jumped on one leg, patting his own behind with his left hand and turning around with the slow speed that such a manuever allowed. Then they separated, and while Jankel clapped his round hands, Ayzik, one hand on his hip, the other over his head, swirled furiously. As this was going on, Jankel yelped, "Hop-la! Hop-la!" and Ayzik replied, "Yoo-ha! Yoo-ha!"

Rudi checked his watch. There was more time left, and a group of four skinny, bruised Mussulmen formed a chorus, singing "Katyusha" and other sentimental Russian and Ukrainian songs. It was well known that the SS Postens loved sentimental tunes.

The soiree finished with the entire Kommando singing, "Mein Yiddische Mame," and then we fell again into marching formation. This time, I could hardly walk at all, but I was not sure whether the reason was my awful shoes, or whether my entire spirit had just fallen into the enemy trap: the place where there was no living, only vegetating, and no walking, only tediously dragging the body and the soul alike.

That evening, seeing the little bridge leading to the Lager had the significance of a homecoming, and for the rest of my existence in Kobier, it was to be for me the symbol of salvation.

However, homecoming was one thing and staying at home something totally different. After the evening report, which like the morning one was short and matter of fact as a report in a camp where people do heavy work should be, and after having received our portions of moldy bread and liverwurst, we returned to our Stube to get some rest. The Slovakian doctor soon came in to inspect our feet for cleanliness. Mine were clean all right, because, in spite of the blisters, I wouldn't have gone to my bunk without washing them first — old habit, going back to the good times. It was also a part of my survival kit: stop caring about cleanliness, and you have just taken the first step toward your tomb. I tried to have the good doctor look at my blisters. His response was only a quick nod.

The next morning, I felt really sick. All over. My feet were swollen and inflamed, and putting on the lambskin shoes was an ordeal. My belly was aching, and I had a powerful Durchfall, either from the old corn soup or from the moldy bread and the slice of spoiled liverwurst, which I should have thrown away but didn't have enough will power to do so. That was definitely a violation of my own code of survival.

In the Quarantane, Stefan and I had decided that it was much wiser to go to work hungry than to risk diarrhea.

I trudged wearily to the latrine, where I joined a long line of Haftlinge hopping from leg to leg and cursing the ones inside for taking too much time. As soon as my bowel movement was over, the pain started again, and I joined the line once more. Finally, I dragged my feet toward my barrack. The tall, skinny Haftling, my first Kobier acquaintance of yesterday, walked over to me and asked me how I was. When I told him, he said I could now see the doctor. I knew from the Quarantane that seeing the doctor was equal to making a decision to go to the gas chamber, and I told the Skinny One so. He clarified things for me.

"It is so in Auschwitz," he said. "Here, they don't make you stay in the hospital but let you remain in the Lager for a day or two, until you are able to return to work. Each of us stays in the Lager from time to time."

It sounded too good to be true, but I was convinced to see the good old Slovak doctor in his Krankenstube. He looked at me with disgust and then at my blisters with even more disgust. He took a pair of scissors and cut all the blisters. I waited for him to dress my feet and to tell me to stay in the camp. Instead, he said, "What are you waiting for? Put on your shoes! The Kommandos are getting ready to go to work!"

I thought he was a sonofabitch and dragged my feet to the Raportplatz. There Reichert helped me with two pieces of string, one sufficient for both shoes, the other to take place of a belt. I blessed him, hoping that the string would do what a rest in the Lager was supposed to achieve.

That morning as we were crossing the little bridge, I said to myself, "See you in the evening." The bridge was my keeper, my family, my warmest hope. As we marched, I kept saying to myself, "I am all right. There is no pain. There is no Durchfall. There is no evil in the world." I kept repeating it, and repeating it, and repeating it, and the road was so long and so tedious. I sang "Erika" and said, "No Durchfall." I sang about the whore in Hamburg, and I said, "There is no pain." But when I worked, there was the pain, and there was the Durchfall. I did the sawing, and the shitting, the barking, and the shitting, the logging, and the shitting. But at lunchtime, I said to myself, "No dice! I have decided to survive!" And I passed my corn soup to Richard who, during his ten years in prison had got used to all sorts of food and didn't seem to suffer at all from the Kobier diet.

The day was almost over, and we were finishing putting the logs in the stacks, when shots were heard from the thicket around us. Hope surged in my chest: "The partisans!"

Everybody knew that wherever there was a big forest, there must be partisans. And it wasn't even important what kind of partisans. The word *partisan* meant to me resistance, armed resistance. Give me a rifle and teach me how to shoot it! In my imagination, I could see myself riding a fast horse (I had never ridden a horse at all), and shooting from the rifle I held with only one hand as I had seen it done in the old silent American movies. My fellow Haftlinge didn't have my imagination. Or maybe they were old timers and knew what was happening. The Skinny One whispered as I was passing him with a movie smile on my lips and a log on my shoulder, "They've shot somebody." Every Haftling was working now even harder than before. A Posten emerged from the woods, beckoned to Kapo Rudi, and said to him, "Imagine — the sonofabitch tried to escape! And he wouldn't stop when I ordered him to!"

Rudi went with his Pipels to identify the man. When they returned, Rudi advised the foremen that it had been the Jew Lemberger, from Berlin. They all discussed the stupidity of the man. How could he hope to escape from here, the poor bastard? This was what I was asking myself. How could he? With all these woods around, and the unfriendly peasants, and the SS probably covering the entire territory? The old timers knew better. "Who's escaping?" whispered the Skinny One. "They shoot us like rabbits. Every weekend. Five of us last week alone."

Now the day's work was really over. Jankel and Ayzik prepared a stretcher from two heavy branches and covered the body with fresh green foliage. This was done according to Rudi's instruction.

"If we meet people from the village on our way back," he said, "they shouldn't see the corpse. It's none of their business."

That evening, Jankel and Ayzik were not requested to perform, and the Kommando marched straight to the Lager, gaily singing, "Erica!" I said hello to my little bridge and sighed with relief. At the gate, the Lagerkommandant, whose title was Herr Oberscharfuhrer as I had learned that day, took a branch off the murdered man's face, looked at him for a moment, and nodded sadly. I could almost hear him saying in his mind, "You Jew bastard. So, for you the whole thing is over."

In Kobier, Durchfall was just one of our physiological miseries. Another was urination. It hit me the very first day, and it was to become worse every day. I had even created a miserable pun in my desperation: urination is my ruination. None of us could find any peace from urinating. Day and night, we had a steady drive to urinate. Sometimes I felt that all my body was melting and pouring away with the urine. At night, danger was added to discomfort, as it was prohibited to use the latrine dressed in anything more than a shirt (wearing pants meant an attempt to escape), the nights were cold, the latrine was close to the fence, and a Posten stood guard right behind the fence. The Skinny One told me that a month ago, when the Lager was still covered with snow, Ayzik had gone to the latrine at night, and the Posten had kept him there for two hours, dancing in the cold. It might have been funny to see the poor bastard jumping in his shirt, but after that Ayzik never went to the latrine at night, and now whenever he needed to urinate, he did it in his soup bowl. By the time I arrived in Kobier, my Kommando had organized an old bucket from the kitchen, and we used this for our night urinal. Of course, it was against the rules, but we always cleaned it very early in the morning and kept it behind the kitchen during the day.

Poor Ayzik's problem was even bigger than the capacity of his share of the bucket. It was my third night in Kobier when at one o'clock Ayzik had to reach once more for his bowl. He used it again a half-hour later, and by two o'clock the bowl was full. There was no room for his urine in the bucket. In fact, should any of us have wanted to urinate, he would have had to use his own bowl, too, but that night it was only Ayzik who couldn't control himself. At two-thirty, he started moaning, and this was when everybody in the Stube woke up. Ayzik was moaning and begging for advice. We all knew what he wanted, but nobody would let him use their bowl. Urine might be a disinfectant, as the Kobier Haftlinge liked to rationalize, but your own urine, and not someone else's. A voice advised Ayzik to forget the danger and use the latrine, but the poor devil didn't dare. Somebody else thought of the drinking cup. It was not big, but it might be a temporary solution, and Ayzik used it. But then, it was three o'clock, and Ayzik needed to urinate again. The poor fellow was crying from pain, and there was no other container available. We all knew that he would have to make an important decision. We were thinking, of course, of his using the latrine. It was certainly danger-ous. Ayzik had been made to dance during his last latrine adventure, but then all the Haftlinge stopped using the latrine at night when another incident occurred a few days after Ayzik's dance: a poor devil had tried to escape from the latrine into his barrack, and the Posten shot him dead just as he was about to enter the Stube. No, Ayzik was not ready to die. While moaning and crying, in a desperate decision he grabbed his drinking cup, now filled with urine, put it to his lips and, as we watched him in fascination, gulped down the liquid, put the empty cup under his penis, and emptied his bladder into it.

Since I'd been a little boy, foreign languages had held a very special fascination for me. When I was six, I learned the basics of Hebrew. In grammar school, I had basic Ukrainian. At ten, I entered the gymnasium and took German and Latin, and at fifteen, I started ancient Greek. After the gymnasium, I studied in Italy, in Belgium, and in France, and accordingly, I learned Italian and French. During the first year of the war, I had learned some Russian, and even some Esperanto, having run across an enthusiast of this artifical language devised for universal understanding.

My knowledge of French made it possible for me to befriend Lucien, one of the ten giants of the Kommando who eradicated the big trees. Lucien was huge, and there was something soothing about him. Whenever I felt miserable, I spent fifteen minutes with Lucien, and it made me feel better. He was French, but not totally. He had come originally from Hungary but had settled in Paris many years ago, and it was there that he had left his wife, an Aryan French-woman, and their six-year-old daughter, when he was taken away by the SS. He liked to talk to me about his family, and I would tell him about Treblinka, and Rabka, and Anka. I told him about Anka when he asked me whether I had a steady girl. Secretly, I had always envied Stefan, and now I was envying Lucien for having somebody close, somebody to think of, to feel warm about. Anka was the only girl I could think of now. I mentioned her to Lucien, and then I couldn't stop wondering what she had really been to me, and how we would act toward each other, should we survive this catastrophe. I embellished her image the best I could and used her name as one of the few lifesavers I had created for myself. The Girl of the Ring was the most important, and as I woke up in the morning, I said good-morning to her, and in the evening I bade her good-night.

My parents were the second lifesaver. I prayed to them each day, using some phrases of the Lord's Prayer: "My Father who art in heaven — my Father, my great Spirit, my Holy Spirit, My Mother, poor Mother, tortured on the earth, but blessed in heaven. Spirits of all my forefathers, pray, implore from the Lord our Father forgive-ness for your son." Such was my daily prayer.

The third lifesaver was the wooden bridge. And now, in my conversations with Lucien, I added the fourth lifesaver, Anka. Lucien's help to me was not purely spiritual. In civilian life, he had been a dentist. As soon as the Kapos had learned about this, they convinced the Lagerkommandant that it would be a splendid idea to have a Lager dentist of their own, and Lucien moved into the Krakenstube as the Slovak doctor's colleague. As soon as this occurred, Lucien was able to give me his soup (by then, my Durchfall was gone, thanks to my abstinence), as the functionaries in the Krankenstube ate potatoes and sausage.

Lucien's help lasted, unfortunately, for not more than a week. The reason was undebatable: all functionaries wore custom-made Lager uniforms; such uniforms had to be paid for with portions of soup and bread; Lucien was now a functionary; he had to use his soup and bread portions to pay the tailor who made his uniform, the stockman who got him a good pair of shoes, and the hatmaker who made his new, fancy cap. I understood this quite well, but Lucien felt so embarrassed that he started avoiding me, and it was not until I was able to give him something of importance that our friendship was renewed. This happened when, during one of our evening reports, Kapo Theo announced that we had all worked well, and that therefore we would be given a bonus: either five figs, or three cigarettes. I had never been a smoker and could have used the figs. However, the temptation to be able to give something to somebody was stronger than my need for the nourishment. I opted for the cigarettes and shortly afterward offered them triumphantly to a blushing Lucien.

Unfortunately, our initial relationahip never came back totally. Oh, yes, we saw each other and conversed, but I read pity in Lucien's eyes, and pity was the last thing I wanted. I could understand it. Of course, I could — he, so big, and so strong, and so lucky — and I, so slim, and so frail, and so hopelessly a part of a Kommando of Mussulmen, all of whom, sooner or later, were to die in the forest. I could understand Lucien's pity, but I didn't have to accept it. Thus, slowly, the distance between us became larger, and I slipped back into the loneliness of a dreamer lost in a crowd of strangers.

After two weeks in Kobier, something unusual happened to me. Although my body was still very thin and, by all human measures, quite weak, I felt inside me a surge of strength, of vitality, of energy, and of new will to beat the system. I started viewing the strange crowd around me not as a crowd, but as individual human beings. I accepted the fact that the biggest part of the Lager population, the Jews from Pruzany, a small town in northeastern Poland, had very little in common with me as far as education was concerned, but I also came to realize that education was perhaps not the most important thing in life, nor was it anything that put a distinguishing mark on its beneficiaries. The Slovak doctor, a person with some of the highest formal educational credentials, was a common rat. The Skinny One from Pruzany was a warm human being who, with all his bruises and his eternal hunger, was able to give me advice and sympathy when I needed it. Richard, the graduate of ten years of prison, who had achieved an avid self-education, had learned a lot and could boast his knowledge, but instead, he chose to admire the beauty of nature in a place where every other day a Haftling was shot in what was later reported as an attempt to escape. I soon realized that there was no substantial difference between Kobier and any community in so-called free society. Both had their rules to be followed (or to be broken); both had their successful citizens, their proletariat, and their criminal element; and both had their authorities to whom, sooner or later, an account had to be rendered. I concluded then that, all things being equal, in Kobier, as in a free society, progress was possible for somebody who tried hard enough.

With this fresh philosophy of survival, I was toiling hard one day in the forest, and to finish the building of my stack of logs faster, I threw one log on each shoulder and trotted with two logs along the usual path.

Suddenly, a Posten's command stopped me short. I felt nervous, and I had every reason: the Haftlinge called this particular Posten the Killer, as he had made a name as the most proficient executioner of the Haftlinge who "tried to escape." He was a handsome young man with very dark, thick hair and dark brown eyes, and he had to his credit two years of humanistic studies in one of the Hungarian universities — he was an ethnic German from Hungary. It would have been a cinch to like him, if not for the fact that he might decide, in the middle of a friendly conversation, to shoot a Haftling right in the head in order to prove to another Posten that he was a reliable shooter. Now, the Killer ordered me to stop, to throw down my two logs, and to approach him.

"Bend down!" the Killer ordered, and I obliged.

"You'll count as I whip you!" he informed me, and I answered with the statutory "Yes, sir, Herr Posten!"

He had in his hand a sturdy new cane, and while he hit me on my buttocks, I counted aloud: "Eins! Zwei! Drei!" I was also looking for the reason that he might have picked me for this unexpected retribution, but all I could think of was that he might have wanted to try out his new cane. I counted to ten, and the Killer ordered me to attention. I faced him now, and our eyes met for an instant. I didn't like it. A Haftling's eyes were not supposed to meet those of a Posten.

"Do you know why you got the beating?" he asked me, while rolling himself a cigarette.

I gave the statutory response, "Yes, sir, Herr Posten!" But then came the surprise.

He asked me, "Why?"

I felt it wasn't fair. He shouldn't ask certain questions. And what would I tell him now?

I replied in an emotionless voice, "I didn't carry a sufficient load of lumber, Herr Posten."

"Wrong," said the Killer. He stopped the rolling of his cigarette, picked up his cane, and brought it down on my head. I saw a million stars, but I didn't budge. I was still all right, according to the regulations.

He put away the cane, went back to his cigarette, and informed me, "It is forbidden to carry the logs on both shoulders. *Verboten!*" And he dismissed me.

My newly found strength helped me to throw both logs on one shoulder and I trotted away as quickly as I could. I thought it had been a narrow escape, and I immediately thanked my father in Heaven.

Early that afternoon, the Lagerkommandant came to visit our Kommando on the work site. He was accompanied by an important figure, the Superintendent of the Department of Forestry, a very high civil-service official. The two of them stopped for a while near Kapo Rudi and the Postenkommandant and watched the Haftlinge as they picked up their logs and trotted with them toward the main road.

A Haftling, one of yesterday's new arrivals (there was a small group of new arrivals every week, to replace the Haftlinge who had been either shot or shipped to the Auschwitz Krankenbau as unable to do the heavy work), was sweating hard, trying to lift a slippery log and put it on his shoulder. He was big, but he didn't seem to be strong at all. Besides, he was lacking all the lifting techniques that one developed after having done this kind of work for some time. The Algerian foreman, Marcel, was yelling at him, and this made the man even more nervous and handicapped his performance altogether. The superintendent pointed at him and asked who he was. Rudi called the man.

"What was your occupation in the civilian life?" he asked.

The man stood to attention. He was heavy, about forty years old,

and his bulging round eyes expressed terror, as he replied, "Accountant, Herr Kapo! In Vienna!"

"Don't you like what you are doing here?" asked the Lagerkommandant. His voice was phlegmatic, almost paternal, and the Haftling suddenly acquired confidence in himself.

"I have a complaint to make," he reported.

"Then report it." The Lagerkommandant frowned slightly.

"I was told in Vienna that I would be working here in my usual
occupation," the man said.

The Lagerkommandant looked at the Superintendent and exchanged glances with Rudi and the Postenkommandant. It was obvious that they found it difficult to keep from laughing.

"Do you need an accountant?" the Superintendent asked the
Lagerkommandant.

"Unfortunately, we already have one," the latter answered with a
solemn air. "But will you accept lighter work meantime?" he asked
the Haftling.

"Yes, sir, Herr Lagerkommandant!" the Accountant replied
briskly. There was joy in his voice. He thought his troubles were over
when the Lagerkommandant recommended to Rudi to get the man a
lighter duty.

When the two officials were gone, Rudi took over. Really, it was
not only Rudi. The Postenkommandant and all the Postens, foremen,
and Pipels became aware of the situation, and all took upon themselves the task of finding the Accountant lighter work. They ordered
him to pick up the heaviest log of all, and as he was anxiously trying
to lift it to his shoulder, they all yelled obscenities, and Marcel and
Erich smashed their sticks on his buttocks. The Accountant was
paralyzed with terror. Now he was totally unable to do any kind of
work. One of the Postens lifted his rifle and shot right above the
man's head. It was supposed to be a joke, but the Accountant became
rigid, foam came out of his mouth, and he fell straight on his back.
Everybody was caught by surprise. The Posten explained that he
hadn't meant to kill the man. Another Posten bent over him and said
that the man was still breathing. The Postenkommandant decided that
the situation couldn't be left in limbo, and he lifted his rifle to finish
off the poor devil. And this was when my life in Kobier took a sudden
turn.

"Herr Postenkommandant," I stood at attention. I wasn't thinking
that what I was doing was butting into an SS man's business, and that
it could easily cost me my own life.

"Herr Postenkommandant," I said, "there's nothing wrong with the man. It's epilepsy. Please give me half an hour, and he'll be as good as new!"

It didn't seem like I was talking. It was somebody else, using my mouth, and my tongue, and my voice. I was terrified at hearing all this coming out of me, and so seemed all the others who were witnessing the scene.

The Postenkommandant stood in front of me, his rifle up and ready to shoot, caught between surprise and disbelief. He was at this moment the highest-ranking official within this little group of people. He had in his hands everybody's life and death. And I was telling him what to do and what not to do. The silence must have lasted just a few seconds. To me — and, I'm sure, to the others — it seemed an eternity.

Then the rifle went down, and a voice said, "I'll give you half an hour. If he's not on his feet by then, I'll shoot both him and you." The voice was coming from the Postenkommandant's mouth, but I felt that what had just happened to me was now happening to him: he must be wondering whose voice it was that was coming from him.

I went to work. Jankel was given permission to help me, and we both carried the Accountant to the edge of a ditch, where there was water used for irrigation. I applied cold compresses and a soothing voice, and soon the foam stopped coming, the color returned to his cheeks, and his breathing became more regular. Within fifteen minutes, the three of us reported to the Postenkommandant, who said, "Saved by the gong!"

I returned to my work, but it was not the same as before. The Pipels, the foremen, the Kapo, and even the Postens looked at me in a way that bordered on respect. A Posten seated along the path where we trotted with our logs stopped me and ordered me to throw down my log. He wanted to learn a little more about me.

"Are you Jewish?" he asked.

"Yes, sir, Herr Posten!"

"But not completely Jewish?" he suggested.

"Not completely, Herr Posten." This was the way to do. Always agree with them.

"Yes, I noticed it immediately," said the Posten. "You do look to me like a better man. Are you a doctor?" He used the German term *mediziner*. I knew that *arzt* meant doctor, and I thought that *mediziner* might mean something like a medical student, or somebody freshly graduated from medical school.

All this would describe my status well enough, and I replied, "Yes, sir, Herr Posten. I'm a *mediziner*."

The Posten ordered another Haftling to pick up my log, and he took me to the central clearing where Rudi and th~ Postenkommandant were.

"He's a doctor," the Posten reported.

Kapo Rudi, surrounded by his Pipels, and the Postenkommandant were eating bread with bacon. Rudi offered me a little piece.

"A doctor? What are we going to do with you? Our Lager doctor would hate competition. Do you know how to use a razor?"

I had never shaved with a regular razor, only with safety razors. These were unavailable in the Lager. We all went once a week to the Krankenstube, where two or three Haftlinge operated on us, trying to keep our cheeks shaven and our heads smooth. They used real razors and haircutters. I had to admit to Rudi that I didn't know how to use a razor, but I swiftly added that I was quick to learn. He thought a little and then decided that something should be done to make my life easier — and I thought that if they just stopped hitting me, my life would be much easier.

Rudi didn't have the power to make me a functionary and to let me stay in the Lager. However, by the same evening, all the Lager knew what had happened at the Kommando site, and from being an unknown part of the Mussulman mass, I had become something of a celebrity.

The next day, at lunch time, Rudi did something I had never seen him do before. He called for the line to form for seconds, a line in which I had never participated because Rudi, like the Schreiber in the Quarantane, used his long ladle to hit Haftlinge quarreling for a little soup. I remained stretched on the fresh grass, my eyes closed in a vain effort to forget that I was hungry.

Rudi gave the seconds to the first four Haftlinge in line; then he stopped the distribution for a moment, and as the rest of the line watched his smallest movement anxiously, he remained pensive. Suddenly, he called aloud, "Doctor!" I opened my eyes and looked at him. Yes, he had me in mind. He was watching me with his green eyes; then he smiled and repeatd, "Doctorchen" — "Little doctor" — and for the first time since I had been in Auschwitz, I received a second. And I had a confirmation of what I had always suspected: man is born with dignity; he dies when his dignity is gone; therefore, if he wants to stick to life, he must strive to keep his dignity intact, regardless of the circumstances.

As spring blossomed, the work in the forest got more hectic, and the shootings because of "attempts to escape" became a daily business. By now, I had learned the practical aspect of the shootings, and it became obvious why the Postenkommandant had wanted to kill the Accountant. There was a bonus for a shooting, if the shot Haftling was an unsuccessful escapee. Thus, had he put a bullet in the head of the Accountant who, he thought, was already dead from a heart attack, the Postenkommandant would have received fifty marks, because he would have declared him as shot during an attempt to escape.

Usually it was decided the night before who would be shot the next day, and the most shootings were done not at our Kommando but at Kapo Alfred's Feldkommando. But we, too, had our good share of them. There was a time when we carried home a corpse every day, and once it was two corpses on one day.

It was already the month of May, the fields bloomed with poppies, the forest smelled of mushrooms, and we shook while doing our usual chores, uncertain whose turn it would be today. The day when a Haftling was to be shot was different from the other days. The Kapos were unusually excited, there was more beating than usual, and the Postens participated in the beatings very actively on such days. The work proceeded in an atmosphere of tremendous tension, which disappeared only after shots were heard, and we knew that for today, the rest of us were probably safe. After the shots came the anticlimax. The Posten who had done the killing advised Rudi of the identity of the killed man. Rudi identified the victim again. All the functionaries wondered about the stupidity of the bastard who thought he could escape. Jankel and Ayzik prepared the stretcher. And the Kommando marched home, singing "Erica."

The first time I found out that the shootings were planned beforehand was when one day, minutes before the arrival of soup, repeated shooting suddenly cut the air. It stopped, then it came again, as from a machine gun. We all held our breath. I thought about the partisans. David, one of Rudi's Pipels, said to the Kapo, "Was it that skinny Jew from Pruzana?"

"No," replied Rudi. "It was that fat, blond Jew with blue eyes. The one who prays all the time."

Indeed it was Berman, an orthodox Jew from Cracow, a man whose life was composed of work, prayer, and hope. A man who wouldn't have killed a fly, or eaten a slice of liverwurst, because it was not kosher. He was lying in the middle of the clearing, with a couple of dozen holes in his body, his log still next to him.

"He was hard to finish off," commented the Killer, who was the one who had shot Berman in an effort to escape right from the very center of the Postenkette — with a log on his shoulder, no doubt to keep him warm at night.

The day after Berman's killing, three Haftlinge got shot at Kapo Alfred's Kommando, and that evening Richard gave me the bad news: "Tomorrow's going to be an important shooting. The Kapos are celebrating together with the Postens. They're all drunk. Rudi was laughing in a way that gave me the shivers."

The morning came, gray and sad. We all had in our hearts the same mute question: Who would it be today?

As we marched to work, it started raining slightly. There was new hope. Usually, when it rained hard, we came back to the Lager early. Now it looked as if the rain might get heavy. Maybe we wouldn't even go as far as the forest. Rudi didn't even order us to sing.

We marched in the rain, and by the time we had reached the clearing, we were drenched. I thought they wouldn't even make us start working. But I was wrong. Rudi raged. He yelled, and whipped, and kicked. I was confused. At first, I thought he wasn't himself today.

Oh, yes, he did have a green triangle, and there was a rumor that he was serving time for murder when he was sent to Auschwitz. Yet he was not all bad. Often he would take a group of us, in the evening after the report, and would hold singing rehearsals behind the latrine. This was his way of teaching us new marching songs, which we'd be singing during our trips to the work site and back. And sometimes, as we were singing the sentimental or heroic marches of the German Army, Rudi would interrupt us and would intone in a very low voice the "International." Thus he implied that he was a communist, and he made us feel as if we had a real brother in him.

Which was the true Rudi? The one singing the "International" or the one yelling now at his own Pipel Max: "You stinking bastard! Hiding here, while all the others are sweating their balls off! March to the logs!" And he struck the boy with a stick, something I had never seen him do before.

The little Pipel, terror in his eyes, rushed to the pile of logs and tried to hoist one on his shoulder.

"You dog!" Rudi was at him again. "Looking for light work? Grab this log here!" He pointed to an enormous piece of wood.

The boy shook, and tried, and couldn't. And Rudi beat him again and again.

"It's bad," Jankel whispered to me, running with a huge log. It was raining steadily. They had to stop this farce.

Rudi looked at his watch. "It's already half past ten! Damn you! Work faster!"

He whipped a couple of Haftlinge who were just passing by. It was hell. It was impossible. People ran like crazy, hoping for the rain to become so heavy that we'd have to go back home. I ran across Max. The little Pipel was soaked to the skin with rain and with sweat. When he looked at me, there was terror in his eyes. I didn't want to think of what by now I knew must be the scope of Rudi's rage. The clouds had now opened up with a downpour, and we waited for Rudi's whistle to fall into formation and march back. And then the shot came. Just one short shot.

Everybody stopped. The Postenkommandant entered the clearing. He was solemn when he said aloud to Rudi, "It was Max. The poor bastard. I called him three times, but he continued running across the Postenkette. I had no choice."

Rudi composed his face into a grimace of sadness and said, "Oh!"

Four men picked up Max. He lay in the ditch, the back part of his skull missing, his eyeglasses intact beside his body.

Raoul, the French Pipel, looked fearfully at Rudi and asked, "Why, Kapo?"

"It must have been because of Kapo Theo," replied Rudi, and he turned around, whistling.

Then it was nothing but the result of a love triangle. An effect of jealousy. A mutual agreement between Rudi and Theo: not mine — not yours. As simple as that.

The next day, it was the Hungarian musician's turn. His name was Matrosz. It seemed he had been a well-known concert violinist. And now the Killer had his eye on him. After all, they were fellow countrymen.

It happened at noon. The soup wagon arrived, Rudi whistled, and we formed a line. Matrosz, his red bowl under an arm, was about to join the line when the Killer noticed him.

"You!" he yelled. "Come here!"

Matrosz stood at attention in front of the Killer. The Posten reached for the Haftling's cap and, with a blasé gesture, thrust it some ten yards away, just beyond a sandy patch that delineated the Postenkette border for the day.

"Pick up your Mutze!" ordered the Killer.

Matrosz looked in fear at his cap, which was lying so close but so far. "It is beyond the Postenkette, Herr Posten," he announced. "I am forbidden to cross the Kette."

"I said, go and pick up your Mutze," the Killer repeated calmly. Matrosz didn't budge.

The Posten hit him, and Matrosz, a little skinny man, fell to the ground.

"Go," said the Killer.

"You intend to kill me!" cried Matrosz in fear.

The Posten grabbed the Haftling by the collar and dragged him toward his cap. As he was pulling, Matrosz clung to the earth, plowing a deep ridge in the sand with his knees. Without even taking his automatic rifle off, the Posten shot Matrosz directly from his shoulder. A stream of blood flew from Matrosz's head, painting the emerald of the grass red beyond the forbidden path.

For the rest of this day, we worked with a feeling of security, so unusual in our everyday life. We hoped that the beast had satisfied his hunger and would let us alone.

The same evening, we learned that the Boxer, one of the giants of the uprooting detail, had been shot. This had been the first shooting at that Kommando. I was told that it had happened as the Boxer was caught cutting a healthy tree. He had done it to complete his day's quota, and he had done it on the express order of the Postenkommandant. But he was noticed by the Superintendent of the Department of Forestry himself, and there were no excuses for killing a healthy tree. The Superintendent shot the Boxer under a half-sawn tree, while the Postenkommandant remarked, "The dog broke a rule. It's just for him to pay for it."

It reminded me of an article I had read in a Polish-language newspaper in Lvov immediately after the German invasion. It was about a Jewish coachman who had whipped his horse. The article warned the Jews that the time of their blood-thirsty lording it was over, and that horses would no longer be beaten with impunity. And at that very time, hundreds of the Jewish intelligentsia of Lvov were being murdered at the Piaskowa Gora.

I cried for the Boxer, because I felt responsible for his death. A few days before, he had beaten me up for no reason at all; he must have been tense, all of us were — but he was so much stronger than I that I felt it unfair of him, and, washing the blood off my lips, I had said, "I don't know why you did it. But I know that you'll pay for it." And now, he had paid for it. And I was sure I had thrown a curse on him. I started believing that a supernatural being was watching over me, and I promised myself that never again would I curse another human being.

With all the killings, our marching songs had become a nightmare, and it was with a feeling of relief that we were finally ordered to shut up once and for all. We were just crossing the little bridge, carrying the body of the day and singing a heroic march. We were dirty with earth and resin, dressed in rags, skinny from hunger, and covered with bruises and ulcerations — and we were Jews. And the words of the march were saying, "We are the Lords of the World!" The comicality of the situation didn't escape the sharp eye of the Lagerkommandant. He rushed out of his cottage and yelled angrily at Rudi: "Stop this nonsense immediately! Once and for all!" I thought with thankfulness that the Germans still had their sense of humor.

My approach to the entire question of survival was quite simple: I had the will to survive, and in order to achieve it I was prepared to do anything, except one: I would never choose to remain alive at the expense of any of my fellow Haftlinge. The first thing I had to do, then, was to become emotionally and physically strong enough to be able to satisfy my keepers. I was successful at that. Within two short weeks, as if touched by a magic wand, I learned how to saw the timber, chop down the trees, thrust the slippery logs over my shoulder, and not show the fatigue.

I also learned how to avoid asking the Slovak doctor for any favors. Once, I had a deep cut in my left thumb, and after a couple of days it became an ugly, purulent ulcer. Remembering that many disinfectants were made with a base of turpentine, and that the turpentine was extracted from tree resin, I loaded the ulcer with fresh sap, and kept repeating this procedure for several days, until my thumb was cured.

My newly acquired image as a young physician with a non-Jewish mother also helped. The Kapos as well as the Postens developed a strange respect for me, which had even reached the point where they stopped beating me, except for the special occasions when the entire Kommando was punished for insufficient productivity.

I even learned to enjoy the beauty of the forest and its magnificent fragrance. And it was just that fragrance that had created a new problem for me: it acted as a tonic, and I was always terribly hungry. It was not just hunger. It was a craving, a pain, a daydream, and a nightmare. In my dreams, I saw myself killing all three Kapos. It was a simple plan. At night, I would slip into the Kapos' quarters, cut off their heads with my hatchet, take from their shelves two loaves of fresh bread and sausage — or, maybe blutwurst, which had much more fat in it — and have a banquet. And after the banquet, I would cut my veins with a knife. Thus, I would die gorged, and in the morning, other Haftlinge would bless me, because there would be no Kapos any longer to torture them. Nobody would even have resented my having eaten all that food, because it wasn't destined for the Haftlinge anyway. But then a new day would come, and I would wake up from my dreams, and the Kapos were still there, and my hunger was still with me. I would stand in the middle of the Raportplatz, the red bowl under my arm, thinking that I would never be able to kill the Kapos. Indeed, I had by now realized that I wouldn't be able to kill anybody. From an enthusiastic, militant student who had returned to Poland to take an active part in the holy war against Hitler, I had become a soft-spoken preacher of brotherhood and forgiveness.

The worst conditions brought out the best in me. I discovered my true self, and I thank God for this. They all viewed me as God's curious miscreation, and while calling me "Doctor," which had become my official name in Kobier, they probably considered me a sort of missionary or halfbaked false prophet whose sport it was to stick his neck out every few days for another imperiled fellow Mussulman.

Then, one day my turn arrived. Rudi summoned me and said, "Doktorchen, a lucky strike! The driver's helper got sick and has been taken to Auschwitz. You'll take his place."

This was a real break. It meant that my worst days were over. It meant working less hard and eating slightly more. It meant standing less on my feet and getting a little more rest. In a quick retrospect, I saw myself the way I had been until now: a skinny Mussulman in a thin, oversized Lager jacket, with a dirty Mutze falling over my eyes, shrinking from the early morning cold, and trying to warm up by holding my hands in the pockets of my striped trousers; pressing my red bowl under my arm, entrusting myself to the Girl of the Ring; then adjusting the spoon that was sticking out of the next-to-the-top button-hole, and going to say hello to Lucien and Richard. Now, all this was over, and as it usually happened with me whenever a part of my life was about to change, I felt sorry and almost unwilling to face an improvement in my condition.

There were two drivers in Kobier: the younger Zdziszek and the older Zbyszek. Both were Poles from Warsaw, and both were charged with identical sets of chores. Their work started about an hour later than that of the Kommandos and consisted of traveling to the forest, loading timber onto the ladder wagons, carrying it to the main road, and unloading the logs into a ditch, from which the wood was later loaded onto a truck that took it to the mill. At midday, the wagons carried soup to the work sites in the forest and in the fields. The entire *Kutcherkommando* was composed of the wagon, two horses, the driver, two Jewish helpers, and a Posten traveling on a bag packed with hay and placed in the rear of the wagon.

All things, then, seemed equal, but they weren't so exactly. Zbyszek, the older driver, was a nice man, and there was by now a sort of friendly relationship between me and him; the younger one, Zdziszek, was immature and overcome with a feeling of power, as in a way, he was the master of life and death over his two Jewish wards. And it was in his Kommando that I was now working, along with Joel, a slim, quiet Jew from Pruzany, a man in his late thirties. While Zdziszek drove the team of horses, Joel and I sat on the floor of the wagon, and the Posten, the ubiquitous rifle on his knees, resting on his hay-stuffed bag, ruled over the three of us. The wagon rode slowly on a narrow path in the forest, until we'd reached one of the stacks prepared by Rudi's Kommando during the preceding several days. The Posten, Joel, and I got off the wagon. Joel and I handed the logs over to Zdziszek, who remained on the cart, while the Posten sat under a bush, rolled himself a cigarette, and hummed a German song.

When the wagon was fully loaded, all of us walked beside it toward the road, where we unloaded the timber into a ditch. We repeated this operation many times, until an imposing heap of wood could be seen in the ditch. The work itself was hard, but there was none of the terrifying kind of rush imposed on the Waldkommando by Rudi, his staff, and the many Postens. Here, we had just one Posten, usually a different one every day, supposedly to make it difficult for us to form a closer relationship with him and perhaps prepare the ground for a successful escape. What was so strange about the Kutcherkommando Postens was that they were all nice to us, even those who only a day before had killed a Haftling in one of the larger Kommandos. Each of them had discussions with us, joked, had a bad word for Hitler's war machine, let us have decent rest periods, and never hit us.

True, their jokes were sometimes not very funny — not to us, that is. Once a Posten put the barrel of his rifle right to my forehead and asked me whether I was afraid of dying. We were at that time on the wagon, traveling leisurely in the heart of the forest, and it had occurred to me that he could easily explain his shooting me as an action taken to stop me from fleeing. I had two possible options: either I was afraid, or I wasn't. Well, if I was going to die, I didn't see any reason to die as a coward. So, I chose the option of courage.

"No, Herr Posten," I assured him, "I'm not afraid of dying."

"But don't you understand," he was curious to know, "that it is only a question of my mood? I can decide to pull the trigger" — and his finger tightened around the trigger — "and all will be over. Now, aren't you really afraid?"

Well, a man is as good as his word. I felt an unpleasant tickling in my stomach, but again I assured him that I was not afraid. He remained in a pensive position — he made me think of Rodin's "Thinker," only in an SS uniform and with a rifle. This must have been a very short exchange, but to me it lasted a long time. I could see Joel shrinking like a turtle receding into his shell, and Zdziszek smiling maliciously. But the Posten laid the rifle on his knees and stated that the Doctor had guts.

On occasion, a Posten would share with us his most intimate feelings. There was a young Slovak Posten who traveled with us sometimes. He was blond, shy, and pleasant, and I was always curious how this kind of a person could become one of the Auschwitz killers. Maybe he read the curiosity in my eyes, or maybe it was a compulsive confession, but he told us one day that he was very unhappy to be there.

"When I enlisted," he said, "it was with the thought that as a soldier I would be able to help my mother. You see, I have an old mother, and there is no one else to help her. I thought I would be sent to the front, and she would be getting my salary. Indeed, I never expected to be sent here to become a murderer."

Sometimes, we were called on to help a Posten in distress. Once, as the wagon journeyed in the shadows of the ancient trees, a fox jumped out of a thicket and stopped in the middle of the path, watching us with curiosity. The Posten, an older man who neither knew anything about the laws of hunting nor was a good shot, decided that he had to get the fox. Zdziszek stopped the wagon, and the Posten shot from his hay bag. Nothing happened. The fox waved good-bye with its tail and disappeared into the forest, and we moved on in search of a stack of logs.

The next day, as we were having our lunch rest together with Rudi's Kommando, the Lagerkommandant and the Forest Superintendent arrived. They wanted to talk to us, to Zdziszek and Joel and me. Zdziszek was the first to be questioned. The superintendent wanted to know whether he had heard a shot the day before. Zdziszek said that he hadn't — definitely no! And he got a powerful blow on his jaw that sent him rolling to the ground. I thought that the superintendent must have been a boxer in his civilian life. Now the Lagerkommandant went to work on Zdziszek. He might not have been a boxer, but my heart bled when I saw him beating up the driver in such a nasty way. Yet Zdziszek didn't say a word. Then they called me. I made believe that I didn't understand any German, and they asked Jankel to interpret. While he was interpreting, I listened and prepared my answers. As Jankel was putting the question about the shooting into Polish, I heard the Lagerkommandant explain to the Postenkommandant that a deer had been found in the forest killed by a Posten's bullet. A deer? The good old Posten had fired at a visible fox and hit an invisible deer! What a laugh! But not just now. They wanted to know whether our Posten had shot the day before, and I told the Lagerkommandant that I couldn't possibly answer such a question: the Posten had been seated behind me, and I was looking forward as the regulations required. How could I know what the Posten was doing?

The Kommandant lifted his arm to hit me, and then let it fall uneasily. He said to the superintendent, "How do you discuss anything with a moron?"

I smiled.

He turned disgustedly to the Kapo Alfred and said, "Tell these idiots that the Posten has already admitted that he shot at a fox. Now he's in the bunker" — that meant "jail" — "and tomorrow he'll be shipped to the front, so he can learn when to shoot and how to shoot." Of course, the other Postens liked us for not having betrayed their comrade, even if our testimony had no real significance, and our relationship with them became even more relaxed.

As it happened, our problem was not the work itself, and not the Postens, but the driver Zdziszek. This eighteen-year-old product of the streets of Warsaw had already had three years of Auschwitz behind him, and most of his education had come from there. He was rough, high-handed, and arbitrary in his manners, and he never thought twice before deciding to beat us up. It was already early summer when the Posten gave us an unscheduled rest on a hot afternoon. Joel hurled himself on the grass and immediately fell asleep, Zdziszek gave one last look at the horses, took off their bits, threw some fodder into their bag, and advised me that he would take a nap, while I'd have to stand by the horses and fan them with the small branch of a beech tree that he handed me now, to drive the flies away. So I fanned the horses, and fanned them, and fanned them with the green branch, and the forest was fragrant, and the air was hot, and with all the beetles buzzing around, I just leaned against one of the horses — and fell asleep standing up.

A burning pain in my chest woke me up. It was Zdziszek's horse whip. The whip hissed a second and a third time, cutting my face and covering it with blood, while Zdziszek yelled that I was a sonofabitch who let the flies eat up a whole horse. This was the last straw, and the same evening I asked Zbyszek whether he could take me on his Kommando. We needed Kapo Theo's permission, but Zbyszek wanted me, and the next day I was a part of his team. My new assignment was to work in the field and, as previously, to carry the soup to work sites.

My diet became richer, now that I was working with Zbyszek. It wasn't that I was receiving larger portions of anything, but Zbyszek closed his eyes to the fact that I was stealing some of the horses' food to enrich my dinner. It was the dry slices of sugar beets, a residue of the sugar-manufacturing process, that the horses got for dessert, and that I adopted as a part of my daily diet. I took a handful of those slices, which looked like potato chips, and threw them in my corn soup, where they soaked for a few minutes, until they became sufficiently soft to eat. Whatever sweetness they still had lent a better taste and, I hoped, substance to my soup. However, my eternally hungry belly was not satisfied even with this new ingredient, and I had to start thinking of another way to get an additional piece of bread. One day — and it was a hot afternoon — as our wagon was slowly rolling through the forest and we approached a sunny clearing, the horses showed an unusual nervousness. Soon we found the reason for this: a snake coiled comfortably in a colorful spiral was sleeping under a bush, enjoying the warmth of the sun. Zbyszek took a swing with a heavy stick, but before it fell on the snake, the animal was gone. At this moment, I had a brilliant idea, "Why don't we look for a nice snake," I suggested to Zbyszek, "and offer it to the Lagerkommandant?"

Our Lagerkommandant had a small zoological garden behind his cottage. He had there a cage with a few local birds; he had a deer, a fox, and a weasel; and I didn't know why he shouldn't have a nice, friendly snake. And should he accept our gift, I didn't see any reason that he shouldn't ask Rudolf, the cook, to give us some of the leftover SS food, instead of throwing away bucketfuls of good potatoes just because he was too anti-Semitic to see the Jews eating something decent. Zbyszek didn't need any such handouts because, as a Pole, he was getting potatoes and meat from Rudolf, but I could use his portion for Richard. Of course, I could not explain all my devious thinking to Zbyszek, so I just appealed to his sense of sportsmanship. Besides, Zbyszek thought that it was a good idea, and with the permission of our Posten, we went looking for snakes. Until that day,

I had never realized how many of them there were in those woods. Green and black, with their SS-like zigzag on the back, they were all over, enjoying a sunbath, but most of them were so alert that we couldn't even approach them before they had already disappeared into some invisible hole in the earth.

I picked up a heavy stick and cut a very tiny fork at one end of it — the way I remembered my old boy-scout books said to do. Zbyszek got a long piece of string, and all that remained to be done was to find a snake nice enough to wait for us. Finally, we found one. It must have been an old snake to let me get this close to it, I thought. And deaf, too. With a quick movement, I got its thin neck into the fork of my stick and pinned the animal to the ground as, by now wide awake and viciously hissing, it threw its long body all over, trying to escape its enslavement. Meanwhile, Zbyszek caught it by the tail, pulled its body up, and fastened it to the stick by wrapping the snake to the wood with several twists of the string. Shortly, the snake was secured to the stick, with only its angry head free and hissing, and as I carried the stick in my hand, I imagined that I must look like Hippocrates himself.

This part of our effort was successful, but the other wasn't. The Lagerkommandant at first liked the present, but he had a swift change of mind within minutes. He was afraid that the snake might be a threat to the rest of his zoo and ordered me to kill it. I pleaded with the man. I remembered having read that poisonous snakes had just two poison-bearing teeth in their mouths, and having had experience in tooth extraction at the Jewish Hospital in Lvov, I offered to extract the poisonous teeth and make the snake amenable to coexistence with the other animals. I would have done anything to get that damned Rudolf to give me the leftover SS potatoes. But nothing doing. Caressing his deer amorously, the Kommandant repeated his order to kill the snake. So, contrary to my original plans, and unwillingly, I did it.

But then a new idea occurred to me. Wristbands! Why hadn't I thought of it before? I ran to Lucien and begged him to give me a few pills of the medicine we were given against the Durchfall; it contained tannin, and I was sure it would do the trick for preserving the snake's skin. I skinned the dead animal, cleaned the skin, and put it into a solution of the medicine. The next day, I started peddling my product: watchbands made of genuine snakeskin.

The first order came from Kapo Rudi, but by the time I thought the skin was ready for use, I also discovered that it was much too thin to be made into a watchband. I consulted Rudi, and we came to the conclusion that I should use his old watchband and glue the snakeskin to it. It proved feasible, and the product was a handsome band. As soon as the Postenkommandant saw it, he wanted Rudi to give it to him, but the Kapo rcommended me. Thus snake-catching and watchband-making became my moonlighting occupation. It brought me an occasional portion of bread and soup, and even a piece of bacon rind given to me now and then by a Posten. Who knows — I might have survived the rest of the war on snakeskins, if not for the fact that one day the Postenkommandant discovered that his beautiful new wristband was in the process of rotting, and soon after, the rest of my clientele had the same experience. Evidently, the medicine was good for Durchfall only, after all, and I had to retreat quickly from my profitable business.

I tried one last zoological adventure, when a mother squirrel fell into Rudi's hands. Our Kommando was returning to the Lager, when Kapo Rudi noticed a squirrel seated on the branch of a tree amidst a small, isolated clump of trees in a clearing. He hit the tree with a hatchet, and the squirrel, scared, jumped to the next tree. Rudi hit again, and the squirrel changed trees. Rudi made a sport out of scaring the animal until, exhausted, it fell off a tree. As he picked the stunned creature up, I noticed that her breasts were heavy with milk and advanced the theory that she either was a mother or was about to become a mother. The little animal soon died, probably from fatigue. Rudi wanted to throw the little body away, but I said that if the litter wasn't born yet, maybe through a Caesarean section we could save the little ones. We carried the squirrel to the Lager, and the Kommandant postponed the evening report to allow me to perform the operation. Alas, the belly of the squirrel was empty, but the excitement lingered even after the report. I started to think that maybe I should stop trying so hard, as somebody might get really angry with me in the end, and my imaginativeness might cost me a little too much. Thus I returned to my skimpy food portions, and the nagging nightmares of hunger.

By now, it was the haying time, and we carried on our wagon heaps of fragrant grass cut by one of Kapo Alfred's Kommandos. We came into closer contact with the local peasants, and once we received a slice of bread from a peasant girl. There was no exchange of words, though, between them and us at any time. I believe they were as scared of the SS as we were.

Rumors started circulating at that time about Polish partisans being in the forest. I don't know how true the rumors were, but some of our

Postens started showing a bit of nervousness each time we were in the woods. Some of them complained that Hitler had promised them a *Blitzkrieg* but had failed to keep his promise. Some said they'd rather be on the front line than in the forest of Kobier. And so one day, unexpectedly, we learned that the camp was to be liquidated immediately, and shortly before the evening report, we were all back in Auschwitz One, the Mother Camp, except that this time we·didn't go into the Quarantane again. We were by now full-fledged Auschwitz Haftlinge.

I watched everything with curiosity: the broad, well-swept streets of the Lager; its two-story brick barracks arranged in neat, even rows; its intense street life. I felt like a provincial thrown into the very heart of the capital city. And I still couldn't believe that I was back here. This time, Auschwitz had for me the meaning of life. Death stayed behind me, in the dark forest of Kobier. I thought of all the people I had met and left there, and I was penetrated by a feeling of awe. My personal God, all the spirits of my loved ones, and the Ring were watching over me closely. My life had never been easy, but so far I was still alive, wasn't I?

I couldn't help noticing that we, the survivors of Kobier, were the worst-dressed people in the Lager. Even the lowest of the low Mussulmen had better clothes and better shoes than we did. With a feeling of disgust, I studied my torn uniform, the wooden shoes, and that disgraceful oversized cap of mine. And I watched with envy some of the pink-cheeked, well-fed Haftlinge in their custom-made suits, whose pants and jackets matched to perfection; whose small, shapely caps made out of gray-and-blue striped wool were boldly pulled toward the back of the head; and whose comfortable calfskin shoes were even better than the ones worn by many civilians in freedom.

But that was only my first impression. Soon, I saw the Mussulmen in a slightly more realistic light. Their uniforms may have been better than ours, but their bodies were in the same bad shape as those of most cf the Kobier workers, and they constantly wandered about, red bowls under their arms, looking for a bite to eat.

After the evening report, I went for a walk on the Lager's main street, and I ran across Stefan almost immediately.

It was an emotional meeting. He wouldn't stop shaking my hand, while repeating, "You're alive! Unbelievable! You're alive!"

He told me that he had learned about Kobier soon after we had left the Quarantane, and that it was common knowledge that the only way to return from Kobier was as a corpse. It is strange how sometimes things look so much worse from a distance than they do to the people who are immersed in them. Stefan looked much better than he had four months ago, when we had been separated.

"Do you remember?" he said, "when they accepted me as an electrician. Well, I'm still with them. Not much food, but it is light work, it's under a roof, and as far as beating goes, the Kapo just gives me an occasional slap in the face."

Stefan took me to his block and scrounged a portion of bread for me. I felt warm with him around. Suddenly, I rediscovered the meaning of friendship.

The next day, our Kobier group started on a new job: road construction. One thing was good about Auschwitz: you did not have to worry about unemployment.

Our work site was some twenty minutes' march from the Lager. It was a very special feeling to see all the Kommandos leaving the Lager at about seven in the morning. A Haftlinge orchestra played various marches next to the main gate, while the Kommandos stamped hard as they passed by the Lagerkommandant. The Postenkommandants left their reports with the Lagerschreiber, reporting the numbers of the Haftlinge in each Kommando. The numbers had to be identical in the evening, when the Kommandos returned from work.

Leaving the Lager behind, each Kommando took its own direction, and soon the regular work day was begun.

The entire Lager of Kobier formed just one work detail, except for the functionaries like the doctor, the dentist, the drivers, and the Kapos. They would be used somewhere else as functionaries, because in Auschwitz, as in our civilian world, once you were somebody, you remained somebody forever after. Our Kommando marched now on a dusty road leading to an empty field where some leftover cabbages and radishes were still waiting invitingly for somebody to pick them. We were to build the next portion of the road across this field.

We were broken into several small groups, each of which had to perform a different task. There was a group of diggers, one of stone breakers, another one of truck workers, and a last one of all-purpose workers, who could be attached to any of the groups, according to the need of the moment. I was a member of this last group.

I discovered that road building is not easy work. We dug the ditches; we filled them with large rocks; we covered those with a layer of stones, which we had previously broken from rocks, using hammers and imagination, as mere physical effort was not sufficient to be a successful stone breaker. While all this was being done, narrow-gauge tracks were set along the ditches, on which we pushed the lorries filled with rocks and earth, bringing them to the spot where these materials were needed. There, we emptied our trucks right into the ditch and then returned for more of the same. Occasionally a lorry capsized, and we had to reload it, spurred into quicker action by the foreman's whipping and the Postens' rhetorical inquiries, "Willst du nicht, oder kannst du nicht?" — "Aren't you willing, or aren't you able?" I disliked even being close to these Postens, as some of them had a steady companion that I hadn't trusted at all since the time of my arrest in Rokiciny: a trained police dog, usually a Doberman or a German shepherd.

In the evening, as tired as we were, we had to face the evening report. It was totally different from that of Kobier, where the count lasted a few minutes, and we could take it easy afterwards, unless there was an occasional evening game such as marching to the main road to load lumber on the lumber-mill trucks. Here, there were no evening chores, but the report itself was usually a lengthy affair, which sometimes extended long into the night if for some reason the count remained incorrect. But on a lucky evening when the report was over within a short hour, washed and refreshed I met with Stefan, and we had our leisurely walk in the main street.

Richard would join us sometimes. He found work in the laundry and was happy with it: he had a roof over his head when it rained, the work was not very hard, and occasionally there was the possibility of organizing an additional portion of soup. Also, from time to time he was able to get hold of a German newspaper, to which the Poles had now the right to subscribe.

"You should see what they're writing," he would say. "It seems to be the beginning of the end."

I thought that it might very well be so, but what was that to me? First of all, would I be alive to see the end? And then, supposing I did see it, I didn't know how much sense my survival would make, with almost everybody I loved dead. Stefan helped me in such moments.

"Sooner or later, you, too, will get a lighter job," he would console me. "The others already have. Marian works in a garage; Szczepan is a Schreiber in a small agricultural Lager; Henek Czernowicki works as a tailor."

I remembered Henek, a handsome man of thirty, who had joined us, handcuffed, on our train from Zakopane to Cracow. He had been in the company of his father and his brother.

"What has happened to his family?" I asked Stefan.

"His brother is also a tailor, and his father is a barber."

Everybody seemed to be all right but me. Sometimes it made me feel as if I were jinxed. But again, what importance could that have? As Father would have said, "Whether you survive or die, it still will not be the end of the world."

The question was whether I wanted to survive. I thought I wanted to. Then there was the other question: What for? It was when Stefan told me about the Warsaw Ghetto uprising that I discovered an answer for the "what for" part of my question.

"When you were in Kobier, we heard a rumor about a Jewish uprising in the Ghetto. It was sometime in April. It seems the boys at Montelupich were right after all: while there is one Jew left, finally to answer violence with violence, and while there is another Jew left to tell the world about it, the cause is not lost."

I wanted to know which cause, and Stefan patted me on the shoulder: "The cause is something that concerns humanity as a whole. A hard test has to be given from time to time, a sort of refresher course, to make the world stop and think again, because we all tend to forget so easily."

"But why always the Jews?" I reacted to Stefan's argument. "Why not the Peruvians, or the polar bears?"

"They, too, have their portion of suffering. Everybody does. But with the Jews, it becomes more evident, because we are everywhere and more visible. Even so, I don't pretend that I accept what's going on, but at least I find a reason to wish that I may survive and become a part of the new world that is going to appear as a final result of this cataclysm."

I thought there was something to think about in Stefan's theory, and I wanted to survive for a cause. I wondered whether I could become a Zionist again. When I was in high school, I had been a Zionist as a way of protest. That was a negative reason. Would I ever find a positive reason?

While our Kommando was laying a new road, in a field a little farther on, a Kommando of women was working at harvesting the vegetables. It wasn't possible to approach them, because there was a heavy Postenkette with all those beautiful, vicious police dogs separating us, but there was nothing to stop me from looking in that direction over my stone-loaded lorry. It had now been six months since I'd seen Anka for the last time. Stefan told me that he had had word from his wife, who was in Birkenau. Stefan's wife was all right. I wondered whether Anka was all right, too. Each time I looked at the women working in the field in front of me, all dressed in ample striped skirts and white aprons, with white kerchiefs on their heads, I thought I saw Anka in each of them. I longed for female company. It came to signify to me the equivalent of warmth, of stability, and of security. Not having a woman companion made me feel even more sharply the precarious condition in which I was existing.

The cabbage picking was finished, and the women were gone. All that was left were some overgrown plants that the farmers couldn't use, and these were added to our menu immediately. We devoured the raw cabbage before the soup, with the soup, and after the soup. We spiced it with some black, very sharp-tasting radishes, which we found in the earth next to the cabbages. We ate with great relish. But then the feast ended with a terrible diarrhea, which hit the entire Kommando at the same time.

The most dramatic moment was on the morning when, as we were marching to work, so many people asked for permission to step out of the ranks in order to have a bowel movement that the Kapo had to refuse, on the grounds that we would make the road dirty. We watched each other in desperation, trying our best to hold on until we reached the field. It was now only a question of a few more minutes, and we'd be safe, when suddenly one man in the group whispered painfully, "I can't keep it anymore!" and gave way. It was like a signal, and a minute later everybody had followed the leader. Now, we all marched in even step, our pants filled with feces, but our faces showing relief. When we reached the work site, the entire Kommando, with the Kapo's permission, lined up in front of the water pump to wash our pants.

I wondered whether this was the bottom of our humiliation. Maybe not everybody saw it as a humiliation, after all. Maybe, in order to survive, it was better not to think about an incident like this and to forget it immediately. Yet, I could neither forget it nor consider it a part of my everyday life, although I was aware that I was playing into my persecutors' hands.

This was on September 9, 1943. The lorry tracks had grown much longer, and the construction of the road was in full swing. As I was working with my shovel and having my gloomy thoughts, the red-headed Kapo, whose name I never knew, approached me and took my shovel into his hands, as if to show me how to use it. As he did so, he whispered, "Italy has surrendered." I thought I hadn't heard him correctly, but he repeated. "Italy — *kaput*!" Then he smiled at me, and gave me back my shovel.

I thought of an old Warsaw Ghetto prediction. It said that it would be easy to predict the end of the war by watching for Italy's surrender, as Germany would fall six months later. Did the Kapo know of the prediction, and was he trying to make a Jewish friend, knowing that the war was going to be over by March 1944? The shovel had become lighter in my hands, and my heart pounded with hope as I proceeded working quickly to make the rest of the day go by faster.

Back in the Lager, Stefan was not so enthusiastic about the news. According to him, Italy hadn't surrendered yet, the entire matter wasn't clear at all, and the hard times were far from being over. As if to confirm Stefan's fears, the following evening, as the Kommandos returned from work, *Lagersperre* was announced. *Lagersperre* meant, literally, the "camp's closure." In reality, it meant that no Kommandos were allowed into their barracks until an SS medical inspection was made. Normally, it meant selection for the gas chamber. All Haftlinge had to undress in front of their barracks, and now, their clothes under their arms, they all filed in front of the SS doctor, Dr. Entress, who, standing on top of a table surrounded by several Scharfuhrers, was deciding who would die and who would live and where the ones who were to survive would live.

I was picked, with about a hundred other semiskeletons, to be transported to the Lager of Buna, which was known as *Bunawerke*. It belonged to the huge German corporation G. E. Farbenindustrie and meant only more work and heavier work; I thought with sadness that this time I might not survive after all. We were packed onto a couple of trucks, and we rolled away from Auschwitz One almost immediately. I was sure that Stefan would worry about me once more.

It was a cold and rainy night when we arrived in Buna. We took a cold shower and went to our bunks in a huge, damp tent. Everything seemed so unfriendly here, so ill-wishing, that I couldn't help thinking that it was again the thing between me and my Fate. A challenge. But this time, I had decided to live, Fate or no Fate, and that I would show them that I would live.

Ayzik was the only person from Kobier who was brought to Buna with me, and in his case, it had become clear from the very first moment that Fate was at work. As we entered the tent, Ayzik found his younger brother, whom he hadn't seen for two years. His brother had had an accident at work, his leg had been amputated, and now the man was dying. Ayzik arrived just in time to say good-bye and to recite Kaddish, the prayer for the dead. I felt there must be a reason for me to have been brought to Buna, too.

The next morning it was raining. Myself and nine other newly arrived Musselmen were taken out of the Lager and into the huge

Buna factory compound, where we were told to start laying sewage pipes. Our minuscule Kommando fell into the hands of an Austrian Kapo who was ghoulish-looking and acted accordingly. Our new work consisted of many activities: we dug a four-yard-deep ditch and built a wooden scaffolding in this ditch; then we laid a section of sewage pipe. As we were doing all this, wet soil was falling on our heads, while the rain was converting the earth under our feet into heavy clay, making it difficult for us to move, and soaking us to the bone.

As we shivered down in the hole, the Kapo bent over us every few minutes, mumbling, "You whorish intelligentsia, you just wait till you get out, and I'll break your bones."

And he kept his promise all right. Whenever any of us was forced to climb up, the Kapo was waiting there to give him a gratuitous whipping, and at the end of the day, he lined us up, soaked and exhausted, and pounded his huge fists on our bare heads. As he was doing this, his gigantic body seemed motionless, almost relaxed, and only the awful arm would fall on us, like a mighty electric hammer.

In spite of this show of dissatisfaction with our work, we all received a bonus at the end of the second week: a coupon which could be exchanged in the local commissary for what I hoped would be an item of food. On a Sunday afternoon, which was the only time we had at Auschwitz, no matter which camp we were in, I went to the commissary and asked the Haftling in charge what could I possibly get for my coupon. He offered a clay pipe, or a postcard, or mustard. As I didn't smoke and didn't have anybody outside to whom to send the card, and as neither the card nor the clay pipe was edible, I chose the mustard. The clerk thrust a couple of spoonfuls of mustard into my bowl, and I left the commissary trying to figure out how to eat it. As soon as I was out, a couple of Haftlinge approached me, offering to buy my mustard. One of them wanted to pay me with a clay pipe, and I refused him immediately. The other man produced a raw potato, but I did not have anywhere to boil it, and I wouldn't eat it raw as most Haftlinge did, because I had always had the impression that much of the diarrhea came from eating raw potatoes. I dismissed this buyer, too, and started eating my mustard. It had the consitency of whipped cream and was tasty. All I had to do was to imagine a Viennese sausage along with it, and I was in business.

The next day, a civilian joined our little Kommando. He was of Czech origin and was living in a nearby town. He was some sort of a licensed plumber or civil engineer, who was supposed to control the technical problems of the pipe laying. He was good to us. He shared with us his coffee and bread, and a couple of times he even scolded the Kapo for mistreating us.

This was something he shouldn't have done. The Ghoul did not accept a civilian's interference with his prerogatives, and we happened to be one of them. The next day, instead of returning to our pipes, we were taken to the Buna railroad station and ordered by the Ghoul to transport bags of cement from a freight car to the warehouse. After Kobier, I thought that never again in my life would I have any difficulty throwing a weight on my shoulders. Little did I know. The small paper bags weighing thirty kilograms had to be grabbed, lifted, turned, and thrown on one's back, all in one quick motion, and it just didn't work that easily. I tried to help Ayzik, and the Ghoul whipped me. Ayzik tried to help me, and the Kapo whipped him. Each of us tried to do it on his own, and the Ghoul whipped each of us. There was no exit from our misery. But that was not the end. Once we'd learned how to land the bag on our shoulders, there was a narrow one-foot-wide iron rail bridging the distance between us and the warehouse, and right under the rail, maybe some ten meters down, was a ditch. I figured that should I fall into the ditch, my bones would be shattered and the bag of cement torn, and a delightful thought occurred to me: the Ghoul would be punished for a torn bag! What a splendid chance to take my revenge on him! But I was too cowardly to do it, so I simply closed my eyes and crossed the bridge, feeling a little like a circus acrobat, only somewhat less sure of myself.

After a few days on this job, I felt that something bad was happening to me, but I still tried to fight until that proverbial last straw. While trying to put the last bag of the day on top of the pyramid of bags we had built during the long hours of our toil, one of our Kommando, a skinny and weak teacher from Pruzana who was known as the worst worker in the detail, accidentally destroyed a part of the pyramid. Many bags slipped to the floor, and I ran to help him to put them back in order. The Ghoul saw what had happened and came running after us. He gave us a beating which eclipsed all the previous ones, and the next morning I was hardly able to stand on my feet. I noticed that my legs had swelled tremendously, and as I walked, I could almost hear the water flowing inside them. I pressed a finger into my thigh, and a deep hole remained. It was edema, and I had to resign myself to going to the Krankenbau, although I knew by now that the Krankenbau was like the antechamber of death. I didn't have anybody here to bid good-bye, and I said to myself that Father had known the real answer to my present predicament: a life more or a life less does not mean the end of the world, even if the life in question happened to be my own.

CHAPTER

10

HOSPITAL

From my very first day in Auschwitz, in the Quarantane, I had been hearing various gloomy stories about the institution called the Krankenbau, but this was the first time I myself had been faced with crossing its threshold, and as I was doing so, I couldn't help feeling that now I was well resigned to accepting without protest whatever would be decided by my owners. I felt that I was just an object, and that as such I was owned by the Germans. And I was sure that this was the feeling of the millions of Jews who had crossed the threshold of the German gas chambers. Therefore, having prepared myself spiritually for the unavoidable and the final, I was surprised when an orderly asked me many questions pertaining to my civilian life. He was sitting at a small table, filling out a form with my answers, while I, dressed just in an undersized shirt, stood in front of him, shaking from cold and trying to figure out why so many questions were being asked from such a little body, which would soon by only a handful of ashes.

There was a chair next to the table, and I asked the orderly whether I could sit down, as my barrellike legs could hardly withstand the featherweight of my body. He frowned in disgust and yelled at me in the elegant German of an educated Jew who still didn't know why

Hitler had put him in a Lager where all those Ostjuden were: "Shut-up, you Mussulman, and wait for my orders!" After another quarter of an hour, he assigned me to a bunk and told me to wait there until the doctor arrived to examine me.

It must have been some two hours later when the doctor came. He was also a Haftling and a Jew. He asked the orderly about the new arrivals and was told about me, "A Mussulman with swollen legs." The doctor glanced at my legs, said it was edema, and asked the orderly to give him my registration cards. The orderly brought two of them: one he had filled out this morning, and the other had traveled with me all the way from the Quarantane.

The doctor read my original registration card, shook my hand, and said, "Colleague, I'm sorry to have kept you waiting. My name is Dr. Kovacs. I'm from Slovakia."

I was too stunned to say a word. Such a show of friendliness was something I could hardly remember had ever existed. All I could do was to smile at Dr. Kovacs, and he exclaimed, "Well, then, things aren't so bad after all, if you're still able to smile! All right, you just keep smiling, and we'll take care of the rest. What you need is a lot of food and rest, and I'll see to it that you get it."

After Dr. Kovacs had left, the orderly came to my bunk, smoothed my blanket, and said with respect, "You should have told me immediately you were a doctor."

After a few hours of sleep and a bowl of boiled farina, called here the *diet soup,* I felt well enough to start showing some interest in my ward companions. It was a good-sized ward, with two-tiered bunks occupying all of it, except for the small section where the orderly's table was, in the very back of the room next to my bunk. All, or almost all, bunks were inhabited, and most of them by Greek Jews from Salonika. All of them spoke French, and I befriended the few closest to my bunk within minutes. They were all poor people, some of them fishermen, some peddlers, who had been transplanted from a city they considered their fatherland to the hostile earth of Buna-werke, and who were still thinking of their odyssey as a nightmare, a routing error. They said their rabbi had told them that they were going to Cracow, where a model ghetto was being prepared, and where they would be given all the help they needed to become a prosperous Jewish center. Not having had anything in their life, they had thought of this transfer as something intended to improve their plight, and they were at a loss to understand why in the world Hitler would want to pay any attention at all to such a poor group of Jews. However, they had been brought into Auschwitz. Many of them had been killed on arrival, and the ones who were left alive had found it very difficult to get used to the roughness of the climate and to the ruthlessness of the treatment. This was why they had become the best clients of the Krankenbau.

I spent the next two days resting, eating, and learning Ladino from my new friends who spoke among themselves that sixteenth-century Spanish which was their Yiddish.

On the third day, I thought I felt well enough to go back to work, but Dr. Kovacs wanted to give me a couple more days to rest.

On the fourth night, I had a dream. The Girl of the Ring bent over me, caressed my cheek, smiled, and said softly, "Watch for this coming Thursday." The dream was vivid, and the Girl's voice was the same I had heard before, the voice that had predicted the cataclysm and had assured me of my survival. In the morning, I related the dream to my Greek friends, and instantly I had become the hero of the ward. The Greeks believed in dreams, and they had a way of interpreting them. Before long, I was informed that this coming Thursday was going to be Rosh Hashana, and suddenly my dream had taken on the stature of a prophecy and the Girl the guise of one of God's messengers. From this point on, the Greeks considered me some sort of a *Tzadik* — one of the Just Ones — and tried to outdo each other in showing respect and love for me. Surrounded by this aura, I could hardly wait for the arrival of Thursday and readied myself for a dignified acceptance of whatever that meaningful day might be bringing for me.

On Thursday morning, the ward took on an air of solemnity. The hours were passing, my Greek friends were keeping silent, and my own feeling of tension was constantly growing more and more acute. It was almost nine o'clock when Dr. Kovacs entered the ward, came to me quickly, and said, "My dear colleague, please get ready! You are going to be introduced to the chief SS doctor of Auschwitz, Dr. Entress, for a job in the Krankenbau. It seems that according to new orders from Berlin, Entress is searching for Haftlinge with medical background in order to assign them to hospital jobs. Good luck to you."

So that was it. So this was what the dream was all about. So perhaps my misery was about to end, and a new chapter of my life would begin. As I was putting on the clothes brought to me by the orderly — the best clothes I had ever had in Auschwitz — the ward remained plunged in almost a religious silence. When Dr. Kovacs called me from the door, and as I walked slowly down the aisle, the

Greeks waved at me from their bunks, saying their Hebrew blessings. I thought that I would like to be assigned to this ward and to help these people, and help them, and help them.

In the admissions ward, Dr. Kovacs gave me last-minute advice. He told me to talk only when ordered and to make my answers clear and concise. A few minutes later, two men entered. One was dressed in a chic Haftling uniform and had an armband reading, "Krankenbau Lageraltester." He was Dr. Kovacs' superior. The other was the dreaded SS doctor, tall, gaunt, and somber-looking behind his black-rimmed eyeglasses and dressed in the black uniform of an SS officer — the same Dr. Entress, an ethnic German born and educated in Poland, who had already dispatched to the gas chambers hundreds of thousands of people. I stood in front of him at attention. This time, I looked him in the eyes — the first time I had looked at an SS man directly. There was a force in me that made me do it.

"Doctor?" asked Entress in a cool voice.

Before I could answer, Kovacs confirmed that I was indeed a doctor.

"Can you find him a job in this Krankenbau?" Entress asked the Lageraltester.

"No, Herr Doktor," the man quickly replied. "There are no openings here."

I stood motionless, my heart pounding like a powerful hammer. It was my life they were talking about. A second of hesitation, and it could be either saved or destroyed. I tried to stay cool, as Entress' eyes reexamined me. Then, suddenly, his decision was made.

"Send him immediately to the Krankenbau of Auschwitz One," he ordered the Lageraltester. "They'll find a job for him."

The introduction was over, but I still remained at attention, even after Entress and the Lageraltester had left.

Dr. Kovacs broke the spell. "Let me be the first one to congratulate you, colleague," he said, and shook my hand warmly.

I wasn't able to talk. All I could do was to keep shaking Kovacs' hand and to let a feeling of immense gratefulness overcome me, flow over me and through me, and flood the world and the people around me. I wanted to tell my Greek friends that they were right, that there was a Holy Power in Buna at the present, and that they all would be saved one day the way I was being saved today. But I wasn't allowed to see my Greek friends again. The ambulance was waiting to transport me to the model Krankenbau of Auschwitz One, the Lager of my origin.

As I look at that moment thirty-five years later, I'm amazed that it didn't occur to me then, as I was being comfortably transported in the ambulance, that I might be being carried to the gas chamber, as this particular automobile did serve, among other things, the purpose of taking individually condemned Haftlinge to the crematorium. No, I was absolutely sure that for me this was the end of one era and the beginning of a new one.

I quickly counted in my head all the people whom I had met during the last year and of whom I had lost all trace. There was no longer any such thing as a lifelong friend or a close relative. There was only the friend you made today for today, as all the yesterdays were gone forever and all the tomorrows were insignificant until they became today. The places — Rokiciny, Montelupich, Zakopane, Kobier — and the people — Anka, Szczepan, Marian, Richard — they had all become just shadows. What about Stefan Blankenheim? A shadow, too. And should I run across him once more, then he'd be my friend of today, our yesterdays having been consigned to the file of things past and forgotten.

I thought that, strangely, wherever I had arrived, the old timers had always told me how lucky I was to have arrived today and not a month ago, when everything had been so much worse. I felt that their lives had been very tough, and that they simply didn't dare to look at the present as being as bad as it really was, fearing that they wouldn't be able to take it. Once it was over, they could afford to expand on its evil features as much as they wanted to. As for me, I looked at things the way they were. In the morning, I prayed to see the evening, and in the evening, I was thankful for having lived a day. My philosophy was still one of surviving at no cost to any of my fellows, but by now it had definitely become one of surviving, regardless of how difficult the circumstances were.

As I have already mentioned, the Krankenbau of Auschwitz One was composed of four blocks, numbered 19, 20, 21, and 28, the last one being a miscellaneous hospital building containing an admissions ward, various medical specialty departments, a couple of small wards, a dietary kitchen, the orderlies' quarters, and the morgue in the basement. Now, at noon of Rosh Hashana of the year 1943, I had been brought to Block 28 and delivered into the hands of an admissions orderly.

In Auschwitz, every Haftling transfer was a complicated affair, in which procedure, discipline, and bureaucracy often created a ridiculous maze of superfluity. Thus, according to the procedure, I took a shower in Buna early in the morning, before being introduced to the Lagerdoktor. Then, I took a shower at eleven, before boarding the ambulance. Now, an hour later, I was given a shower in Block 28, in order to become qualified for admission. In spite of the fact that I had been transferred here as a member of the medical staff, and not as a patient, my clothes were taken away — the good clothes I had so admired that very morning — and I had been given a skimpy shirt and told to stay in a bunk in the admissions room until further notice. My plight was further complicated by the fact that the admissions Stubendienst, a fat man of fifty-five, with small, round, bleary eyes that looked somewhat lost in a head continuously shaking due to a nervous disorder, simply didn't seem to hear me telling him that I had been assigned to the Krankenbau by Dr. Entress, and that I was supposed to get a job here. Mr. Sobkowiak, the Stubendienst, just kept repeating that he would send me tomorrow to any of the out-of-Lager work details, and that was it. When I asked him to give me my clothes, he said he couldn't do that until I had been introduced, tomorrow morning, to the SS doctor, along with all other patients. I said that I had just been introduced to Dr. Entress a few hours ago, but to this he said that the introduction I was talking about had been done there, and that I needed now an introduction here. There was definitely nothing I could do with Mr. Sobkowiak. In desperation, and hungry, I lay down on my bunk, hoping that the hours between now and tomorrow would not be too lengthy for me.

An hour later, the Stubendienst approached my bunk. He had a slip of paper in his hand, and he read my name aloud while his head shook desperately.

"Is this you?" he asked, and when I said yes, he ordered me out of the bunk and to his table. There, as I stood in my shirt, he started taking my vital statistics again. As he was doing this, the door opened and a man of about thirty-five — handsome in his custom-made uniform, which stressed the beauty of his athletic body — came into the ward. He approached the table, his hands clasped behind his back, and glanced into the Stubendienst's book.

"A new arrival, Herr Blockaltester!" The Stubendienst snapped to attention, trying to stop his head from shaking.

"Physician?" asked the Blockaltester in a deep voice. It sounded like something between a question and a statement.

"Yes, sir, Herr Blockaltester!" I snapped to attention, feeling ludicrous in my shirt.

The Blockaltester said my name aloud. His face was pensive, as if he was trying to remember where he could have heard my name before. He said to the Stubendienst, "Give him a job in this room, Sobkowiak, until we find something better."

"Mr. Ratajczak liked you," stated Sobkowiak, as soon as the door had closed behind the Blockaltester.

Now *my* face must have become pensive. I did know the name Ratajczak, but I couldn't remember from where. Maybe he was an athlete. He looked like one. Maybe he had been at some time or other on a Polish national team. I didn't know. All I knew was that he had been nice to me, and for this I was grateful.

Meanwhile, Sobkowiak was trying to decide about a job for me. Finally, he came up with a plan. I was to become a helper to his helper, Jozek Wolny.

He called, "Jozek! Jozek!" and a bulky figure with flat feet slowly approached the table. He had heavy, expressionless features, and he stood at attention in front of Sobkowiak, trying to pull in his bulging belly. He spoke only Polish, and now Sobkowiak advised him in Polish that I would be his aide, along with Tazartes.

Jozek Wolny waved at me and led me slowly to the end of the ward, along an aisle between two rows of three-tiered bunks. There, he sat on a bunk, sighed deeply and, in Polish, addressed a slim man of thirty, with a handsome face and bright eyes: "Listen, Tazartes, this is my second helper. From now on, you and he will wash the ward three times a day and make up all the bunks, *verstehen*?"

The German finale of Wolny's Polish speech seemed to be the most important part for Tazartes, as he smiled obligingly and repeated, "*Verstehen*!"

I must have looked puzzled; Wolny said immediately to me, "That Greek doesn't understand one word of what I'm saying."

Now that I knew that Tazartes was Greek, I introduced myself in French, and within minutes we all were friends, as from this point on Jozek Wolny didn't have to worry about making himself understood, and Tazartes didn't have to worry about being beaten for not understanding, and I didn't have to worry about my skimpy shirt. Both Wolny and Tazartes, out of mere happiness over the new development, gave me a pair of pants, a jacket, and a pair of shoes, and I could now go out for a walk in the Lager.

Or I thought I could. At the entrance to my block, a doorkeeper was seated who wouldn't let me out, in spite of my reassurance that it was all right, that I was now a member of this block and would be back in time for the curfew. I really wanted to get out, in the hope that

I might run across Stefan and get a piece of bread from him. I was famished. Now all that was left for me to do was to have a conversation with Tazartes. He told me that my going out was out of the question until I had been introduced officially, tomorrow morning, to Dr. Entress. He also told me it was fortunate that I hadn't been able to get out, because the doorkeeper wouldn't have let me back in later.

When the evening report was over, and many Haftlinge started coming in for emergency treatment, a change of dressing, or a visit with a doctor, I went into the long, narrow hall of the block, to watch the traffic. And, lo and behold! Whom did I see but Stefan, of course, who had come to get a couple of aspirins for his cold.

Our meeting was exceedingly warm, as I was now sure to get something to eat, while he had the surprise of his life, having thought that my transport to Buna had simply been another name for a liquidation in the gas chamber; many of the Haftlinge who had been picked that night by Dr. Entress had gone to Birkenau and to the gas chambers. Good Stefan was so excited, he forgot about his aspirins and ran to his block to get me a portion of bread. He looked well and kept assuring me that he could now well afford to be generous with me, but I knew that bread was bread, that anybody who could afford to give it away could also buy other goods or services with it, and that Stefan was simply being generous.

While we were talking, I watched the intense activity of the infirmary, thinking that maybe tomorrow I, too, would be working in this large cement room helping the sick. The dispensary must have been about fifty meters long and twenty wide. It was divided lengthwise, at about two thirds of its width, by a meter-high metal-pipe barrier, at the narrower side of which medics, supervised by a Haftling physician, were busy dressing the ulcers and wounds of the Haftlinge lined up in front of each medic on the other side of the barrier. Of course, the term *medic* does not reflect the medical knowledge or the degree of devotion displayed by the Haftlinge working in such a capacity there, but I suppose that this is the closest translation for their official title, *Krankenpfleger,* or *Pfleger* for short, a term applied to all the workers in the Krankenbau, whether they had to deal with the sick, sit at the door, peel potatoes for the dietary kitchens, or load corpses on the crematory truck. Thus I, too, was now a Pfleger, although I didn't yet know what kind of function I would eventually have, after my temporary assignment as an aide to an aide to the Stubendienst.

Behind the Pflegers, along the wall, was a row of tables filled with jars, bottles, and large rolls of paper bandages. At the left side of the room, was a wooden partition with a reception window in it, at which the longest line of Haftlinge was formed, since in order to be seen by a doctor or treated by a Pfleger, each Haftling had to get his sick card, and such cards were dispensed through the window by an administration Pfleger. A dispensary doctor was seated at a little table next to the window, quickly examining one Haftling after another and writing on the sick cards his diagnosis and his instructions for the Pflegers or for the pharmacist, who was located at the opposite side of the room. Once a sick Haftling had been seen by this physician, there were three possibilities for him: treatment by a Pfleger, medicine from the pharmacist, or a return the next morning for presentation to the SS doctor and a recommendation for a period of stay either in his own block, if it was only a question of a couple of days of bed rest, or an admission to the Kranbenbau as a patient.

The traffic in the infirmary was heavy, and I couldn't help wondering how all these people dared to come here, to the Kranbenbau, the antechamber to death. So I asked Stefan, and he assured me that now most people were admitted, treated, and then released to go back to work, although usually not on the same detail.

All this ado went on for a long time, and Stefan had to leave me. But it was all right; he knew where to find me, and I hoped to be able to look him up in his block tomorrow night.

I returned to my Stube, where I learned from Tazartes about his plan for me. He had started a service business for himself: he washed and pressed shirts for some Polish functionaries in the block, shined their shoes, and alternated for each of them in soup-barrel carrying and barrel washing (everybody in the block, except for the Blockaltester, the doctors, and the Stubendienste was supposed to have his turn in the kitchen), and for this he got an occasional portion of bread or soup. Now he offered me partnership in his business. He said that there was a sufficient number of potential customers for both of us. It was his way of saying thank you, for finally being able to understand what Jozek Wolny wanted of him.

The morning came, and once more, naked and dripping after a cold shower, I followed a long line of sick Haftlinge to be introduced to Dr. Entress. This time, the introduction was less dignified than yesterday in Buna. I stood in front of him naked, wet, and shaking from cold and uncertainty, as the Polish chief doctor introduced me. I was the very last one on the line of the Haftlinge that had just been introduced to him, and I couldn't help thinking that my fate was fully in the hands of the Polish doctor. And what if he said, "Herr Doktor, this is a Haftling who has Durchfall"?

But Entress showed an excellent memory. He gave me a quick glance and said to Ratajczak the Blockaltester, who stood next to the Polish doctor, "I remember him from yesterday. Find him a job here." And the presentation was over.

Soon I dressed in my clothes of last evening and went to my Stube, which was the admissions ward, to wait there for my eventual assignment. Presently, the Polish doctor came in and asked the Stubendienst Sobkowiak to give him my registration card. As Sobkowiak, his head shaking, was trying to find my papers, another Polish Haftling, who had previously been seated at Sobkowiak's table, stood up at attention in front of the doctor. The doctor himself, a stocky man probably five foot eight or so, looked very important with a band on his arm reading, "K.B. Lageraltester," and wearing a short, black woolen jacket over his custom-made uniform. There was something in his movements and his posture that reminded me of Mussolini. Now Sobkowiak handed him my registration card, and the doctor perused it. He looked at me critically, and said in Polish, "Where are you from?"

"From Lvov, sir."

"Then you're a Bolshevik!" There was sarcasm in his voice. "A Bolshevik from Lvov! We'll cut your testicles off! A Bolshevik!"

I didn't know whether to take this as a joke, or what. I smiled shyly. There was no smile in his eyes, and no encouragement in his voice. He kept watching me as a viper might watch his prey. Yet I didn't think he could mean any harm, until the second Haftling, Sobkowiak's friend, dared to interject a word. "I beg your pardon, Dr. Dehring," he addressed the doctor. "I am from Lvov myself, but I'm far from being a Bolshevik."

He was short and husky, about sixty years old. His voice was deep and warm, and I felt more assured as he glanced at me with his wise, gray-blue eyes.

"There goes Kurylowicz, defending a Jew again!" jeered Dr. Dehring. "When will you learn that all the Jews are Bolsheviks!"

I stood at attention in front of Dr. Dehring, not knowing whether it would be proper for me to say something in my defense. Kurylowicz gave me a glance, and I could read in it, "Let me do the talking." But this was the end of anybody's talking.

Dehring addressed me in disgust, "You watch yourself! Otherwise . . . ." and he drew an upward spiral with a finger, as if to say, "You'll go up with the smoke." And he left.

And, strangely, it was not I but Kurylowicz who emitted a sign of relief at this point. He said, "Be very careful, colleague. Never talk to Dr. Dehring. Who knows how many people have finished in the gas chamber because of him? You've got to make yourself invisible, as he doesn't seem to have much sympathy for you."

As he was telling me all this, suddenly I realized who Kurylowicz was. When I was a little boy, he was the secretary of the powerful union of the railway workers at the time, who became instrumental in Marshall Pilsudski's coup d'etat. Kurylowicz — Pilsudski's man. And a very decent person. To expose himself like this for a Jew! And it seemed to me suddenly that my life would be brighter from now on, now that I had met another rare, decent person in the world.

This was the beginning of my life in the Auschwitz Krankenbau, Block 28.

My new job was a far cry from what I had hoped it would be. My first working morning was spent, along with Tazartes, washing the wooden floor of the admissions room, while Jozek Wolny followed slowly, drying the floor with a broom wrapped in a rag. After that we made up the bunks. At seven in the morning, patients started arriving. They were coming from the shower and were shaking from cold, as water dripped down their emaciated bodies. After awhile, there was a sizeable group of patients gathered in the front of the admissions room. Now the admissions doctor examined the patients quickly, filling out their history cards. The ones who had already been examined gathered next to the window that Kurylowicz had opened to make the floor dry faster. They shook even more from cold, and some of them tried to get unobtrusively into the nearest aisle, where they hoped to avoid the draft and perhaps sit down for a moment on a bunk. From time to time, the deep basso of Kurylowicz chased them out, "Get out of there! *Verboten* to sit on the bunks!" After an hour, tired of waiting, the patients started to whisper among themselves and soon the room was filled with humming. The basso of Kurolowicz was heard again: "Silence! Or I'll chase you out into the hall!" It seemed to be Kurylowicz's function to forbid and threaten in his deep voice, and while he was forbidding, Wolny, Tazartes, and I sat in the far corner of the room, just waiting.

Suddenly, the doorkeeper yelled from the entrance of the block, "Lagerarzt!!!"

Sobkowiak and Kurylowicz chased the patients out of the room and into the hall. Naked and barefoot, they ran along the long corridor and formed a line in the dispensary, waiting on the cold concrete floor for the arrival of the German doctor. They were all emaciated and covered with ulcers, abscesses, and bruises, and a good portion of them looked just like skeletons covered with skin.

Now the doctor came in. It was again Dr. Entress, as it was an important function of the Lagerarzt each morning to see the Haftlinge who claimed sickness and to make a wise decision as to their immediate destiny. He stood in the middle of the dispensary with a Scharfuhrer at his right and Dr. Dehring at his left. Slim, in a black uniform, a black SS cap, and dark-rimmed glasses, and without a smile, Entress looked like Death in person. The patients approached him one by one and handed their cards to Dehring. He read the diagnosis aloud, and Entress barked a short, "Eins! Zwei! Kranken-bau!" This meant a day or two of block rest, or admittance into the Krankenbau. But occasionally, Entress didn't speak. He just moved his hand faintly, and the Scharfurhrer took the patient's card from Dehring.

The introduction of the patients to the doctor was over, and they ran along the corridor towards the admissions room, slapping their bare feet on the concrete floor. Shortly, the assignment started. The admissions doctor wrote the number of the hospital block to which the patient was to be taken, and as soon as a group for one block was ready, Wolny, Tazartes, and I gave each patient a coat and a pair of wooden sandals and led them all to the assigned block: surgery to 21, Durchfall to 19, miscellaneous to 20. As we were crossing the street, their wooden sabots rattled, and I had a strange impression that it was not the sabots but their bones that rattled, so skeletal were some of them.

Finally, all patients had been taken to their hospital blocks, and only a small group was left: the ones whose cards had been taken by the Scharfuhrer. Jozek Wolny took over. They followed him indifferently along the corridor and out. They turned to the right, and around the corner of Block 28. Then the clatter of their sabots died down, as they descended the stairway leading to the morgue. Tazartes didn't want to tell me what was happening in the morgue, but later that night Jozek Wolny explained that the Scharfuhrer practiced intracardiac injections of some sort of poison. Usually, according to Wolny, it was one of the Haftling doctors who did it, but now that this doctor had been transferred to another Lager, it was the Scharfuhrer's function.

After the patients were all gone, Tazartes and I washed the floor once more, and in two trips, we brought two barrels of soup from the

Lager kitchen. At noon, the soup was distributed among the Pflegers and the patients of our block. Tazartes and I washed the barrels in the bathroom and returned them to the kitchen. Later in the afternoon, we brought from the kitchen a barrel of hot water with herbs, which was intermittently called tea or coffee. It was distributed to the patients only, as the Pflegers didn't want it. We washed the barrel and returned it to the kitchen. Then, again, we washed the floor in the admissions room.

After the evening report, while the dispensary Pflegers were treating the outpatients, Tazartes and I were told that we couldn't leave the block, as we were needed in the morgue, to help load the crematory truck. It was a gloomy task, and I didn't want to do it, nor did Tazartes, but as he was already an old timer here and also could make believe that he had not understood the order, he disappeared at the very moment when the truck arrived, and I found myself working with the morgue team, known as the *Leichenkommando*. It was a huge truck, lined inside with sheet metal. It was also taller than most trucks. Two fellows from the Leichenkommando, a Yugoslav Jew, Herman, and a Slovak Jew, Otto, brought the bodies from the basement morgue and lined them quickly and neatly along the side-walk of the back entrance to Block 28. The third fellow from the team, the Pole Kostek, needed my help to throw the bodies on the truck. He taught me how to do it. He grasped the corpse by the hands, I by the feet, and swinging it slowly to the count of, "One — two — and — three!!!" we hurled it up, as if throwing it out of a sling. The corpse fell on the sheet-metal lining with a metallic bang. This meant that our thrust was well coordinated. Sometimes several bangs were heard: this signified bad coordination. As Kostek and I were hurling the corpses, Otto and Herman rushed out the rest of the bodies, now carrying two to a stretcher. As soon as they had emptied the morgue, they joined us in loading the truck. They were very good at it. They grasped the naked corpses, smelling of pus and bearing their registration numbers scribbled with a marker on their chests, and hurled them up almost with elegance. But then, they were professionals.

After the loading was over, they invited me to their quarters and offered me a bowl of cold soup. They lived in a cozy room adjacent to the morgue. There was also a fourth man, a terribly fat Pole, Wojtek, who weighed possibly four hundred pounds. He lived there, too. He was the Kapo of the Leichenkommando, but he didn't do anything at all. How could he, with all that fat?

And thus, my first work day in Block 28 was over.

It didn't take long for me to find out that my being a Pfleger did not necessarily mean that I was one. I was the last arrival, and a Jew to boot, so what did I dare to expect? Mine was definitely not a "function." Along with Tazartes, I scrubbed the floors, made the bunks, carried barrels of soup back and forth, and washed them. Without Tazartes (the bastard knew how to disappear at the proper moment), I helped the Leichenkommando in their crematory task. With Tazartes, in our free moments, I washed the clothes of the Polish functionaries in Block 28, for which they paid us. We were also supposed to be paid by them for carrying the soup barrels for each of them, but they usually forgot the payment, and we knew better than to remind them about it.

With all this, I was satisfied with my work. I had a roof over my head, and each time I remembered the horrid working conditions in Buna, I sighed with relief. And I finally was not hungry. The Poles paid us for our work with their Lager soup, because they had packages from home and didn't care for rotten turnips. Sometimes they paid us with a portion of Lager bread, usually after having kept it long enough so that it had become moldy. I am not sure they did this on purpose — I mean, waiting for the bread to spoil before giving it to us. I suppose it was rather a question of some kind of "inflation." In Auschwitz, bread was considered money in its lowest denominaiton — something like an American nickel — and the owner of a portion of bread could buy things with it. But if he did not make his purchase early enough, his money would become moldy and lose a part of its value. Then the owner would pay Tazartes and me with his "inflated" money.

The Polish functionaries in Block 28 had their own home-made dinners. They had contacts in the Lager kitchen and in the SS warehouse, and they organized such delicacies as whole cubes of margarine (about a pound a cube), SS sausages (called SS because these short, straight, delightfully smoked sausages were made for the consumption of the SS guards only), bacon, potatoes, and onions. With such of God's blessings as these, they cooked their midday dinners, adding an occasional piece of meat. When one of these functionaries was in a particularly good mood, he would let me or Tazartes wash his soup bowl, leaving in it a piece of sauteed potato for us, so that we could reminisce about the good times of yesteryear.

Sometimes, we ran into a minor difficulty, like the time Tazartes discovered the miraculous influence of chlorine on dirty shirt collars, and we applied it to a beautiful blue shirt belonging to the assistant pharmacist of Block 28. That time, we got an equitable distribution of slaps instead of soup, but we deserved them, and besides, they were nothing in comparison with a beating in Bunawerke.

All this was a part of our normal work day. Occasionally, we were called for a special chore. It could be collecting the body of a Haftling who had died suddenly in his block, or unloading a freight train that had brought in bags of chemicals. On one of these occasions, a group of Pflegers, accompanied by a Posten, went to the railroad platform to unload two boxcars of barrels containing chlorine powder. It was a change of routine for us, and we didn't treat it as much of a job. At the end of the unloading, all covered with white, flourlike powder, we started pushing the chlorine barrels into what the Posten called the warehouse.

It was the first time I had been in this warehouse, and I curiously examined this low structure, consisting of heavy brick walls without windows and small round chimneys with fans, which I assumed were used for ventilation instead of windows. We rolled the barrels through a heavy sliding door that separated a kind of an antechamber from the large, low-ceilinged room in which the barrels were stocked. I noticed in one of the walls of the antechamber a recess, something like a niche or a built-in cupboard. It was filled with a pyramid of metal cans similar to the ones used for preserved meat, only somewhat wider and taller. I took a closer look and noticed that there was a cross and a name engraved on each can.

I could only assume what it was, but after we had returned to our block and were taking a shower, I learned the details. Herman of the Leichenkommando, who was a real old timer in Auschwitz, said that the warehouse had been the first gas chamber and crematory of Auschwitz; he called it a "showcase theater." He remembered when the first group of Russian prisoners of war had been poisoned here with the Cyclon B gas. After that, it had been used on several occasions to poison the first Polish prisoners at Auschwitz. At that time, the Lager administration still cared about appearances, and so the families of the victims were sent notices saying that their dear ones were dead and that, for a fee, an urn containing the ashes of the deceased would be sent to the bereaved family. The death notice also said that the prisoner had died of a heart attack or pneumonia, but it failed to say that the ashes were the residue of a cremation of some five or six bodies at a time and that, consequently, each urn was actually a mass grave. Eventually, the administration stopped advising the families and transferred the operation of gassing to a real death factory in Birkenau, some three kilometers away. The urns in the warehouse were a reminder of the old times, or they might have been destined by the administration to become museum pieces or collector's items.

After Herman finished recounting what he knew, Jozek Wolny had something to add, too. He also was an old timer, and he remembered the way it used to be in Block 28. His "used to be" was a reference to a time not so distant in our everyday parlance: Perhaps three or four months.

Wolny said that the Scharfuhrer had come to the admissions room every morning an hour before the Lagerarzt, picked his twenty Mussulmen and took them down to the morgue. At that time, he practiced the intracardiac injections of phenol. He was enthusiastic about his work, and it was his dream to become a real expert. Twenty must have been his lucky number because whenever he couldn't get his twenty Mussulmen in the admissions room, he went back to the Lager and rounded up enough working Haftlinge to bring the number up to twenty. Jozek Wolny was always present at the killings, and he had all sorts of reminiscences. Usually, it was a simple thing: an injection, a few seconds of spasms, and the Mussulman was dead. You just heard a rattle in his throat, then he'd become black, he swelled, his tongue came out, and everything was over.

On one occasion, Wolny had witnessed a scene he couldn't forget. As the doorkeeper was piling the corpses along one wall of the morgue, one of the corpses started crawling out from under the heap. He was black and swollen like the others, but he breathed heavily and moved. "Like a worm," said Wolny. As he got out from under the heap of bodies, the doorkeeper grabbed a crowbar and split his head in two.

Wolny looked around with suspicion, and whispered, "That sonofabitch doorkeeper is now a Pfleger, and he'd do the same to me if he knew I told you this story."

Sielecki, the assistant pharmacist in the infirmary, wrinkled his overly long nose: "There's no need for injections now. They do it now only for sport. The real thing is done in Birkenau. Five hundred people gassed at a clip and burned in a couple of hours."

At this point, I came out with something everybody else judged as the most idiotic statement of the century. I said, "My God! When the world comes to know all this!"

They all laughed.

"They know it!" exclaimed Sielecki. "And, what's more, they like the idea of the Jews being exterminated like rodents! The Germans are finally doing what the others didn't even dare to dream of. The Germans are just doing the dirty work for all the rest of the world. Isn't it so, Wolny?"

Sielecki was Jewish. Wolny was Polish, and Wolny's word was the Bible for Sielecki. And now, Wolny nodded slowly. Yes, he agreed. The world knew it, and if the Allied powers and the Vatican had strongly protested, the Germans might have reconsidered. The world knew but did not protest.

I couldn't accept that. I said that I wanted to survive so that I could write a book about it and let the world know. But they all laughed at me. They said that nobody would read such a book. Or if they read it, they'd say that these were all ugly fables. They would sue me for libel. Or they would call me a sadist, a sick man. But most probably, nobody would want to publish such a book. So the general consensus was that I should forget all this, if I survived. But then, an even more general consensus was that neither I nor any other Jew in any concentration camp would be allowed to survive.

I disliked working with the Leichenkommando for many reasons. Each corpse I helped thrust up on the crematory truck was a reason. But there was also something else. The Pole Kostek took to addressing me as Moritz. "Moritz" was a name used by the Germans in caricatures of Jews, and I didn't feel I was such a caricature. Herman and Otto, the two Jews on the Leichenkommando, learned from Kostek, and they, too, started addressing me as Moritz. So one Friday morning, when Kostek stuck his head into the admissions room and yelled, "Get ready, Moritz! It's the Black Wall Day!" I buttoned my jacket, put on my Mutze, went down to the morgue, and said coolly to Kostek, "Stop calling me Moritz."

The Pole was speechless. Herman and Otto looked on in awe. The three of them were tall, and strong, and well fed, and I, a Mussulman, was telling them what not to call me!

"My name is Franek." What's more, I was even telling them what to call me!

"That sonofabitch, look at him!" Kostek burst out. "What are you, a big shot!"

The big, brawny fellow towered over me, ready for a scramble. I looked into his eyes and repeated coolly, "My name is Franek, and this is how you are going to call me."

I was very steady, very calm, and the silence that followed was very awkward.

And suddenly, something happened to Kostek. He smiled and stretched out his hand. And he said, "Are we friends, Franek?"

As we were shaking hands, I knew that Herman and Otto started respecting me. I thought that, regardless of the circumstances, dignity is a part of man, and when he loses it, he loses a large part of himself.

"We'd better be on our way, Franek," said Herman. "The Black Wall is about to start."

There were two categories of punishment in Auschwitz: an informal one, where a foreman, a Kapo, or an SS guard beat up or killed a Haftling; and a formal one, where the sentence was read in front of the Lager, and the punishment was dispensed during a special Lager report. The formal punishment could be for a minor transgression such as smoking during the working hours. In such cases, the transgressor himself carried from the Bunker (this was the official name given to Block 11, the jailhouse of Auschwitz One) a slanted, narrow table called the *goat,* put it in the middle of the Raportplatz, bent over it, and received his twenty or thirty whips on the buttocks. This whipping was called the *payoff* and it usually took place on a Saturday evening. The man who administered it was Jacob, the gigantic Jew, the Kapo of the Bunker.

Jacob was a controversial figure. Before the war, he had appeared at small-town fairs in northeastern Poland as a performer, showing his strength by bending and breaking horse shoes with his bare hands. The SS admired his brute strength and had made Jacob the Bunker Kapo. As such, he was responsible for everything that happened in the Bunker and was also its official executioner; in addition to the payoff whippings, Jacob was the one who prepared the gallows and the rope for public hangings and who executed the hangings in the presence of the Auschwitz administration and in front of the Haftlinge population. Just by looking at him there was no doubt that Jacob was able to kill. He was a primitive man, some three hundred and fifty pounds of muscle and no brain. The language he spoke was a strange combination of Yiddish and some animal-like sounds. Yet, he had a strange sense of justice and loyalty. Haftlinge who served time in the Bunker told stories about Jacob: how he would help the good and punish the evil—the latter presumedly being stool pigeons. It happened that Haftlinge thrown into the Bunker by the SS to spy on the others were eventually found with their necks broken. Much later, I came to know that a few politically-initiated Haftlinge had had a short-wave radio in the Bunker, and that Jacob was its trustee. For us, the Jewish Haftlinge, Jacob was a symbol of strength, resistance, and revenge, and we admired him for exactly the same reasons for which the Polish functionaries hated him. I personally knew Jacob, as he would drop into the infirmary for an occasional chat with Sielecki, whom he knew from the town of Prozana.

Serious crimes called for severe punishment: a few days of solitary confinement in the Bunker, the loss of one's function, or a transfer to a different camp. But this kind of punishment was seldom given to a Jewish Haftling, who normally received an informal punishment, or if his crime was meaningful enough, the most serious punishment in Auschwitz: the gallows. Of course, for a really important crime, a non-Jewish Haftling, too, could be sentenced to hanging.

And then there was the Black Wall.

When we arrived in Block 21, there were already a few Pflegers in the surgery room on the second floor. The window facing the Bunker was covered with a blanket. This was the standing order for Black Wall days: windows facing the yard of the Bunker were to be covered, and Haftlinge were prohibited from looking at what was about to happen in the yard.

Through the folds of the blanket, I could see unusual traffic in the yard. Jacob and his assistant, a skinny, serious, middle-aged man, placed a large black screen along the back wall of the yard. Then they brought out of the Bunker a small table and two chairs.

When the stage was set, a group of civilian prisoners was led out of the Bunker. There were two women among them. They were lined up in front of the table. Now, an SS man—probably an officer—accompanied by a Scharfuhrer came out of the Bunker. He sat at the table, took out some documents from the briefcase he brought with him, and read aloud. He probably called the prisoners' names, because as he was reading, they approached the table one after another, listened to what he was reading to them, and returned to the line. The reading was soon finished, the table and the chairs taken back into the Bunker, and the officer and the Scharfuhrer, guns in their hands, took their places at both sides of the black screen. In one hand, the officer had a sheet of paper—probably a list of names—from which he called out a name. The prisoner refused to approach the Black Wall. He yelled something back at the officer. Now Jacob came out of the Bunker, grabbed the prisoner by the collar of his jacket, and dragged him toward the officer. I remembered the killing of the musician Matrosz in Kobier. A Pfleger at the window cursed, "That sonofabitch Jacob! One day we'll make our accounts with him! The fuckin' Jew!"

The officer said something to the prisoner, and the man fell to his knees. The officer shot him through the neck, and the man fell. Jacob grabbed him by the hair and dragged him toward the wall of the Bunker. The executions proceeded, and in less than ten minutes all was over. As the two SS men left the yard, Kostek said in a whisper, as if they could hear him, "Now, it's our turn."

The earth under the Black Wall was soaked with blood, but it didn't seem too bad to Kostek.

"Once they killed so many of them that we worked with blood up to our ankles," he said matter-of-factly.

Otto confirmed this: "Now, it's peanuts. It was quite different when I first arrived. My group was lodged in the Bunker. They called it the *Straffkommando*—the punitive detail. We worked only a couple of hundred yards beyond the walls of the Lager. Every morning, before leaving, the Kapo received his orders as to how many of us were supposed to return. It was up to him how to dispose of the ones who were chosen to die. If he was in a good mood, then all right, he asked a Posten to shoot the Haftling. At least, it was nice and clean. But if the Kapo was in a bad mood, wow! He beat up the man something awful! And then, when the man was lying on the ground, the Kapo would lay a shovel on his throat—the handle of a shovel, you know—and he see-sawed on it, until the man's throat was smashed. Only ten of us are still alive today out of the initial one hundred and thirty!"

We carried the bodies of the dead civilians to the morgue. If not for the fact that they were dead, they seemed to me like normal human beings, well fed and heavy—so totally different from the emaciated bodies of the Haftlinge that we handled each day. Suddenly I felt the shiver a live person feels when he is in the presence of death. I realized that these were truly dead people, while the dead bodies of Haftlinge seemed unreal—more like puppets or mannequins.

With the coming of the rainy season, I could appreciate my working in the Krankenbau more than ever. By that time, the morning report had been abolished in Auschwitz, to increase our productivity. However, there were still the evening reports, and those were still lengthy. The work details that returned from their jobs outside the Lager still had to stand in front of their blocks, sometimes for hours, drenching in the rain, while we, the Pflegers, just lined up in the halls of our blocks for a quick count by the Blockaltesters, who then reported to the Scharfuhrer.

I saw Stefan seldom, usually on Sunday afternoons, being so terribly busy with my official and unofficial activities. Even on Sundays, before meeting Stefan, Tazartes and I took care of our laundry business behind Block 28, while the remaining seventeen thousand Haftlinge had their *Bettruhe:* "bed rest" on Sunday afternoon was a part of the Auschwitz constitution, and whether you felt like sleeping or not, you had to be in your bunk. Except, of course, for Tazartes and myself. We laid two wooden boards on four stools next to the entrance of the morgue, filled a couple of buckets with cold water, and scrubbed the clothes of the Polish functionaries with rice brushes. There were some Jewish functionaries in the block, too, for example, Otto and Herman, but they washed their own clothes, and Tazartes and I considered them simply stingy. We felt that they did it themselves in order to avoid giving us a portion of soup, and it was only about a year later that I had a chance to revise my feeling about this. A year later I myself was a functionary, and I helped a Jewish boy from Lodz to become a *Laufer* ("messenger") for our block. One day I caught him polishing my shoes, and I scolded him terribly for it. I wanted to help him, but I didn't want him to feel humiliated. Maybe this was why Otto and Herman did their own laundry.

We washed all articles of clothing: shirts, underwear, Lager uniforms, and overcoats. Washing these clothes was like living again in freedom. While all the Mussulmen and a good number of the functionaries in the Lager wore badly made, often torn or patched uniforms—old, worn shirts and underwear that wasn't even good enough to be used as rags—the clothes we received for washing were custom-made of excellent fabric by some of the best tailors in Europe. All this clothing originated from what was known in Auschwitz as *Canada*. Canada was actually a sorting Kommando that worked near the crematories in Birkenau and was tantamount to a luxury department store. Anything of importance, starting with good, warm blankets and finishing with expensive jewelry, was stored in Canada—just long enough to make up a transport of all those goods to be shipped back to Germany. However, the Haftlinge who had the money could buy from Canada Kommando whatever they desired, as it seemed to be impossible for the administration to keep an exact account of the innumerable articles flowing through Canada.

Just as the people in a free society feel they must keep up with the Joneses, so the Auschwitz aristocracy kept up with their own peers, by purchasing various Canada objects. A better person in Auschwitz had to have a Canada blanket—a fluffy thing made of Scottish wool—and Canada shoes, and Canada shirts and underwear, and his uniform had to be made by one of the Jewish tailors who came to Auschwitz from all the capitals of Europe.

The commerce of Auschwitz had to be scientifically organized so that all those things could be smuggled into the Lager. Again, as in a free society, there were distributors, traveling salesmen, and retailers. The Canada Haftlinge usually handed their goods to less conspicuous people, whose Kommando happened to be working nearby, as the Canada people were often thoroughly searched by the SS. Once the goods were smuggled into the Lager, they were picked up by their Canada owners, and the smugglers were paid, usually with a portion of bread or, if the article was very costly, with margarine. The Canada people then had the goods offered to the consumer by their block representatives, who made their profit when the final sale was consummated. Because of the various values and the diversity of the articles offered for sale, a complete monetary system had to be developed. A portion of the Lager bread was, as I mentioned before, the lowest monetary denomination. It was called *Porcja* ("portion"), and it equaled four cigarettes. The next highest denomination was *Kostka* ("cube"), a cube of regular Auschwitz margarine, about half a pound. Kostka equaled twelve cigarettes. The next denomination was *Esmanska,* which was a sausage made for the SS personnel. This was equal to twenty cigarettes. Of equal value to the Esmanska was the *Puszka* ("can"), which was a can of beef stew. These two were interchangeable, because sometimes it was difficult to procure an Esmanska on a short notice. All these were "small change". There was also what we called "soft money" in Auschwitz: a fifth of vodka, which had a value of fifty cigarettes. And there was "hard money": a fifth of Bon-Gout, the 186-proof Polish monopoly alcohol, which had a value of eighty cigarettes. This duality of money—food products and cigarettes—served an important purpose, as the sellers needed food, and the ultimate consumers, our aristocracy, were not hungry and could stock cigarettes and alcohol instead of keeping such messy things as bread and margarine.

At that time, the first Italian Jews arrived in Auschwitz. They had become Mussulmen to the worst degree, having worked in a coal mine, not being used to the beating, to the lack of food, or to the Polish climate; and, last but not least, not being able to understand either German or Polish. Nevertheless, some of them had not lost their Mediterranean ways: one introduced himself as a famous tenor from La Scala, and for a bowl of soup, he sang *Martha* in the laboratory room to a group of Pflegers; another one, by the name of Piperno, said that he had had a huge fleet of taxi cabs and a luxury restaurant in Rome. They were all hungry, and all were anxious to tell somebody their problems. I happened to be handy, being fluent in the Italian language. Night after night, I was called into the infirmary as a translator, and in no time at all, I had a number of new friends. Indeed, when some ten years later I needed a witness to testify that I had been in Auschwitz, one of them, Dr. Teo Ducci, was to vouch for me.

One morning, I got up with a strange feeling of darkness around me. Even the light bulbs seemed to be black. I tried to make up my bed but couldn't lift my left arm. Tazartes advised Sobkowiak, who told me to approach his desk and stuck a thermometer into my mouth. Kurylowicz read the temperature and whistled.

"Forty-one!" This meant about 104° Fahrenheit. "How do you feel, colleague?"

"It is just blackness around me. And my head turns. And I can't lift my arm."

Kurylowicz tried to lift my left arm. It hurt, and the arm didn't yield. He touched the armpit.

"It's swollen. We'd better show it to Dr. Smerek." This was one of the admissions doctors who slept in our ward.

Dr. Smerek examined me briefly. Then he asked, "Have you worked lately in the morgue?"

"Yes. The last time two days ago."

Dr. Smerek turned to Kurylowicz:

"He must be immediately referred to Block 21. He has septicemia."

I felt as if I were surrounded by a thick fog. Odd pictures and strange words were reaching me from far away. Ratajczak, the Blockaltester, stood at the foot of my bunk, his hands clasped behind his back, and looked at me gently. Dr. Fajkiel was mixing his medications on a table in the corner of the ward.

"Wladzio," said Ratajczak to Fajkiel, "try to save him. Just tell me which medications you need, and I'll get them for you."

Then, again, emptiness. Tazartes, Sielecki the pharmacist, Kostek, and some others appeared at my bunk. They told me they had come to say good-bye.

"You're a nice fellow," said Kostek. "We're going to miss you."

Tazartes was sobbing.

For a moment, I woke up from my stupor and smiled at them.

That night, another patient was dying in a nearby bunk. He raved and complained until his last breath. Later in the night, they took away his body. I fell back into a stupor.

Suddenly, Auschwitz and the universe were one and the same. Auschwitz meant thirty blocks, meant seventeen thousand human beings, meant sixteen and one half thousand Mussulmen and five hundred functionaries. I was now at the center of the universe and around me I saw the amorphous Mussulmen population: long processions of odd figures meandered, skeletons covered with sunburned skin, clad in rags, their mouths always open, white paper bandages around their heads, always roaming around silently, bent toward the earth looking for a potato peel or a rotten turnip; coming out of the darkness, they became clear, then again disappeared into the darkness. One of the figures straightened up and turned toward me his skinny, blackened face; I recognized Matrosz, the Hungarian musician murdered in Kobier. "It is your turn now," the phantom said gloomily.

I saw the functionaries. They had names, they had faces, they had importance. Now I, the medic, the laundryman, the mortician, now I was one of the five hundred. When I die, the football-faced Wojtek, with his jellylike, huge belly, seated like a Buddha in the antechamber to eternity, would ask, "Did you prepare the flowers?" as Kostek and Herman carried my body to the morgue. Wojtek always said that whenever a functionary died. It was supposed to be a joke.

My hallucinations changed, and I now saw the ambulance car from Birkenau. It came to Block 28 twice a week, carrying a few patients from the women's camp for the X ray, and a few females willing to sell themselves for an Esmanska: *"Cherchez la femme."* The male Scharfuhrer was bribed. The female Scharfuhrer was bribed. The female Haftling doctor was bribed. Now a line of functionaries formed at Block 28, during the working hours, while the Mussulmen were away from the Lager and unaware of the fact that life was still going on here. There was a line in front of the X ray room; and one in front of the watch-repair room in the attic; a line in front of the minor-surgery room; and one, the most impressive one, on the stairway leading to the antechamber to eternity, the small room next to the morgue. Each of the people in line had a Kostka, or an Esmanska under the arm. Only Hilda, the pretty blond SS Scharfuhrer, was paid in gold by one of the Blockaltesters, the handsome Mucha, for giving him her favors in his private office.

The picture changed again and again.

Jurek, the medic, brought me back to reality. He pricked my arm with some shots and wanted me to swallow six pills. I couldn't. My throat felt narrow, and I felt like vomiting, but Jurek stood over me, like a hangman, forcing me to take them all.

Then I had a guest. Through the fog of stupor, I saw the face of a good giant bending above me.

"I am Bronek Umschweif," said my guest. He smiled a gentle smile. "Stefan Blankenheim sent me. He had a premonition. He went to your block, and they told him. He is not allowed to visit you. I can, because I work in a laboratory and have the right to enter the ward. Stefan wants to know what he can do for you."

I regained consciousness.

"You must do me a favor," I said feverishly. I took two portions of white bread lying at the head of my bunk—a special bread given to the very sick patients only. "Please give this to Stefan."

"No, Stefan will not accept it. He wants to help you. Maybe I could bring you something to eat?"

"Please!" I felt my stupor returning. "Please! This is just a small part of my debt."

"I'll give it to Stefan. But what can I do for you?"

"Drink. Something to drink." I started feeling incoherent. "Mother used to give me lemonade. It was tart. Refreshing."

"I'll bring you lemonade. I can make it from citric acid and sugar. I'll also bring you milk. My wife is working in the garden near the laboratory, and we have a son of six, for whom we receive milk."

I was conscious again: "Wife? Son?"

"The Gestapo brought us from Lvov, on a special order from Berlin. I'm a chemist. I was working on something important. My wife and son are living here, in Block 10. But I'll leave you now. You must be tired."

I was burning with fever. The feverish activity of Auschwitz encircled me. In the general confusion, the masks of the elite mixed with the skeletal buttocks of the Mussulmen. All of them turned around each other, and all of them whirled around me in a strange harlequinade. I didn't know any longer whether the world extended free and wide, beyond the barbed wire of Auschwitz, or whether it was I who lived in the only real world, the Lager, separated from the huge concentration camp of the Big War, where people suffered and died and longed for a rest in the quiet of Auschwitz.

The morning came, and to everybody's disbelief, I was still alive. The medic gave me injections and fed me sulfa pills delivered by Ratajczak. The fever still ran high. In my moments of lucidity, I tried to cheat on the medic, holding the thermometer outside my armpit, to keep the registered temperature lower. This maneuver was to no avail, as during the few seconds the thermometer remained in my armpit, it hit its highest. This made me worry, as it would mean prompt selection for the gas chamber.

Bronek Umschweif returned in the evening. He spoke with Dr. Fajkiel, asking him to do for me the best he could, and to Bronek's amazement, he was told that much more important people had also asked him to help me.

Bronek brought me tea mixed with citric acid. As he was feeding it to me with a teaspoon, I closed my eyes, and saw a green field with a forest in the background, a cottage drowning in flowers, and a peasant girl bent over her plants. That was on our way to Treblinka. Suddenly, I felt a strong desire to press my cheek to the dew-covered grass. The reality and the delirium were blending again.

"Do you remember what a carrot looks like? Yes, a carrot. That is what I want: a carrot!"

"I'll get you a carrot." Bronek smiled.

The next day, he brought me a carrot. A carrot and a small grater, as he knew that I wasn't able to swallow anything solid. He grated the carrot, squeezed its juice, and fed it to me. Then, he gave me a little milk. As he was leaving, I asked him to take my portion of the white bread to Stefan. This had become a ritual.

On the third day, with the fever still running very high, a new symptom appeared: the swelling in my armpit became much bigger, and I had difficulty breathing. I continued trying to fool the medic with the thermometer, but it continued showing a very high temperature. Meanwhile, the left side of my chest became hard to the touch, and I felt a terrible burden inside. Strange changes were taking place in my body, and Dr. Fajkiel had difficulty understanding them. He had me X-rayed, and found pleurisy. He consulted another doctor, Dr. Grabczynski, a husky man with a coarse, healthy voice, who examined me carefully and said, "I think this is a phlegmone subpectoralis sinistra. It's a difficult proposition. However, now we might have a chance to save you, colleague." He spoke directly to me. "This is how your septicemia became centralized. We'll transfer you tonight to surgery, and we'll get to work on you as soon as possible."

I had time before the transfer, and for the first time in three days, I dragged myself out to the hall and to the bathroom. My head was whirling, my ears were humming, and the world around me was wrapped in a yellowish fog. The urinals were attached to both sides of a partition in the middle of the bathroom. As I tried to urinate, I thought I saw a phantom at the other side of the partition. He was tall, and pale, and clad in a long nightshirt. He was urinating, too. I reached out with my right arm. I said, "Piotr?" and he put a finger to his lips. Then Piotr was alive. Then the Gestapo hadn't killed him. Then Rebecca was mistaken.

"I don't think I can make it," I whispered.

He took me under my arm and led me back to my bunk. As I lay down, he sat at the edge of the bunk and whispered, "Don't tell anybody we are friends. You just met me, understand? I'm here as a Ukrainian, and I want it to stay that way. I'd better go now. I'll try to visit you later."

That evening, Dr. Grabczynski examined me again and decided that he had to make an incision in order to see better what was to be done. He wasn't even sure where to make the incision. Dr. Steinberg, his assistant, a Jew from Odessa brought to Auschwitz from Paris, said that there was no need for any incision, as I was a goner anyway. However, Grabczynski had made up his mind. He made an incision in my chest and failed to locate the right abcess. Only a little thick, black blood came out, and my temperature jumped.

The next morning, I was again on the table. Grabczynski made an incision in my left chest and the left armpit. A bit of pus came out, and my temperature went up once again. I was given a drain. A medic threaded a pair of long, curved pincers through my chest and my armpit, placed a piece of gauze between the jaws of the pincers, and pulled the pincers until one end of the gauze came out of the cut in my chest. This was the drain, and it was to be changed twice a day.

By the time Dr. Grabczynski made the third incision the morning after, the entire left side of my torso was swollen with pus. As I was going to surgery, I could hear the pus bubbling in my chest. Yet nothing of importance happened. I was scheduled for a fourth incision that same evening.

Steinberg said to Grabczynski, "Well, wasn't I right? We'll be singing Kaddish for him tonight."

I had never said Kaddish for my parents: I had not been on speaking terms with the God of Israel, after Treblinka. And I knew that Steinberg would not say Kaddish for me. He was cold and unfriendly.

"Kaddish might be your business, colleague, but incision is mine," said Grabczynski. "I have not given up."

I was on the table for the fourth time in two days. I counted slowly,

"One, two, three, four," while inhaling the chlorethyl. My thoughts became confused, and I started falling rapidly into an abyss. I saw myself lying on hot sand in the desert. The sun was burning, and I was thirsty.

I whispered, "Water!"

A doctor was standing above me, Dr. Gordon from Vilna. He was nice to everybody, and he addressed every patient as "colleague," so that all the medics kidded him, saying that Gordon had thieves for colleagues. He was very nice, but now he said to me, "You will have no water; you didn't give water to others, when they were thirsty."

I thought of Father, as he went thirsty to the gas chamber. And Mother had been thirsty. And I hadn't given them water. And Gordon laughed, and laughed, and laughed. I woke up. A medic was dressing me.

I whispered, "Doctor, I can breathe easier."

Grabczynski smiled warmly. "This time, I got it. A bull's eye!"

"Pus burst out like a fountain," said Gordon. "Now colleague, everything is going to be all right, and you'll be as good as new."

"Provided he eats a lot!" This was said by another doctor who had just come into the surgery. He was Kuba Wolman, a young, rosy-cheeked, blond Jewish doctor from Lodz.

For the next three weeks, I lived in a world filled with fog and visions. During my brief moments of consciousness, I could see human faces bent above me. At such moments, I smiled shyly at all those people I didn't know and apologized for the awful smell of the pus emanating from me. My body was immersed in pus, and I smelled just like the corpses down there in the morgue.

The medics didn't seem to mind. They changed my dressing twice a day, cleaned my bunk, and changed my shirt.

Then, at long last the fever started subsiding. One morning, I was trying to cope with a bowl of tea that the Stubendienst had brought me, when Kuba Wolman arrived. He put his hand on my forehead, and his blue eyes smiled cheerfully as he yelled, "Gordon! Come over here! The fever's gone!"

Gordon, an unusually shy, modest man of thirty-five, took my pulse and then said, "Welcome to this world, colleague. I'll send you some soup."

In the evening of that day, Bronek came in. His face was beaming. "I spoke with Grabczynski and Fajkiel. You are out of danger. It's a miracle!"

"I am so grateful to you."

"Nonsense! Someday it will be your turn to help. I'd better go, to give the good news to Stefan. He's waiting in front of the block. He has been waiting there for a month."

A whole month. I thought it was a miracle there hadn't been a selection during that period of time.

Before leaving, Bronek asked me what I would like to eat, and I said, "Blutwurst. The butt portion, where there is a lot of fat. And bread."

"Blutwurst and bread it will be. My wife, Niusia, will be happy to hear the news. She knows all about you and has been worrying all this time."

Many changes had occurred in the Lager, while I was fighting for my life. Dehring had been released, and Fajkiel had become the head of the Krankenbau. Entress had been transferred, and a seemingly less bloodthirsty SS doctor, Dr. Koenig, had taken over as Lagerarzt. These changes accounted for the lack of selections for the gas chamber during the previous month. Had there been a selection, I would have surely gone.

Although usually slim, at this time I weighed less than eighty pounds, and the skin was hanging off my buttocks in loose folds. I was a total Mussulman.

Dr. Wolman and Dr. Gordon kept assuring me that I would be back to normal in no time, and that they would get me a function in their block. Ratajczak paid me a visit and assured me that a position was waiting for me in Block 28.

Suddenly one morning, Block 21 bustled with unusual activity. The Pflegers were running, cleaning, washing, and arranging the bunks. The new SS doctor, the Lagerarzt, was coming to make a selection for the gas chamber. It all seemed so illogical: I was coming back to normal after a month and a half of victorious struggle for life, only to be chosen for the gas chamber, when otherwise my chances had seemed to be so good.

A long line of naked patients formed in the central aisle of the ward, waiting for inspection. The chief Stubendienst called the names and handed each patient his hospital card. The Blockaltester and the Pflegers stood between the patients and the bunks, to make sure that nobody avoided the inspection.

Sudden silence fell on the ward. The chief Stubendienst yelled at the door, "Ward Number One! Ten Pflegers, seventy-eight patients, all present and accounted for!"

The Lagerarzt, his Scharfuhrer, and Dr. Fajkiel entered the ward and went to the end of the main aisle, where a table and a chair had been prepared for them. The Lagerarzt leaned his booted foot against the chair and glanced coolly at the line of patients.

Fajkiel took the card from the first patient in line and read aloud, "Flu. Accepted to the hospital for five days. Three days are over. No temperature."

The Lagerarzt glanced at the patient through his eyeglasses. Then he took the card from Fajkiel and handed it over to the Scharfuhrer. This meant the gas.

As the Lagerarzt took the second patient's card, Fajkiel walked along the line, persuing the cards. He saw me. He stopped in front of me, hiding me from view, and whispered, "Run! Hide in any upper bunk!" He slipped my card into his pocket.

With some hesitation, I left the line. The Blockaltester, who had heard Fajkiel, pushed me swiftly between the bunks, and I climbed into the top one, and laid down, my heart pounding.

Meanwhile, the first patients started coming back to their bunks, and it became practically impossible for the Lagerarzt to know who had missed the inspection. I felt more at ease and could watch the selection.

It was a quick procedure. A glance at the card, a glance at the patient, a verdict. Before long, the line in the central aisle had disappeared, and now Dr. Wolman was leading the Lagerarzt through the labyrinth of bunks, stopping from time to time in front of one of the bedridden patients who hadn't been able to stand in line. Wolman was leading the doctor in a complicated way, so as to avoid showing him a seventy-three-year old Dutch patient who was lying in the bunk after a hernia operation. I thought that took guts, because, if discovered, Wolman himself ran the risk of being sent to gas.

Now, this part of the inspection, too, was over, and the commission left. After the deep silence during the selection, the ward was humming with excitement.

That same afternoon, the patients selected by the Lagerarzt were taken away.

A few days later, although still a patient, I started helping Gordon and Wolman in various ward chores. I was under the command of the Stubendienst, a limping, one-eyed German who disliked me from the very first day and made me perform the most unpleasant duties in the ward. I helped carry patients to other blocks, gave out urine pans at night, washed the floors in the ward, cleaned bed-ridden patients, and did all sorts of minor ward jobs.

The new Lagerarzt, Dr. Koenig, became a steady visitor to Block 21. Taking advantage of this special opportunity, he was improving his skills in all sorts of surgery. He did it very systematically. First, it was the appendicitis patients. Any Haftling who had ever complained of pain in the right side of his abdomen was summoned into the block, and Dr. Koenig performed the appendectomy on him. After a couple of weeks of appendectomies, Dr. Koenig showed an interest in hernias. Each morning, he would select patients who had presented themselves because of a bad cold, ulcers, or diarrhea and operate on them for hernia. Hernia inguinalis, scrotalis, umbilicalis—it made no difference. Then, he switched to hooked toes. The Lager was combed in search of Haftlinge whose big toe overlapped the second toe, and in spite of all their protestations, Dr. Koenig made them undergo cosmetic surgery.

Occasionally, a whole group of German physicians cooperated on a project. They would pick a group of Jewish Haftlinge, and apply to their thighs various ointments, ichthyolic, boric, or nitrate of silver. A week later, portions of flesh were removed for laboratory examination, leaving the patients for months to come with ugly, festering wounds on their bodies.

A group of six Jews had their testicles removed, after which their sexual responses were examined. They were stripped naked, put next to naked women, and examined for erection. They were then kept in ice water for a number of minutes and again examined for erection.

Another group of four Jews underwent the testing of a truth serum. They were all given a cup of coffee containing the truth medicine in various concentrations. All four fell asleep, and only one woke up again.

Dr. Mengele at Birkenau studied twins. Twin siblings were searched for in each incoming transport, to be kept alive for his research. As soon as this became known, on a number of occasions children of equal age who were strangers were paired by their doomed parents, in the hope that their lives might be saved.

But the most serious tests were being performed in Block 10, the mystery block, where the only women in Auschwitz One were staying: ten prostitutes who worked in the Lager's bordello (to be used by the German Haftlinge only); Bronek's wife, Niusia, with their little son, Oles; and an indefinite number of women on whom unknown tests were being performed by a group of German doctors helped by a Jewish Haftling, Dr. Samuel, supposedly a specialist in genetics. Nobody knew what was going on, but sperm was occasionally taken from a few Jewish Haftlinge, and an abortion was occasionally performed in Block 21.

Selections went on as before, but they had become less frequent, and unlike previously, in the present selections only the seriously ill were sent to the gas chambers, unless a given case was of special interest to the German doctors' research. An example was the case of a young Jewish butcher by the name of Malinowski, who developed a cancer of the testicles. Dr. Koenig first removed one testicle. As the cancer continued, he removed the second testicle. However, a new growth had appeared. Malinowski suffered excruciating pain, but Dr. Koenig was not yet ready to send him to the gas. Every other day, he took photographs of the new growth, until it had become the size of a cauliflower, at which point Malinowski died in his bunk.

The time was passing, and from a patient I had become an almost-ex-patient, still working on the ward as a medic, but already seeing the end of this assignment, because with each day that passed, the one-eyed Stubendienst hated me more and more, and tried to have me sent back to an outside Kommando. I lost my hope of being retransferred to Block 28, as Ratajczak had been freed and replaced by a new Polish Haftling, whom I didn't know, and who, I was told, was rabidly anti-Semitic.

Finally, the day of my discharge from Block 21 had arrived. Along with a group of ex-patients, I was in line in the main aisle of the ward. We were all given the usual torn uniform and wooden shoes, a soup bowl, and a spoon, and we were waiting for a Pfleger to take us to one of the outside-Kommando blocks. Once more, it seemed to me that the song was over. I prayed in my thoughts to my parents and then to the Girl of the Ring. She had promised. She had told me that I would survive, and so far I had. But to go to an outside Kommando in my present condition meant bringing me closer to death. I thought of the beatings, and the shootings, and the lengthy roll calls in snow or rain. And then I had been healthy!

A Stubendienst's helper arrived to pick up our transfer papers. So this was it. Then, as the group was about to leave, the Krankenbau-schreiber rushed in, yelling "107455!"

I had a sudden feeling of anxiety as I stepped out of the group.

"By the order of Dr. Fajkiel, you will report to Block 28 as a dispensary medic."

Lady Luck seemed once again to have touched me. The Block-altester who had taken over after Ratajczak left showed me a great deal of goodwill and friendliness. Perhaps Ratajczak had had a talk with him before leaving Auschwitz.

I was assigned my own bunk in the ward where thirty other Pflegers lived, on the second floor, and I was assigned a space in a metal cabinet similar to a locker—in short, I had become a functionary. Imagine my feeling at being an equal of those for whom I had been washing laundry only a few short months ago.

My job was in the dispensary, where I started working the next morning. The schedule was simple. The first patients arrived at six in the morning, before the details started going to work. As soon as these patients had been taken care of, the Pflegers washed the dispensary and went upstairs to their room, leaving the first floor clean and empty, ready for the daily inspection of the patients by the SS Lagerarzt.

At eleven o'clock we attended to the patients who had been permitted to remain in the Lager for a few days, and who now came to the dispensary to have their dressings changed or to receive their medications for the day. At three o'clock more such cases came for treatment.

It was only in the evening, immediately after the report, that the really hard work was begun. At this hour, new patients arrived for the dispensary doctor's examination; old patients came for a change of dressing or for their daily treatment, like, for example, having their herpes smeared with iodine; and then there were the chronic everyday patients, who came to the dispensary with a hidden hope that perhaps this time the doctor would discover some mysterious disease which would entitle them to a few days' rest in camp. They all lined up in front of the Pflegers, each holding a hospital card on which the doctor had written the diagnosis and the prescription. The Pflegers worked swiftly, some of them knowing what they were doing and some simply considering a patient some sort of a bundle that was supposed to be wrapped up into a couple of yards of paper dressing.

At first, the patients avoided me. Just as in regular society, it took time and good work to develop a following. Within a few days, however, mine was the longest line in the dispensary. I found it difficult to understand the reason for this fast change, until Stefan, who was a regular patient of the infirmary, told me that there was a rumor among the patients that I was generous in dispensing the medications.

And then I recognized my newly acquired power. A Polish Haftling working for the SS kitchen came one evening to have his boils treated. As I was getting ready to apply some ointment to his neck, he said, "Hey, Pfleger! I'd like an extra treatment, get it? I'm going to take good care of you."

Vitamin pills were a rarity in Europe during the war and were considered a valuable commodity. In Auschwitz they went for the value of gold; the Krankenbau got its supply of vitamins and other cherished medications from the Canada warehouse. I took a few vitamin pills from the pharmacist Sielecki, handed them to the patient, and said with an air of complicity, "One in the morning, one in the evening. And return in two days."

And this was how I started to "organize" the better things of life. Two days later, my new patient brought me sugar. The rumor went around, and the number of my patients with means soon increased. My space in the locker started filling up with sausages, margarine, bread, and canned meat.

At that time, Auschwitz was full of all sorts of rumors. It was said that the selections for the gas chamber would be discontinued; that the SS were going to yield the rule of the camp to the Wehrmacht, the regular army, that the Jews would be spared. As if to substantiate the rumors, a movie theater was opened, and some privileged Aryan Haftlinge received tickets from their Kapos. However, the most important improvement occurred with the introduction of a full-time brothel.

Brothel facilities had been in existence in Auschwitz for quite some time. Ten German prostitutes lived in Block 10 and worked in a small block next to the camp's main gate, servicing the German Haftlinge functionaries.

Now, a new, more complete system was devised. Ten Polish and Russian prostitutes had been added and were also moved into Block 10. They were supposed to service all non-German Aryan Haftlinge. All the Haftlinge of the Aryan group, not just the functionaries, could now use the brothel — the *Puff,* as it was called in Auschwitz — provided that they had earned the necessary tickets, which were given out in the work details as a bonus for productivity. The small block was fixed up for the occasion, the tickets became an additional item on the camp's black market, and lines of happy customers formed around the block at the scheduled hours.

However, a minor problem developed in Block 10, where the balance of the tenants were the women on whom various medical experiments were being conducted. Here also lived Bronek's wife, Niusia, with their little son. The women were indignant at the addition of ten more prostitutes, not having been happy with the presence of the original ten. Now they decided to do something about it. They wrote a petition; and another petition; they vocalized their protest; they threatened to go on a hunger strike. And one evening, as Bronek, Stefan, and I stood under a first-floor window of Block 10 to say hello to Niusia, the little six-year-old Oles exclaimed excitedly, "Daddy, Daddy! All those whores are finally gone!"

The administration had yielded to pressure, and the twenty prostitutes had been moved to a recently built, minuscule women's camp, about a mile away from the barbed wire, where they were to live from then on. Their work was to continue in the Puff inside the camp, and from that day on, as all the details made their morning march out of the camp to the brisk sound of the Haftlinge orchestra, a small group marched in the opposite direction. As it stopped for a moment in front of the sentry booth, its leader, an SS Scharfuhrer, snapped to attention and reported, "The Whore Kommando, twenty strong! All present and accounted for!"

Sometimes the SS would let a couple of girls remain in the Puff overnight. When this happened, some of the more intrepid Auschwitz functionaries considered it a personal challenge to make an unscheduled visit to the Puff. Some such visits had an unexpected ending, and they accordingly entered the camp's history.

One example was the famous climb of Kapo Albrecht. He serenaded a girl. She asked whether he had brought the promised bottle of vodka. He answered positively. She threw him a rope from the second-floor window. He started his famous climb. And when he was almost at the window, she asked him to show the bottle. He said he would have it tomorrow, and she let the rope go. He wound up in the hospital block for surgery, with a broken arm, and the entire camp had a laugh at his expense.

All the camp knew the handsome, tall young man who, in his Haftling uniform, black boots, and black cap — the marks of the Lager's fire brigade — stood every evening under the Puff, leaning against a tiny tree looking up at the second-story window in which his sweetheart sat sighing for him.

The young man was known as "Irka." Irka is a girl's name in Polish, and it is odd for a man to have a girl's name. But for him it wasn't. He was in love, and his sweetheart was a whore whose name was Irka. Thus, the young fireman was also called "Irka."

The two usually just looked at each other. On rare occasions, they talked. No one knew what they were talking about, but the theory was that the theme was pure love. Some in the camp joked that they were discussing what their children would be when the war was over, and the decision was that should they be males, they would all be firemen; and should they be females . . .

"Irka" was an important functionary and he had important friends, so it was easy for him to "organize" the best delicacies of Auschwitz and send them to Irka. Among his friends was the head butcher of the SS kitchen.

One day, Irka received a package from the camp. It was about a foot and a half long, wrapped nicely in paper, and decorated with a ribbon organized from Canada. She knew it must be a gift from "Irka," and from its dimensions, she deducted that it was an SS sausage. She was unwrapping the gift at the very moment when her sweetheart, back from duty, took his usual position under the tiny tree.

Now the gift was unwrapped, and Irka became red with anger. She yelled, "You son of a bitch!" and hurled the gift out of the window and straight onto the fireman's head.

The source of the problem was the head butcher and his sense of humor. In the slaughterhouse of Auschwitz every little bit of the animal was utilized, but in this case the butcher decided to keep the penis of a horse and to have it delivered to Irka as her lover's gift.

This was the end of the romance, but the beginning of just another legend among the people of Auschwitz.

I felt very lonely. Now that I didn't have my hunger to think about, I secretly envied the people who had somebody to care for. Bronek had his wife and son; Stefan discovered a way of corresponding with his wife; Sielecki the pharmacist had found himself a fat girl in the women's camp to whom he was sending packages. All the Polish functionaries had somebody whom they could see and help. Thus it was a great day for me when Bronek brought me a note from the new women's camp where the prostitutes lived.

It was from Anka, and it was short and to the point: "I've been transferred here from Birkenau."

I felt a tremendous urge to help her, to do things for her, maybe even to see her.

The Haftlinge of Auschwitz could be very cruel—but they could also be very sentimental. Practically everybody offered his help. As I was making up the first package, some of the Pflegers threw in a piece of white bread or a portion of sausage. It felt unreal for me to prepare a package. Until now, I had seen only the Poles and Sielecki prepare packages. But me? Sending a package? To a Jewish girl? I felt I was alive and, what's more, that my being alive had been officially acknowledged.

Bronek had Niusia deliver the package. A regular correspondence was begun: Anka would write what she needed; I would organize and send it to her. I didn't feel lonely any longer. I was constantly busy thinking what to organize and anticipating the pleasure she would feel in receiving it.

At first, she needed just food, food, and more food. After that, she asked for better clothing. Later, she was interested in lipstick and cologne. Finally, she asked for an iron ring. It was considered chic at that time to have an iron ring bearing the owner's registration number. One could be ordered from any Haftling working in the machine shop, and the usual price was a couple of portions of bread and a double portion of sausage.

Anka got all she wanted.

And then, one day, with some important Pflegers' help, I had her brought to Block 28 for a visit.

Now she was sitting in the waiting room of the block, silent and smiling oddly, and I was standing in front of her, trying desperately to say something. She looked different in her Lager uniform: a striped dress, a dotted apron, and a white kerchief. Her hair was cut short.

She broke the silence. She asked, "Have you had any love affairs all this time?"

"No." I was taken aback.

"Neither have I." She still wouldn't look straight at me, and she still had that undefined smile.

I felt awkward. I sat on a bench, at a distance. I asked, "How have you been?"

"I had typhus. They shaved off my hair."

Every couple of minutes, another Pfleger stuck his head in the door and looked at her with curiosity. The time started to drag for me. I didn't know what to talk about with her. I sighed with relief when the woman doctor called the girls back to the ambulance car.

Later, the Pflegers surrounded me, to express their sorrow that I hadn't had a chance to make love to Anka. They offered to arrange a private room for us, when she came the next time.

But, somehow I knew there wouldn't be any next time.

That was the last time I saw Anka.

This was the beginning of the summer of 1944. New rumors were circulating around Auschwitz. They contradicted each other. Again, there was talk of the Wehrmacht taking over Auschwitz and all the other camps. That was good. Then there were rumors that weekly selections for the gas would be reinstated. That was bad. That a Puff for the Jews would be opened. That was good. That all the Jewish Haftlinge were to be called out to the front of the Lager during one of the evening reports in order to be taken to the gas chambers. That was bad. That ditches were being built in Birkenau, to offer resistance to the advancing Russian Army. That was good. That all the Polish Haftlinge would go away on a transport, and that Auschwitz would become a purely Jewish camp. That was bad.

The atmosphere of the Lager had become tense. The Haftlinge had to find an outlet for their frustrations, and the anxiety of Auschwitz was suddenly directed against individual new arrivals—single prisoners transferred to Auschwitz from other camps or prisons. Each new arrival was accompanied by a full report of his previous activities, and through the Schreibstube, the main administrative office, the functionaries knew the histories of the new arrivals and spread this knowledge throughout the camp. Then the camp's brutal vengeance would befall the individual.

The first revenge was taken on a Jew from Belgium. It was in early evening, immediately after the report, and the Pflegers of Block 28 were busy in the dispensary. A noise was heard at the far end of the camp. We were accustomed to occasional scuffles among the Haftlinge, and nobody paid any attention to the disturbance. Soon, the noise came closer and became more distinct, more threatening. We crowded in the door of our block to watch a mob of Haftlinge coming along the main street toward the Krankenbau. In front of them was a man whom they kicked and beat, on whom they spat, and at whom they yelled, "Kill the sonofabitch!"

The mob consisted of everybody: of the Poles, the Russians, and the Jews, even the German Kapos.

A Scharfuhrer appeared, and the mob stopped in silence. And in this silence, the high-pitched squeak of the persecuted wretch was heard. The Scharfuhrer passed by as if nothing had been happening.

Triumphantly the mob again fell on the man, whom they called a collaborator, and he would have been torn apart if not for another Scharfuhrer, who came out of the Bunker to take the victim into the jail, to protect him from his fellow prisoners.

Another time, a Polish collaborator arrived from the prison of Myslovitz. The mob used a different technique with him. The man was beaten up in his block and then driven out into the street. There, the mob marched after him slowly and threatening, forced him to walk toward the barbed wire, where he would be electrocuted by mere contact with the wire. Until only a year ago, dozens of Haftlinge had thrown themselves on the wire each night, to have it done with. The mob wanted this man to finish the same way. They were all over him. He suddenly broke down, and with a penetrating scream, he jumped on the wire. Nothing happened. The electric current had been disconnected. The crowd roared at the SS guard at the other side of the wire, "Shoot him! Shoot him!" But the guard turned his back.

The man was spared that day. But he was admitted to the Krankenbau, where he was declared dead from exhaustion two days later.

One Sunday afternoon, the Pflegers were called to one of the blocks, to take care of a man who had tried to hang himself from his bunk but had been cut down by the Blockaltester. That same night, he was found hanged again—this time for good. The rumor went around that he had been forced to hang himself, and that he had been cut down the first time because it had been decided that one hanging was not enough for him.

Even the Krankenbau had its frustrations, its tensions, and its hatreds. Every now and then, a scuffle broke out between a Jewish and a Russian Pfleger; a Polish functionary slapped his Jewish colleague; a Slovak Jew abused a Polish Jew. The Blockaltesters and the Jewish old timers intervened when this happened; sometimes Dr. Fajkiel was called in, and even, on occasion, Mr. Cyrankiewicz, a Polish Haftling of political stature who after the war was to become the first Prime Minister of the new Poland.

Of the many rumors, one at least proved true. Trenches were being built in Birkenau. Their purpose, though, was different from what the rumors so hopefully stated.

At the beginning of July, large transports of Hungarian Jews started arriving. There were five crematories in Birkenau, each of which had five ovens. Each oven could take two corpses at one time. The cremation time was about half an hour. That meant 2,400 bodies could be burned in twenty-four hours. Much better productivity was needed to accommodate the tens of thousands of Hungarian arrivals. The trenches were the solution.

One foggy morning, the nauseating smoke of burning flesh invaded Auschwitz One. I knew that smell: it was Treblinka.

I became frantic with an indescribable feeling of horror, panic, and despair. I ran from Haftling to Haftling, trying to share my feelings, but none of them seemed to understand me. They were good people, but they had become desensitized. Most of them just shrugged me off. As far as they were concerned, the SS really could be burning people alive, and they still wouldn't respond.

Only Richard, my old Kobier friend, found the time for a quick comment: "I had a chance to read Goebbel's last article in the *Reich*. One had to expect it. The Hungarian Jews were the last Jews in Europe still left alone."

While the Hungarian community was being destroyed, the Auschwitz people had a picnic. The things brought by the new arrivals started a wave of new business, as Canada was overflowing with woolen blankets, luxurious underwear, gold, watches, and jewelry.

The food itself in Auschwitz became more substantial. Several times a week, there was an extra portion of bread soup for everybody. In this soup, besides bread, could be found pastries, dried fruit, and even an occasional comb or piece of toilet soap. The old-time Mussulmen suddenly grew fat, and even the least enterprising Haftlinge started organizing.

Then the first Hungarian Jews appeared in the Lager. These were the lucky ones who had been spared the gas chambers. These people, who only two weeks before had been sleeping in their own beds, who even now looked well-fed and healthy, were lining up in the dispensary, scared and helpless.

And the heavy smoke during the day, and the red flames at night, over there beyond the barbed wire of Auschwitz, were proof that the extermination was in full swing.

These new Haftlinge were different from most previous new arrivals. Many of them were orthodox Jews, and they tried to keep their religion alive. In mournful groups, they gathered at dawn behind their blocks, tefilin on their foreheads, reciting praises to God and prayers for the dead.

They weren't allowed to do this for long, as one evening the Lagerkommandant commented, "It has come to my attention that the Jews are using some kind of radio transmitter that is unknown to us and are trying to contact the enemy! From now on, any Haftling caught with an antenna on his head will be shot!" This was the end of the public prayer.

The Hungarian Jews, however, attempted to keep their religion intact in another way. They tried to remain kosher, and in circumstances where a tiny chunk of meat could mean a day of life, they refused to eat the only real food we received twice a week: a tiny piece of sausage or of blutwurst.

The Hungarian Jews were decent and pious, but they, too, had their moments of anger. They saw around them Polish Jews, some of whom were functionaries, and most of whom had by now developed ways to outsmart the three-month survival theory and were doing comparatively well. The Hungarians compared their own lot with that of the Polish Jews, and they decided that it was not the SS but the Polish Jews who were responsible for their tragedy. They developed a hatred against the Polish Jews — a hatred that was to last long after the war was over, and that even today can still be detected lingering in the old survivors.

Some Hungarians had relatively good luck. The Krankenbau filled up with Hungarian physicians, and machine shops and garment details also acquired a number of Hungarian Jews. Dr. Mengele kept Hungarian twins and Hungarian dwarfs alive.

But over there, behind the barbed wire, the huge fire kept burning and burning.

This was my time of plenty.

I remembered the time when one of the Polish Pflegers handed me his bowl containing some remnants of a potato and said, "Here, have some decent food. And wash my bowl after you're done." Those had been my lucky moments. I had felt even luckier when they paid me for laundering their clothes. Once I had been paid with a whole small loaf of bread, which a Polish Pfleger had received from home. I carried the loaf under my arm and dreamed of enjoying it to my full satisfaction. I had decided I would eat only a slice that evening and would keep the rest for Sunday afternoon. I sat on my bunk in the admissions room and called Tazartes for a treat. Tazartes sat down and took out his jackknife. I pulled out a large carton from under the bunk. All Polish Pflegers had such boxes, except that theirs were filled with all sorts of good things. Each time a Pole sat down to a meal, he would pull out his box, cut off slices of home-made bread and small pieces of pork fat, and eat in solemn silence. Tazartes and I loved this procedure, and we, too, fixed cardboard boxes for ourselves. Now my box was open in front of me. It was empty. "One day," I dreamed, "one day I'll have in it pork and sausage. Esmanska and Kostka." I cut a slice from my loaf of bread. It smelled of mildew. I cut a second slice. Feverishly, I cut the entire loaf. It was mildewed through and through. My dream of home-made, freshly baked, aromatic bread was dead. I felt like crying.

"I knew they wouldn't give you good bread," said Tazartes sadly, folding his jackknife. "They are getting so much from home they cannot finish it. But they wouldn't give a piece of good bread to a Jew. Not even when it's coming to him."

Now my box was full, but Tazartes was gone. He had been sent away on a transport when I was sick.

Now I was helping others. Every evening, the Italian Piperno came for his bowl of soup; and the young Sonnino, who had two huge ulcerations on his legs, left there from some medical tests; and a Hungarian youth who worked in a machine shop. Stefan liked the special soup given to patients with stomach ulcers: cold oats with sugar. I gave it to him from time to time. But most of the things I organized went to Anka. By now it had become some sort of duty for me to keep sending her things. Otherwise our relationship was one of indifference to each other, with her asking for more unusual things each time, and disdaining me for being able to send her only the necessary, everyday staples.

Before the Hungarian transports, some of the original Auschwitz problems had become almost extinct. The fleas and lice were gone, and ulcers and diarrhea were rare.

Now, with the new arrivals, it all started all over again. The dispensary was filled with Haftlinge with festering wounds, ulcers, and abscesses, and diarrhea became again a daily guest. Block 19 was filled with Durchfall cases, the selections for the gas chambers returned, and large trucks filled with patients, clad only in their shirts traveled to what they were told were the "rest camps."

One afternoon, a group of unusual-looking Haftlinge arrived. Their bodies were swollen from beating, their eyes looked glassy and empty of emotion, and they spoke and walked like zombies. The last time I had seen people looking like this was in Treblinka. And sure enough, these were the workers of the crematory in Birkenau. It was a weak point with all of us, the people of Auschwitz: we despised those who worked in the gas chambers and the crematories, and we never gave a thought to the possibility that any one of us could be chosen by the SS to become one of the despised ones. Now, curiosity being stronger than aversion, we asked them some basic questions. They were Jews from Athens who had worked in the crematory for a couple of months. Today they had been put on a transport. In Block 28 we all knew where the transport would finish, but nobody had the heart to tell them.

That same evening, the crematory workers were taken to Canada.

There they were gassed in the chamber where clothing was normally disinfected. Their bodies were burned that same night by the SS themselves, so that the news wouldn't reach the remaining members of the Crematory Kommando. But in one way or another, all of Auschwitz came to know it the very next day.

The liquidation of a part of the crematory detail was greeted in Auschwitz as good news. Everybody seemed to agree that this was the beginning of a complete liquidation of the gas chambers and the crematories, and the first step back toward civilization. Obviously, the Germans intended to get rid of all traces of their crimes, and a new hope surged for the Auschwitz population.

As if in support of this theory, Dr. Koenig was transferred elsewhere, and the position of Lagerarzt was given to Dr. Klein, an elderly gentleman of Hungarian origin, short and plump, with gray hair and grey melancholy eyes. His personality was the opposite of what Auschwitz had had for Lagerarzt until now. The others had all been slim men, with pale, cadaverous faces, with cold eyes, and with narrow lips unable to smile. The usually well-informed sources were saying that Dr. Klein played the violin, was a lover of classical music, and was an absolute enemy of selections for the gas chambers.

The patients of the Krankenbau were now treated better than before, and Auschwitz started having guests from the outside world. These were sundry so-called international press commissions, composed of Italian, Slovakian, Hungarian, and Japanese journalists. They were given a guided tour of Auschwitz, and before each such visit, the Krankenbau blocks were thoroughly scrubbed and disinfected, the first and second tiers of bunks covered with impeccably white sheets, and the patients wrapped in cotton gauze instead of the usual paper bandages.

It was also at about this time that the first swallows of freedom started visiting the camp. Every morning, at eleven sharp, the sirens wailed, and all the SS staff left the Lager, just as the rules required. The first plane arrived. It flew so high that it was difficult to see it, until it drew a huge semicircle of white smoke, to match the outlines of the camp. We thought this was a sign for the bombers that we, the Haftlinge, lived there, and that we were not to be touched. A few minutes later, the bombers arrived. The German antiaircraft artillery, posted a couple of miles outside the camp, opened fire. Splinters rained on the roof of Block 28, while the dispensary Pflegers, stretchers readied for emergency, gathered in the corridor, listening with pleasure to the faraway outbursts of the friendly bombs. The bombs were exploding majestically, and each explosion sounded to me like the clapping of a hammer driving nails into the lid of the coffin of the Nazi Empire.

In midsummer 1944, the first witnesses of German defeat had arrived and were brought to the dispensary for first aid. They wore torn camp uniforms, many of them were barefoot, and all were dirty and exhausted. They came from Majdanek, a concentration camp in eastern Poland. According to their tales, the Russians had broken the front line at Lublin, and Majdanek had had to be evacuated so unexpectedly that the entire procedure took less than an hour, and some of the SS guards had fled without their jackets on.

A young Polish physician, Jaronski, who had worked in the Krankenbau of Majdanek, told me more about that camp. He said that about one thousand people had been evacuated. Some couldn't march and had been shot on the road. The women and most of the men had been taken to Birkenau, and only a small part came to Auschwitz.

A few days later, after we had become closer, Jaronski told me more. There had been seventeen thousand Jews in Majdanek, living in entire family groups. The camp had been divided into five parts, called *fields*. In two of the fields lived Polish Haftlinge, in one the Russians, in the fourth one the Jews, while the fifth field was taken up by the Krankenbau. There was also a central field, where the daily report was held.

Life in Majdanek had been about the same for everybody, except perhaps for the Russians, who reacted worse than the rest of the Haftlinge to diarrhea and had died like flies during the winter of 1942. Jaronski told of sick Russian soldiers who had been thrown out of the barracks during that harsh Polish winter and left to die from the cold. He said that later the life in Majdanek had become more endurable. Everybody worked, and everybody had enough food to survive. This idyll lasted until November 17, 1943. On that day, the camp was awoken earlier than usual. Everybody entered the central field for the morning report, except for the Jews, who were all marched into the Krankenbau field. The entire camp was surrounded by the SS, but the heaviest concentration was around the Krankenbau, where machine-gun nests were fixed, and a triple line of armed SS took position.

The Polish and Russian Haftlinge were kept all day in the central field, from which they could hear uninterrupted shooting in the Krankenbau. In the evening, it was all over. The Krankenbau was drowning in blood. Jaronski found in his ward a friend of his, a Jewish physician, hanging from a belt, while his wife lay on a bunk, her veins cut. Out of the seventeen thousand Jews, not one remained alive.

A few months later, other Jews were brought into Majdanek, and some of them had now come to Auschwitz. Jaronski estimated the entire number of the remaining Majdanek Jews to be close to two hundred.

In Auschwitz One, there had always been a few Gypsy Haftlinge, mainly German, who had been brought here as antisocial elements and wore black triangles on their uniforms, just like the Russians. They were treated a little bit better than the Jews and a little worse than the Poles, in spite of the fact that they were fully settled German citizens. In fact, some of the German Gypsies had served in the Wehrmacht until a time, towards the end of the war, when they were brought to Auschwitz directly from the front.

In Auschwitz Two — that is, in Birkenau — there was a Gypsy camp, where real, nomadic Gypsies lived. They were never given the same attention as the other Auschwitz Haftlinge. They weren't tattooed with the registration number; they didn't receive the camp uniforms; and their families were not separated. Instead, they were crammed into wooden barracks in a muddy, dirty, waterless, and sewerless corner of Birkenau, men, women, and children together. For a short time, their only co-tenants were the Jews from the Czech ghetto of Teresina, before the latter were sent to the gas chambers.

One day, everything suddenly changed. Two nice, clean blocks in Auschwitz One were surrounded by a single barbed-wire fence, and the Gypsy families were brought in. They were told that the situation was only temporary and that their ultimate destination would be resettlement to the eastern province of the Ukraine, where they would be set free to become farmers and artisans.

The arrival of the Gypsies was like a fresh breeze. The Gypsy girls swirled about in their large, colorful skirts, arousing sexual desire among the curious Auschwitz Haftlinge. The Gypsy men played their mandolins, and the Gypsy children cried.

A wave of margarine, sausage, and bread was temporarily directed toward these two unusual blocks, swarming with life, rebellion, and the promise of freedom.

There was a little Gypsy Pfleger in Block 28. He was of a middle-class family, from Berlin. His name was Harry. Until the arrival of the Gypsy families, Harry had been considered a German, and nobody had thought of changing his status.

But Harry fell in love with a Gypsy girl. He spent every free moment with her, within the new Gypsy camp.

The last of the Gypsies had been brought into the two blocks, soldiers, noncoms, and officers, who had arrived directly from the Ukrainian front.

New rumors started circulating: all the Gypsies would go free, provided they would let themselves be sterilized. The soldier Gypsies objected violently, and it seemed for a while that they would either be forcibly sterilized or let go as they were.

Then uglier rumors started. These were about the extermination of the Gypsies.

The transport date was set.

Little Harry went from one Pfleger to another to say good-bye. He could have remained with us, because the decree regarding the Gypsies did not apply to the ones who had been tattooed. But Harry was in love. The Lagerarzt himself gave him permission to follow the Gypsy camp.

They left Auschwitz One that same night, with their bundles, with their pieces of old furniture, and with their mandolins.

The next day, at noon, an elderly Jew arrived in Block 28. He was short and had a slightly curved back and gray, uncut hair. He was dressed in a much-used civilian suit and had come from the old Gypsy camp in Birkenau. His name was Dr. Fischer, and he was a noted Czech psychiatrist, a disciple of Freud. He was the bearer of the sad news.

A group of Jews with whom he had been staying in the old Gypsy camp had been added to the transport of Gypsies from Auschwitz One. They had all been gassed in Birkenau. Dr. Fischer was the only survivor, and the Lagerarzt had had him transferred to Block 28 in Auschwitz One.

Auschwitz was full of activity. New arrivals were coming; transports were leaving; individual Haftlinge were escaping. Most of the escapees were caught and brought back; some of them were punished by hanging; some were sent away on a transport to another camp. All this was logical.

But then, one day, an illogical thing happened. At the evening count, it appeared that there was one Haftling more in Auschwitz than the books showed. The count was taken many more times that night, and each time, there was that one, inexplicable Haftling too many. Late that night, the mystery was cleared up.

It had all begun the day before, when a group of Krankenbau patients were selected for the gas chamber and segregated in Block 19, awaiting the trucks.

The night passed, early morning arrived, and the crematory trucks hadn't arrived yet. This was sufficient time for one of the selected patients to sneak out of Block 19, join a work detail, and leave the Lager for the day. During the morning, the trucks arrived and transported the rest of the group to the gas chamber. Thus the patient who had sneaked out had been officially transported to Birkenau, gassed, cremated, and otherwise disposed of.

The question remained: What was to be done with him now? In a way, it was double jeopardy. Could a person be killed twice? The Blockaltester of Block 19 spoke with him. The Krankenbaualtester spoke with him. Finally, the Lagerkommandant himself came over to Block 19 to speak with him. Everybody wanted to know why he had done what he did, and to everybody he gave the same answer: he had wanted to prove that he was still ready, able, and willing to work. And when the Lagerkommandant said angrily that he had been selected to go to a rest camp, the man answered that he felt fine and, indeed, did not need a rest. It seems that this time the joke was on the camp administration. They left the man alone.

A lot of punishment was dispensed in Auschwitz during the late summer and the early fall of 1944. It started with a Hungarian Jew who thought it possible to escape without any help from an outside source. He was caught in no time at all, sentenced that same day, and hanged in the Raportplatz during the evening count. While his skinny body was swinging from the gallows, the Haftlinge were ordered to march by and look at him, so that they would learn about the futility of any such hope. Yet, soon afterwards, a Slovak Jew who was the Schreiber of the crematories tried his luck. It took the SS two weeks to catch him. Now, he was standing under the gallows, his hands tied behind him, and Jacob the Bunker Kapo was trying the strength of the rope before throwing the noose around his neck. Then the unexpected happened: the trap opened, the rope broke, and the man fell into the hole.

The scene was unreal. The Lagerkommandant and his SS cohorts were confused, and we were choking from emotion, as the Slovak — his hands still tied behind his back, the purple imprint of the rope around his neck, and hiccupping violently — was being marched away from the gallows and toward the Bunker.

That night, Auschwitz was talking about the miracle. All pointed to the only possible reason why the Slovak was not put back on the gallows right then and there: the German mentality would not allow a man to be hanged twice.

But we soon found out that the Slovak was shot in his cell later that same night, and Jacob was thrown into the Bunker, under the suspicion of having engineered the event.

Jacob did not remain a prisoner for long. After a few days, he was reinstated as the Bunker Kapo.

And the hangings went on.

The sirens announcing an escape could be heard more and more often. After they stopped, hours of expectancy slowly passed. And then the Haftling would be brought back. On rare occasions, in spite of the dogs, the guards, and the spies, the flight was a success. Sometimes it took many days to find and catch the runaway.

Edek was a Polish Haftling whose imprisonment in Auschwitz had been one of the longest. His tattoo number was only slightly higher than 500. He had an important function, a good life, and no need to escape.

Mala was a Jewish girl from Belgium. She was a relative newcomer to Birkenau, and although she held a good position, she was just a Jew, and her plight was as unpredictable as any other Jew's.

Edek and Mala fell in love.

The time came now for Edek to use all the influence he had, as a long-time Haftling, to help Mala.

Edek knew that the only sure way for a Jew to survive Auschwitz was to be away from it. He thought he could arrange an escape.

Everything was prepared with utmost care. The Polish underground outside Auschwitz was of help, and so were some people inside the Lager. Mala left the camp dressed as an SS woman. Edek escaped separately. They were to meet in a prearranged place.

Two weeks had already gone by, and there was no sign of the fugitives. The camp was praying for the couple.

Then, late one day, on a sunny afternoon, a loud drumming was heard at the main gate of Auschwitz. A few SS men marched down the middle of the main street, the sides of which were crowded with curious Haftlinge.

A small group followed. First, came the Scharfuhrer, a gun in his hand. Ten steps behind him walked Edek, a big, handsome fellow, still dressed in good civilian clothes. He walked passively, as if in a dream. A drum was suspended from his neck, on which he beat the rhythm. A poster was hanging on his back, announcing: "Hurra! Hurra! Ich bin schon wieder da!" — "Hurrah! Hurrah! I'm here again!" Two SS men walked alongside Edek.

Ten steps behind Edek walked Mala. She was frail, little, and pretty.

A few days later, Edek was sentenced to be transferred to another camp, and for Mala, the sentence was death by hanging.

In the middle of the Raportplatz, the gallows was erected. Mala stood under the noose with her hands behind her — tied, we assumed. Beside her, the Lagerkommandant read the verdict aloud from the papers he held in his hand. He finished reading and turned to Mala. Gloom hung over the Lager.

In the silence, suddenly, the frail Jewish girl from Belgium raised her right hand and slapped the Lagerkommandant. Then she collapsed, bleeding profusely from her veins, which she had been able to cut with a razor slipped to her beforehand by a well-wisher. The same person must have cut the rope that bound Mala's hands.

Mala wasn't fit for hanging anymore, and the SS rushed her to the gas chamber, to kill her before she died on her own.

But the rumor of Auschwitz was kind. It said that Mala died before reaching the gas chamber.

Life went on in the Krankenbau, with the Pflegers trying to kill time the best way they could.

In Block 28, three Jehovah's Witnesses — a huge Netherlander, a shy Slovak, and a dwarf German — had secret evening meetings with Jewish Mussulmen from the Lager. The theme was the Day of Atonement; the goal was conversion; the tool was the distribution of free soup. Irked by other Pflegers' jests, the Witnesses decided to prove that their Jewish disciples were intent on conversion, not on the soup, and they cut out the food. This was the end of the meetings.

In Block 21, the Pflegers introduced a ritual of initiation, according to which each new Pfleger had his groin pasted with glue.

The Pflegers of Blocks 20 and 19 waged a war of water syringes.

Rich Pflegers held heavy drinking parties at night, and the day after, the Scharfuhrer looked for alcohol in the Pflegers' ward in Block 21.

While this life of leisure was going on, the Allied airplanes were flying over Auschwitz every day and every night.

And they were bombing every day and every night.

At eleven in the morning, it was the British. They finished their daily chore at six in the evening. Three hours later, it was the Russians.

The British used smoky semicircles to outline the camp, while the Russians threw a number of flaming rockets into the sky, which served the same purpose at night. We called the British circles "the smoke," and the Russian rockets "Stalin's Christmas trees." Soon, we were divided into three groups, living by three different philosophies. One group loved the British bombardment but hated the Russian. The second group enjoyed the Russian bombardment but was afraid of the British. The third group, to which I belonged, loved the entire show.

The only ones who seemed to dislike the whole idea of bombing were the SS. A few times, I heard the Scharfuhrer say with envy, "You bastards are at least sure that nobody intends to bomb you!"

September 13, 1944, arrived. The day started as usual: morning visit by the Lagerarzt; our morning work with the patients; the daily eleven o'clock siren; the usual semicircle of smoke above the Lager. Then unusual things started happening. The air squad arrived but, instead of continuing their flight as usual, the planes discharged their bombs right on the Lager. Unbelieving, we stood in the corridor of Block 28 with our stretchers at the ready, while all around us there was whistling and bursting, exploding and shaking. When you are under a heavy bombardment, it is difficult to measure the time: seconds become minutes; minutes become hours; then, when it's all over, time seems to have been at a standstill all along.

When the bombardment was finally over, a messenger arrived from the main gate, yelling for the emergency Pflegers. Stretchers in our hands, we all ran. Pflegers from the other blocks joined us. In no time, we reached the small women's camp and the wooden barracks housing the garment shops. There was pain, destruction, and death all over. Buried under the smoking debris lay moaning Haftlinge and their SS guards side by side.

All that September day, we worked feverishly, searching out the wounded and carrying them to all the available Krankenbau blocks. All bunks and floors were filled with the wounded. The most dreadful cases appeared. A man lay on the floor looking like a porcupine, with splinters of wood sticking out of every square inch of his body. People whose chests had been smashed were faintly begging for some air. Haftlinge who had marched off to their work four hours ago were numbly massaging their legless hips.

Outside, behind Block 28, the dead were being collected. At first, we put the SS guards and the Haftlinge on the same heap. Later, we were ordered to load the SS bodies on a truck, which carried them away, leaving only the shredded corpses of the Haftlinge next to the block. A Jewish Haftling came in search of his father. He recognized him by his shoes, cried in desperation, and said Kaddish in front of a huge heap of massacred bodies.

The Lagerarzt, Dr. Klein, brought a bouquet of flowers for the Haftlinge victims of the British air raid. More than three hundred were killed that day.

The bombings became the order of the day. The British with their ribbons of smoke or the Russians with their Stalin's Christmas trees seemed to be there all the time. Buna and Unionwerke, two huge German industries of artificial rubber and ammunitions, which were spread all over the Auschwitz territory outside the barbed wire, were being bombed daily. The Pflegers in Block 28 spent most of their time standing in the corridor with the stretchers and waiting for somebody to tell them where to go. What we considered a picnic at the beginning had become an oppression. Up there, in the dark sky of the night, the falling bombs and the Christmas trees gave the camp a festive look, but down here we were bowed under the oppressive hiss of the diving planes, tense and no longer sure of our untouchability.

Meanwhile, the selections for the gas chambers and the death penalty were reinstated. Yet, even under these conditions, Dr. Klein seemed to be somewhat better than any of his predecessors. Like the others, he did select people for the gas, but unlike the others, he did it in absentia. He arrived in the Krankenbau office late at night, asked for the patients' files, and made the selections from the sick cards, without ever facing the patients.

In one of these selections, an elderly Haftling from Paris, a certain Mr. Fink, was chosen for the gas. He looked very much like Dr. Klein, with his soft, gray eyes and gray hair. He had an Aryan wife and a daughter back in Paris, and he was a well-to-do perfume manufacturer. So when he approached me to tell me about his mishap, I couldn't help but suggest that he see Dr. Klein and beg for his life. I felt that Dr. Klein wouldn't refuse. But Mr. Fink was a proud man who wouldn't beg, and two days later, on October 4, he was taken away.

At that time, I learned about the existence of an underground movement in Auschwitz. One evening, Kuba Wolman asked me whether I thought that I could get together a fighting cell in Block 28. The cell was supposed to consist of me and four trusted persons. This was about as much as Wolman knew at this time. Further orders were to arrive soon. I enrolled the three morgue Pflegers and one of the dispensary people I thought good for it. There was a promise in this for me. Finally, I would be actively involved instead of waiting for somebody else to settle my accounts with the Nazis. I dreamed about a rifle and about doing heroic acts.

A few days passed by. Wolman returned to ask me about the progress of my mission. New orders were to follow two days later, and with them, we were to receive some arms.

The tense hours of expectation passed slowly.

A gloomy October day arrived, with the sky heavily overcast and with a light drizzle falling on the camp. The details left for work, as usual, and we were doing our chores leisurely, hopeful that because of the clouds, no bombers would arrive today.

Everything went as usual until the lunch hour. Then, in the early afternoon, small firearms were heard from the general direction of Birkenau. Though not many at first, the shots soon became frequent and intense. Rifles, pistols, and even hand grenades could be heard very clearly. The camp stood still, waiting for an explanation.

I went to Wolman, to ask him whether this was *the* hour. He too was at a loss, not having received any new orders.

The shooting continued. It sounded like a battle. Sometimes it was nearing. Then it faded away.

Back in Block 28, I ran across Kurylowicz. Red with excitement, the old man hissed, "The crematories!" But this was as much as he knew.

The work details started reentering the Lager. They were bunched up, the everyday camp discipline not manifest any longer.

Stefan came to Block 28 to see me. He rubbed his fine, bony hands nervously and said, "As I was coming back, I noticed armed SS surrounding the camp by the hundreds."

"Do you think this is the repetition of Majdanek?" We looked at each other with worry.

The shooting subsided. Then it burst out again; this time it was orderly and well organized. It all stopped an hour later.

The details formed silently next to their barracks, waiting for the evening count. The report took only a few minutes, and the details were dismissed as if nothing had happened.

A little later, the news came to Block 28. Old man Kurylowicz, surrounded by a group of Pflegers, told the story he had heard from a well-informed source. It was the crematory all right.

The crematory detail had received a tip that they would be dispatched to the gas chamber that very same day, and on the spur of the moment, they had decided to resist. Everything happened suddenly. There was no time for any coordination. They disarmed a few guards and turned their newly acquired weapons against the arriving reinforcements. The crematory Kapo was thrown alive into the oven, after which a part of the detail crossed the railroad tracks and took up a position behind the boxcars, from where they shot at the approaching SS. At one moment, it seemed as if the uprising was destined to succeed. But the SS were too well organized, too well armed, and too numerous for the bunch of desperado Haftlinge.

Several platoons of the SS sent to the rescue surrounded the rebels. The Haftlinge who had weapons fought until they were shot, like soldiers. The others were driven to the railroad platform, where they were swiftly divided into several groups and executed, group by group. The first ones were ordered to lie down, and the crematory Scharfuhrer himself, a gun in his hand, went from one to the other, shooting them in the back of the head. The other groups were ordered to lie down on the bodies of their colleagues, to be executed by the enraged SS guards. The Auschwitz crematory detail had been annihilated.

The next day, Wolman told me that all action was being postponed. The crematory uprising had been due to an SS provocation caused by the rumors of an underground resistance. The SS had a good number of spies in the camp, and they wanted to bring the resistance into the open. Now they had discovered that at least some of the weapons used in the uprising had come from the Unionwerke and were supposed to be distributed among the potential fighting cells of Auschwitz. A few days later, five Jewish girls working in the Unionwerke were arrested for having supplied the crematory detail with grenades. They were promptly sentenced and executed. As the five were going to the gallows, they sang "Hatikvah," the anthem of Jewish hope for a rebirth of the State of Israel.

It was a rare thing to see a Jew serving in the fashionable regiments of the Polish Ulans. Stasiek Lowenstein, a distinguished-looking gentleman of fifty-two, was a major of the Ulans. Years back, he had been a well-known playboy in Lvov. Now, he was lying in Block 21 with prostate disease and saw himself as a nonentity.

"My boy," he said to me once, "it has always been my fate to be just the shadow of somebody of importance. You probably know that my father was a famous man?"

I knew. The elder Lowenstein had been a statesman and a noted lawyer; the cream of the Jewish society of Poland.

"When I was a boy," continued Stasiek, "everybody pointed to me in the street, saying, 'There goes the son of the famous Lowenstein.' Later in life, I married a beautiful woman. Everybody in Lvov pointed at me, saying, 'There goes the husband of that exquisite Margot.' She was splendid. And she was so much younger than I. We had a son. He would now be fourteen. They killed both of them, Margot and my son, two years ago. My son. My son was a mathematical genius at the age of eleven. It was my dream to be pointed at one day in the future by the people of Lvov, who would say, 'There goes the father of that famous Lowenstein.' "

That was the dream. The reality was that Lowenstein the Playboy and Lowenstein the Shadow stopped existing when Lowenstein the Man took over, to become a courier in the Polish underground and to work in Hungary in the Polish-British Intelligence. When things became too hot, the English sent an airplane to pick him up, but he refused to go, feeling that there were things still to be done.

The Gestapo caught up with him finally, but he had a prostate attack during the interrogation. He was transferred temporarily to Auschwitz for treatment. His fame preceded him, and the Krankenbau society of Auschwitz received him with the honors due a senior statesman. The Polish underground planned an escape for him the moment he was well enough to withstand the effort.

The Gestapo didn't give him a chance. Stasiek Lowenstein was still sick in bed when the crematory ambulance came to pick him up.

Stasiek Lowenstein lay on a stretcher in the courtyard between Block 21 and Block 22. Many Pflegers came to say good-bye.

Stasiek asked, "Am I going to die like a soldier or like a rat?"

Kuba Wolman had seen the pickup paper. He said, "Like a soldier."

Stasiek said, "When the time comes, tell my comrades that I did not betray one name, regardless of the torture. And that I was glad to die for Poland."

And so ended the story of the man who had failed to anticipate in his dream that one day the people of Lvov might point at him, saying, "Here goes THE Lowenstein."

Retaliations for the crematory uprising started almost immediately. Every day, large groups of Polish Haftlinge were concentrated in newly created "transport blocks," from where they were being taken to different Lagers all over Germany. Auschwitz was being emptied rapidly.

For the Poles, it was a punishment to be taken away from a camp where they had grown roots. For the Jews, it looked like a death sentence. We felt this, and the Poles did, too. This was confirmed by one of the Pflegers of Block 28 when it was his turn to leave. He took me up to the attic and led me into a tiny room, with just one bunk as furniture. He pushed the bunk away, pressed on the wooden wall behind it, and exposed a small passage leading into a corner under the roof.

"I prepared this hideout for myself, two years ago," he said. "I'm not sure it will help you, because they say that the SS will burn Auschwitz together with the Jews in it. Or maybe they will first finish you off, and then they'll burn the camp. Anyhow, there is also a chance that they will take you to the gas chambers. In such a case, you can try to hide here."

Yet not all the Poles were taken away. In Block 28, Kurylowicz was left, and Dr. Kapuscinski from Warsaw, and Dr. Wasilewski, an ophthalmologist and an anti-Semite, whose sister was a famous communist writer and, possibly, *not* an anti-Semite. A few Poles remained in each block. It was the general feeling that they would be taken on a transport on the eve of the extermination of the Jews.

The routine of Auschwitz had also changed. New functionaries had to be installed to substitute for the Polish ones. Block 28 had received a German Blockaltester, Adolph, who bragged that his reason for being in Auschwitz was his long-standing membership in the German Communist Party, and who drank an awful lot of vodka. Weiss, a Slovak Jew, became the Schreiber of the block, while I had become the Schreiber of the dispensary. Now, we all had important titles, but no food. Along with the Poles went the beautifully developed Auschwitz marketing system which we had endearingly called organizing. There was no more hard money (pure spirit), or soft money (vodka), or small change (kostka, esmanska, and cigarettes). There was no more Canada, with its supply of fancy everyday goods, as well as expensive jewelry. There were no sellers, and there were no buyers. Hunger had returned to Auschwitz.

Up to now, I had supplied Anka with almost all she wanted. Times having changed, I considered it a stroke of good luck if I could send her a portion of bread or a bowl of cereal.

Anka didn't seem to understand the new circumstances. One evening, a German Kapo came to Block 28, bringing me a letter from her. She had never written me a letter before. Instead, hers were usually order slips, asking for certain things in certain quantities. This time, it was serious. She called me inefficient, expressed her contempt of me, and cited the example of others who had kept delivering. It was an ultimatum.

I sighed, and tore up the letter. I was fed up with Anka and her demands. Longingly, I thought of the time at Rokiciny Malopolskie when Martin had written me from Warsaw: "Bergman has a wonderful position for you, provided you come to Warsaw without Anka." At that time, I had felt heroic, and indignant, and chivalrous. Now, I felt simply nauseated. Until now, Anka had been for me a point of reference, a link between the past and the present. The past had faded away, and I felt that I no longer needed her. I stopped even needing myself. I had become an obsolete tool. I told myself that should I ever again be able to "organize," I would give my help to somebody who really needed it.

The picture of Auschwitz started changing once again. Small groups of non-Jews were being brought in daily from France, Holland, and Italy. Most of the new arrivals received good functions, and soon Auschwitz started organizing again. But it was not like in the old times, because the new tenants lacked the Polish generosity. However, they, too, had their abscesses, their festering ulcers, and their sundry diseases, which qualified them to become a source of new organization. Also, the few leftover Poles had become more active on the Auschwitz market, and meat, bread, and margarine soon reappeared.

One day, a short, husky Pole from Silesia came to the dispensary. He had a favor to ask. There was a barber from Marseille whom he wanted to protect from being sent to Birkenau, and he was asking to have him admitted to the hospital for a few days. As I was about to help him, he noticed that his number and mine were almost equal, which meant that we had come from the same Quarantane group. He became sentimental about me and invited me to his block that evening. He was a big-time organizer. There was a warehouse of riches under his mattress: SS sausages galore, and margarine, and even a full half of a hog. From that time on, I visited him twice a week, and abundance returned once more to my locker.

Reassuring news was arriving from Birkenau. The gas chambers were being disassembled, and only one crematory was supposed to remain, to take care of the Haftlinge whose deaths were due to natural causes. Rumor wanted Auschwitz to become a labor camp, and all my dreams of armed insurrection, revenge, and heroics were put aside. I felt disappointed. It was as if somebody had robbed me of the last chance of contributing to the lofty effort of keeping alive all that was noble and beautiful.

For all practical purposes, I was in a great position. Like other functionaries, I had a sharp-looking uniform, custom-made for me by one of the best tailors from Lvov. I wore my cap aslant, the way the Polish functionaries had in the good old times. But that was my outside. Inside, I felt empty and useless. I wanted to help somebody in need. Occasionally, I would fix a nice dinner for Stefan and Bronek, but that was not the same as helping the needy.

One day, Kuba Wolman paid me a visit, accompanied by a fourteen-year-old boy from Lodz named Jurek, and asked whether I could arrange to have the boy assigned to Block 28 as a messenger, in which case he would try to do the same for the boy's younger brother, Rysio, in Block 21. I used all my powers of persuasion on the chief doctor of the block and on the Blockaltester, Adolph, and finally I succeeded. Jurek became the official *Laufer* ("messenger") of Block 28. At the same time, he became my ward. I finally had somebody to care for.

Jurek tried to please me in various ways: he wanted to polish my shoes and wanted to cook for me. I didn't let him. I wanted to be on the giving side and didn't want to receive anything in exchange. Then Jurek told me about his family: that they had been rich before the war, that they had a piece of land in Palestine, and that he expected me to join him and Rysio there, once the war was over. For Jurek the war was as good as over, now that he didn't have to work any longer in the stable in a little camp outside Auschwitz, from which he had come to us.

Big changes were taking place in the Lager meanwhile. The Lagerarzt, Dr. Klein, was removed, and a young Dr. Fischer took over. Before leaving, Dr. Klein made a surprise appearance in Block 28. He requested that all the staff be assembled in the corridor, and he delivered a short speech. His gray eyes were moist as he said: "I beg your forgiveness for any atrocities I might have commited during my tenure as Lagerarzt. I was forced to follow the orders. There is just one thing that I would like to say to you at this point: may you all return to your homes very soon and forget this terrible war, and may God bless you in your new beginnings."

My throat was choked with emotion. The speech had sounded so final that I felt as if I were a free man. And for a Lagerarzt to say something like this? It seemed like a dream. I didn't know at that point that the "I was forced to follow the orders" would soon become the excuse of every Nazi dignitary.

Young Dr. Fischer's main job was to order the execution of the unsuccessful runaways. But now that most Poles were gone there weren't many escape attempts: the Jews didn't have a place to escape to, and the French, the Dutch, and the Italians didn't have any reason to escape as they were treated better than the others. The discipline kept slackening; nobody really knew any longer what to expect. The guards themselves didn't know what was going on. They had become milder in their manners, and our Scharfuhrer could often be seen drunk with the vodka supplied to him by one of the remaining Polish functionaries.

Then, shortly before Christmas, five Haftlinge escaped. They were caught almost immediately, and five gallows were raised for them. Three of them were Polish, two German. While the camp watched in silence, the five of them were hanged simultaneously. Before the nooses were thrown around their necks, the Poles intoned "Jeszcze Polska nie zginela," the first words of the Polish anthem, and the Germans yelled, "Down with Hitler!"

The day after, Christmas 1944 arrived, and the Haftlinge received their once-a-year bonus: a Christmas stew made with real meat.

It was now New Year's Eve.

Some of the Pflegers went to a show organized by a group of functionaries, where an Italian opera singer was supposed to sing a few arias, a young Austrian Haftling would play the mandolin, and a Polish performer would whistle. Others were drinking in the laboratory. I had had a little dinner with Stefan, Bronek, Jurek, and Rysio, and now I was lying on my bunk, thinking of the two years I had spent in the Lager.

It had been two years of a hard struggle for survival, during which from a Kobier Mussulman I had become a Krankenbau functionary in Auschwitz One. I had one good thing to say about myself: amidst all that struggle, amidst the most horrifying brutality, surrounded by a society whose basic law was "Kill, or be killed," I never hurt anybody, and yet I had been able to remain human and to achieve. The same went for Stefan and Bronek. I thought of the legend of Sodom and Gomorrha, and of the Ten Just Men who couldn't be found. In Auschwitz, God would be able to find His Ten Just Men, and more.

Then, I thought of other Jewish Haftlinge. Many of them were having sex in exchange for sausages or margarine. I was feeding

Jurek instead. I felt like somebody carrying a piece of ice in his chest. I was in mourning, and people in mourning aren't interested in sex, because sex is celebration.

I thought of Wanda, and her last words: "Keep believing in your Ring." The Girl of the Ring had been my only woman throughout all this time, beginning with Treblinka. Did she exist? Was I ever going to find out?

Suddenly, the door to the Pflegerstube opened, and a group of Pfegers came in with a drunken Blockaltester Adolph at its head. They were hailing the New Year. It was midnight, December 31, 1944.

The next two weeks were uneventful. The bombings had stopped, and there were no selections for the gas chambers. There were only the rumors. Rumors about the front line approaching. Rumors about Germany asking the Allies for peace. Rumors about the camps being dissolved.

At two o'clock in the morning, on January 17, 1945, Blockaltester Adolph came hastily to the Pflegerstube and summoned the Schreiber, Weiss. Nothing like this had happened before, and we felt uneasy. We thought that we might be taken to the gas.

Weiss returned within a few minutes and asked me and a couple of other Pflegers to come with him to the administration office.

There, we saw the Lagerarzt, Dr. Fischer, dressed in a heavy fur coat, burning documents in a small iron stove. We were ordered to burn all the patients' cards and death certificates. We built a large fire between Blocks 21 and 20 and started destroying the files of the Auschwitz Krankenbau. At the same time, functionaries in the camp's main administration office were burning the general files. Now we knew that Auschwitz was being liquidated. No documentation would remain for the world to learn about the camp. Maybe we would survive to tell. But maybe we, too, would soon burn the way these papers were burning now.

And the papers kept burning and burning. Until this moment, we had never realized that there were so many documents in Auschwitz. The Pflegers kept bringing out piles and piles of records from all the blocks of the Krankenbau, the flames were devouring them, the Scharfuhrer kept yelling, "Faster! Faster!" — and the papers never seemed to diminish. So many people had gone through Auschwitz, and so many of them had remained forever, between the blocks of the Krankenbau and the gates of the crematories, that the auto-da-fe of their histories seemed to take on the significance of a memorial candle.

At dawn, Dr. Fischer left the camp in a car that had been waiting for him all this time in front of Block 21. Other Pflegers took a turn at the fire, and Sielecki and I returned to Block 28. From the second-story windows, we could see columns of women dressed in thin coats and kerchieves, marching slowly outside the barbed wire. The small women's camp was being evacuated.

Stefan came to see me. He wanted to find out whether I had any better knowledge than he of what was going on. He said that it was official. Auschwitz was to be evacuated today. He knew it from Bronek, who had already left with Niusia and Oles in the laboratory Sturmfuhrer's car. Bronek was too precious for the Germans to leave him alone even at this very last moment.

I didn't know what to say to Stefan. He planned on joining his wife's column. He was sure the guards wouldn't mind, as long as he was a part of the official evacuation. As I was being recalled to Block 21 to continue burning the files, I just had enough time to ask Stefan to return later, so that we might decide together what to do.

Richard came to say good-bye. His block was going to be the first one to leave. He told me that Kapo Schultz was joining their block. Kapo Schultz was a bloodthirsty Jewish Kapo from the Unionwerke ammunitions factory. He was known for beating the male Jewish Haftlinge working for him and for sexually abusing the Jewish females. He was hated by everybody, and during the previous New Year's Eve, he had been beaten up severely by unknown persons and thrown on a heap of garbage in the middle of Auschwitz, to freeze to death. He had survived, but in spite of a broken arm and broken ribs, he had refused to go to the Krankenbau, and now he was escaping the wrath of Auschwitz by going away with the Germans.

By now, one block after another was emptying. I went back to Block 28, to hear the latest news from Kurylowicz. The sturdy little old man was talking in his basso voice to a group of Pflegers.

"As soon as the camp has been evacuated, the patients in the Krankenbau will be gassed in their blocks, and the camp will be burned. A special Kommando of the Gestapo is already in the Lager."

I noticed the pharmacist Sielecki, with a knapsack on his shoulders, and asked him about his intentions, as the Krankenbau had not yet been ordered to evacuate.

"I'm going with my friend Braun," Sielecki said. His friend Braun worked in Canada and usually had the most reliable information. "Braun said that all those who remain in the camp will be killed."

I said good-bye to Sielecki and went to Block 21, to see Kuba Wolman. He was the first person to tell me that he was staying. He, Gordon, and Steinberg had been ordered to remain with the patients, and a train was supposed to pick them all up the next day. Things were becoming more and more embroiled. I asked Gordon whether he thought that it was safe to stay. He smiled with his usual shy smile and said, "I don't know, colleague. The point is that the sick need us. If you feel you'd like to try to stay, I can hide you in the sewer, where I have already hidden another person."

I needed a little time to analyze the situation. I left Block 21 and sat in front of it, on a bench. By now, the camp seemed empty. The sun was setting slowly, and soon the dusk would be falling, and the Krankenbau workers would leave. Suppose I left with the rest of them. I might reach another camp. But what situation would I be in then? I would have to start all over from scratch. But then, who knew whether I'd ever reach another camp? With all the snow, and the cold, and the hunger. So, suppose I stayed. What if Kurylowicz was right? What if the special Kommando gassed us all and burned the camp? But then, how did I know that would not happen in another camp? And still another? There seemed to be no logical answer. I made one quick decision. If I was to die, let me die looking decent. I felt a revulsion toward dying as a Mussulman.

Jurek and Rysio came to ask me about my decision. They were afraid of staying, and I told them that they would have to make up their own minds. It was a difficult moment for the two boys. They wanted to live, and they counted on my good star. It was a third boy, their little friend Max, who made the decision. "Whatever Mr. Franek does, I do," he said. He knew my history of Treblinka and the rest. Jurek assented. His brother, Rysio, cried and cursed me. He wouldn't leave Auschwitz without the other two, and he hated me for not wanting to leave.

We went to Gordon, who took us down to the backyard of Block 21. There he lifted a slab of cement and uncovered an entrance to the camp's sewer. We entered and crouched under the slab, with which Gordon closed the opening. The long wait started.

The Krankenbau was getting ready for evacuation. We could hear muffled traffic right above our heads. The patients who were able to walk were being put in formation. Then the Pflegers fell into ranks, and the roll call was read. For the first time, instead of calling the

Haftlinge by their numbers, the Schreiber used our real names. When my name was called, there was no answer. Blockaltester Adolph sent somebody to look for me. The man returned soon. I was nowhere to be found. My heart was pounding. I had had no idea that suddenly it would become so important for the camp of Auschwitz to find me. For a second, I regretted ever having become a functionary. Had I remained a simple Haftling, nobody would have bothered looking for me.

Rysio, next to me, was terrified. He whispered, "Will they come here and find us?"

I shushed him. We could hear them; they might hear us.

The Scharfuhrer yelled my name. The Blockaltester suggested that I might already have left with my friends. The Scharfuhrer mumbled, "He'd better have!" I realized that he was drunk.

He then addressed the Pflegers officially left behind: "You'd better make sure that the Krankenbau is in tip-top condition. The blocks must be shiny! So that we will not be taken for slobs by the Russians, when they arrive." He reconsidered what he was saying and corrected his address: "I'll be back tomorrow to pick you up! If things aren't smooth in the Krankenbau, I'll settle accounts with you!"

The command was given, and the groups moved. Feet beat rhythmically over our heads. The Krankenbau had evacuated Auschwitz.

Deep silence followed. We waited, counting the minutes — no, the seconds. If Kurylowicz was right, the special Kommando would start the gassing of the patients about now. Then would come the burning of the Lager. We waited an eternity. We had lost all sense of time.

Several steps were heard in the yard above us. The steps stopped right over our heads. We heard the lifting of the cement lid. I quickly remembered Rokiciny Malopolskie. Were these the Gestapo? Were they coming for us?

The lid was removed, and we saw the darkness of night up there.

And in the tense, desperate silence, the voice of Gordon was heard: "Come out, colleagues! The Lager is evacuated."

Back in Block 21, the patients and the remaining Pflegers were still waiting for further news, not sure whether the worst was still to come. A German Pfleger, George, who had remained at his own request, went out into the camp to see what was going on. He came back within minutes, urging that we organize an expedition to the kitchen warehouse. He had found out that a number of Haftlinge had stayed hidden in various corners of the Lager, and had now come out, broken the doors to the warehouse, and begun plundering the food.

We all felt better. As long as there was plunder, everything was perfectly normal. We formed several teams, using the more able of the patients, and went to work, organizing wooden cases of margarine, condensed milk, sugar, and canned meat. We had a moment of elation as we discussed the beautiful meals we would be able to prepare for ourselves and for the patients. As we were going back and forth with the cases, an SS man passed by, making believe that he didn't notice us. We liked the situation, but we also realized that Auschwitz wasn't rid of the SS yet. In Block 21, some Pflegers and patients had opened the cans of meat and were eating it cold.

"Careful, colleagues," urged Gordon. "Too much of it at once might cost you your lives."

At two-thirty in the morning, I went out to take a rest on the bench. I felt guilty about Stefan. Why hadn't I advised him to stay in the camp? Wouldn't it be nice to be together now? To be able to say to each other, "We made it"? At this very moment, somewhere in the snow, Stefan might be dragging along, not even knowing where his wife was. I leaned against the wall of the block, listening to the far rumbling of artillery and watching faraway flashes of light.

"The front line must be very close now," said a competent basso voice.

I looked around. Kurylowicz stood in the door of Block 21. As I smiled at him, the old man seemed slightly embarrassed. He said, "Then our colleague decided to stay, after all?"

"I just followed your recommendation, Mr. Kurylowicz," I answered.

"The front is so close that they could be here tomorrow," said Kurylowicz, changing the subject.

By the morning, the artillery had stopped. I went around the camp cautiously. It was a rude awakening. With all the evacuation, there were still numerous Haftlinge around and, surprisingly, quite a few SS men. In the kitchen, I found a cook and a Scharfuhrer. I asked the cook about the evacuation of the camp, and he laughed: "You sonsofabitch think this is it? Alive and free? You just wait and see when the trains come to pick you up! Sonsofabitch thieves of food!"

Going back to Block 21, I ran into Dr. Kapuscinski. He was overjoyed to see me.

"Colleague," he said, "I need you urgently! As soon as Block 28 had been evacuated, a new group arrived from an outside camp. It is hell over there. They're dirty and they smell. We must do something about it!"

A group of new arrivals would explain the presence in the camp of so many SS men. They were probably the ones who had accompanied the new group to Auschwitz. It was not good to have unknown SS guards around. It is easy to be finished off by somebody who has never seen you before. I followed Kapuscinski to Block 28.

The showplace of the Krankenbau until yesterday, Block 28 was now a picture of filth and misery. Unshaven, dirty Mussulmen were lying on the floor of the dispensary, some of them scratching themselves, some eating pieces of bread. The stench of pus saturated the premises.

I looked into the Pflegers' quarters upstairs and into the ward, and I figured that we should have the new arrivals take a shower and assign them the bunks upstairs, thus reestablishing some order in the block.

I returned to the dispensary and delivered a short speech to the people there. I explained to them what was to be done and I told them why I thought it would be good for them. Nobody budged. I said that I would like them to form a line in front of the reception window, so that each of them could be examined by a doctor and receive his medical treatment card. Nobody budged.

I realized what I had to do. "Damn you!" I yelled, putting my legs astride, my hand on a hip, the way the Kapos always did. "Fall in line! March!"

And the miracle happened. In seconds, an orderly line of people was standing in front of the admissions room, waiting for further orders. The discipline of Auschwitz was still alive.

In the final analysis, my efforts proved useless. Before we even started registering the new group, their Scharfuhrer called them out and led them away from Auschwitz. Only one of them, a Hungarian doctor named Farkasz, remained, hidden by me in one of the upstairs rooms.

Every hour or so, a small SS squad entered Auschwitz One. They had a bite to eat, announced that the pickup trains would be there any moment, and left for their destination.

The afternoon arrived, and no more SS squads came in. No trains arrived either. Some Haftlinge gathered in small groups in the main street, looking up at the watchtowers, from which the last SS guards, in their machine-gun nests, were watching the activity in the camp.

Early evening fell on the Lager, and we discovered that the electricity and the water had been turned off.

The Pflegers held an emergency session. It became obvious that, with the electricity missing, the barbed wires had become harmless, and now it would be easy to escape from the camp. It was also obvious that there were too many sick people in the Krankenbau who wouldn't be able to help themselves without us around. Unequivocally, we decided to remain in the camp.

One of the cases organized by us the day before contained candles. These would solve the problem of light. The water was a tougher nut to crack. There was an old well in the camp, and we organized several squads of the less sick patients and started a water transport operation. We pulled the water out with buckets, filled the wooden kitchen barrels, and distributed it among blocks the way we used to distribute soup. It was hard work, and the quantity of water thus obtained was far below our needs.

The third day after the evacuation arrived. Again, teams of SS came in, ate, told us of the imminent arrival of the pickup trains, and left. Nobody believed them this time. Some of the Haftlinge hiding in the camp became arrogant and started pilfering the kitchen warehouse at noon, heedless of the kitchen Scharfuhrer. At first, the SS man yelled. Then he took out his gun and shot several times into the mob, dispersing the pilferers, who left three wounded comrades behind. We took them to Block 21, where Steinberg, Wasilewski, and the newly arrived Dr. Farkasz performed surgery, but to no avail. One man died on the table, the other two a couple of hours later. We took them to the morgue, where a few more corpses had been waiting to be picked up from the time before the evacuation.

We found hiding in the Lager a Jewish ex-fireman named Adam, with whose help we improved our water delivery system. Adam taught us how to use a manual water pump and the hoses from the fire department. Now we were able to pump the water faster and in larger quantities. This helped us with washing the patients and the blocks, and with preparing hot meals. The worst problem was now the toilets. We couldn't allow the use of the toilets because they couldn't be flushed properly. Yet, we certainly needed the toilets. We decided that the toilets could be flushed with buckets of water, provided that no paper was used. We installed a wooden barrel in each toilet room, and this was where the paper went. The barrels were emptied once a day.

The rumble of artillery was heard again on the third day, only this time much closer. In the afternoon, the only SS guards in the camp were again the ones in the watchtowers.

On the fourth day, a squad of SS rushed into the camp. They told us that they had come to take the Haftlinge with them. As they were eating cold meat from the cans they had received from us, we were overwhelmed by anxiety. Was it really to be so, that with freedom around the corner we would be taken away to the old life of uncertainty? The SS guards in the watchtowers were making sure that we wouldn't escape, and the artillery pounded closer and closer. Then the SS squad that was supposed to take us away disappeared. With heavy hearts, we took care of the sick, washed the blocks, and cooked the meals.

It was past noon when another SS squad rushed in. They ate hurriedly and left. After that, every fifteen minutes another SS squad rushed in and out. At two o'clock, the last squad went. And at two-thirty, January 21, 1945, our hearts swelled with emotion as we saw the watchtower guards hastily leave their positions and their machine guns and run away. Auschwitz seemed at last to be free.

LIBERATION

It was big. It was unreal. It was unbelievable. There were no Haftlinge any longer. There were only the people of Auschwitz. The people of Auschwitz, who reacted, each in his own, private way, as one reacts to things that are big, unreal, and unbelievable.

A small group of people gathered at the main gate, over which the motto, "Arbeit macht frei," gave the promise the Germans had never intended to keep. They crossed through the gate, in and out, and again out and in, as if to make sure that nobody would shoot them from a convenient hideout. Nobody shot, and their freedom had been marked symbolically.

This group started swelling with people hidden all over Auschwitz. Within minutes, a solemn throng was standing in front of the gate. Adam the Fireman brought a pair of large shears, approached the barbed-wire fence, and cut a strand. Nothing happened to him, so the people of Auschwitz knew that there was no hidden electricity in the wires. A man left the throng, took the shears from Adam, and cut into the wire violently. He cut and cut, as if he wanted to cut his way out of the Lager, oblivious of the wide-open gate.

Asta, a hunchbacked Pipel of one of the Blockaltesters, followed by Jurek and Rysio, climbed one of the watchtowers and yelled, "We've got the machine gun!"

The throng at the gate was composed mainly of Musselmen, whose emaciated faces showed curiosity rather than emotion. Here and there could be seen a custom-made cap worn at a slant by one of the few Polish functionaries who had remained in Auschwitz, hidden until the last moment.

Someone in the crowd yelled, "To the SS warehouse!"

The mass of people moved slowly toward the building in which the choicest foods previously available for Canada gold only, were stored. As the heavy door of the building was cracking under the pressure of the Auschwitz people, Krankenbau squads were quickly formed, to save for the hospital whatever was possible.

The door fell, and the mob, like living lava, flowed over the warehouse. Until a moment ago, silent, they were now roaring with greed, joy, and pain. The warehouse was sacked. Torn bags of white flour, coffee, cocoa, and sugar, huge blocks of margarine or butter, cases of wines and liquors were thrown on the floor, pulled out into the street, stamped on and crushed. The people of Auschwitz were drinking alcohol, they were pouring wine over the heads of their comrades, they were sobbing, and crying, and screaming.

Auschwitz was taken by a paroxysm of freedom. The mob writhed in convulsion. Spirits and wines flowed over the snow of the main street in narrow streams, blending in the middle of the road into a river of alcoholic exuberance.

An emaciated, unshaven, dirty-looking man was running along the street, his cheeks aflame, pulling his hair and yelling, "Freedom! Give me my freedom!"

Amidst this storm of emotions, stood silently a tall, skinny man in a torn coat. An enamel bowl bulged under his arm as he watched the events with an absent smile. Perhaps, he was hoping for a portion of soup.

The new situation called for special action. The staff of the Krankenbau sat for a short but important conference. In a concise speech, Gordon described the latest events and ended by saying, "Thus, we must decide about our next move. It is not clear at all whether we will be free tomorrow, but we are free today. Therefore I don't think anybody should be blamed for trying to save himself by leaving the camp now. As a matter of fact, many of the people who were hiding in the camp have already left. Even some of our own Krankenbau staff have done so."

In fact, I had seen Dr. Wasilewski and an Italian doctor leave Auschwitz, carrying a valise of laryngological instruments.

Meanwhile Gordon continued: "Whoever wants to leave now will not be considered a coward. However, we do have to think of some seven hundred patients who cannot be left alone. I just wanted you to know that nobody can be blamed, no matter what his decision. I am staying."

He finished, and calmly sat down. There was a short silence, and then, as one man, Kapuscinski, Wolman, Steinberg, and I said, "Staying."

"Who wants to leave?" said Adam the Fireman. He was talking for himself and for Jurek, Rysio, and Asta. Lately, they had become very friendly and had formed a compact group of their own. "We are all staying," said Adam.

Steinberg rose. After the evacuation, he had been nominated the Lageraltester of the Krankenbau. Now he took to exercising his prerogatives. "Colleague Gordon will take care of the hygiene in Block 21. Colleague Wolman will supervise the general business of the Krankenbau. Professor Kapuscinski and colleague Franek will take care of Block 28."

The conference seemed to have come to a close, but Gordon wanted to add a point.

"Colleagues," he said shyly. "Let us take an oath. We don't know for how long. Maybe for a day only. Maybe for much longer. But let us take an oath not to drink until we are officially free. We must give a good example to the people of Auschwitz. We also need all the cool heads we can use. And also," now his voice was reduced to almost a whisper, "when the Russians come, we must show them that we deserve freedom." Good, precious Gordon, who called everybody "Colleague," had a deep conviction that with the arrival of the Russians, Justice itself would be returned to the world.

The day went by, and still another day. We were hearing artillery fire all the time, but it seemed to remain at the same distance as before. Rumors started circulating that a special Gestapo Kommando would come to pick us up, and this is when some of the hospital attendants, selected by us from the less sick patients, left Auschwitz.

The seventh day after the evacuation had arrived.

It was two in the afternoon. The patients had just finished eating their midday meal, and the Stubendienste were collecting the dirty bowls. I dropped into Block 21 for a chat with Kuba Wolman.

Shortly after me, the doorkeeper rushed into the ward. He was out of breath and looked pale as he announced almost in a whisper, "They want Dr. Wolman downstairs."

We thought for a moment, "Who are, 'they'?" But we didn't have to think very long, as the well-known harsh command came from the first floor: *"Rrraus!* Everybody out! The chief doctor report to me immediately!"

Then, the rumors had been correct. At the eve, perhaps, of liberation, they had come to take us away. My mind was working fast. Now that they would be taking away all the patients and the Pflegers, there was no need for me any longer, and I had to do what I had to do to save myself. I looked out of the window. Five Gestapo men were standing in front of Block 21. The same in front of Block 28. And more of them along the main street. All of them were holding tommy guns at the ready. I looked down the second-floor stairway. Another one was standing in the hall, yelling to hurry up. As the patients were rushing outside, he kept barking, "German Haftlinge in the first group! Other Aryans in the second group! Jews in the third group!"

I made up my mind.

"I'm not going," I said to Gordon and Wolman. "I'll hide in the attic."

"The attic won't help," said Wolman. "They'll kill everybody outside and inside and will burn the blocks."

"I'll take my risk." I was thinking longingly of the little hideout in the attic of Block 28, where I could be so cozy, but which was now inaccessible to me.

Jurek, Rysio, and Max came running, terrified.

"What do we do!"

This time, I decided for them. "You'll come with me to the attic."

One by one, Jurek, Rysio, Asta, Adam, and Max climbed the stepladder to the attic. I shook hands with Gordon and Wolman. We all knew this might be our final good-bye.

The Gestapo man kept yelling downstairs: "Everybody out! Whoever is caught inside will be shot on the spot!"

I climbed into the attic and pulled the ladder in. I closed the trapdoor. The die was cast.

Without my knowing so at this time, Kurylowicz was casting his die in the morgue of Block 28, getting rid of his clothes, scribbling his tattoo number on his chest, and lying down amidst the corpses in expectation of the crematory truck, the only well-fed body in a heap of emaciated Musselmen.

All three groups of patients and Pflegers were marched off as we were waiting in the attic, motionless and speechless, counting each precious second that was passing by.

It was a timeless moment. Minutes, hours, centuries? As we were waiting, I prayed what would perhaps be my last prayer to the Girl of the Ring.

The outside silence was suddenly filled with voices. I tried to catch the sound and to analyze it. Were these German voices? Gestapo voices? Was this it?

We heard steps on the second floor. Then the trap door was moved, and a head appeared in the opening. It was the German Pfleger, George. He announced merrily: "Gentlemen, you can come out! The nightmare is over."

Everybody was talking wildly, everybody was talking miracle. They were recounting the song of their march to the main gate, and how they had been stopped there, each group separately, all surrounded by the Gestapo men from Kattowitz — this was as much as they could find out — ready to shoot. About thirty Gestapo men, and their chief yelling, "I want the Jews separately, understand?"

Then, a car arrived, and another Gestapo man ran to the head of the Kommando group. He said something to the chief Gestapo man, and then the chief yelled again, "Wait here! The Jews separately!" — and they were all gone.

The patients and the Pflegers stood there, in front of the gate, waiting for further developments. Time was passing, and dusk had fallen on the camp, and they were still waiting.

Then a column of men and women appeared outside of the gate. They wore civilian clothes, but it was obvious that they were Haftlinge. They stopped in front of the gate. The people outside the camp and the people inside the camp looked at each other. "Where are we?" asked a woman.

"In Auschwitz One," was the answer.

"And who are you?"

"Haftlinge from Birkenau" was the answer. "The special Kommando took us out of the camp and left us alone in the middle of the road. We decided to keep marching. And then we arrived here."

"Any Germans on the road?"

"No. But many dead Haftlinge."

And suddenly, everything had become clear as a spring day. We were free. Nobody knew how, or why. And nobody wanted to know. All everybody wanted was to go back to the blocks, and lie down, and warm up, and stay alive.

Starting with the eighth day after the evacuation, we finally saw the first of the Wehrmacht. The soldiers, in small groups of three or four, their white camouflage sheets dirtied by the battle, their faces un-shaven and haggard, stopped in Auschwitz, asked for a piece of bread and a glass of water, and continued westward. We gave them the bread and the water and weren't quite sure whether to feel pity or satisfaction. They were not the SS or the Gestapo. We didn't have any quarrel with them.

Meanwhile we tried to make life in the Krankenbau as normal as possible. With the arrival of the Birkenau Haftlinge, the activity in the dispensary had become almost frantic. Empty blocks in the camp became inhabited by the new population, where the women played the most important role, and Auschwitz was now more like a little town on the eastern border of Poland than a German concentration camp.

The food warehouse in the Krankenbau had reached imposing dimensions. A small room in Block 21 had been converted into something that resembled a well-supplied grocery store, with all the pounds of margarine, cases of canned meat, bagfuls of flour, dried peas and macaroni, not to mention the liquors and the wines.

Our patients received one good hot meal a day, as well as portions of cold food, which they ate in the morning and in the evening. A stronger group of Pflegers had been organized, who took the best possible care of the cleanliness of the patients and the hospital blocks. What could not be helped were the nonhospital blocks in the camp, inhabited now by the Birkenau arrivals. Though they were once members of the Hungarian Jewish middle class, having been subjected to the daily humiliation of Birkenau, they now needed much more than a couple of days of freedom to become clean and civilized again.

On the ninth day after the evacuation, heavy artillery fire was heard very close. At noon, a Russian and a German plane had a dramatic dog fight not more than fifty yards above the Auschwitz Raportplatz.

Anyone who could stand on his feet watched the fight. At two o'clock, two German soldiers entered the camp. They were dirty and hungry. As they were eating the bread I had given them, one of them said, "You won't be bothered for much longer. This time tomorrow, you'll be free."

About two hundred yards beyond the walls of Auschwitz, behind Block 21, flowed the river Sola. The river was spanned by a bridge built by one of the Haftling details. The bridge cost many a Haftling his life, but I am sure none of its builders had ever dreamed of the possibility that the victorious German troops would one day march on the Sola bridge westward instead of eastward. On the evening of the ninth day after the evacuation, columns of German trucks, guns, and infantry crossed the bridge and crowded the road along the walls of Auschwitz in a never-ending retreat. From our second-story windows, we watched the defeated army trudging westward. Now and then, a Russian fighter plane machine-gunned them or dropped a bomb. The column continued its somber march throughout the night. The humming of engines and the bustle of people and of horses could be heard without interruption.

In the Krankenbau, we were waiting for the grand moment when the Germans would blow up the Sola bridge. We knew it had to be done, and for us the blowing up of the bridge had become the symbol of Freedom with a capital *F*.

It was late at night, and we were lying in our bunks in Block 21, too excited to sleep and too impatient to think. We were listening to the sounds reaching us from the outside, and only now and then somebody would remark, "Who knows what will happen to this block, when the bridge goes up?" And then, "Should we transfer the patients to a block further up?" The strange thing was that we didn't think of the most obvious and, clearly, the simplest answer: to leave the block, each of us as an individual, and each of us to save his own skin. Each of us, whose only worry during the past years had been to save his own life, suddenly felt an obligation toward the patients. It was as if we owed the world an act of sacrifice for all the years of our passive acceptance of humiliation, while the soldiers out there were fighting for the survival of our dignity.

Early in the morning, a couple of us ventured toward the river. The bridge was still there.

We went on with our usual morning chores. In the surgery, the anesthesia of the first patient was about to start when a deafening explosion was heard. The block shook mightily, then everything quieted down. We crowded the windows. The bridge was gone.

"Finis of Solabrucke," somebody whispered piously. It sounded like an "Amen."

Now we noticed on this side of the river, under a tree on a small hill, a group of German soldiers manning a machine gun.

Steinberg recalled us to reality. "Back to the surgery!" he ordered. "War or no war, the work has to be done."

We worked on our patients feverishly, listening to the intriguing noises outside. Some of the patients were standing in the windows, relaying the latest news. The Pflegers were taking turns in the surgery, to let their colleagues watch the spectacle from the windows.

Out there, a full-scale war was being fought. German soldiers could be seen in the field beyond the camp's wall, stopping, kneeling, shooting toward the river, standing up and running. The air was filled with the crackling of machine guns, rifles, and small arms. A low, powerful German tank appeared on the road. It was moving slowly toward the river, shooting from its cannon. A short while later, it was on its way back, going westward toward the woods, into which the last infantry soldiers were disappearing.

"Don't stay in the window," warned Steinberg.

"Shhh!" I said to him. "It looks beautiful!"

A fiery bomb hit the upper corner of the surgery room. A patient fell from a table. The cabinet, the tools, the gauze — everything, including the Pflegers, was on the floor.

"I told you so!" hissed Steinberg from under the stretcher.

We put the room back together in no time and went on with our work. Time was passing swiftly. It was two o'clock, and we had just finished dressing the last patient of the morning, when the hunchbacked Asta ran into the room, his eyes almost out of their sockets with excitement, and yelled, "The Russians are in Auschwitz!"

This was, then, the moment for which we had been living all these years. All the suffering, the blood, and the tears — all these had been endured so that we could hear this short, simple announcement.

The Russians, three unshaven soldiers covered with dirty camouflage sheets, were slowly walking down the middle of the main street of Auschwitz. They were clutching their tommy guns at the ready and looking around them suspiciously.

A group of the Krankenbau inhabitants went out, uncertain what to do. And indeed, what was there to do? What is a man to do who, after having been locked in death row for years, is suddenly told that he is free to go?

The emotion was visible. The people of Auschwitz had tears choking their throats. There was some hesitation. And then, as if in mute agreement, their arms open wide, they ran toward the Russian soldiers. In a frenzy, the short, shy Gordon was embracing the tallest of the Russians, while the others crowded around the soldiers, weeping, touching them, and thanking them. Somebody knelt in the snow and kissed the torn boot of a Soviet warrior.

Strangled with emotion, I stood aside and watched. Why couldn't this have happened on that terrible September day, in 1942, when my family was being murdered in Treblinka? How many horrifying events had there been since then, how many human lives wasted? And all this could have been spared the world by just one little happy ending, as in the movies. Tears were choking me as I watched the three soldiers, who were bearing the outburst of emotion of these strange people patiently and awkwardly. Finally, the tall one, who sported a thick mustache, asked, "Where are we?"

"In Auschwitz, colleague," sobbed Gordon. "In Auschwitz."

"What is Auschwitz?" asked the soldier.

"It is a concentration camp, comrade. A death camp. You saved our lives, comrade." Gordon spoke Russian, his city of origin being Vilna. Now he dropped his usual "colleague," and switched to the Russian "comrade." "You have just saved the lives of one thousand people, and we thank you for it," finished Gordon.

"Where are the Germans?" asked the soldier in a matter-of-fact voice.

"They ran away!" The people of Auschwitz were pointing toward the west. "They saw you, and ran away!"

"Then we'd better follow them," said the soldier.

"Please, do not leave us! Not just yet!" begged Gordon.

"We cannot let the Germans escape," retorted the soldier.

Through the haze of the days just past, I saw the light. I said, "We'd like to offer you a glass of vodka, comrades."

In a small room to the right of the entrance to Block 21, we set a little table. There was vodka, cognac, and sausage. We filled large cups, which the soldiers drank in one swift draught. The tall soldier sighed, wiped his mustache with the back of his hand, and hinted at a second cup. The cups were filled again, this time also for the Pflegers, and Gordon made a toast.

"To the Red Army," he said. "To our liberators. To Comrade . . ." he waited for the name. The soldier said, "Woroblewski." "To Comrade Woroblewski," finished Gordon.

We all drank, standing. Our time of prohibition was over.

We asked the soldiers to take a tour of the wards, so that our patients might feel the joy of the moment. As we led the three soldiers along the aisles, even the sickest of the patients managed to raise their bodies on the bunks to catch a sight of Freedom. Some patients only sobbed. The others cheered loudly.

The three soldiers had their third cup of vodka before starting again after the Germans. By then, a confusion of voices was heard at the entrance of Block 21, and a small group of Soviet soldiers burst in.

The group consisted of five young men and a young woman; all were about seventeen years of age and all had guns in each of their hands.

This was the end of Auschwitz One, the SS concentration camp, and the beginning of a new era.

Almost as soon as the first Russian soldiers left Auschwitz in pursuit of the Germans, the influx of Russian high-echelon officers and newsmen started. They sat with us in the administration room all night long, smoking, drinking, asking questions, taking notes, and making comments of disbelief.

Gordon had become the official spokesman of the camp of Auschwitz. In a dull, monotonous voice he was telling the Lager story over and over again: "There have been two levels of authority: the SS and the Haftlinge.

There would come that inevitable, painful question, "So how come there are still Jews left in Auschwitz?"

"It is a miracle," Gordon would say, after which he explained the history of the last ten days of our lives.

It was now almost dawn. While Gordon was repeating his story for possibly the hundredth time, I lay on a bunk and watched the Russian officers with their broad chests. They were wearing fur caps and golden insignias on their shoulders. They were different now from the simple, unadorned officers of 1939, who, besides being the subject of funny jokes, had also awakened tender feelings. There seemed to be no place for either amusement or tenderness this time. These officers were harsh in their manners and full of self-importance.

I watched them and couldn't believe that these men were actually the Russians. I was still afraid that, suddenly, they might throw off their long Soviet coats, to say, "Fooled you, haven't we!" and to show us the death's head, the Gestapo insignia. It didn't seem true, but then what was the truth? Now, soon, I'd be free to go. To go where? I realized more dramatically than ever that there was no place for me to go, no people for me to embrace. A deep sadness enveloped me.

The new morning had arrived. The roads along the walls of Auschwitz were now crowded with the Russian military columns. An army physician, a Tatar with the rank of major, stopped in Block 21 for a visit. He was the head of the front hospital in this zone and was fully aware of his importance.

After having listened to Gordon's tale, he said, "All of you, comrades, will receive medals, for having saved your patients. You'll receive medals."

Gordon didn't want any medal. What he, what we all, wanted was to have the sick transferred to a decent hospital, away from the combat zone. I suggested that if the major could lend us a dozen horse carriages, we would transport our very sick patients to the civilian hospital in the town of Oswiecim, at the other side of the river. There, we figured, they would be safe, at least, from any unforeseen complications at the front line.

"No," said the major. Medals yes, horse carriages no.

"But should the Germans return, even for an hour all these people might be destroyed," ventured Gordon.

The major knew better. "The Germans," he said, "will never return."

As he was saying this an aide-de-camp burst in and whispered something in the major's ear. The major left so quickly that he didn't even say good-bye to us heroes.

I looked out of the window. At the other side of the wall, the Russian convoy was driving wildly toward us and the river, while some infantry men took cover behind trees and bushes, shooting toward the woods, from where the German infantrymen had suddenly erupted. Then a Russian tank came from the east and rolled toward the woods, all the time spitting fire. The Russians reorganized quickly and followed the tank. Half an hour later, the westward march had resumed.

That afternoon, Russian soldiers dug ditches outside Block 21, right under the surgery room. A little later, two guns were placed in the ditches, and Block 21 started shaking from the incessant gun fire.

This situation lasted for two days. At the end of the second day, the guns were pulled out of the emplacements, and the front line moved westward.

For the next three days, Auschwitz was the main road into Germany. Supply columns kept pouring through the front gate, and after having crossed the length of the main street, they went through an enormous breach in the barbed wire, at the opposite end of the camp, and continued toward the woods. The days were hectic, the nights noisy, and the once-impeccable main street took on the appearance of an Oriental bazaar.

Various commissions of the military and civilians were in and out each day, visiting the bunker, listening to the tale of the Black Wall, touching the wooden pay-off goat, and taking pictures of the bodies that had been lying in the morgue since the beginning of the evacuation, but that had not yet decayed because of the below-zero temperature.

One day, a military commission took Gordon, Wolman, and me to Birkenau, to view the gas chambers. It was a sad, snowy afternoon, and the camp looked like an old, abandoned cemetery. We left the jeeps among the dark barracks of Birkenau and went by foot toward the crematories. Gordon had spent some time in Birkenau, before having become a Pfleger in Auschwitz One. Now he served as a guide.

"There were five gas chambers with their crematories on this very spot," he explained. "In October, the Germans started disassembling them, to erase the traces of their crimes. Here, where you can see just a flat space covered with snow, and where possibly next spring flowers will bloom, millions of people lost their lives. Just one gas chamber remained until the end, but even this one, it seems, has been destroyed."

We entered the demolished gas chamber. The heavy posts made of iron and cement that had supported the roof were half-collapsed. We could still see the vents up in the roof, and a pillar made of iron mesh was still intact.

"Here's how the Germans injected the lethal gas into the chambers," explained Gordon. "In the first place, the chamber was filled so full of people that they would literally choke from the lack of oxygen. Children and the sick were often thrown on the heads of standing people. The temperature in the chamber rose considerably, which was a necessary condition for the gas to become volatile. It just wouldn't work under 27 degrees centigrade. Once the people were in, the chambers were sealed, and the air was sucked out through the vents in the ceiling. As soon as that was done, the last part of the operation was performed, a crematory Scharfuhrer threw the open gas cans into this iron mesh pillar. As you can see, these were underground chambers, and these pillars ended above the roof as little chimneys above the ground. The gas cans were thrown into these chimneys, and then each chimney was sealed with a hermetic lid. Once inside the pillar, the gas emanated into the chamber through the iron mesh, and there was no way that anyone could reach through the mesh, to cover the can and stop the gas from working."

Gordon knew this part of the story from a young Hungarian Jew who had come to Auschwitz with the last of the new arrivals, and who had survived a gassing in the chamber.

"Strange," said one of the Russians, "that nobody ever rebelled."

"People sometimes did, but it was a lost cause. The Germans seemed to enjoy a little resistance. They would shoot into the crowd and set their dogs on the people on such occasions. They also liked to throw sick people into the flames alive and to throw infants up in the air and shoot at them."

We left the gas chamber.

"There, you see?" said Gordon, indicating a low chimney sticking out of the ground. "This is what I've just described."

I noticed that one of the Russian officers looked in a different direction and furtively rubbed his eyes.

The people of Auschwitz were trying their best to make a new beginning. While the Mussulmen in the Krankenbau suddenly started dying like flies (something that was explained by the Russian-Jewish doctor, the new head of our hospital, as being due to nervous relaxation following a long period of nervous tension), other ex-prisoners were quickly pairing up and creating makeshift families.

Adam the Fireman met a Polish girl from the nearby town of Oswiecim, when she came to the camp with other town folks in search of clothing and bedding, and he convinced her easily to remain with him. They moved into a corner of a large room where a dozen other people were staying and remained there as man and wife.

Asta befriended a Russian girl, an ex-prisoner of Birkenau, and moved with her next to Adam.

Various men from Auschwitz and women from Birkenau moved together into a number of empty blocks, each couple occupying a small room, if they were lucky enough to find one, or into large communal quarters which they shared with other couples. This was not a situation that was easy to accept for Steinberg, who cursed at them all in Rumanian, or to the conservative Gordon, whose immediate reaction was to swear that he would never marry again, having lost his wife and child.

A few single women moved into Block 28. I gave a small room, on the top floor, to two Jewish girls, one from Hungary, the other from Yugoslavia, and a corner in one of the large wards to two teenage French girls who were also Jewish. It was a pleasure to watch the two teenagers, Sarah and Charlotte, take care of their corner, which in a very short time they had converted into a real home.

The other two girls were older, and they had other interests than decorating their Auschwitz abode. The Yugoslav girl seemed to have lost her sense of social balance. One day, a man ran to me, still red from embarrassment, complaining about her behavior. It seems that while he was sitting on the toilet, she had come into the bathroom, sat on the other bowl, relieved herself, and asked him to pass the paper. He resented this, while she evidently didn't see anything wrong in it. Not everybody had been affected by Auschwitz in the same way.

Meanwhile the Russians had converted Auschwitz One into a front-line military hospital. A couple of additional blocks had been appropriated and various departments created. Each department was supervised by a Russian military doctor, while Steinberg, Gordon, Wolman, and I were assigned to help, each in a different department. There were only the four of us, because Dr. Kapuscinski had left a couple of days before, after having refused to testify against the Nazis on the grounds that although he knew about the killings, he had never seen one with his own eyes. Besides he felt there was no longer any need for him. Other Poles had left even earlier.

The Russian chief doctor, an extremely severe Jew from the Ukraine, introduced a new system. Every morning, at seven o'clock, all the physicians gathered in his office to report on the previous day's hospital activities and to discuss the plans for today. After everything had been approved by the chief, we went to the pharmacy, where the medications approved for that day were dispensed, and then we went to do our chores.

Block 28 had become the dermatology department, and this was where I worked. I had only one small ward where the few bed-ridden patients lay, most of my work being done in the dispensary. Thus my block had more room than the other blocks, and the Russians established their officers' kitchen and the officers' mess. The Russian cook, having soon discovered that one of the medications dispensed in the pharmacy was pure alcohol (which we administered in the evening instead of barbiturates), made himself a steady guest of mine, proposing to exchange goulash for the spirits. He would have embarrassed me forever, if the military police hadn't jailed him for having stolen a watch from a civilian.

Something had to be done regarding the cleanliness of Auschwitz, and the Russians soon found a way. One morning, they brought into the camp a group of German civilians from the town of Oswiecim and turned them over to Steinberg, saying that these people would be back every morning to clean the camp and that ex-prisoners should supervise them. Asta, Jurek, Rysio, and Adam advanced their services, and they were nominated the supervisors of the group. Asta, the hunch-backed ex-Pipel, put his heart and soul into the new assignment. He found some old armbands reading, "Oberkapo" and "Kapo," and he handed them over to two Germans of his choice, instructing them to make sure that the rest of the group worked effectively. To make his intentions clear, he gave each of the two supervisors a stick and promised cigarettes for work well done. Everything went smoothly. The new supervisors belabored their fellow Germans in a most unheard-of way, making them bring Auschwitz into its former condition of cleanliness, and they made us see that you didn't have to be Jewish to yield to fear. To break the boredom of the workday, the boys also made the Germans march, sing, and take their hats off to each passing Russian soldier.

This was also the time when some Russian soldiers settled their accounts with the Nazis in the most expeditious possible way. A few times each day, a Russian soldier brought an SS man to the camp, ordered him to take off his boots (boots were an important spoil to the Russians), and shot him against a wall.

The Russian administration of the new front-line hospital decided that now that the ex-Haftlinge were free people who had just joined the new society, it was proper to confiscate the food supplies accumulated by Block 21. When I asked the chief doctor for an explanation, he said that the sick would receive the same food that the Russian soldiers were eating, while we, the Pflegers, would be using the officers' mess. Several horse carts stopped in front of Block 21, and some Russian soldiers emptied our magnificent larder.

After that, a Politruk, a political army commissar, addressed me in rather crude language and ordered me to follow him. We went to the attic of Block 28, accompanied by a soldier, and stopped in front of a wooden trough filled with a white powder.

The Politruk pointed dramatically to the trough and asked, "And what is this?"

I said, "Plaster."

He said, "Liar!" Then he took a pinch of the powder and deposited it in his mouth. He quickly spat it out, reddened, and yelled, "So it's plaster! But I know that you are hiding flour! We will have no bourgeois tricks here! I said that all the food must be surrendered: then, all the food will be surrendered!"

I was afraid that he might know about some other things, too. I had some meat cans hidden in my secret place in the attic. But he was just guessing. Cursing me and the entire Auschwitz population, he led the way out of the block and to the waiting carts, filled by now with cases of margarine, sacks of flour and peas, and cases of vodka, cognac, and wine. I thought that Gordon didn't have to worry anymore. None of us would get drunk. I also knew that in one way or another the Politruk would make me pay for the embarrassment I had just caused him.

The face of Auschwitz was changing swiftly. The Polish Red Cross had sent in some volunteers to help the sick. The white-aproned women roamed through the blocks, complaining of the harsh conditions of their work and of the smelly patients, and collecting food and clothing, which they sent daily to their families in Cracow. Every day, Polish peasants from the neighboring villages visited the camp, exchanging bread, eggs, and milk for clothing, bedding, and anything at all that Auschwitz still could offer. The camp had lost its original traits, and by now it had become difficult to discern between the old Haftling and a plunderer from outside. This situation lasted for many days, until the Politruk, annoyed by what was going on, stormed the plundering peasants with a gun in his hand, yelling, "You blood suckers! These people have paid dearly for the things you are robbing! It's all theirs! I'll shoot on sight, if I catch anyone carrying things away!"

A couple of days later, Polish army trucks invaded Auschwitz, taking away clothing, furniture, medical equipment — in short, all that had remained. It became more and more evident that soon nothing would be left here to remind the world that this was the place where millions of Jews had been exterminated and their possessions accumulated to become the spoils of the murderers. Most of the Jewish belongings had been stolen by the Nazis; some of them snatched by the women from the Polish Red Cross; portions of them had been "organized" by the camp's functionaries; now the Polish government was plundering the rest. Everybody was complaining about the dirt, the disease, and the poverty of Auschwitz, but nobody gave a thought to the possibility of starting to rehabilitate the ex-Mussulmen by giving them what, by their right, legitimately belonged to them.

Some of the soldiers in the new Polish army were Jewish. I asked one of them how it felt to be a fighter.

"It feels good," he said, "because we have somebody to fight against. Yet we don't have much to fight for. No kin of mine have survived, I have no home, and I seriously wonder whether I have a fatherland."

I was living in sadness and dejection. I had no kin left either, or home, or fatherland. It had been a long time, since I had cut my ties with Poland. By now, I also knew that Russia would give me no comfort either. I befriended a Russian woman doctor, a major in the army, who confessed to me that she was Jewish but was hiding it, because of the strong anti-Semitism among her colleagues. She would have liked to defect to the West, but her family was living in Charkov, and she couldn't afford to expose them. The Russian anti-Semitism was becoming more evident every day in the behavior of the Politruk, and even the Russian-Jewish chief doctor was showing strong signs of anti-Semitism, maybe to please the Politruk.

One day, the Politruk called me to his office. He was all smiles, and he said, "We've cleared your case, comrade, and I want to be the first one to congratulate you. Today is Saturday. This coming Monday, you'll report to the Soviet Draft Board in Kattowitz. You'll be inducted as a lieutenant. You deserve it. And you will still be on time to do some shooting in Berlin."

I knew he would repay me for his embarrassment. To fight? For whom? For what cause? I said calmly, "Sorry, comrade. I am an Ecuadorian citizen."

He looked bewildered. He didn't believe his ears. Then, he roared, "You rabble! I'll show you Ecuador! You're from Lvov, and you'll report on Monday to the Draft Board! Dismissed!"

I was totally depressed as I started on my way back to Block 28. I didn't want any part of it. I didn't want to kill or to be killed. I just wanted to be let alone.

A military limousine was parked in front of the block. A Polish soldier was waiting next to it. Somebody pointed at me and said, "This is Dr. Franek."

The soldier snapped to attention and recited, "I have an order from Miss Anna to bring you to Cracow!"

I asked, "Who is Miss Anna?"

"The colonel's secretary. She said I mustn't return without you."

I didn't know any Miss Anna, but that was beside the point. Here was an opportunity to escape, and I wouldn't miss it. I asked the soldier for an hour's time. I went to the clothing warehouse, where a few pieces of garments were still hanging, and took off my Haftling uniform. I put on a pair of civilian trousers that were too large for me, an old blazer, and a navy blue woolen coat. I reported to the Red Cross office, where I requested and received an identity card made out to an ex-prisoner of French origin. My name became François Carter. Then I went to my attic hideaway and filled a small valise with cans of meat and a Canada blanket. I was ready for a new beginning.

We traveled back to Cracow by the same road that, two years before, had brought me to Auschwitz. I left behind me the camp, and a tremendously important part of my life.

But I didn't know what was in front of me. I watched the leafless trees at the edge of the road passing by. I had no feelings, no dreams, no desires. I still felt as if I were living in a deep freeze. I thought,

"Nothing has happened to me during all these years. I've been living in a state of separation from reality, frozen into 1939, and once the frost has thawed away, I will find again my old self, unscathed by the events and oblivious of the lapsed five years."

But was I really going to find myself? I had no family, no friends, and no past. My life would have to be started from scratch. Was I going to find enough strength to do it? Was I going to find purpose?

Suddenly, the well-known voice of the Girl of the Ring seemed to address me: "Remember. I promised. Trust me."

I awoke to reality. We were going to Miss Anna.

ZIONISTS AND SMUGGLERS

The ways of fate are unfathomable. Miss Anna was no one else but Rebecca, a good friend from student days at the Russian University in Lvov. She had heard from the first returnees from Auschwitz that I was alive, and she wanted to help me.

We were sitting in her office in the government building in Cracow. I watched her with curiosity. From the pretty little provincial girl she had been when we first met, she had become a sophisticated young woman, wearing a gray sport suit and smoking a cigarette.

"I don't remember you smoking before."

"I didn't. I do a lot of things now that I didn't before."

"What is your position here anyway?"

"Officially, I'm the colonel's secretary. In reality, I run the colonel and his office. During the last two years, I've become deeply involved with the party — the underground and all. It didn't happen overnight, and it was not easy. After you left, I went to a Polish home as a maid. Someone denounced me, and when the Gestapo came for me, I jumped out of the second-story window and escaped. It took me some time before I found a contact with the underground. But even then, nobody cared about how I was managing to survive. Believe me, it has been rough."

"I saw Piotr in Auschwitz." I thought I was giving her surprising news about her boyfriend. But she wasn't surprised at all.

"I know that he was in Auschwitz. I sent him food parcels all the time, and it never occurred to him to ask me where I had got the money to buy all that butter, and sausage, and bacon, and white bread. You wouldn't believe what Piotr wrote me once: 'I am fed up with all that *brot und butter.* I would like you to send me some oranges!' "

"I saw Piotr exactly twice. He didn't want to see me after the second time because he was afraid it might expose him. He was living in one of the hospital blocks, as an incurably ill tuberculosis patient. Nobody touched him, as he had, obviously, some excellent connections. He was there as a Ukrainian. His only activity was to read and to write."

"You mean to say that with all that he received from me, he never offered you anything?"

"No, he never did. But I don't mind. One less person to say 'thank you' to. Besides, I survived, so what's the difference."

There was a moment of silence. Then Rebecca said, "Do you want to know how I managed?"

"No." I really didn't want to hear. I wanted to see her the way she had been four years ago, a pretty, rosy-cheeked girl with a huge bow in her hair, who had just been overcome by Piotr's big-city sophistication and his blasé manners.

She laughed. "Oh, yes! You will listen! I've got a lover. How about that? A married man, to boot. A Ukrainian, in addition. And it is thanks to that man that Piotr could have his *brot und butter.* Even now, this man wants me to go away with him. He wants to drop everything, his wife and children, and go with me to France, or wherever I wish."

"And what do you wish?" I watched her uneasily, feeling that maybe it would have been better if we had not met.

"I?" She shrugged her shoulders. "I am still waiting for Piotr. He was the first man I loved."

"And if he doesn't come back? And if he's dead?"

"Then I might wait forever."

An uneasy silence followed. Rebecca broke it.

"I have a nice apartment," she said. "You can stay with me, except for two days a week, when my lover comes for a visit. He's quite jealous."

"Thank you, but no. I think I'll go to the Jewish Committee. I can sleep there for a couple of nights until I decide on my next step."

I picked up my valise.

"You can leave your things with me," she said. "You can pick them up when you are set. I understand you. And you can always come to my office if you want to see me. Remember, my offer is open."

I left Rebecca and walked in the streets of Cracow without purpose. At one point, I took a streetcar.

"I'm from Auschwitz," I said, when the conductor asked me for the fare. Other passengers looked at me with curiosity. Somebody whispered, "And I thought the Germans had gassed them all." I felt a deep bitterness coming over me. I got up, said, "I'm sorry, if I strike you as being alive. I'm the ghost of your past. I came to see if you know the feeling of remorse. Put your minds at ease. Soon, I'll be gone forever."

I entered the drab office of the Jewish Committee, and on a table lay a big open notebook. In it were written names of survivors and of people looking for survivors. I perused it. No one was looking for me, and the names in it were strange to me.

I noticed in the office a small group of people whom I knew from Auschwitz. I shook the hand of a tall, skinny fellow: "I remember you. Your name is Elih." He was a member of the fire brigade in Auschwitz.

"I remember you, too," said Elih. He smiled and exposed an empty space where a front tooth used to be. "Meet my fiancée." He introduced to me a plump, shy girl in her late teens. "And this is her sister, and her sister's boyfriend, and her aunt, and her cousin." Then, he said to them, "This is Dr. Franek from the Krankenbau."

"What are you doing in Cracow?" I asked.

"We have just found an apartment and are going to move in today. Would you like to join us?"

"I don't know. I'll have to think about it."

The aunt took me under the arm, scrutinized me for a moment, and said, "You are going to stay with us. This is definite."

Next morning, I went to see the Gunthers. It felt strange to enter the large building where, two years ago, I had lived a free man and a Pole. I seemed to feel around me all the others: Martin, Wanda, Adam, Anka, and Ostrowicz. My heart was pounding as I went upstairs, and after a moment of hesitation, I rang the bell.

The door opened, and Miss Gunther appeared. She looked at me, suddenly clasped her hands, and exclaimed, "Mother! Quickly! Mother!"

I said, "Good morning."

The old lady screamed from the other room, "Mr. Franek!" and came running. "I recognized you by your voice!"

The two ladies shook my hands with affection. They took me into the living room and pushed me into an armchair. Without allowing me any time for explanations, the older Mrs. Gunther inquired, "And how's your brother?"

Everything suddenly seemed so senseless. All the masquerading, all the effort to appear Polish, my green hair, and all the rest — all useless.

"You knew then that he was my brother," I said, "and not just a business partner?"

Mrs. Gunther sat down.

"Of course we knew. We just wanted to help."

I took her hand and kissed it.

"Oh, stop it, now!" the lady wiped her eyes with a handkerchief.

"And what ever happened to all the others?" I asked.

"My God," she sighed. "Do you remember? I asked you to stay with us for Christmas, because I was afraid that something might happen to you. One never knows. The day after you left, the Gestapo came to us to arrest the two gentlemen and the lady. Do you remember them? Two days later they were shot as members of the underground, God bless their souls. Their names appeared on the list of the executed resistance members."

Then Mrs. Gunther still didn't know that Zula Ginczanka and her husband had been Jewish, and that they had died as involuntary heroes of the Polish underground.

"I have spent these two years in Auschwitz," I said. "And I don't know whether my brother is dead or alive. I suppose if he's alive, he'll pay you a visit. Will you kindly tell him that he can find me through the Jewish Comittee? I'll be registered with the Commission for the Ex-Prisoners of German Concentration Camps."

"And the young lady?"

"Oh, she too, was in Auschwitz. I have no idea what has happened to her."

On the morning of the third day, I was disgusted with Cracow and with my freedom. The Poles around me were, at best, indifferent. The Jews felt that the world owed them everything. The aunt in the group with whom I was staying wanted me to marry her niece, even though nobody knew whether the niece's husband was dead or alive.

I went out early and took a long walk around Cracow. The city, not so terribly damaged by the war, was trying to put itself back into shape. Polish militiamen were rounding up people in the streets, to make them clean the rubbish left over by the bombings of buildings and bridges. A militiaman approached me. I didn't feel like participating in the patriotic effort of cleaning the city, and I showed him my Red Cross papers. He told me that I had to go just the same. I answered in French. It worked. He left me alone.

I passed a corner where Polish prostitutes were attending to their work first thing in the morning. One of them accosted me, "Shall we go?"

I said, "I'm Jewish."

She answered, "Money is money."

Life was coming back to normality.

I continued to wander around the city. I had ambivalent feelings about the worth of my survival. Why me and not the others? Was my survival for my benefit, or was it to make me suffer a little bit more? Here I was, a man with a blank slate for a past, without family, without friends — even my old name was gone — surrounded by unfriendly strangers in the middle of a city in ruins.

Yet, not all the people were bad. I thought of the Polish clerk in the hotel in Warsaw who had protected us against the Gestapo on our return from Treblinka. And the Gunthers. People had helped us, me and Martin. Who knew what had happened to Martin?

I went to the Planty Park where I sat on the bench on which Wanda had said her good-bye to me. I felt lonely, and it occurred to me that the only home suitable for me was, after all, Auschwitz. I felt like going back to the camp.

I went to Rebecca. I would take her to lunch and discuss my plans with her. Plans? If I had any.

Rebecca was busy writing reports and asked me to wait for her. After a few minutes, I became restless and felt an urge to get out and go.

I left her office, crossed the marketplace, and entered the *Sukiennice,* a sixteenth-century bazaar, now full of people, bustle, and commerce.

A strange force kept pulling me. Like a zombie, I crossed the bazaar and left it at the opposite end. There, in front of me, a man with a briefcase was crossing the street. I wasn't a bit surprised. I just said, "Hello, Martin."

He stopped. It was obvious that he didn't trust his ears. He looked straight ahead, not daring to turn his head toward me.

"This is me, Franek," I said. I spoke softly, without emotion.

Slowly, very slowly, Martin turned his head and looked at me. Then he fainted.

This was how Martin and I got back together after the war.

As we were going to his home, Martin was trying to tell me his story in as few words as he could. He had fainted because he thought he'd seen a ghost. Helena Bergman had visited Rokiciny Malopolskie after we had been arrested, and some peasants had shown her my grave. Now that he found me, Martin felt that his happiness was complete. He was employed by the Polish Ministry of Finance and was living temporarily in one large room in a building belonging to the Polish government. All the employees of the ministry were living there.

And Martin had a woman.

"You will now meet a person whom you'll admire," he told me as we were approaching his house. "Oh, and please — I will introduce you to my neighbors as a cousin of mine, back from Auschwitz. Because they all think that I'm Polish. My name is still the same: Alfred Stelmachiewicz."

As we were entering the hall of the building, Martin whispered to me, "I hope you'll forgive me. You know — the fact that I have somebody. That I'm forgetting Pola."

"Who am I to forgive?" I answered.

We met, and I felt ill at ease. Maybe it was because she was trying so hard to be nice. I couldn't lay my finger on it, but there was something about her that made me feel uncomfortable.

This was Easter week, and the holiday could be felt all around that building of Ministry of Finance employees. Martin's woman friend set a nice table, but before we could sit down and have our dinner, the neighbors kept dropping in for vodka and a bite, and before long everybody was drunk and happy.

This holiday spirit lasted for several days. I didn't mind. During the years of hunger, I had developed a peculiar way of absorbing food. I had become like a camel. I could eat whenever I was offered food, because I lacked a control device that would tell me when to stop. I had lunch at Martin's, after which I had lunch in the apartment where I stayed with my Auschwitz group. One of Martin's Polish neighbors had vodka with me in the morning, at noon, and in the evening. I drank it constantly, but I became drunk only after the last glass, when I knew for sure that there would be no more vodka that day.

My eating habits were just one of the traits of my new personality. There was more to it, and Martin once expressed it in this way: "You are not the person you used to be. It's hard to describe. What comes to my mind is stone. Or wood. There is something wooden in you. You are cold and unresponsive, and one has the impression that words, things, events just slip off your skin, without ever penetrating it."

This must have been the protective shield I had developed to survive the unsurvivable. Now I wasn't able to get rid of it and might wear it for days, or months, or even years.

I learned more about Martin and his lady friend. After I went to prison, Martin, helped by Bergman, had taken a supervisory position in a certified accountants' office run by a civilian German and employing more than twenty accountants, some of whom were Germans, but most of whom were Poles. One of the Poles was the lady's husband. After having found one day that this woman and her husband were Jewish, Martin fell in love with her, and now that the war was over in this part of the world, she had decided to divorce her husband and marry Martin. In fact, she expected to go to Lodz in a few days, where her husband was now staying, to start the steps toward the divorce. For Martin, this was his first real love.

As much as Martin loved me, I could not rid myself of the impression that I was just one person too many in their household. I visited Kurylowicz, who meantime had become a special minister for the Affairs of Ex-Prisoners of Nazi Concentration Camps, to ask him for help. Kurylowicz had his residence and office in the elegant Hotel Francuzki, and he was genuinely glad to see me. I didn't want to waste his time and went right to the reason of my visit.

"I need a job. When I was leaving Auschwitz, I forgot about such minor necessities of civilian life as the money. I have a little, of course, because I've sold a few cans of meat, and I've received some from the Jewish Committee. But this is not the kind of life I want to have. I cannot remain a charity case. I feel there must be something I could offer, and for which I could be entitled to compensation. You know me well, and if you will not help me, who will?"

Kurylowicz thought for a minute and then said, "I must be very candid with you. I could get you a job, but somewhere in a small town, because they don't want any Jews in Cracow."

"How about my living under an assumed name, as a Pole?"

"I'm sorry, colleague. A new law is being prepared right now, to the effect that all changes of name must be approved by the courts, and whoever assumes a new name must, in addition, retain his old one."

"This means, then, that if a Mr. Cohen assumes the name of Poniatowski, he's going to be known as Mr. Cohen-Poniatowski? But this law is aimed against the Jews!"

"Exactly. I must tell you that things aren't any better for you now than they were under Hitler. And indeed, I would be very reluctant to give you a job in a small town, because you might easily be destroyed there by the Land Army." The Polish underground had been divided during the Nazi occupation into the People's Army, a socialist faction, in which even some Jews had served, and the Land Army, which was a fascist organization that had previously fought the Germans and was now killing the Jewish survivors.

"Then, Mr. Kurylowicz, what do I do?"

"It might be bitter, what I'm going to tell you, but it will be practical. Look at me: I'm Polish. I have an important position. But if I were your age and without a family, I would leave Poland, never to return."

As the old man Kurylowicz spoke, I knew he was sincere.

When I told Martin about my conversation with Kurylowicz, he concurred fully and advised me to leave Poland, the sooner the better. I was puzzled and a little disappointed. I had expected my brother to want me to stay with him. After all, we were the only surviving members of our family. I asked him about his plans.

"With me, it's different," he said. "I have my Polish name, and nobody thinks for a moment that I am a Jew. My papers are authentic. I have a position. I have security. And last, but not the least, I'm so much older than you that even the thought of a drastic change scares me."

I didn't feel hurt. My brother didn't want me. But then I thought of all the other circumstances surrounding my life. All my friends were gone. I would have to begin life from scratch. What difference did it make, then, whether I began it in Poland or elsewhere?

The practical side of the story was that I didn't really know how to go about leaving Poland. I had heard from some Jewish ex-prisoners that there was an organization which was smuggling Jews out of Poland to Palestine. I had to find this organization.

I discussed the plan with my group in the apartment, and everybody, except the aunt and her niece, wanted to leave Poland. We decided that each of us would go around Cracow, gathering any information that would lead us to the organization.

One of the girls in the group finally made a contact. She led me to a small apartment in the Old Jewish quarter. There, a man scrutinized me suspiciously, asked me whether I spoke Yiddish, and wanted to know about my Zionist connections. The whole thing didn't seem to be very promising. I didn't speak Yiddish, and the Zionist group with whom I had been connected as a boy was the Hanoar Hazioni, a middle-of-the-road youth party, which did not please my interviewer. But then he discovered that I spoke several languages, and his face brightened. I would be a perfect leader of the group of Jews who were first on the list to leave Poland. He took my address and said that I would be advised on a very short notice.

The waiting period started. Martin inquired every day whether I had any news. His lady friend had gone to Lodz to make her divorce final, and he was living under constant tension. He wanted to see me off and her back.

Two weeks had passed. Then, late one morning, as I was cooking a pot of borsht for Martin and me, Elih arrived. He was out of breath as he said, "We have just been summoned. We have one hour's time."

I left a note of good-bye for Martin. I also left him my good Auschwitz coat, my suit, and the valise with the remaining cans of meat. I put on a laborer's overalls, as instructed by the organization, took my Canada blanket, and left. Two hours later, I was assigned a group of people, a part of which consisted of my own Auschwitz group, and was ordered to report to the next point of the organization, in the town of Rzeszow.

CHAPTER
13

AMCHU

A   stands for Anti-Semitism.
M stands for Murder.
C   stands for Cruelty to Man by Man.
H   stands for Hatred universal.
U   stands for Under your eyes, oh God, under
   your eyes has all this happened.

But the initiated know: Amchu, means Thy People, God,
Thy Chosen People.

Oh, God, how could you!

. . .Avec leurs chats,
   Avec leurs chiens,
   Avec pour vivre quels moyens,
   Les gens s'en vont,
   Les gens d'ici,
   Par la Grand' Route,
   A l'Infini . . .

   Verhaeren

One of the men in charge of the operation of leading Jewish survivors out of Poland briefed me on the project.

The unofficial name of it was the *Organization*. Its Hebrew name was *Aliyah Dalet,* Return to Palestine Number IV. The project was run by a coordinated effort of all Zionist parties, from the leftist *Hashomer* to the right-wing *Betar,* it was coordinated by the people of the Jewish underground army in Palestine, *Palmach,* and it was funded by the money contributed by the Jewish communities in U.S.A., and the rest of the countries untouched directly by the Nazi furor.

A trail had been created similar to the American underground railroad of the time preceding the Civil War, which went from Poland to Slovakia, Hungary, Rumania, Austria, and Yugoslavia, and converged in Italy, where the survivors were clandestinely placed on small ships, which in sporadic sallies tried to reach the shores of the Holy Land.

There were small offices along the trail, where the groups of survivors stopped for a day or two to be fed, get a night's sleep, and receive the instructions how to get to the next such office. These offices were run by one or two people, usually members of the left-wing Hashomer, and they were called *points.* Thus, the proper execution of the Aliyah Dalet was based on the wanderings of groups of Jews from one point to another, until they would reach Italy, and from one of the southern ports of that country, Bari, would be smuggled in small groups to Palestine.

I was given a twenty-member group consisting of males and females who were either survivors of the Nazi concentration camps, or refugees from the Russian internment in the faraway Kazakhstan.

We traveled by freight trains, by narrow-gauge mountain trains, and by foot. During our migration, we learned that some of the managers of the points were dishonest; that all of them were partial to the left-wing members of my group; that the Jews of Hungary and Slovakia hated the Polish Jews, and refused them all help on the illogical grounds that those of the Slovakians and Hungarians who had suffered or perished in the Nazi camps did so not because of the SS, but because of the doings of the Polish Jews.

During our travel, we ran across other groups. Everybody watched everybody else with mistrust and suspicion, and for mutual identification, instead of a "Good morning," the Hebrew word "Amchu" was used, "Your People, oh, Lord!"

People in my group, who hadn't known each other at the beginning of our journey, had coupled up after one day of travel, and after that, during the stuffy nights spent on the floor of the tiny rooms of the points, everybody around me was copulating. Their ways were different from mine; their values foreign. I wanted to become one of them, but I couldn't. And they, too, had their reservations. They treated me with deference, and called me by my Organization name "Doctor Franek," but they never accepted me as one of them. I didn't speak Yiddish; I was sophisticated; for them, I remained an eternal "Yecke," a Jewish Gentile, a person to use when in need, but not one to share with.

Then, I suddenly acquired at one of the points four additional members, the brothers Bielski. The four brothers had been partisans in the forests of northern Poland. They had saved over two hundred women, children, and old people in a village they had created in the midst of wilderness; and had been given by the Russians the medals of Heroes of U.S.S.R. Finally, oblivious of their Soviet honors, the Bielski brothers joined the 1945 movement of the return to the Holy Land. I became very close to them. They were the ones who felt as alien to the rest of the survivors as I did, but who knew how to fight their alienation. They were incessantly drunk. And now, I, too, had found my way to fight back: I drank with the brothers Bielski, I drank with them to the bottom, I drank, until I couldn't think, until my brain became numb, and my eyes saw the world through a thick haze which separated me from the ugly reality of loneliness, dejection, and defeat.

And after a long and painful journey, we reached a point where we were destined to remain for the next six weeks: Alba Julia, Rumania.

Alba Julia was a charming town in Transylvania, the Jewish population of which spoke Rumanian, Hungarian, and German, and had miraculously escaped serious harm from the Nazis, or from the Rumanian fascist Iron Guard. They extended a helping hand to the survivors, seven groups of whom, one hundred forty people, converged on this small provincial capital.

The underground railroad point in Alba Julia was immeasurably better than any of the points we had visited before. It was fairly large, consisting of three wooden barracks shaped in the letter "U". Each barrack was divided into a goodly number of minuscule rooms, which offered some degree of privacy to people who for years had known no privacy; there was a long banister in front of every barrack, which gave it the feeling of a porch; and the entire compound was protected by a high brick wall, with a narrow gate in it, permitting a person to come in, or go out, and keeping the unwanted strangers away. Before the war, this compound had been a brothel, but the owner, a well-to-do Orthodox Jew, lent it now to the Zionist project for the survivors to enjoy.

The majority of the point's inhabitants were left-wingers; the official language was Yiddish; and I, once more, became a "Yecke."

The point badly needed medical services, and in this I proved quite functional. I established connections with the Jewish physicians of Alba Julia, who promised to help without payment; I persuaded the local hospital to extend such help to people in need of X-rays and surgeries; and I improved the already existing small dispensary within the compound.

I also befriended a few members of the right-wing Betar, with whose help as interpreters — they all spoke Yiddish — I introduced such improvements as a primitive shower in the yard of the compound, made out of a pail attached to an overhead wooden beam, which could be pulled by a rope; and, the most important of all, a clean new outhouse.

Many other things occurred during the weeks of our stay in Alba Julia. Our people, hungry for normal life, found here its beginnings. Some of the refugees made friends with the local Jews. Toward the end of our four-week stay, many love affairs had been initiated, two of them resulting in refugee boys marrying local girls. Several local Jews, and even one Rumanian gentile, courted our girls. We had picnics and shows organized by me and my new friends, in which many local Jews took part.

The curtain finally fell on the Alba Julia episode, and, being too numerous to continue together, we were split into several groups. I led a group of people to the city of Temesvar.

At the point of Temesvar, I had even more of a chance than before to watch the special treatment enjoyed by the members of the Zionist left-wing. While the few non-leftists were thriving on a piece of bread and sausage, the Shomer people, the leftists, were having dinners in restaurants, eating fresh fruit, and going to the movies. My political sympathies definitely started leaning toward the right.

Our next stop after Temesvar was a Red Cross camp in the small Yugoslav town of Vielikaja Kikinda, immediately past the Rumanian border. We stayed there less than a day and continued to Belgrade, where we stayed in a point — an empty apartment — managed also by a left-winger. We had three days at our disposal, and during that time I roamed around the city, admiring its beauty and watching the innumerable Yugoslav partisans who crowded the streets, ill-dressed, often barefoot, cuddling their dearest possession — their guns — and looking suspiciously at everybody.

Then came Zagreb and soon, Ljubljana, where we stayed overnight in the Red Cross building. Finally, we found ourselves traveling on a freight train going to Italy.

It was in 1935 that I had come for the first time to Italy. I was eighteen years old, and it was my first independent trip abroad. I was traveling the same road now, but the circumstances were different. Yet the beautiful mountains around me hadn't changed. They were still warm, and still majestic, and they inspired in me a sudden urge to move, to do, to achieve. The train stopped in the middle of the war-damaged but still beautiful countryside. Far among the hills a church belfry could be seen. All was quiet, and I felt in my mouth the distinct taste of the tart, red Tuscan wine. Years back, I had drunk it with my meals in Pisa. The students called it *vino nero,* and it was served in carafes. Suddenly, I longed for money. I would love to return here one day as a tourist. Then, I'd have my *vino nero,* and I'd enjoy Italy.

In Udine, the members of the Jewish Brigade of the British Army were waiting for us at the station. We were taken to a villa occupied by the Brigade, where we could wash and refresh ourselves. Immediately after breakfast, soldiers from the Brigade went around in search of members of the Hashomer Hatzair, the leftist group, whom they transported to a beautiful villa in Mestre, while the rest of us were taken to a refugee camp in Bologna. After two days, we were taken to our final destination, a large Jewish camp in the Military Academy of Modena.

In Modena, the long-nourished antagonism changed into rancor when it appeared that the only groups being taken from here to a transshipment camp in the vicinity of Bari, from which people were being shipped clandestinely to Palestine, were the left-wingers. About two thousand people who had no political affiliation or who belonged to the middle-of-the-road or the rightist Zionist groups were left in Modena in dirt, hunger, and oblivion. We were issued identity cards which classified us as *displaced persons.* It was like going back to the concentration camp days. After a week in the military academy, I decided to act.

I convoked a secret conference of representatives of the groups of people who felt that they were being hurt. Our most immediate need was to improve the situation of the camp. We needed cots and mattresses, soap and detergent, a dispensary, and more and better food. There was a commission of the American Joint Action Committee in Modena, but so far the only thing they had given the camp were two truckloads of mezuzahs, the Hebrew blessings that are hung on the doors of Jewish dwellings. Otherwise, the camp was under the direct authority of the American army, while it was fed and policed by the Italians.

I could well understand that the Italians didn't have enough food for themselves, let alone the displaced persons. If we wanted our plight to become better, we had to address ourselves to the Joint Action Committee and to the Americans. Handwritten leaflets were sent around, and a general meeting of the displaced persons was called in the yard of the academy. It was an afternoon of action. Surrounded by my bodyguards, I climbed on a barrel to deliver my first revolutionary speech. At the last moment, it occurred to me that I would be expected to deliver my speech in Yiddish. I decided to try a subterfuge. I would speak in German, which because of my Polish accent would not be so terribly German, and the people would take it for Yiddish. Or else, I could use any language. They wouldn't be listening to the words anyway. They had come here to protest, and protest they did.

I lifted a fist and roared, "We're fed up with the Lagers!"

The crowd murmured approvingly.

"What we want is freedom!"

The murmur became more intense.

"We want bread! We want clean mattresses! We want medical care! We want decent treatment!"

With each of the slogans uttered, the behavior of the crowd became more threatening. Finally, I implored, "Let's go on a hunger strike! Let us refuse the charity rations, and let us demand the return of what is rightfully ours: our human dignity!" The crowd became frantic. They yelled, they cried, and they threatened. And when the two American MPs arrived to arrest me, the crowd ripped me out of their hands and pushed them aside. Other MPs arrived, shooting repeatedly in the air.

I stood again in front of the crowd and said, "We ask to be seen by the camp director."

This was an American captain. He was arriving at this moment, accompanied by a woman representative of the Joint Action Committee and by the chief of the Italian police.

An immediate meeting was arranged. Accompanied by two of my advisers, I sat down in the captain's office. We were invited to state our complaints, and they listened. Dirt. Rats. A cup of water with a spoonful of powdered milk and a slice of bread for breakfast. A pint of soup at noon and in the evening. A lot of sickness, but no medication.

At the end of my expose, the American captain said, "So what do you want us to do? We have our own problems."

"And this demonstration. Such a shame!" added the lady from the Joint Action.

I became incensed.

"Not a demonstration, lady," I said. "A hunger strike. We will fight to be recognized as normal human beings, equal to you and to these gentlemen!"

The conference was over. The authorities hadn't taken me seriously, although the captain warned me to stop the nonsense if I wanted to stay a free man.

The same evening, two thousand people, old and young, went on a hunger strike. They refused the water with the milk powder. They refused the soup. Twenty hours went by. We had permitted the children to be fed, but even they had refused to accept food.

At noon of the second day, I was called for another conference with the camp authorities. This time, I was treated with courtesy. They seemed to have gotten our message. As we were discussing various facets of the situation, we witnessed a scene through an open window that added some validity to our arguments.

A mother was leading her seven-year-old child to the kitchen when the boy suddenly jumped back and yelled, "I will not eat, mother! I am on a hunger strike!"

At least some improvements were won: more soup, more bread, and some cheese from the Italians; more bunks, a dispensary, and a promise to disinfect the camp from the Americans; and a promise of more worldly help than the mezuzahs from the Joint Action Committee.

But this was not all I wanted. The two thousand Jews in the camp of Modena wanted to go to Palestine, and there were rumors that the first groups of refugees were already being shipped out of Bari through the underground Aliyah Dalet. Forgotten by all the Zionist parties, these people in Modena had to be helped by somebody. My companions and I worked out a plan, according to which we would send a group of ten each day to Bari. Once there, they were to ask the local point for help, lest the Italian authorities become curious about the refugee Jews sleeping in the street.

Oh, those hectic days! Those mystery-wrapped nights! All my efforts went into finding a way to transfer to Bari the displaced persons about whom nobody seemed to care. There was no problem traveling to Bari. Once on the train, anybody could travel. The problem was that each person had some belongings, and as this was all they had in this world, it had to go with them to Bari.

The camp of Modena was guarded heavily by the Italian police and the American MPs. Although during the day the refugees could come and go as they pleased, they were forbidden to carry out any bundles. At night, there was a curfew. I had to create a system by which the bundles would be smuggled out of the camp.

My knowledge of Italian came in handy. I rented a room in town, because my plan was based on a slow but continuous movement of the belongings out of the camp, and the room was to become our warehouse. The people who were interested in participating in my "Operation Bari" chipped in with money, and soon we had enough to pay for the room.

The next step followed. The candidates for the trip would go to the room several times a day, wearing a couple of changes of clothes, and then take the clothes off and pack them in the room. A squad of young men specialized in getting small bundles out of the camp at night, using long ropes, muscles, and courage. After one week of such work, the first group of people was ready to go.

Every two or three days, a small group of my people left Modena. And after several such groups had reached Bari, the people at the point there got the message. They sent to me two representatives of a left-of-center Zionist group called Gordonia. After some bickering, they made an agreement with me, according to which the consecutive transports of my people to Bari would follow an agreed-upon schedule; at the point in Bari, they would see to it that my people became a part of the Aliyah Dalet. My Modena-Bari underground train had become legitimate.

The moment came, finally, when the people of my original group decided to transfer to Bari. At that moment, I stepped down. There were still a few people in Modena who had been with me in Alba Julia, and I thought I would make an effort to improve my existence and theirs. I wanted one day to go with these few people to Palestine so that we could build our own kibbutz. For this, we needed money. And I had just found out how the money could be made.

Some of the more enlightened Jewish refugees were making a lot of money by smuggling foreign currency between various countries.

They were using the road through Austria. I decided to use the Yugoslavian passage. Accompanied by my two bodyguards, Itzke and Mischka, two ex-partisans in Russia, I bought English pounds with my thirty dollars, and I embarked on my first smuggling adventure.

It was nice to travel across all of Italy, with nobody to take orders from, with no luggage, without even a decent suit of clothes. I dressed in my old blue overalls, a pair of oversized black shoes, and one change of underwear. I didn't have socks, and I didn't think I needed any. My two bodyguards, Itzke and Mischka, although somewhat better dressed, also looked far from elegant. Of course, we had no money, except for the English pounds, which I intended to multiply during my projected smuggling trips. But at that time, money was no object. One traveled gratis and was fed in various Red Cross stations. We didn't need any hotel rooms; a bench in a railroad station or in a park would do just as well. We even passed one night in a convent. Everything was new and exciting. Before long, we reached Trieste. The first difficult part of our assignment was before us: we had to cross Yugoslavia in order to reach Rumania.

Nobody asked us any questions.

We arrived in Ljubljana the same afternoon, registered at the local Red Cross as Polish refugees going back home, got a cot and some food, and the next day were on our way to Zagreb.

Then things became slightly more complicated. The Yugoslav partisans, who were the bona fide police force of that country, inspected the train every hour or so. They wanted to see the passengers' papers and interrogated each suspicious person at length. I had the Red Cross papers made expressly for this occasion. I spoke to the partisans in Polish, they spoke to me in Croatian, everybody understood everybody, and that evening, we reached Zagreb.

Here, we went directly to the point, where the Jewish manager wanted to know who had allowed us to leave Italy and come to Yugoslavia, and who would be responsible for us, should anything go wrong. He didn't waste any food on us, but let us spend the night at the point. The morning after, we left for Belgrade.

In Belgrade, we reported to the point, only to be told that we had no business to be there. We went to the Red Cross station, had a bite to eat, and that same night left for Vielikaja Kikinda. In the morning, we boarded a freight train on its way to Rumania. At noon, we were in Temesvar. I felt the taste of victory. Half of the assignment was over.

I got into the smuggling of foreign currency without the most elementary knowledge of it. The first thing I found hard to understand was that there were two kinds of English pounds in Italy: the one-pound notes printed on solid paper and the five-pound notes printed on tissue paper. In Rumania, they wanted only the tissue-paper notes, and this was what I had. I had bought these pounds for one simple reason. In Italy, the one-pound notes cost $2.80 each, while the tissue-paper pounds cost seventy American cents per pound. In Rumania, I sold my pounds in a couple of minutes at $2.50 per pound. With this money, I purchased German schillings, at 10 cents per schilling. For the amount of schillings I now had, I would receive in Italy $300. I felt smart, and rich, and anxious to bring the good tidings to my group in Modena.

Before leaving Temesvar, we visited the point in that city. As soon as the manager heard that we were leaving for Italy, he prepared a group of Jewish refugees for me to take along. I didn't mind the assignment. It gave me the feeling of being fully utilized, and it would also obligate the points in Yugoslavia to give us a helping hand.

This time, the crossing of Yugoslavia was just a routine matter.

I deposited my group of refugees in Milan, bought over four hundred English pounds, and in two days was ready for a return trip.

We traveled again the same route, using the same means, and seeing the same people. We had no problems at the points in Yugoslavia, because we were going to pick up another group of refugees in Temesvar, and also I was carrying some papers from the Zionist leaders in Italy urging the points to give us their full assistance. We reached Temesvar, and once more, we made a killing. The pounds were sold within minutes, and with the money thus obtained, I bought some schillings and some gold coins. The burden of the money had become somewhat more complicated, and we had to make cloth belts, which we stuffed with the schillings, and which we wrapped around ourselves.

By our third trip, everything seemed so routine that we no longer saw the dangers that might have been evident to somebody new in this game.

This time we went to Bucharest, as I had much money to sell and would want much money to buy, and it seemed to me that the Temesvar market might not be large enough. We spent a week in Bucharest, and this time we got several belts full of schillings and a small canvas pouch filled with gold coins. According to my figures, one more trip was needed to give us enough money to take my group to Palestine and start a small kibbutz of our own.

We left Bucharest accompanied by a Jewish couple from Poland and another one from Rumania. In Temesvar, still another couple from Poland were added, and away we went. As we arrived in Vielikaja Kikinda and were on our way to the Red Cross camp, something unprecedented happened. We were arrested by a Yugoslav partisan.

The man was barefoot, but the rifle in his hands was persuasive. We were taken to exactly the same place next to the railroad station where the Red Cross had functioned until a week ago. Only this time, the place was filled with Yugoslav peasants waiting for the train, while some Yugoslav police officers were working in the office where the Red Cross had been. They examined our papers, scratched their heads, and told us to join the peasants in the yard.

I considered this a good sign. Probably now we would be given something to eat, and then we would be allowed to take the train to Belgrade.

Instead, the evening arrived, and there had been no food and no instructions for us.

We passed the night in the yard, and in the morning we were called again to the office of the police. The officers didn't want to take upon themselves the responsibility of releasing us, and they decided to send us to the headquarters of the political police in Petrovgrad, the largest town nearby.

We left on a train, accompanied by two armed partisans. The police in Petrovgrad didn't know what to do with us either. For the time being, they placed us in something resembling a prison cell, telling us that this was simply a temporary arrangement. The tiny Jewish community in Petrovgrad, having learned about our plight, made an effort to show us their full sympathy. On the afternoon of the second day of our confinement, the door of our cell opened, and four Jewish women came in, carrying platters of steaming goulash, vegetables, fruit, and bread. The women were accompanied by the head of the Jewish community in Petrovgrad, to whom I stealthily consigned the documents I was supposed to have passed to the leader of the Jewish community in Belgrade. The man promised that the documents would be delivered to the right place within a day.

The next day, we were sent back to Vielikaja Kikinda for the police of that town to worry about us. We arrived at the crowded station of the little town at night. The train going to Belgrade had just arrived, and the confusion all around us was enormous. Only one partisan was guarding us this time, and the crowd separated him from us for a minute. I decided to make a move. Itzke and Mischka were carrying the belts with the schillings, while I had the pouch with the gold coins.

I slipped the pouch to Itzke and hissed, "You and Mischka board the train. Take the two Polish couples with you. The Rumanian couple will stay with me, and we'll divert the partisan's attention. See you in Milan."

While the Rumanian couple and I crowded the poor partisan, the rest of the group boarded the train and left for Belgrade. Slowly, the noise, the traffic, and the confusion died down, and in the desolate station of Vielikaja Kikinda remained the partisan with his rifle, the Rumanian couple, and I.

The partisan didn't understand what had hit him. He watched his three wards with amazement. It was easy to tell that he was trying to perform in his head an utterly complicated computing operation. The three of us were standing there indifferent, waiting for further developments.

"Weren't you nine?" the partisan finally asked.

"Yes, we *are* nine," I confirmed.

"So where are the others?"

"I don't know," I shrugged my shoulders. "We don't know each other."

"But aren't they here?" The partisan was showing signs of distress.

I looked around me. "I don't see anybody. Do you?" This was addressed to the Rumanians.

"No."

"So where are they?" the partisan was visibly nervous.

"Maybe in the station building."

The partisan took us all inside and inquired at the station master's office. The missing six were nowhere to be found.

"What am I going to do?" The partisan was in despair.

"What were you supposed to do?" I asked.

"I was to take you to the headquarters."

"So, maybe they are at the headquarters."

The partisan cheered up a little. Yes, maybe I was right.

We started walking on a long, dark road leading from the station into town, where the police headquarters was located. It never occurred to the partisan to make a telephone call and have the whole thing cleared up. Now it had become my worry to delay our arrival at the headquarters as long as possible, to allow the group to reach Belgrade before a message might reach the police of the capital. My brain was working feverishly. All we needed were three hours. How to get a respite?

I asked the Rumanian girl, "Would you be able to make believe that you are very sick?"

"Yes, of course," she answered. "I was an amateur actress. I can faint, if you want me to."

The comedy started. As the girl fainted, her husband played the role of a desperate companion. He wrung his hands and repeated "Oh, my God! Oh, my God!" while I knelt down next to the girl lying on the pavement and massaged her temples. The partisan paced around us, mumbling into his chin.

I addressed him with all the seriousness required by the situation, "This girl is very ill. She must be taken to the hospital. Otherwise . . ." I looked up toward the sky and sighed.

The partisan was out of his wits. He didn't know what to do. I made a suggestion.

"Why don't you ask at one of the homes along the road if you can make a call. To the hospital. To send an ambulance."

I accompanied the partisan to the nearest house, from which he made the telephone call to the hospital and was promised an ambulance. He did not think of telephoning the police headquarters.

We waited in the empty street for about twenty minutes. The clacking of horse hoofs was heard from afar. The ambulance was arriving. Slowly, from the darkness, emerged a hearse pulled by two black horses. Two orderlies jumped out, laid the girl on a stretcher, and pushed it into the hearse, just like a coffin. The husband, the partisan, and I climbed into the hearse, and the ambulance rolled in a slow, dignified way toward the hospital.

The woman doctor who received us was smart, perceptive, and cooperative. She also happened to be Jewish. She examined the girl and said to the partisan, "It is not very serious. However, I must keep her in the hospital for observation. For a few days. And it would be helpful if her husband remained with her."

It was already morning when the partisan and I reached the headquarters. I was not worried any longer. By now, Itzke and the group were in the point, and the money was safe. As far as my situation was concerned, I would have only one answer: I didn't know of any group. We just happened to travel together. And I had no idea of how and when they had disappeared.

I was yelled at, threatened, searched, and shut up in a cell. I still didn't worry. They had nothing on me. Sooner or later, they would let me go.

I spent one week in jail, during which time I befriended one of the political policemen. He had a Jewish mother and wanted to help me. I asked him to put me in touch with the local Jewish community. Through them, I sent a message to the point in Belgrade, asking them to get me out. The head of the community seemed very distressed when he brought me what he thought must be a coded message: "OZNA (Yugoslav Political Police) has caught Dr. Franek? Let OZNA hang Dr. Franek."

I must say I didn't know much about OZNA if I thought for a minute that they would get tired of investigating me and would let me go. Each day of my stay in jail, I was taken to the office upstairs, where all possible means were used to trick me into an admission of guilt. They were not sure what they wanted of me, but they did sense that I had something to hide, and they wanted to squeeze it out of me. One thing they didn't use was brute force, and for this I was grateful.

At the end of my stay, I was brought in front of a Jewish OZNA officer, who for the last time asked me the standard set of questions and then said angrily, "Maybe you're not a spy. I don't know. But you have broken the most basic law of courtesy. You have come to Yugoslavia without a visa. Coming to a country without a visa is like entering a room without knocking on the door."

I reminded him that this was the end of a long war. That many people found themselves in many countries in which they didn't want to be in the first place. And that many people were trying to return to their countries of origin, with the help of all the governments involved. And that the Red Cross papers were accepted as tantamount to a visa. All my persuasion was in vain. He was angry.

He said, "If you want to come to Yugoslavia, you'll need a visa."

"Where do I get it?"

"In one of the Yugoslav consulates abroad."

"Abroad?"

"Yes. You will be reshipped today to Rumania."

"But this is ridiculous! I am not a Rumanian citizen. And what if Rumania doesn't let me in?"

"That is your problem."

That afternoon, a special locomotive pulled into the station of Vielikaja Kikinda. Accompanied by an armed partisan, I climbed onto the locomotive. The engineer pulled on the rod, and the siren emitted a long, sad sound. I felt the grandeur of the occasion. I,

Doctor Franek, was being expelled from a country and transported toward another country in my personal locomotive. I felt like Lenin. I was poor at this moment, the only money I had on me was a fifty-franc Swiss note in my shoe. But I breathed with pride and excitement.

It was a short trip. The locomotive let me out at the Rumanian border, handing me over to the Rumanian chief of police. He, in turn, put me under guard in a room at the railroad station, promising to reship me to Yugoslavia on the first available train.

The same night I was back at the Yugoslav border, and again that same night I was returned to the Rumanian station. In my head, I had a picture of a man without country who, for the rest of his life, would travel between the two borders.

I spent the day at the Rumanian border, waiting for the night train to Yugoslavia. It was already late in the evening when my Rumanian guard left the room to attend to his physiological needs. A freight train was passing through the station going toward Hungary. It was loaded with coal, and a moment later it carried me, hidden in a pile of the black pebbles. I was on my way toward Arad, a Rumanian city at the border of Hungary.

In Arad I changed trains and boarded a transport of Russian soldiers on their way to Budapest.

I journeyed on the roof of the train, where I met another Polish Jew. He was traveling for business, and he had an address in Budapest that he had been told to go to.

As the train arrived in Budapest that night, we joined three other Jews and followed them to an apartment where the new class of post-war Jewish businessmen gathered. The apartment belonged to a Hungarian Jew, who was selling floor space at a premium by the square foot. The traffic in the apartment was brisk, and people came and went, buying and selling foreign currency, saccharine, flints for cigarette lighters, and, as rumor had it, German cocaine.

Next day, I visited the point in Budapest. They refused to help me. It appeared that all the points in Yugoslavia and Hungary had been advised not to give me any help.

I spent a few days in the apartment, where I got in touch with a small group of the businessmen — frankly, I'd call them smugglers — who were readying themselves to leave for Austria. I contributed a little money and joined the group.

That same night I left Budapest in the company of a small group of Jewish smugglers. We traveled on a Russian army truck to a small town near the Hungarian-Austrian border. The Russian soldier drove wildly on a road full of bumps and potholes and at one point hit something hard. A sound was heard similar to when one smashes an air-filled paper bag, and the soldier cursed, "That sonofabitch of a dog! Shouldn't be roaming the streets!"

The truck reached town before dawn, and we entered the dreary little house that was to be our meeting point with the Hungarian guide who was supposed to take us into Austria the next night.

At nightfall, we started toward the border. It was a complicated frontier line. The first portion of it was guarded by the Hungarians. Further on, there was a zone guarded by the Russians. Still further, we would have to cross the British line, and only then would we reach the railroad station from which the train would take us to Gratz.

The night was terribly dark, and we couldn't see more than a couple of yards in front of us. We followed our guide in a single file, each man watching the silhouette of the one preceding him. Time passed slowly. It started to rain. The mountains themselves had disappeared in the darkness, and danger seemed to be lurking everywhere. Nobody talked. Nobody smoked. We hardly dared to breathe. The file stopped, and the order was whispered, "Pay the guide," Each of us passed his share to the man in front of him. The file moved again. We walked and walked. It felt as if we were walking in circles. We stopped. Nobody knew why. Then, a desperate whisper from the front of the file: "The guide is gone!"

The night had become even darker, and the rain was falling harder. Shivering, I approached the man at the head of the file.

"Have we been going straight all the time?" I asked.

"Yes. I'm sure we have. I'm sure this is the way to the border," he waved his hand toward the darkness. "Maybe that's why the guide left."

"Then, let's continue. We have little choice, do we?"

We started again. Now I was walking beside the first man in the file. Our walk seemed to have no end. The smugglers were getting tired, as each of them was carrying a valise full of merchandise. I offered to help the man next to me, but he refused. He didn't trust anybody. We kept walking, but our confidence was withering. I still had that very strange feeling that we had been walking the whole time on one spot, that it was the night that was really moving around us, and that the dawn would find us at exactly the same place we had started from.

Then something new occurred. The smuggler walking next to me collided against something — or was it somebody?

An angry curse was heard in Russian: "You sonofabitch! Where do you think you are going!!"

We had run directly into a Russian border guard. He grabbed the smuggler by the collar with one hand and pulled his sleeve with the other. The sleeve yielded at the shoulder seam, and a package of bank notes fell on the ground. The Russian grabbed it and shone a flashlight on it. I saw a stack of one-hundred-dollar bills wrapped up in large Russian five-hundred-ruble notes.

The soldier cursed, took the rubles, and throwing the dollars on the ground, yelled, "You are still carrying that German shit! You spies!"

"We are Jews. Refugees," mumbled the smuggler.

The Russian eased his tommy gun. He said, "Jews?" Then he added, "Go to the devil! But don't tell anybody about the rubles, or I'll shoot you all!"

The smuggler picked up his dollars, and we rushed into the darkness. By now the group had disintegrated, and each of us went his own way.

I don't know how long I walked. At one point, an English sentry yelled at me from far away. I didn't stop, and he fired a few shots. I kept going until, at last, at dawn, I came to a peasant's hut. I was thirsty and hungry. I knocked at the door and said that I wanted to buy something to eat. All he had was hard cider. I drank it and inquired about the railroad station. He said it was half a mile from the hut. I inquired about Gratz. The train would leave in another hour or so.

I stopped in Gratz for only one day. My grandparents on my mother's side had lived in Gratz. And aunts and uncles, and cousins. I knew they were all gone.

That same day, I left for Klagenfurt, where there was a large refugee camp. I registered as a Frenchman on his way back home. As it happened, the fellows in the administration were French, and a group of Italian repatriates were about to leave for Udine. I was given the documents of the Italians and was made the official leader of the group. One of the Italians on the train mistook me for a German in disguise. He introduced himself as a tailor from Naples, returning home from a job in Germany. He offered me room and board in his home in Naples and swore that we, the fascists, would help each other forever after.

This was the first time after the war that I had traveled anywhere legitimately. I had my papers and I had the official papers for my group. In Udine, I telephoned the camp administration to send trucks for the new arrivals. I handed the documents to my new friend from Naples, telling him that I had a mission to accomplish, and I took a train for Venice.

The ways of Fate are indeed very strange. As I was leaving my train in Venice, the first familiar face that caught my eyes was that of Itzke.

"What are you doing here?" I asked. "We were supposed to meet in Milan."

Itzke was surprised, too. Soon I knew why. He mumbled something about a car accident he and the others had had while going in a taxi from Yugoslavia to Trieste, and how the little bag of gold coins had been lost. All he still had was the belt full of the schillings, which he had on him and which he returned to me promptly. This would account for about one tenth of all the money we had made. I inquired about Mischka. Itzke took me to his room and asked me to wait while he went to summon Mischka. That was the last time I saw Itzke and the last time I heard of Mischka.

By stealing that money, they had destroyed my dream of a kibbutz in Palestine for me and my little group of refugees, who were still waiting in the camp at Milan. I didn't have the courage to face them. They wouldn't believe my story.

I went to see my direct supervisor, who was in charge of the transshipments of the refugees to Palestine. I wanted sympathy from him for what had happened to me in Yugoslavia, and revenge for the way I had been treated by the left-wing Zionist administrators of the Organization. His reaction was bland and meaningless.

He said, "What's the big deal? You are free, and you are here. Just forget the whole thing, and go back to work."

That was my good-bye to involvement in Zionism.

I sadly counted my losses. All my friends were gone. My family was gone. My idealism was gone. Behind me — the void. Ahead — no purpose.

I had reached the most dangerous crossroad of my life.

During the weeks that followed, I rented a furnished room over a wine store in Modena. My landlady was an old Italian widow who ran the store during the day, and was a combination of mother and counselor to me in the evening. I often traveled to Rome and Naples, buying things and selling things, and trying to stay alive, without exactly knowing why I should bother.

I was lonely. I could see all of them in my mind: Father and Mother, Pola, Adam, Wanda, Stefan, and Bronek — all my friends, all the people who were the background for the panorama of my life. I could see them laughing and crying, arguing and agreeing, accepting and refusing — and all of them slowly disappearing into an abyss. I knew that there was no meeting again. I had witnessed the demise of millions, but not one ghost had crossed my road. They were all gone forever, and there I was standing between the world that is and the world that was. My past, the factor that adds depth to human life, had been erased, and without it I found myself a pathetic flat figure pasted against the background of a two-dimensional society. The present had refused to accept me as a part of it. My brother Martin had sent me away. My brother Gustav who was living in Palestine, and to whom I had dispatched a joyous telegram of survival, cabled me in response the address of our brother Max in the United States. By doing so, he had washed his hands. There were no open arms for me. I felt betrayed by my brothers, by the Zionist movement, and by God Himself.

One day, I and two other Polish Jews rented a chauffeur-driven car to get from Rome to Modena. The car got stalled when we were deep in the Appenine Mountains. For a whole night we waited for help while we froze. Finally, at early dawn, two trucks arrived. They were loaded to capacity with fresh Tuscan chestnuts, but the driver of the second truck offered me and my traveling companions a lift on top of the heap of chestnuts. A little bit farther on, the trucks stopped again, to pick up two girls. One of them climbed into the driver's cabin; the other sat on top of the chestnuts with us.

I was frozen and half-asleep. While my companions were trying to make conversation with the girl, I fell into a deep slumber. All around me was gray and blue. I dreamed of Mother the way I had seen her the last time, on the train to Treblinka. She caressed my cheek. I felt something soft and warm around my throat, and a melodious, familiar voice said, "Take it. You are cold."

My brain worked hard, going backward, laboring through the darkness of the ages. I knew the voice. It was not just sympathy. It was much more. It was not Mother. It was . . . It was . . .

And I knew. I knew for certain. I opened my eyes. I was wide awake. The exquisite oval of the beautiful face was above me. She was smiling with warmth.

It was the Girl of the Ring.

EPILOGUE

Her name was Ione. We married shortly thereafter, and a daughter was born, whom we called Aurora — the symbol of a new beginning.

Martin joined us in Rome. He felt dejected after his lady friend had returned to her husband and offered Martin a *ménage a trois*. This arrangement went against Martin's moral fiber. He had left his woman, his Polish name, his secure position, and his home, and came to Italy. To die. He was forty-four years old when he committed suicide a few months later. I buried him on the afternoon before Yom Kippur, in September 1947 — two months after Aurora's birth.

He left me a note — I suppose, the note was intended for all his brothers — which I quote verbatim: "The explanation is simple. There are no secrets to hide. Those who know me are aware of it. I have lived an honest life. After this war — so tragic for us Jews — I had a justifiable hope of being able to start a normal and settled life in my fatherland: Palestine. I have been waiting, every moment I was ready to depart, but my hope was in vain. For the world, we have been a plaything, sometimes pleasant, sometimes not so. I have no will any longer to live like an animal — without work, without a today, and without a tomorrow. This is all I have to say in my justification."

After all we had been through, Martin still considered his suicide a crime against God that needed a justification. I accepted his decision, but didn't agree with it, because I am convinced that life has a meaning. His ability to survive Treblinka and the war must have had a purpose, and his crime was not so much against God as it was a breach of that purpose. Had he remained alive, he would have witnessed the birth of the State of Israel and, perhaps, he would be living there today.

The great day had arrived.

When Ione and I, with Aurora in Ione's arms, arrived at the Colosseum, the throng had already assembled. Here and there, one could hear an outburst of voices, but then all noise died out, and the world stood still.

In front of the silent multitude, not more than a hundred yards beyond, stood the Arch of Titus. A curse attached to it for twenty centuries had prohibited the descendants of the dispersed Hebrew nation to walk through this arch until the day when the old land of Israel was reinstated as a free country, and the destroyed temple was restored to its ancient splendor, as a shrine of God, Justice, and Peace.

The Great Rabbi of Rome raised his arms toward the sky. The deep furrows running from both sides of his aquiline nose to the long white beard were wet with tears. His eyes were closed, his lips whispered holy words, and he looked like a prophet, clad in his white priestly vestments.

Suddenly, he started, as if awakened from a deep dream. He opened his eyes and fixed them on the arch. His face shone with joy, as he stepped forward.

The assembly moved slowly behind the leader. In an orderly fashion, the first rows passed under the arch and stepped on the ancient Roman Forum. The basso-relievo on the arch, representing the triumph of Titus over the Holy City and her defenders, seemed to say, "Two thousand years ago, we passed here, carrying on our shoulders the burden of golden candelabras, of deceived faith, and of lost hope. Now, it is up to you to return to the people of Israel that which was theirs."

Somewhere in the multitude, a voice shyly began a Hebrew chant. Another voice joined the first, and then still another, and another, and then they all merged in a powerful anthem.

The blue sky of an early May magnified the anthem in a joyous echo, while the despair of the past became a hope for the future. The solemn procession of the people, freed from a bimillennial slavery and filled with a new dignity, passed under the Arch of Titus. Ione with Aurora in her arms closed the procession.

* * *

It has been more than thirty-five years since I was liberated from Auschwitz. I know now that the Ring was a symbol of a cycle of growth through pain, suffering, mourning, and occasional joy. I had been treading its slippery edge, like an acrobat walking a tightrope, with a precipice to my right and a precipice to my left, to return at the end to the very point of departure.

Old people die, but not the old rings. Maybe somewhere in the world, somebody is wearing my ring on his finger. Please take a hard look at your ring. It could be mine. But even if it isn't, it might be a depository of a profound human drama, and it might have a magic that will answer to your call. Look at it with reverence, and then, notwithstanding your religious faith, I beg you to say along with me a Kaddish for all those who were and aren't any more.

All the events told in these pages are true. All the people I have introduced to you existed once upon a time. They have crossed these pages, leaving only a gentle shadow of remembrance. All the things I have told you about took place once upon a time. Once upon a time, all this was a real life. Today, it sounds like a fable.

Today, all of it seems to me a dream. A dream, and a nightmare, and then again a dream. And there is no awakening.

Yet, there is a reality, an indestructible Spirit of Hope, which came to me in the shape of a ring, but which since has become my spiritual companion forever: The Girl of the Ring.

Aurora 1988

ABOUT THE AUTHOR

After a long career with the New York State Department of Labor, Frank Stiffel is now doing what he has always wanted, pursuing a career as a writer. He lives in New York City with his family.